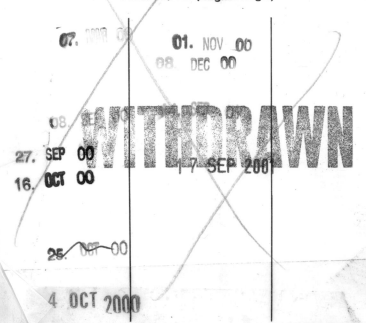

ISSUES IN CONTEMPORARY RELIGION

Series editors: Christopher Lamb and M. Darrol Bryant

The volumes in this series are interdisciplinary and present their subjects from global and cross-religious perspectives, examining issues that cut across traditions and emerge in distinctive ways in different religions and cultural settings. Based on sound scholarship, the books are intended for undergraduate courses and for professionals involved in inter-faith dialogue.

Also available in this series:

Dan Cohn-Sherbok, *Understanding the Holocaust: An Introduction*

Christopher Lamb and M. Darrol Bryant (eds),
Religious Conversion: Contemporary Practices and Controversies

Exploring
New Religions

George D. Chryssides

CASSELL
London and New York

Cassell
Wellington House, 125 Strand, London WC2R 0BB
370 Lexington Avenue, New York, NY 10017–6550

First published 1999

British Library Cataloguing in Publication Data
A catalogue record for this book is available from the British Library.
ISBN 0–304–33651-3 (hardback)
    0–304–33652-1 (paperback)

Library of Congress Cataloging-in-Publication Data

Chryssides, George D., 1945–
    Exploring new religions / George D. Chryssides
       p. cm. – (Issues in contemporary religion)
    Includes bibliographical references and index.
    ISBN 0-304-33651-3 (hardcover). – ISBN 0-304-33652-1 (pbk.)
    1. Religions. 2. Cults.   I. Title. II. Series.
  BL85.C49   2000
  291′.046–dc21
                                          99-30475
                                              CIP

Typeset by Bookens Ltd, Royston, Hertfordshire
Printed and bound in Great Britain by Biddles Ltd, Guildford and King's Lynn

Contents

To Margaret

Acknowledgements

This book would not have been possible without the help of a number of people, including members of new religious movements. I should therefore like to express my thanks to the following: Bill and June Thompstone, Stephen Morris (Jehovah's Witnesses), Bryan Grant and John Burton (Church of Jesus Christ of Latter-day Saints), Steven Upton (Spiritualist National Union), Mark Brann, William Chasseaud, David and Patricia Earle, Robin Marsh, George Robertson (Unification Church), Mick 'Temp' Haines (Jesus Army), Rachel and Gideon Scott (The Family), Graeme Wilson, Barbara Bradley, Sheila Macdonald (Church of Scientology), Rasamandala and Indriyesha (ISKCON), Subhuti and Naghabodhi (Western Buddhist Order), Stephen Potter (NKT). Audrey Chaytor (FAIR), Eileen Barker and the staff of INFORM have also given invaluable assistance. Dr Jean-François Mayer patiently answered my numerous questions on the Solar Temple.

Acknowledgements are also due to Kevin Tingay for answering queries about Theosophy, and to Preston D. Hunter on statistical information. Professor Brian Bocking (SOAS, University of London) has kindly given permission for me to use sections of an article in Diskus, entitled 'New religious movements: some problems of definition' (1994), and the Lindsey Press Publications Panel has authorized the reproduction of some material on the New Age. I have also been helped by contributors to the Nurel e-mail list, co-ordinated by Professor Irving Hexham at the University of Calgary.

Thanks are due to students and staff at the University of Wolverhampton. Several students brought back up-dated information while studying the 'module' on New Religious Movements and helped to stimulate ideas. The faculty's Research Executive allocated time to work on the project. Among colleagues, I am grateful to Deirdre Burke, Joyce Miller, Susan Arblaster and Sandeep Chohan,

ACKNOWLEDGEMENTS

who have made invaluable comments and sat through several research seminars based on sections of this book. Particular thanks are due to Ron Geaves, who made many valuable suggestions on preliminary drafts.

Above all, thanks are due to my wife Margaret, who not only provided encouragement, but scrutinized the text, discussed it and assisted with background research.

Introduction

Providing solid and up-to-date analysis of the new religious movements (NRMs) that are covered in this volume has proved to be quite an ambitious task. Not only is the subject matter complex, but NRMs are volatile, and it is likely that, even before this book reaches the public, affairs will have moved on. I can therefore do no more than offer a snapshot of NRMs as I have found them at the turn of the millennium.

One or two words of explanation of matters of policy may be useful. Part of the volatility of NRMs involves changes of name: 'Rajneesh' becomes 'Osho', the 'Children of God' become 'The Family of Love' and now 'The Family'. Unless the discussion dictates otherwise, I have always used the most recent name, with one exception. The name 'Unification Church' has become so widely known, and it has taken the UC decades to persuade the media to use this name in preference to the pejorative label 'Moonies'; the new name 'Family Federation for World Peace and Unification' is at present little known, and is likely to cause bewilderment rather than intelligibility. In any case, the name change is so recent that it remains to be seen whether this is a permanent change or a passing experiment.

'Political correctness' is always a problem when dealing with religions that are sometimes very traditionalist in their expression. Scientologists never use gender-inclusive language; Unificationists always use the term 'Old Testament', which many Jews now find offensive, and their *Divine Principle* does not seem to consider the possibility that its central figures might have been female rather than male. In general, I have chosen to use politically correct forms of expression where these do not affect the essence of a religious group's teaching: since Scientologists really mean 'men and women', I have usually avoided using the word 'men' to embrace both genders. On the other hand, I think it would be improper to amend the Unificationists' term 'Old Testament Era' to something like 'Ancient Hebrew Era', and it would simply be wrong to talk about a coming messiah as 'he or she' – notwithstanding those who support equal opportunities – when the expectation is clearly of a male figure. Also, where a group is typically male, like the Latter-day Saints' Twelve Apostles, it would be misleading to use gender-inclusive language, which might wrongly imply that one might find women amongst their numbers.

When examining a religious group's origins, it is not always possible to disentangle myth and history. No doubt numerous stories of NRMs' founder-leaders are pieces of modern hagiography, but discussing their claims to be historical truth would be distracting as well as irrelevant to my aims. I have tried to avoid inserting too many words like 'supposedly', or 'it is believed that', which could be construed as sneering at the believers' claims. If a reader's credulity is sometimes stretched beyond its limits, he or she should not assume that the author's is not!

Quoting Christian scripture posed another problem. Latter-day Saints and The Family prefer the King James (Authorized) Version; the Jehovah's Witnesses use their own New World Translation; other groups have their own favoured modern translation, and I normally quote from the New International Version when given a choice. When quoting Christian scripture I have normally used the translation that is actually used by the religious group under discussion, bearing in mind the date at which a scripture might have been quoted. Although this involves some unevenness when quoting scripture, I thought it important to indicate the exact scriptural sources that underpin an NRM's beliefs and practices.

1. Methodological issues

New religious movements (NRMs) is a topic on which there are many opinions, but fewer reliable sources. Until the 1970s there was virtually no serious academic study of the phenomenon. Traditional theology, as I studied it in the late 1960s, was essentially a quest for religious truth, and it was implicitly assumed, I think, that groups such as the Latter-day Saints (the Mormons) and the Jehovah's Witnesses had little claim to be serious contenders in theological debate. If the subject of NRMs ever crossed the minds of university teaching staff, they may well have thought their absurdity to be plainly evident. Was it not obviously absurd to claim that an angel showed Joseph Smith golden plates, that the world had ended in 1914, or that illness is the product of the mind?

The 1960s, however, saw a substantial influx of immigrant communities into Britain from India, Pakistan and Bangladesh, and it was understandable that Christian churches and British universities should channel some of their energies into understanding the faiths of the new settlers, principally Hinduism, Islam and Sikhism. The study of the major religions gained momentum, but little attention was paid to the minor ones.

Initially the academic interest in NRMs came from sociologists, principally in the context of the sociology of deviance. The new religions were interesting, not because of their doctrines, but because of the societal factors that gave rise to the phenomenon and the group dynamics that existed within such organizations. One of the first such studies was John Lofland's *Doomsday Cult* (1966), in which the author, as an observer, studied the early methods of proselytization of the Unification Church in its early years in the USA. The fact that Lofland nowhere disclosed the identity of the 'Doomsday Cult', for reasons of 'confidentiality', indicates that he did not consider the group's identity to be particularly important.

1

Indeed, Lofland mentions that his initial decision to make contact with the 'Divine Precepts' (his cryptonym for followers of the Unificationists' *Divine Principle)* was fortuitously occasioned by the cancellation of a flying saucer convention that he had planned to attend one evening! Of course, Lofland was not to know the extent to which the UC would gain such wide media attention, and his work remains a highly important early study. From the 1970s onwards the sociologists have tended to corner the market of academic studies of NRMs. Their treatment acknowledges NRMs' existence as an interesting societal phenomenon, but remains neutral on the question of whether the beliefs and practices of these religious minorities are themselves worthy of study from a distinctively Religious Studies perspective.

Although there is a surfeit of books on the 'cults', there is a singular lack of serious academic studies that have treated the ideas of a new religion as a topic worthy of study in its own right. There are a few exceptions, such as Kim Knott's *My Sweet Lord* (1986) and my own *The Advent of Sun Myung Moon* (1991). As my students embarked on the study of new religious movements, it quickly became clear that a general introduction was needed that presented their fundamental tenets in as impartial and empathetic a manner as possible – something akin to Walter Martin's *The Kingdom of the Cults* (1965/1985), but with much more substance and without its Christian polemic.

In what follows, I have attempted to set out the key ideas of a number of NRMs, focusing on their origins, beliefs and practices. Since there are estimated to be some 600 NRMs in Britain alone, and over 2000 in the USA, it would be plainly impossible to cover them all. What follows is a sample of new religious movements: I have attempted to categorize them within a typology, taking three or four representative samples of the particular genre which each respective chapter addresses. While this is intended to ensure that fairly sustained treatment is given to each group under discussion, the inevitable result is that certain NRMs can only be mentioned in passing, and in some cases not at all. I had initially hoped to give coverage to Meher Baba, Sahaja Yoga, Elan Vital (formerly the Divine Light Mission), the Worldwide Church of God, the Church Universal and Triumphant and the Word-Faith Movement among others, but to do so would have necessitated scant treatment, rendering the book quite inadequate.

Methodology

The approach that I have adopted is a broadly phenomenological one, in which I have aimed at empathetic (which is quite different from sympathetic) understanding. I have attempted to combine NRMs' own source material, other academic writing, and whatever counter-cult material helps to shed light on NRMs' origins, beliefs and practices. This has been supplemented wherever possible with conversations with adherents, together with participant-observer fieldwork. Obviously there are some groups where this was not possible, most obviously the 'suicide cults' which are discussed in Chapter 2.

To pursue this particular approach to new religious movements is not to suggest that other concerns are inappropriate or less important than my own. On the contrary, issues concerning brainwashing, leadership styles, living conditions and so on are perfectly legitimate issues. Questions about orthodoxy and heresy are absolutely vital issues for evangelical Christians, for whom it is a very live concern as to whether one can be 'saved' while remaining a member of an NRM. Such questions remain largely unaddressed in this book, not through lack of concern, but because of the parameters I have set myself. Readers who wish to find 'cult critiques' will find no shortage of sources.

It is popularly believed that the world-view of NRMs is incoherent: words like 'bizarre', 'absurd', 'naive' and 'irrational' are frequently used to describe their doctrines. Indeed one writer (Christopher Evans) has seen fit to entitle an entire book on NRMs *Cults of Unreason*. With few exceptions, the teachings of NRMs are considerably more sophisticated than their critics allow, and their detractors would do well to ascertain the true nature of their opposition. Mainstream Christians who believe that the Jehovah's Witnesses read only certain sections of their Bible, like the Book of Revelation, and take verses out of context are unlikely to make a serious impact on the Witnesses, who systematically study all of the Judaeo-Christian scriptures and whose publishers are thoroughly trained for their door-to-door work.

Although different religious communities lay different degrees of emphasis on the doctrinal aspects of their faith, it is their fundamental teachings that are the driving force of the organization. Even if it were true that many NRMs are headed by a megalomaniac leader whose main interest was personal power or material wealth, these aims would be unlikely to attract even the most gullible of followers. Those who decide to follow a religion do so because they are impressed by its ideals and its outlook on the world. Although NRMs often need followers to raise money, create ritual activities or encourage followers to become politically active, none of these activities make sense without a set of fundamental beliefs that underpins them. An NRM's teachings are the fuel by which the religion is driven, and without which it would fail.

What is a new religious movement?

Before proceeding further, we need a working definition of 'new religious movement'. The term is used widely by academics, in preference to the terms 'sect' and 'cult', and covers a large number of disparate groups. 'Sect' was the term that tended to be used in connection with the older wave of new religious movements, the term 'cult' gaining momentum from the 1970s onwards. (There were earlier precedents: William C. Irvine's *Timely Warnings*, published as early as 1917, used the term 'cult', as did Gaius Glenn Atkins in his *Modern Cults and Religious Movements* (1923), and the Unitarian writer Herbert Crabtree (1932).) Although academic works on NRMs now tend to avoid the terms 'sect' and 'cult' in this connection, both terms have an academic pedigree that can be traced back to Max Weber, who distinguished between 'church' and 'sect', a dichotomy which was further elaborated by his pupil Ernst Troeltsch. Weber (1922/1965) and Troeltsch (1931) regarded the church as the dominant form of religion, the established institution which reflects and accommodates the values of the civil society with which it co-exists. Citizens have an almost automatic right to belong to the 'church', gaining membership by birth, rather than by any conscious adult decision to join which stems from conviction. Thus in England, for example, the Church of England's parish system confers an automatic belonging to a parish, with the entitlement to use the established church for the various rites of passage. The practice of infant baptism, used in all Christian churches where Christianity is the dominant religion, ensures membership as a birthright rather than through a later decision to belong. The church accommodates the values and goals of civic society, legitimating the affairs of state and providing ceremonial backing for state events, such as coronations, royal weddings and parliamentary events. Although those who complain when the established church's clergy bless nuclear submarines or hunting parties may have moral arguments for their objections, it is in the nature of established religion to accommodate activities that are sanctioned within society more widely. There is a serious point behind the description of the Church of England as 'the Conservative Party at prayer'! The church, then, incorporates a mix of people, some more committed than others; as Weber wrote, it is 'an institution, necessarily including both the just and the unjust' (Weber, 1930/1976, p. 144).

The sect contrasts with the church on virtually all the points mentioned above, according to Weber and Troeltsch. The sect tends to be small, unlike the established religion which dominates the culture and constitutes the religion of the majority. Rather than sanctioning the affairs of the state, sects often renounce the goals of the dominant culture, opposing civil authorities. Such opposition can either be active (for example, the refusal of Jehovah's Witnesses to take part in armed conflict, the celebration of public holidays such as Christmas and Easter, or the acceptance of certain forms of medical treatment such as blood transfusion) or passive (in cases where the sect simply is indifferent to societal values, withdrawing from them, as can be seen in monastic or closed religious communities). The Amish and the Hutterites are examples of the latter. Because the sect cannot accept the values of the dominant culture, it follows that those who seek to belong are those who are disenchanted with the norms of prevailing society: the 'disaffected' and the 'alienated', who, according to Troeltsch, belong to the lower and more disadvantaged social classes.

Membership of the sect is not automatic. In most sects, neophytes enter by means of conscious decision, often publicly professed, in which they affirm their commitment to the sect's aims and values. Their applications to join will have been scrutinized by more senior members, who must satisfy themselves that the potential new member is committed to the strict moral discipline that membership entails. Belonging is thus dependent on merit rather than by birthright, and the sect characteristically imposes sanctions on those who do not live up to the expected standards. (The Jehovah's Witnesses are well known for their practice of 'disfellowshipping' wayward members.)

On this analysis, the sect by its very nature is unstable. Weber believed that, with the passage of time, there would be a tendency for the sect either to become accommodated within the church structure, as was the case with Pietism, or else the sect would become 'routinized' and come more closely to resemble the established church, existing as an independent organization. The second generation of adherents comes into the movement as a result of their parents' belonging, rather than from conscious application for membership. If a sect is headed by a charismatic leader, the void left by the leader's death tends to be filled by a successor who has 'legal-rational authority' set up from within the sect's institutional structures, rather than the charismatic authority that gave the movement its original impetus.

Weber and Troeltsch spoke of the 'church' as the entity that contrasted with the 'sect'. This was, of course, because of the fact that they lived within a culture where Christianity was the dominant religion. Their analysis, however, need not merely apply to Christian-dominated cultures, since similar contrasts could be drawn between other world religions that dominate different cultures in other parts of the globe, and minority religious groups that set themselves up in contrast to the dominant religion.

Sects, too, can admit of a variety of genres, and later sociologists defined typologies of sects. Thus J. M. Yinger (1946/1961) distinguished between 'acceptance sects', 'aggressive sects' and 'avoidance sects'. The first category was a movement within an institution seeking reform or renewal, such as the nineteenth-century Oxford Movement; a more recent example is Opus Dei. The second type totally rejects society: Yinger cites the Anabaptists. The 'avoidance sects' are those who detach themselves from the world, emphasizing other-worldliness, such as the Holiness churches.

Bryan Wilson (1961) defines an alternative typology: conversionist sects, adventist/revolutionist sects, introversionist/pietist sects and gnostic sects. The first category consists of Christian fundamentalist groups who evangelize, aiming to win the entire world for Christ; examples are the Salvation Army and the Pentecostalist churches. The adventist sects emphasize the imminent end of the present world order, emphasizing acceptance of the sect's doctrines rather than a personal conversion experience, such as the Jehovah's Witnesses and the Christadelphians. The introversionist groups correspond roughly with Yinger's 'acceptance sects', while the gnostic sects offer a body of esoteric teachings enabling the seeker to progress towards a better state of prosperity, health and personal success: examples are Christian Science and New Thought.

In addition to Weber's church/sect typology, Troeltsch added a third category: 'mysticism'. The term is somewhat misleading, since Troeltsch was thinking not so much of those who claimed to have a verbally inexpressible experience of oneness with God (the more generally accepted definition amongst theologians and philosophers of religion), but rather what he saw as a growing individualism, in which seekers quested for a personal religious experience that was independent of the fellowship of a religious community.

Howard Becker claimed that this phenomenon was a relatively unstructured form of religious expression by those who sought 'purely personal ecstatic experience, salvation, comfort, and mental or physical healing' (Becker, 1932, p. 627; quoted in Hill, 1972, p. 156.) As examples of 'cults' in this sense, Becker cited Spiritualism, Theosophy, Christian Science, 'and a variety of "pseudo-Hinduisms" linked with "Swamis and Yogis who consent, for a consideration, to carry their messages to the materialistic Western world"' (Becker, 1932, p. 628).

Becker's examples are interesting, for these movements in reality are not so much characterized by the intensity of religious ('mystical') experience that they offer, but for the distance at which they are removed from the 'church' (in the Weber–Troeltsch sense). These groups do not lay claim to be a rival form of Christianity, but have their own independent existence apart from the Christian faith. Yinger, who was Becker's student, carried the latter's thought a stage further by distinguishing between (1) the 'established sect', which is the sect which had become routinized and institutionalized; (2) the 'sect' *simpliciter,* which is the somewhat fluid group of adherents held together by a common religious experience (equivalent to Becker's 'cult'); and (3) the 'cult', a term which spans 'groups that are similar to sects, but represent a sharper break, in religious terms, from the dominant religious tradition of a society' (Yinger, 1946/1961, p. 154; quoted in Hill, 1972, p. 157).

It should be noticed that there is no consistent, agreed sociological definition of 'sect' and 'cult', and there seem to be various criteria by means of which a religious movement is designated as 'cultic': (1) the intensity of religious (mystical) experience which it offers; (2) its looseness of organization; and (3) its lack of proximity to the dominant religion.

All these are certainly elements that are, arguably, characteristics of 'cults'. I have already mentioned the role played by religious experience. The second feature – structural looseness – is one that is commonly associated with cults: one talks, for example, about a film or television series having a 'cult following', meaning that there is public approbation of (one might even say devotion to) the film or series, accompanied by 'cultic' activities, such as reading stories about the characters or the actors, or acquiring memorabilia as tangible demonstrations of one's approbation. This does not occur within any institutional organized structure; it is, rather, up to each individual to decide the exact form in which to express one's devotion. A cult in this sense, however, is very different from many of the new religious movements that are rife at the present time: the Unification Church, ISKCON (International Society for Krishna Consciousness) and the Church of Scientology, to name but three examples, are very tightly structured, and indeed the anti-cultist criticism that such movements have an authoritarian leadership only has plausibility if there is a definite structure by means of which a leader's authority can be imposed.

It is really the third feature – the lack of proximity to the dominant religion – that characterizes the new wave of NRMs. With the exception of the examples cited by Becker, the older new religions tended to be the 'Christian deviations', as Horton Davies has called them: sects that lay claim to be Christian, but whose Christian identity has been questioned by mainstream Christianity. The newer NRMs tend to be either versions of Christianity which have been laced with oriental religions (such as the Unification Church), expressions of a traditional religion other than Christianity (ISKCON, the New Kadampa Tradition, Sufism) or a completely novel religion (such as Scientology).

Church (or better, religion), sect and cult (understood in the sense of a movement that is loosely organized) form more of a continuum than a sharp distinction. Thus, loosely organized veneration can become embodied in a more definite structure, creating a 'sect'; a sect, as it comes to attract second and third generations of followers, takes on the features more appropriately associated with the 'church', and may best be described as a denomination.

The church–sect–cult typology and NRMs

The analyses offered by Weber, Troeltsch, Becker and Yinger are useful in demonstrating the development of some, although not all, new religions, demonstrating, for example, how a nebulous group that surrounds a charismatic leader can acquire a structure by 'routinization' and institutionalization. Yinger's and Wilson's studies are important in identifying various sub-categories of the 'sect', demonstrating that there are important differences among them: they are by no means all the same, as some of the less reflective anti-cult literature implies. As we have seen, however, the word 'church' is no longer appropriate, since the term limits the discussion to societies where Christianity is the dominant religion. As globalization gains momentum, the Weber–Troelsch model creates paradoxes: for example, the Soka Gakkai would be a sect in Japan, but a cult in Britain, while the Jehovah's Witnesses would be sectarian in the Christian-secularist west, but cultic in China and Korea.

It is clear that the word 'cult', as used by modern sociologists, cannot properly characterize groups such as the Unification Church, ISKCON and the Church of Scientology. Troeltsch's notion of its preoccupation with the mystical is a characterization which seems no more true of the Jehovah's Witnesses than the Church of England or of L. Ron Hubbard rather than Meister Eckhart. The majority of social scientists now tend to prefer 'heterodoxy' or deviance from the dominant culture as the cult's distinguishing feature.

Whichever definition is favoured, however, a cult is normally regarded as something which is loosely organized, and probably in a relatively undeveloped state of being, prior to its becoming more formally organized as a 'sect' (Campbell, 1972, pp. 119–35). This characterization of the cult, of course, stands in sharp contrast to the impression of the NRM which is perpetuated by the counter-cult movement, which claims that 'the cults' *are* tightly controlled by an authoritarian leader, with very strict rules about morality, commitment and community living which are rigorously enforced.

'New religions' or 'minority religions'?

The sensitivity of defining what is and what is not a new religious movement may raise the question of what is to be gained by continuing to use the concept of the NRM as a category for academic study. Instead of organizing student courses on new religious movements, perhaps one could less contentiously devise programmes on 'minority religions'.

The possible use of the expression 'minority religions' rather than 'new religious movements' raises a number of issues. What is and is not a minority religion varies according to place. Mormons constitute a religious minority on a worldwide scale, but not in Utah – a situation that is, arguably, little different from that of the Sikhs, who are a religious minority everywhere except the Punjab. Should a book or a course on minority religions include one, but not the other? If so, on what grounds? Minority religions are certainly not congruent with the cluster of religions that fall into the category of NRMs: a study of the former would certainly have to envelop older groups such as Quakers, Unitarians and Swedenborgians. To substitute 'religious minorities' for 'new religious movements' would therefore cause a shift in the centre of gravity in current academic work.

Although studies of religious minorities may have their merits, there are important reasons for continuing to use the term 'NRM', and to continue to study the cluster of groups to which it refers. First, this cluster of groups has emerged to a large degree from controversies in western society in recent times, and it is an important duty of academics to contribute to public debate. 'Cult controversies' would be much the poorer if academics shifted the ground and focused more widely on religious minorities. Critics of 'cults' have already marked out a number of groups for attention: this can be readily seen from consulting the pages of journals such as *FAIR News* and *Reachout Quarterly,* as well as visiting the web pages of cult-monitoring organizations such as the American Family Foundation. The agenda has already been set.

There is a further, perhaps more important, reason for continuing to explore NRMs rather than some slightly different category of religious groups. By examining forms of religion that are less than 150 – and in some cases less than 50 – years old, we can see how a religious organization develops in its initial stages. In what kinds of situation can a new form of spirituality emerge? What factors might serve to determine whether a new expression of religion succeeds or fails? What features does a charismatic leader have, and to what extent is charismatic leadership an important feature of an emergent religion? How do doctrines and practices emerge? How are they affected by key events, such as political occurrences, internal conflicts or prophecies that seem to fail? When the founder-leader dies, how does the group routinize and institutionalize the charisma? How is the status of the founder-leader affected by the memories of his or her followers? How does public perception of an emergent religion alter through time? How does an expression of religion change in order to attract converts within a new culture? All these are important questions in the study of religion: not only are they of intrinsic interest, but in witnessing the early development of religions before our very eyes we may also be afforded some clues as to the nature of early developments within what are now traditional world religions.

'N', 'R' and 'M'

The acronym 'NRM', which is the preferred term in academic circles, signals three key components: 'new', 'religious' and 'movement'. Each of these elements requires some comment.

New

First of all, 'new'. As I have already mentioned, some of the so-called new religions can boast a long pedigree. The Soka Gakkai, the Reiyukai and the Rissho-kosei-kai can claim to be exponents of the teachings of Nichiren (1222–82), the controversial thirteenth-century Buddhist teacher. ISKCON claims to derive from the teachings of Krishna, whom devotees regard as a real historical figure who lived in and around the holy city of Vrindaban some five thousand years ago. The Jehovah's Witnesses and the Church of Jesus Christ of Latter-day Saints insist that they are reviving the authentic Church, which became apostate through the passage of time.

The question of whether a religious group is an authentic expression of an ancient and lost tradition is notoriously difficult to

11

settle, and is partly historical and partly theological. Discussions of such matters would take us far beyond the scope of the present study, and I propose to leave these to the historians and theologians of their respective traditions. To cut several long stories short, it can be said that verdicts by mainstream traditions are unequivocally negative – a point whose importance will emerge shortly. Whether or not these restorationists receive a fair and unbiased hearing from the mainstream can be debated, but, whatever the merits of their claims to authenticity, it is preferable that the term 'NRM' should be defined in such a way as to avoid adjudicating on these delicate matters.

What is crucial, therefore, in deciding whether or not an organization belongs to the category is whether it arose in recent times *as an institution*. (An institution need not be a legal entity such as a charity, but simply an organized group that has internal social cohesion.) Taking this as the yardstick, there can be no doubt that, as an organization, ISKCON was founded in 1965, that the Soka Gakkai dates from 1930, that Watchtower Bible and Tract Society was founded in 1884, and that the name 'Jehovah's Witnesses' was not officially used until as recently as 1931. Institutionally, then, these organizations are not ancient, but recent.

One convenient benchmark that is frequently used as a watershed for separating 'old' and 'new' religions is the Second World War. Peter Clarke, for example, takes as his scope 'those new religions that have emerged in Britain since 1945' (Clarke, 1987, p. 5). Eileen Barker opts for a somewhat later boundary; she writes:

> The term new religious movement (NRM) is used to cover a disparate collection of organizations, most of which have emerged in their present form since the 1950s, and most of which offer some kind of answer to questions of a fundamental religious, spiritual or philosophical nature. (Barker, 1989, p. 9)

Other scholars believe that the real explosion of new religions came even later, identifying the 1960s and 1970s as the period of their real rise (Melton and Moore, 1982; Beckford, 1985; Nelson, 1987).

There are several problems in using a 'western post-war' rule of thumb to demarcate the new religions. First, there is a degree of parochialness in confining one's scope to Britain, or even the west, and this limited scope does not in fact reflect the work of scholars like Barker and Clarke. Clarke in particular has done much important work on new religions in Brazil, and movements like the Pacific cargo cults and African NRMs – of which there are said to be some 10,000 – are as much part of the NRM phenomenon, even though they are not included in the present study. The restriction of the term 'new' to the post-Second World War period entails that subsequent generations of scholars will be obliged to redefine the term. Post-Second World War will no longer be 'new' in two centuries' time, when – one imagines – even newer religious movements will have arisen, providing further subject matter for scholarly research.

Perhaps even more worryingly, a post-Second World War criterion fails to correspond to our intuitive identification of new religious movements, and indeed the subject area which is in reality demarcated by scholars such as Clarke, Barker, Melton and Moore, and indeed nearly all students of religion. If a new religious movement is indeed to be equated with a group which arose after 1945, it will simply not do to exclude the United Reformed Church on the grounds that it resulted from the merger of two older denominations; nor is it satisfactory to include Jehovah's Witnesses and Mormons on the ground that they are 'nearly new' or 'sufficiently similar' to those groups that unarguably fall within the researcher's declared agenda. Indeed the anti-cult criterion – 'new and disliked' – seems more reliable in distinguishing between those religions which we would intuitively wish to classify as NRMs and those which we would not.

A new religious movement, I suggest, can simply be defined as a 'recent' phenomenon. By 'recent' I mean recent in inception, not in its arrival in Britain or in any other country in the world. Thus mainstream forms of Hinduism, Buddhism, Islam and Sikhism do not count as new religions, even though they may be new to the west. I prefer to leave the precise definition of 'recent' fairly vague, rather than to specify an exact cut-off point, before which an organization can no longer be regarded as 'new'. The Unification Church, The Family, the Scientologists and the International Society for Krishna Consciousness are certainly recent; the Quakers and the Unitarians are certainly not; and the Latter-day Saints and the Jehovah's Witnesses are sufficiently recent to be of interest to the student of new religions.

The somewhat vague nature of this definition need not worry us unduly. The word 'new' is inherently nebulous: do I possess a 'new' car, for example, if I have purchased a second-hand one three months ago? The fact that there are such borderline cases does not mean that 'new' and 'old' are not appropriate distinctions to make about cars or religions. Indeed the somewhat nebulous definition of 'new' takes into account the fact that currently new religions will age, and perhaps in some cases become the older more established religions of the future.

What is religion?

I turn now to the 'R' of 'NRM'. What counts as a religion is equally problematic. Much has been written within the study of religions on the topic, and I can do little more than mention the key types of definition and suggest a somewhat dogmatic answer. E. B. Tylor, one of the early pioneers of what was then called 'comparative religion', suggested that religion was 'belief in supernatural beings'. 'Supernaturalist' definitions of this kind have largely fallen into disfavour in the study of religion today, mainly because they tend to focus on the doctrinal element of religion – a key element in Christianity, of course, but one which commands less importance in the other major world traditions. Even in Christianity, despite its history of creeds, confessions and definitions of orthodoxy and heresy, most – if not all – Christians would agree that there is more to the Christian faith than belief: there is worship, the sacraments, a whole way of living, and means of salvation that offers hope of a life to come.

For reasons such as this, many sociologists of religion operate with a 'functional' definition of religion: the important feature of religion is what it does for its followers, rather than what may exist in a supernatural realm. Thus Yinger defines religion as follows:

> Religion, then, can be defined as a system of beliefs and practices by means of which a group of people struggles with these ultimate problems of human life. It expresses their refusal to capitulate to death, to give up in the face of frustration, to allow hostility to tear apart their human aspirations. (Yinger, 1970, p. 12)

Hence, a religion enables its followers to come to terms with key events in their lives, for example, by rites of passage and by doctrinal explanations about matters such as suffering and death.

Another approach to defining religion is to consider the characteristic forms religion takes. Most religions involve myths,

14

rituals, ceremonies, beliefs, symbols, sacred texts and so on. In his various writings, Ninian Smart has identified several broad categories of component which are salient features of most, if not all, religions: the experiential, the mythic, the doctrinal, the ethical, the ritual, and the social/institutional (Smart, 1995, p. 7). He calls these the six 'dimensions' of religion.

It is not possible to enter into debate here about the merits of these various attempts to define religion. Suffice it to say that our definition must satisfy a number of conditions: it should be a definition that is accredited within the study of religions, it should be non-judgemental and non-arbitrary (that is to say, once the definition is established, groups should not be included or excluded because they are disliked or suspected of malpractices – there are bad religions as well as good ones), and it should encompass the cluster of religious groups which are typically studied in this area and brought under the general umbrella of 'NRMs'. For the purposes of the present study, then, we might say that a group of people constitutes a religious group if they operate functionally as a religion – that is to say, if they offer a means of coping with the key events and the adversities and misfortunes of life, using the key characteristics of religious practice which are identified by scholars such as Smart.

One or two further observations on the nature of religion will be relevant in the subsequent discussion. Religions tend to have overarching goals that seem humanly impossible to attain. The salvation of the world, the enlightenment of all living beings, or the ultimate triumph of good over evil are all goals which, from a human standpoint, are unattainable. Followers of religions are not like social workers or relief organizations that simply focus on one specific type of problem, such as crime or poverty: the goal is nothing short of the transformation of the entire human race, or even the entire world. In order to achieve this, two elements are needed. First, a religion typically identifies a root problem that it claims is the cause of all ill: for the Christian it is 'sin', for the Buddhist *dukkha* (unsatisfactoriness), for the Hindu *maya* (illusion). The world is not brought to perfection simply by patching up a few human problems, by building a few more homes for the destitute, or raising money for famine relief: religions aim to treat the cause, not the symptoms. Allied to this, there is a second characteristic of religion: religions hold that the world's problems are not solved by human effort alone, but require supernatural aid. For some followers of religion, this means miraculous intervention; for others, it is constant prayer or meditation, in which powers that transcend the human realm are invoked and employed.

If at times religions may seem to be uninvolved, even unconcerned about suffering in the world, this may be because they are seeking the means to achieve a more radical remedy for the cause of ill. The monk who lives apart from the world does little that is of direct benefit for those who suffer; however, since he has renounced the worldly quest for wealth and material comfort, and is developing the virtues of purity and compassion, he is removing from within himself the causes of the world's ills, and serves as an example to those who want to purify their own lives, and not merely offer first aid for specific human problems.

New religious movements are sometimes accused of not being 'genuine religions', but rather business companies or political organizations. One important way of verifying a movement's claim to a religious identity can be found by examining its ultimate aims. If the Unification Church were only attempting to secure the triumph of democracy over communism, then it would indeed be nothing more than a political organization; however, since it seeks to achieve the restoration and salvation of all humanity, and employs prayer and study as means of furthering its ultimate goals, its identity is more authentically religious.

Movements

The 'M' of 'NRM has not received as much discussion from scholars as it really merits, and no doubt seems much less problematic than the categories 'new' and 'religion'. However, its appropriateness in categorizing groups such as the Unification Church, ISKCON, the Church of Scientology and the like may legitimately be questioned. A 'movement', strictly speaking, is distinct from an organization. It is a current that moves within a wider organization, or within society as a whole. Thus one talks about Christianity's 'charismatic movement', 'the Human Potential Movement' and 'the New Age movement'. While an organization is clearly defined, with a definite structure, leadership and hierarchy, making it obvious who are inside and who are outside, a 'movement' is much more nebulous.

There is no single group to which 'the charismatics' or 'the New Agers' belong, and which might serve to define whether or not one was a charismatic or a New Ager. One can suggest a number of characteristics that are typically found amongst New Agers (as I shall do in Chapter 9), but not every New Ager possesses them all by any means. The word 'current' is often used as a near synonym for 'movement': just as one can be in the midst or at the edge of a water current, the same goes for currents of thought; those who are affected by the charismatic or the New Age movements are charismatics or New Agers to a greater or lesser degree.

This contrasts with new religions, in which, by and large, it is fairly obvious who belong and who do not. There are some problem areas: until recently, the Church of Scientology did not have formal membership, but counted as Scientologists anyone who had undergone a Dianetics course; the Unification Church is now less interested in membership than in persuading couples – who may or may not be members – to undergo the marriage Blessing. However, in sociological terms, there is a tendency towards 'institutionalization'; what starts out as a loosely organized movement, often centred around a charismatic leader, becomes a structured organization with clearly defined tenets, rituals and criteria for determining who belong and who do not. The leader's authority becomes 'institutional' and not simply charismatic, or, following the leader's death, institutional structures determine the succession. Although new in character, the vast majority of new religions have progressed beyond the stage of being movements, and even at very early stages assumed an organizational structure. That being so, it may reasonably be questioned whether the term 'movement' is an appropriate description for organizations which are highly structured and 'institutionalized'.

It is difficult, perhaps even impossible, to suggest a preferable term that will successfully encompass all that currently falls into the category 'NRM'. Many of the new religions are too large simply to be called 'groups', and others are too small or too young to be categorized as 'institutions' or 'organizations'. To call them 'religions' could suggest that they had acquired the status of the world's major traditions – a claim that probably only the Baha'i faith would wish to make about itself. Other organizations such as *est* and Transcendental Meditation would wish to claim that they were not religions at all. An expression such as 'new forms of spirituality' might more successfully encapsulate a subject matter that ranges from the nebulous New Age to the highly structured Church of Jesus Christ of Latter-day Saints.

Whatever the merits of some alternative descriptor, the term 'NRM' is now so widely used in academic circles that it would seem perverse to try to amend it. If the word 'movement' reminds us that new religions *move,* then this at least is a benefit. Not infrequently, critics view NRMs as if they are static and monolithic, or at least expect them to be so. Thus Jehovah's Witnesses have been criticized for having celebrated Christmas in the past and the Mormons on the grounds that their early leader Brigham Young drank tea and coffee. Such criticisms ignore the fact that religions develop over time. The Jehovah's Witnesses did not decide to forgo Christmas celebrations until the 1930s – which only serves to show that it took several decades for them to define their stance on the Church's festival year (Watchtower, 1993, p. 79). Similarly, Mormon food and drink laws were not systematically enforced until around the end of the nineteenth century. Even today, there are different schools of thought amongst Mormons on how precisely they should be interpreted.

Some further defining characteristics

Although an NRM's three key characteristics are ostensibly being new, religious and a movement (or at least a group or organization), there are some additional factors that are relevant to categorizing a movement as an NRM.

An NRM is outside the mainstream. In many cases, the traditional religions have taken NRMs to task for heretical beliefs or unorthodox practices, claiming that they are not authentic forms of the mainstream religion to which many of them claim to belong. For the Christian evangelical, for example, the Mormons and the Unification Church have undoubtedly hit on raw nerves when they claim respectively that Joseph Smith received a new revelation of Jesus Christ, and that the new messiahs are now on earth to complete Jesus' unfinished work.

The movements that we instinctively classify as NRMs find difficulty in securing a position within mainstream religious orthodoxy or orthopraxy. For example, when the Unification

Church applied for membership of various national Councils of Churches, it was consistently turned down, and the Jehovah's Witnesses and the Mormons would not particularly wish to be part of mainstream Christianity (although of course they would still classify themselves as 'Christian'), since they consider all the mainstream churches to be in serious error. As I have already mentioned, the Soka Gakkai is often regarded as an inauthentic form of Buddhism amongst Buddhists more widely. Not only did Nichiren, their historical founder-leader, regard all other forms of Buddhism as inadequate, but other Buddhists, conversely, often regard them as 'not truly Buddhist'. For many years the UK Buddhist Society's directory did not list them at all; in the most recent edition they have secured a single entry, and the directory now carries a disclaimer stating that inclusion does not indicate endorsement or authenticity (Buddhist Society, 1991, p ii).

The criterion of being 'outside the mainstream' does not merely encompass those groups that are 'on the fringe' of a major world religion, but find difficulty in securing adequate recognition. Additionally, there exists a cluster of religious groups which are 'free-standing' and which cannot be obviously related to any single mainstream tradition. For example, there is the group of religions which Paul Heelas characterizes as the 'self religions' – a category which embraces movements such as Exegesis (Programmes Ltd), Rebirthing, Transcendental Meditation and the Church of Scientology (Heelas, 1982). Such groups, of course, have no particular desire to be aligned with a major world tradition, although some groups may sometimes claim to draw on mainstream traditions – Hinduism and Buddhism in the case of Scientology (Church of Scientology, 1994, p. xxvii). The fact that they are 'free-standing' and hence lack a specific religious identity contributes to the anti-cult feeling that their goals are unclear and possibly sinister.

ISKCON is perhaps more of a problem. Not only does it claim to be the world's oldest religious tradition, stemming from the ancient Vedic tradition, but it has a large following of those who are Hindu by birth, and is accepted by the National Council of Hindu Temples in the UK. There are of course many problems in defining what is 'mainstream' in such a diverse set of traditions that comprise the Hindu religions and in which there is no tightly defined hierarchy to define orthodoxy and orthopraxy. However, there are certain aspects of ISKCON that mark them out from traditional Hinduism,

19

as it is found in western society. As I have discussed elsewhere (Chryssides, 1994a), most Hindu families in the west still maintain a form of the caste system, which is determined by birth, and which is evident in their social contacts and their marriage arrangements. ISKCON has called into question conventional Hindu attitudes to caste, by attributing to the Bhagavad Gita the teaching that the original four varnas referred to societal function rather than to social status, and that the true brahmin is the one who understands 'Supreme Absolute Truth' (Satsvarupa, 1983, pp. 74–5). Caste, according to Prabhupada and his disciples, is not something which is gained by heredity, and indeed it would not be possible for the western convert, who embraces ISKCON's beliefs and practice, to find a niche in a caste system which belongs to a different society and has operated in a very rigid manner for millennia. A further implication of this is that the western leaders, who have acquired what effectively amounts to brahmin status within the organization, enjoy the somewhat controversial status of white western brahmins. Although this may not seem incongruous to westerners who remain outside any caste system, it is certainly a remarkable feature to the Hindu, and arouses comment particularly inside India. In Vrindaban, for example, where its international headquarters are situated, ISKCON is regarded as an unusual expression of Hinduism.

The NRM attracts converts from the indigenous culture. Although issues of evangelization tactics, 'recruitment' and brainwashing have assumed a certain importance in academic study (Barker, 1984; Clarke, 1987), the concept of conversion is seldom, if ever, regarded as a defining characteristic. Proselytizing methods loom much larger in the anti-cultists' discussion of the phenomenon, and anti-cult leaflets which state that 'anyone is vulnerable' make the point that members of the public may find themselves converting to a religion which often appears to others to be socially unacceptable or culturally inappropriate (FAIR, 1990, p. 4).

The fact that NRMs attract converts clearly seems an important feature in determining which organizations come under the scope of cult-monitoring activity, not to mention academic scrutiny. Evangelical Christians in particular are concerned that NRMs attract converts whose indigenous religious identity might find a more conventional expression in western Christianity. Conversion (or 'recruitment') is thus seen as demanding apostasy from a religion which is believed to offer 'the truth', or from a conventional way of living which values material possessions, comfort and a lifestyle consisting of conventional secular occupations such as medicine, teaching and so on. The fact that the lifestyle afforded by the NRM is sometimes radically different from western cultural expectations is a common source of difficulty between NRM converts and their families. To the parents whose child was destined to become a lawyer, a teacher or a social worker, life as a sannyasin symbolizes 'dropping out' or failure; for the convert, by contrast, to live an unexamined conventional lifestyle is failure, compared with the spiritual liberation that the NRM is claimed to afford.

The proselytizing aspect of the phenomenon is highly relevant to our initial decision as to which religious movements might count as NRMs. As Barker has pointed out (1989, pp. 11–13), one important characteristic of new religious movements is the first-generation convert. What the new religious movements lack, in contrast with older religions, are family traditions of belonging: because NRMs are new, members belong by choice rather than habit. Even in the case of NRMs that do not actively proselytize, such as the Gurdjieff Society, belonging has come about by converting to the movement, rather than a long-standing family tradition.

As NRMs become older, of course, a second generation arises, and, as time goes on, the proportion of first-generation converts declines. This has already happened in the case of the Mormons and Jehovah's Witnesses, and we are beginning to see this in the Unification Church and ISKCON, where members try to ensure that their children are brought up within these movements and remain in them as they mature. When this occurs, these movements are less likely to be viewed as 'threatening to society' since they can no longer justly be accused of 'splitting up families' to the same degree: on the contrary, membership is more likely to be a contributory factor to family coherence and stability, as is the case with established Christian denominations.

Some problems

There are always problematic cases that appear to defy one's categories. Opus Dei, for example, often regarded as a 'cult' by its critics, nonetheless consists of members of the Roman Catholic Church, and hence is not 'outside the mainstream'. Is it an NRM any more than the Sea of Faith, which is a group of liberal Christians in Britain and New Zealand – mainly Protestant, and with a few Unitarians – for whom it is a forum for exploring radical reinterpretations of the Christian faith? No doubt there are more serious concerns about Opus Dei because of practices such as self-flagellation, but many Protestants strongly disapprove of the Sea of Faith for theological reasons, since many of its members reject the notion of a transcendent God and are unable to accept Jesus Christ as fully divine.

One might also consider whether Pentecostalism should be counted as an NRM. The Pentecostalist churches in Britain have not sought membership of the Council of Churches for Britain and Ireland, and hence remain outside the mainstream. The 'revival' of glossolaliation is a recent phenomenon, dating back to 1906, when some Christians in Los Angeles began to experience 'baptism in the Holy Spirit'. Whether the tongue-speaking of modern Pentecostalists is a revival of the original Pentecost experience described in Acts 2 is debatable. Luke's account is itself unclear as to whether the disciples' speech was miraculously translated into a multiplicity of languages, or whether the critics who accused them of drunken babbling were hearing something like the sounds one hears in Pentecostalist worship. Since sound-recording is a recent invention, we have no way of establishing whether glossolaliation has a long or a lost tradition, or whether it is really something new.

No doubt Pentecostalists have escaped inclusion under the umbrella of 'cults' for several reasons. They are theologically orthodox, with the exception of the 'Oneness Pentecostalists', who contend, in common with Unitarians, Jehovah's Witnesses and Latter-day Saints, that the doctrine of the Trinity is not to be found in scripture, and who have now become a target of evangelical Christian counter-cultists. The charismatic revival of the 1960s, further renewed by the Toronto Blessing of 1994, enabled glossolaliation to spread into some mainstream Protestant churches, thus bringing the phenomenon of 'tongues' into the mainstream.

Such movements are borderline cases of NRMs. While I have not given them coverage in the present volume, they are a salutary reminder that the boundaries between mainstream religion and NRMs are by no means clear-cut. There is still a tendency to equate NRMs, like 'cults' with groups that are disliked, if not by the researcher, at least by the public or by religious believers more widely. Perhaps the time has come to consider whether our boundaries are arbitrary and need some slight rearrangement.

Typologies of NRMs

There are many more NRMs in existence than can be manageably dealt with in a single volume. If we are to understand them, it is therefore necessary to devise some of kind of typology, by means of which we can classify new religious movements.

Counter-cultist typologies

For some considerable time, counter-cultists tended to suggest that 'cults' possessed more or less identical features, and it is still not uncommon for counter-cult organizations to formulate 'marks of a cult' such as authoritarian leadership, enforced obedience, illegal activities, control over members' sexual mores, and the acquisition of members' financial assets to augment the leaders' personal fortune. More recently, however, at least two British counter-cult groups have identified two major types of NRM: (1) 'self-improvement/counselling' and (2) new religious movements. Presumably this distinction relates to a perceived difference between movements that appear distinctively religious in character, and those which lack overtly religious features (at least as traditionally understood) and emphasize human potential. In this latter category would fall Dianetics, Programmes Ltd (formerly Exegesis), *est* and Transcendental Meditation.

As a consequence of the somewhat negative portrayal of 'cults' by their critics, the term 'destructive cult' has sometimes been used as a label for new religious movements. Thus Eli Shapiro (1977) itemizes several features which are supposedly characteristic of the 'destructive cult': total obedience, separation from society, discouragement of education, hatred of parents and other authority figures, disregard for bodily welfare, communal living, psychological coercion which makes disengagement virtually impossible, and, finally, brainwashing – a familiar list! As examples of destructive cults, Shapiro cites ISKCON, the Unification Church, the Divine Light Mission, the Church of Scientology and the Children of God. Shapiro provides no examples of benign cults, and it is unclear whether he believes the epithet 'destructive' applies to all NRMs, or whether he is suggesting a possible typology in which NRMs can be categorized into 'destructive' and 'benign'.

The essential problem, of course, about such a typology is that, apart from obvious disasters such as the Peoples Temple, the Waco community, the Solar Temple and Heaven's Gate, the question of whether an NRM is destructive or beneficial is subjective to a high degree. Not only will members testify to the benefits of belonging, but even ex-members are not unanimously hostile to movements that they left, sometimes claiming that they helped with their spiritual quest at the time, or that they offered 'this-worldly' benefits such as administrative skills, public speaking or learning trades that are needed within the movement. This is not to say that there are no malpractices within NRMs, but to categorize NRMs as 'destructive' or 'benign' would be to ignore the enormous complexity of NRMs, as well as the variety of people who join them and who benefit or are harmed to different degrees and in different ways.

Christian and counterfeit-Christian cults

Because evangelical Protestant Christianity has a supreme interest in saving people's souls, it is perhaps understandable that some Christian writers have sought to classify religious movements in terms of their approximation to authentic Christianity. In his book *Cult Critiques* (1995), Doug Harris distinguishes between 'counterfeit-Christian cults', 'Christian cults', 'commune cults' and 'personality cults'. The first category embraces the Jehovah's Witnesses, the Latter-day Saints, Christadelphians and Christian Scientists, while the second encompasses the Central Church of Christ, The Family, Seventh-day Adventists and the Word-Faith Movement. Interestingly, the Unification Church and the Worldwide Church of God are judged to be neither Christian nor counterfeit-Christian, but 'personality cults', presumably because of the prominence given by their members to Sun Myung Moon and Herbert W. Armstrong respectively.

If it is indeed the case that Jesus Christ offers the sole means of salvation, as evangelical Christians believe, then clearly it is important to ascertain whether any of the new religions can serve as a vehicle to mediate the divine grace to make available the effects of Christ's redeeming work. Indeed, if counterfeit-Christian groups exist, it is all the more important to identify them and unmask them, for, if the Christian evangelical is right, then followers of such groups are doubly mistaken. Not only are they mistaken in accepting a set of false beliefs and practices, but they are also mistaken in presuming that such falsehoods mediate salvation, when they do not. At least ISKCON devotees or Scientologists are under no illusion that their chosen spiritual home offers Christ's salvation. Just as the possessor of counterfeit money is, arguably, in a worse position that someone who has no money at all, and who therefore has a true understanding of his or her financial state, so those who fall victim to the spiritual counterfeits can have a false sense of security, supposing their eternal salvation is assured, when this is far from the case.

What appears to be decisive for Harris in determining a group's claim to a Christian identity is not merely its acceptance of Christ's saving work, but its ability to accept the credal affirmations of mainstream Christianity. One common feature of Harris's 'counter-feit-Christian' groups is that they characteristically reject doctrines such as the Trinity and Christ's oneness with the Father. This contrasts with The Family, who, much as their views of sex and family life may attract forceful criticism, nevertheless openly affirm the historical doctrines of the Christian Church, and hence are presumed to possess the means of salvation.

Although it is important for evangelical Christians to draw a distinction between Christian and pseudo-Christian cults, it is the Church itself that has the sole responsibility for defining the bounds between orthodoxy and heresy. Heresy is not a category that can simply be applied at will to a religious group whose teachings one rejects; something is only heretical if the Church as a whole or a mainstream Christian denomination has formally pronounced a belief heretical: it is not the task of a scholar of religion to do the Church's work for it. As to the question of which NRMs offer salvation, I think it would be rash in the extreme to venture an opinion. Even scholars within mainstream Christianity have acknowledged that this is an extremely difficult, even impossible question to settle. St Augustine, for example, claimed that the marks of the true Church were invisible ones, known only to God, who would divide the wheat from the chaff when the Heavenly City was finally complete.

World-affirming, world-renouncing and world-accommodating religions

I turn to typologies devised within academic circles. The best-known typology of NRMs is Roy Wallis's distinction between 'world-affirming', 'world-renouncing' and 'world-accommodating' religions. Wallis notes that certain religions share 'the common characteristic of accepting most of the goals and values of the wider society but providing new means to achieve them' (Wallis, 1985, p. 5). Thus organizations like Scientology and *est* endorse conventional societal values, such as the value of a better job, a high IQ or more successful personal relationships, but suggest novel means by which these can be attained. In common with society at large, they prize the material world, viewing it as fundamentally good and worth entering into. In pursuit of worldly values, such religions will often use worldly means such as present-day marketing techniques, and charge normal (or even high) prices for courses, just as one would in the secular world. Such religions are to be classified as 'world-affirming'. As examples of world-affirming NRMs, Wallis cites Transcendental Meditation, the Human Potential Movement, *est*, Silva Mind Control and Scientology.

By contrast, other religious movements view the secular world as fundamentally corrupt, and emphasize the need to separate oneself from it. In many cases, such separation is physical and not merely emotional, and followers of such 'world-renouncing' religions separate off from the world into their own discrete communities. Conventional values are rejected: one abandons one's family life and career in favour of a spiritual monastic-style community. Conventional sexual relationships are often renounced in favour of celibacy. Belonging involves total commitment. The secular world, being corrupt, is irredeemable, and those who belong to world-renouncing religions will often predict an imminent eschaton which will bring to an end the present world order. Thus Christian-orientated groups will predict an imminent return of Christ, while ISKCON devotees will preach that humankind is living in the *kali yuga*, the dark age which will finally end with Krishna absorbing the universe into himself and re-creating it. As examples of world rejecting NRMs, Wallis cites the Unification Church, ISKCON, CoG (now The Family) and the Peoples Temple.

Wallis claims to identify a third category of religious movement which lies between the two extremes. The 'world-accommodating' religion (Wallis's third category) does not entirely reject societal norms and values, but rather teaches that humanity has fallen away from some divine plan. The remedy for such backsliding is not world-renunciation, but rather a renewed fervour within one's spiritual life. Wallis cites Neo-Pentecostalism and the Charismatic Renewal Movement as examples of world-accommodating forms of spirituality. While phenomena such as glossolaliation and prophecy are not features of secular society, such 'gifts' can be practised without the follower having to abandon his or her secular job, family, education or secular ambitions.

As world-rejecting movements develop, they can find difficulty in sustaining their separatist structure. Gaining finances and support can become a problem; and members become older and themselves sometimes want to settle into more conventional family life. Accordingly, it has become possible to join ISKCON and the Unification Church without being committed to the community living and austere lifestyle that have been associated with such movements.

Wallis's scheme has the undoubted advantage of demonstrating how different NRMs (as well as traditional religions) come to terms with one important and fundamental question, namely how the material world is to be valued. Wallis also has the merit of showing not only that different NRMs can answer the question in different ways, but that, with the passage of time, an NRM can move from one end of the spectrum towards the other. The world-rejecting can through time become world-accommodating.

Wallis's classification is rather broad, and a rather blunt instrument by which to classify NRMs. Where, for example, should one place Roman Catholicism, which has a majority of lay members who pursue a secular world-affirming lifestyle, but yet which maintains a celibate priesthood and monastic orders which separate themselves from the world in pursuit of the spiritual life?

By simultaneously spanning both the teachings and the practices of religions, it is hard to see how Wallis could deal with the very complex attitude to the world displayed by certain groups, which cannot straightforwardly be labelled 'world-affirming', 'world-rejecting' or 'world-accommodating'. The Jehovah's Witnesses provide one such example. They are an entirely lay movement with no priesthood or monastic orders (world-affirming), although one might argue that they form their own distinct community (world-rejecting). They pursue the family life and normal forms of employment (world-

27

affirming), yet their imminent expectation of an end to the present world causes them to place little value on worldly wealth and investment (world-rejecting). They teach that the world is currently under Satan's control (world-rejecting), but that key events in world history are predicted in the Bible and are part of God's plan of salvation (world-affirming). Although they expect an imminent end to the present world order (world-rejecting), their interpretation of the Bible leads them to believe that the earth will be renewed, and that all those who are 'in the truth', but who do not belong to the 144,000, will live under Christ's rule in an earthly paradise.

Wallis's scheme is highly problematical as a typology of NRMs. This is largely because, as a sociologist, he has tended to treat them in terms of their societal, empirically obvious characteristics. NRMs are much more complex, having teachings that are much more sophisticated and intricate than certainly their critics and indeed many academics often allow. Rather than classify religions crudely into these three categories, it would be more accurate to say that all religions possess world-affirming, world-renouncing and world-accommodating characteristics, and that most religions possess all three in varying degrees.

Turner's taxonomy

Another kind of typology comes from Harold W. Turner (1998). Turner distinguishes between: (1) 'neo-primal'; (2) NRMs that synthesize; (3) 'Hebraist'; and (4) independent churches. The first type attempts to revive the traditional primal religions that existed before the advent of Christian missionaries, while the second combines features of primal religions with Christian missionary elements. Hebraist groups endeavour to return to the Jewish scriptures, allowing no status to Jesus of Nazareth, either as a divine or semi-divine being or as a saviour figure. Independent churches acknowledge Jesus as more than a historical human being, but are not allied to mainstream church councils, and often have their own idiosyncratic features. Examples of these four categories respectively are the Godianism (an east Nigerian neo-primal religion), the Unification Church (which combines Korean folk shamanism with Christianity), the Rastafarians and the Aladura.

It will be immediately obvious that Turner's scheme is designed to encompass only those new religions that arise from the interaction between Judaeo-Christianity and primal religions – a phenomenon which has been Turner's life-long interest, particularly with reference to Africa. The scheme usefully points to the fact that, far from straightforwardly converting primal races to the Christian faith, Christian mission resulted in a number of different reactions. As I have pointed out elsewhere (Chryssides, 1994a), there is no agreed distinction between culture and religion, and, when those who espoused primal religions expressed a wish to convert to Christianity, it would be immediately apparent what this entailed, in terms of giving up elements of one's previous life. One example which has typically aroused controversy is ancestor veneration, often called 'ancestor worship' by missionaries. Was ancestor veneration a violation of the first of the ten Mosaic commandments, which proscribes worship of any being other than Yahweh, or was it merely an innocuous folk practice? 'Worship', of course, was a piece of English vocabulary, and hence was the missionaries' term, not that of the culture from which the practice derived. Was the practice really 'worship', or was it no more than a means of showing respect for one's forebears? It was inevitable that different missionaries and different converts – over whom missionaries had various degrees of control – should reach different decisions, with the result that some converts made quite a radical break with their past lives, while others felt able to synthesize, freely combining elements of folk culture and religion with Christianity. Other reactions to the Christian message might include renewed vigour for one's previous faith – a phenomenon which one often finds when a religion is challenged by another (Chryssides, 1994a). Another scenario is that people can abandon their previous primal religion as a result of hearing a garbled version of the gospel message, perhaps as a result of hearing a new convert, who was little acquainted with the Bible, and had little understanding. This phenomenon certainly occurred in Korea, and accounts for the rise of a number of New Christian groups there, although not for the Unification Church itself.

Turner's scheme provides a useful tool for understanding the character of a number of NRMs. Some are concerned to return their origins, which they perceive as being threatened. Others – like the Unification Church – are innovative, emphasizing continuing revelation and seeing no reason to preserve either Korean indigenous religion or mainstream Christianity in their historical forms. A

29

further, important, phenomenon to recognize is that, just as primal cultures can wish to preserve their tradition, so New Christian groups can feel a need to recapture a lost past. For example, the Latter-day Saints and the Jehovah's Witnesses might both be described as 'restorationist' groups, seeking to recapture first-century Christianity, which they believe has been lost in layers of tradition and apostasy.

Turner's scheme proved suitable for his own purposes, but it is of course incomplete, being incapable of accommodating religions that are neither primal in character nor related to the Judaeo-Christian tradition. As Turner himself would acknowledge, the scheme cannot incorporate groups like Scientology, ISKCON or the Soka Gakkai. Nonetheless, Turner's emphasis on primal religions is important, particularly in view of renewed interest in primal societies in recent times, for example, shamanism, Native American religion, pre-Christian Celtic religion and magic.

Melton and Moore

In their book *The Cult Experience* J. Gordon Melton and Robert L. Moore propose an eight-fold typology. New religions, they claim, can be divided into: (1) Latter-day Saints; (2) communalists; (3) metaphysicians; (4) psychic-spiritualist; (5) Ancient Wisdom schools; (6) magical groups; (7) Eastern religions; and (8) Middle Eastern faiths (Melton and Moore, 1982, pp. 19–20).

Defining the Latter-day Saints as a single category may seem initially surprising, but it should be remembered that there around 40 different Mormon or Mormon-derived groups that emanate from Joseph Smith (Melton, 1996). The second category (communalists) embraces groups that share community living, ranging from the Amish to The Family (formerly the Children of God). The meta-physicians are those who derive their thinking from Phineas Parkhurst Quimby, denying the reality of evil in their quest for health, wealth or happiness. The psychic-spiritualist groups emphasize the paranormal, typically employing mediums in their endeavours to contact the spirit world. The Ancient Wisdom groups tend to be esoteric and occultist, denying their wisdom to the wider public, but espousing teachings which professedly come from ancient sources such as Egypt or Atlantis. Magical groups are self-explanatory, and incorporate witches and pagans. Eastern religions derive from Hinduism and Buddhism principally, but also other eastern faiths, while the Middle Eastern faiths are based on Judaism or Islam, often in their mystical forms, such as Sufism.

Melton and Moore's scheme is largely based on the historical developments of American religious alternatives, with the exception of the communalist category, where there does not appear to be any direct influence between groups as diverse as the Bruderhof, the Amish, The Family and the Unification Church. There are a few groups that are difficult to place in this scheme: Scientology has no obvious niche, nor do the Raëllians and other such groups that base their teachings on extra-terrestrial communication. Perhaps it is inevitable that no completely definitive scheme can be devised, and that there will always remain a residue of groups that must be labelled 'miscellaneous'. As William Bainbridge writes, 'we will recognize that each religious organization is unique and cannot be placed perfectly in any category ... We will view religion not as a set of distinct organizations arranged in conceptual boxes, but as dynamic systems of beliefs, practices, socioeconomic structures and human beings' (Bainbridge, 1997, p. 25).

Towards a typology

How does one arrive at an appropriate typology? The above typologies need not be seen as mutually incompatible or competing, since a typology is, to a large extent, a classification system that is designed to suit one's particular purposes. Just as a computer can classify files according to icon, size, kind, name or date, depending on what the operator wants to achieve, so each typology can effectively serve a particular set of requirements. Those who are keen to trace the historical development of NRMs would do well to note Melton and Moore's categorizations. Evangelical Christians who believe that they can determine which groups mediate the proper means of salvation would do well to consider Harris's scheme. Those who are interested in the interaction between traditional faiths and primal religions will see merit in Turner's taxonomy, whereas sociologists who are examining the ways in which NRMs interact with society will no doubt be helped by Wallis.

There are two basic requirements for a taxonomy. First, it should be exhaustive, enabling no religion to elude the parameters it sets. Second, it should highlight distinctions that are genuine and, as far as possible, unproblematic. (The 'benign'/'destructive' typology fails on the second requirement, since it is simply possible to apportion each NRM unequivocally into one of these two categories.) My own arrangement of NRMs relates to the major tradition to which they are aligned, where one exists. Thus one can distinguish 'New Christian' groups, Hindu and Hindu-related organizations, new forms of Buddhism and groups that originated from Islam. If space had permitted, it would also have possible to identify and discuss new Jewish groups, such as the messianic and Lubavich Jews, as well as Sikh-related groups such as Healthy Happy and Holy (3H). Additionally, there exist groups that do not relate in any obvious way to any single world religion: the Church of Scientology, for example, appears superficially to emphasize self-improvement, although Scientologists will often contend that the ideas of their founder-leader L. Ron Hubbard are derived at least in part from Hinduism and Buddhism. This cluster of religions – if religions they are – I have brought under the umbrella term 'Human Potential Movement'. The New Age, of course, is notoriously difficult to pigeon-hole, and I shall consider whether this can strictly be called a new religion: it is certainly a recent form of alternative spirituality, and its very pervasiveness merits inclusion in this volume.

It may be better to view my attempt at taxonomy, not so much as an attempt to find neat pigeon-holes into which various new religions fit, but rather as a set of ingredients which different NRMs possess in differing degrees. Most religions have syncretized with the passage of time, a phenomenon that causes certain groups such as Latter-day Saints and Jehovah's Witnesses to try to recapture the lost 'purity' of a tradition. Particularly in the case of NRMs there is often no single category into which to fit. The Rastafarians, for example, would not claim to be Jewish, yet they use Hebrew scriptures and not Christian ones, and can be viewed as a reaction against Christianity, combining these features with a 'Back to Africa' ideology which has often been more political than religious. In what follows, with the exception of Chapter 2, I propose to categorize the NRMs under discussion in terms of their principal religious ingredients. While this has its problems, it has the merit of bringing to the fore the salient beliefs and practices, and the sources from which they originate.

2. The 'suicide cults'

One word that is most frequently associated with 'cults' is the word 'problem', and it is an interesting exercise to see how long it is before a journalist or an author of a book on new religions – even an academic one – introduces the word into the discussion. Although the most commonly experienced problems associated with NRM membership are family relationships, financial commitments and alleged 'brainwashing', it is remarkable how frequently the counter-cult movement remind its readers of 'mass suicides', particularly those of Jonestown and Waco. It is extremely doubtful whether Jim Jones' Peoples Temple, the Waco community, the Solar Temple or Heaven's Gate would have attracted much attention, even amongst academics, if it had not been for their catastrophic endings, but the inevitable publicity that ensued, as well as the fears that NRM membership entails a similar risk, makes these 'suicide cults' a suitable cluster of groups to examine here. These four groups were markedly different in character: the Peoples Temple was a fairly radical expression of a Christian social gospel; the Branch Davidians were a fundamentalist Christian group in the Adventist tradition; the Solar Temple was in the Templar tradition; and Heaven's Gate was a UFO group that combined its UFOlogy with biblical exegesis. Of these groups, the Adventists are probably most significant in terms of the wider dissemination of their constituent ideas, and I have given substantial emphasis to their historical origins, since Advent-ism has been an important influence on a variety of New Christian organizations, including the Jehovah's Witnesses.

The Peoples Temple

Jim Jones' Peoples Temple has become the archetypal 'destructive cult'. Ever since 919 people at Jonestown lost their lives in the tragic event of 18 November 1978, the Jonestown massacre has featured in nearly every anti-cult book, and is constantly revived as a reminder of the dangers of 'bizarre cults'. How such a large group of people could be brought to commit suicide *en masse* is something that does not admit of a ready explanation. The event was so extraordinary that some commentators have – perhaps understandably – resorted to conspiracy theories: Jones, they argue, was no mere clergyman, but a CIA agent commissioned to conduct an experiment in thought control (Church of Scientology, 1995). The most commonly offered theory, however, is that the group was an example of religion gone wrong, a fanatical group into which its members were brainwashed, and would do anything that Jim Jones, its authoritarian 'messianic' leader, commanded.

The notion of 'brainwashing' had been rife for some 25 years before the Jonestown massacre, having had its origin in the treatment of US prisoners of war during the Korean War of 1950–3. In its wake a number of psychological studies were carried out to ascertain the extent to and the conditions under which experimental subjects would radically alter their behaviour in conformity to group pressure or in obedience to an authority figure. An example of the former was Solomon Ashe's experiments, where subjects were shown pictures of lines of unequal length, but apparently preferred to conform to previously agreed suggestions of confederates of the experimenter rather than declare what their senses ought clearly to have suggested. Stanley Milgram (1974) was notorious for his experiments, described in his *Obedience to Authority,* in which volunteers demonstrated their preparedness to obey the instructions of the experimenter, a presumed 'authority figure', who sanctioned the administration of high-voltage electric shocks to others.

For those who were nervous about the rise of the 'cults' two well-publicized events in the 1960s and 1970s helped to fuel such fears. One concerned the Charles Manson murders of the late 1960s: Manson's community was not a religious group, but to many it served to illustrate the lengths to which members of a group would go under the direction of a leader who maintained power over them. (Manson was an anti-establishment 'hippie messiah', who ordered his followers to undertake multiple random killings in California.) The other was the case of Patty Hearst, the daughter of a respectable wealthy American family, who suddenly vanished from her home, to reappear as an active member of the Symbionese Liberation Army. In the face of the argument that no normal young woman would voluntarily undergo such a transformation, many concluded that her metamorphosis was evidence of brainwashing. It is not surprising that the brainwashing theory should emerge as the most favoured popular explanation for the mass suicide at the Peoples Temple.

Like a number of individuals who have been responsible for human tragedies on a vast scale, Jones has become demonized and regarded as the archetypal authoritarian leader, who demanded and received unquestioning obedience from his followers, to the extent that they were prepared to sacrifice not only their own lives, but to murder their own young children for Jones' cause. Certainly things went very wrong with the Peoples Temple, particularly in its final period following its emigration to Guyana. However, it would be naive to suppose that Jones was simply a charismatic leader who could make his followers do anything, or that he had a hypnotic hold over the members, eliciting obedience at all times. The Peoples Temple had its attractions, and afforded positive reasons for belonging. In a letter to her family, one member wrote the following:

> You obviously think that the Peoples Temple is just another cult or religious fanatic place or something like that. Well, I'm kind of offended that you think I would stoop so low as to join some weirdo group. I think I am a pretty sensible person and I can tell what's real and what's not. People have a hard time fooling me. The reason I think that the Temple is great is not just because Jim Jones can make people cough up cancers but because there is the largest group of people I have ever seen who are concerned about the world and are fighting for truth and justice for the world ... it's the only place I have seen real true Christianity being practiced. (Moore, 1985, p. 93)

Jim Jones

James Warren Jones (1931–78) was born in Indiana. After commencing work in a hospital, he began his college education. Ever since his youth he engaged in street preaching, proclaiming the theme of human brotherhood to mixed-race audiences. In 1949 he married Marceline Baldwin, a white Methodist, who encouraged him in his campaign for racial justice. (Some reports of Jones state that Marceline was descended from Cherokee Indians, enabling Jones to claim that his family were 'bi-racial'.) Drawn towards communism, the couple attended various local communist rallies, and America's McCarthy era only served to strengthen their determination. Jones believed that he could use the Church as a vehicle for the proclamation of communism. In 1952 Jones became a student pastor in Sommerset Southside Methodist Church; however, the congregation did not support his quest for racial integration, and Jones felt that he had no option but to leave. His search for a community of like-minded people took him to the Seventh Day Baptists and to Pentecostalists. At a Pentecostalist convention, a woman pastor picked Jones out from the congregation and declared, 'I perceive that you are a prophet that shall go around the world ... And tonight you shall begin your ministry' (Hall, 1987, p. 18). Jones, in turn, called people out from the congregation and began to administer spiritual healing: this marked the beginning of his ministry as a revivalist preacher and healer.

In 1954 Jones founded his own religious community, called 'Community Unity'. It was renamed 'Wings of Deliverance' in 1955, and later in the same year it became the Peoples Temple. (It was so-called because of the Pentecostalist use of the term 'Temple', signifying the place where the Holy Spirit dwelt.) It had a choir and a youth group and a reputation for a healing ministry, and it proclaimed a 'social gospel'. It was therefore understandable that it attracted a healthily growing congregation. In addition to the regular worship, Jim and Marceline continued their work with the poor and disadvantaged, even using their own home as a nursing home, providing accommodation for various people of mixed race, with a basement restaurant, where free food was provided for the poor. Their resident community became known as their 'rainbow family'. In the late 1950s Jones visited Father Divine's Peace Mission in Philadelphia, and borrowed several of Divine's ideas for a ministry to the dispossessed. The practice of Jones' followers of calling him 'Dad' was derived from Father Divine's mission. The Peoples Temple experienced some harassment, particularly from the substantial racist elements within the locality, and Jones' church was daubed with swastikas on several occasions.

In 1959 the Peoples Temple affiliated with the Disciples of Christ under the name of the 'Peoples Temple Christian Church, Full Gospel'. The Disciples of Christ is a mainstream denomination, being affiliated to local and national councils of churches. It is important to note, therefore, that, at least in its American period, the

Peoples Temple was a mainstream Christian community, and not an NRM that existed on Christianity's fringes. In 1964 the Disciples of Christ ordained Jones as a full minister. He continued to proclaim his social gospel, and actively campaigned for social justice within his locality. In 1961, for example, he was made Executive Director of the Indianapolis Human Rights Commission.

Jones was no Christian fundamentalist: he preached a social gospel, being more interested in people's physical needs than in some metaphysical world which may or may not be inhabited by a mysterious transcendent God. Jones emphatically rejected the traditional supernatural 'sky God' of Christianity – the 'buzzard God', as he called him, who hovered over humanity, swooping down occasionally to mete out punishment or misfortune to unlucky victims. If it seems strange for a Christian minister apparently to deny the existence of the God of theism, it should be remembered that Jones was by no means unique in this regard. A substantial sector of mainstream Christianity had found problems with traditional theism, as was witnessed by the provocative 'death of God' movement of the 1960s, spearheaded by Thomas J.J. Altizer and William Hamilton. Jones himself stated, 'I am God', although it is difficult to know precisely what he meant by this. Jones was more of a social activist than a theologian, and it may be inappropriate to expect retrospectively to be able to scrutinize such claims for exact meanings. It is unclear whether he was asserting some special status exclusively for himself, or encouraging all his congregation to discover a god who resides within each individual. Certainly Jones believed that salvation was to be found, not in some other world beyond the present physical world, but by working towards the betterment of human life on earth, here and now.

Jones' claims about his relationship with Jesus are certainly bold. On one occasion he is reported to have said:

> I have put on Christ, you see. I have followed after the example of Christ. When you see me ... it's no longer Jim Jones here. I'm crucified with Christ, nevertheless I live, yet not I, but Christ that lives here. Now Christ is in this body ... You will not get Christ's blessing in Jim Jones' blessing until you walk like Jim Jones, until you talk like Jim Jones, until you act like Jim Jones, until you look like Jim Jones. How long will I be with you until you understand that *I* am no longer a man, but a Principle. I am the Way, the Truth, and the Light. No one can come to the Father but through me. (Moore, 1985, p. 155)

Jones reinforced his status by his healing ministry, which continued within the congregations which he led. However, it is generally acknowledged that not all his healings were genuine: some were deliberately faked, the justification being that they served to increase people's faith. On numerous occasions Jones claimed to have extracted cancerous tumours from people's bodies, when in fact he had previously secreted chicken's livers and produced them by sleight of hand. On one occasion Jones instructed Timothy Stoen, a prominent Temple member, to feign serious stomach pains for the duration of a service until the point at which the former would perform a miraculous healing.

Jones certainly claimed to possess extraordinary powers, claiming psychic abilities, power to heal the sick and even raise the dead, as well as the gift of prophecy. Such pronouncements were based on the belief that Christ's followers would be imbued with the nine gifts of the Spirit mentioned by Paul: 'the word of wisdom, the word of knowledge, faith, gifts of healing, working of miracles, prophecy, discerning spirits, diverse tongues and the interpretation of tongues' (1 Corinthians 12:8–10). Some of his followers appeared to be convinced that he had such powers, believing, for example, that in Jonestown he could clairvoyantly bring news of someone's relative in a distant part of the globe. Jones's detractors, however, contend that his aides were instructed to search through the camp's refuse where such information could readily be found.

The thrust of Jones' ministry, in sum, was the betterment of the human condition and the alleviation of suffering. These social concerns caused Jones to introduce a somewhat unorthodox element in his teaching – belief in reincarnation. This was certainly unusual in a what was officially still part of a mainstream Christian denomination, but Jones used the doctrine to explain how justice and hope were possible, averring that qualities such as gender, class and race were all transient and could be changed in one's next rebirth. According to Galanter, Jones claimed himself to be the reincarnation of Jesus, as well as 'Akhenaton, the Buddha, Lenin and Father Divine' (Galanter, 1979). However, if Jones did say this he could hardly have been serious since his own life was contemporaneous with Father Divine's.

Jones' preaching about human justice was also accompanied by apocalyptic interests. He frequently preached about an imminent end of the world, which would be destroyed by a nuclear holocaust. One source claims that Jones actually named a date on which this cataclysmic event would occur – 15 July 1967 – but when this day came and went, he simply claimed to have privileged secret knowledge of the revised date. In January 1962 Jones happened to read an article in the magazine *Esquire,* entitled 'Nine places in the world to hide'. The article enumerated nine places where a community might experience seclusion and escape the effects of a nuclear holocaust. Faced with mounting opposition, Jones began to consider the possibility of having his own secluded community, sheltered from the effects of the outside world. The article mentioned Cuba, but the 1962 Cuban missile crisis ruled the country out, since Jones was American. Jones also visited Brazil and Guyana during the same year. Redwood Valley in California was another 'safe place' designated in the article, and Jones decided to relocate the Peoples Temple there, moving to Ukiah, California in 1965. There the church was known as the Peoples Temple of the Disciples of Christ – still a congregation in a mainstream denomination.

The California church undertook a number of social projects. There were counsellors who offered legal and welfare advice to the community; a number of old people's homes were established, and also a farm for the mentally retarded. The policy of the church was that no one should ever be turned away, and hence it found itself visited by drug addicts and criminals, a number of whom successfully reformed as a result of their contact with the Peoples Temple.

Although in measurable terms the Peoples Temple appeared to be thriving during this stage of its evolution, the late 1960s can also be said to mark the beginnings of its downfall. In 1969 Jones had an affair with Carolyn Layton. From this time on Marceline's influence seems to have declined, and this occurrence also marks the beginning of a number of sexual misdemeanours on Jones' part. In 1973 Jones was arrested for indecent behaviour in a public lavatory in Los Angeles, and when he eventually established his community in Guyana Jones had various sexual relationships with members of the community there. There were also other unusual elements establishing themselves within Jones' community. Even before the emigration to Guyana, Jones had a firm control on his members. He made them write 'confessions' of their misdemeanours: some members wrote brief accounts of having stolen pieces of cake from the kitchen, or becoming irritable with someone, but Jones encouraged them to confess that they had all taken part in homosexual or lesbian relationships.

Perhaps unsurprisingly, the Peoples Temple had begun to attract adverse publicity not only because of Jones' sexual entanglements and his controls on the congregation, but because of ex-members, some of whom had left because they could not support Jones' campaign for social justice. They began to sensationalize some of the Peoples Temple's activities, and the media began to give the church negative publicity. A group called 'Concerned Relatives' was formed in opposition to Jones, and with the aim of enabling members to disengage. The Treasury Department and the Internal Revenue Service both began investigations into the Temple, which Jones and his followers regarded as persecution. It was becoming apparent that Jones' aim of establishing social justice within the local communities was failing, and therefore the idea of setting up a totally new community, free from external prejudice and harassment, and which could itself embody the principles of social justice, had a decided appeal.

In 1973 Jones and his followers started planning the next, more ambitious migration – to Guyana. Apart from offering the possibility of living in seclusion, Guyana was the only English-speaking country in South America. The land that became Jonestown was situated in an isolated part of Guyana, some 140 miles from Georgetown, the capital. An advance party was sent out in 1974 to explore the possibility of developing 300 acres of land offered by the Guyana government, and the Board of Directors of the Peoples Temple made the decision to move. The community that moved in with Jones was predominantly black, although headed up by Jones and some 70 white members who had constituted the main leadership in the Californian church. It should be noted that Jones's followers were a mixed-race community, and not drawn from the beatnik or hippie counter-culture. Many were disadvantaged, and some were trying to rehabilitate themselves after prison sentences or drug or alcohol abuse.

The ambitious nature of the Jonestown project should not be underestimated. The community was about to move into a tropical jungle, without water supplies, sanitation, electrical power, buildings and roads, and to establish itself from scratch. Wells had to be dug, generators brought in, equipment transported. In addition to the hard work, the tropical climate and primitive conditions posed serious health risks, and it is remarkable that the pioneers did not die from disease. The settlers developed the land, building cottages and workshops, cultivated fruit and vegetables, and reared chickens and pigs. It became a virtually self-sufficient community, with its own educational system and its own caring facilities for the old and the sick. The community intended to lead a pure lifestyle, and alcohol, tobacco and drugs were not permitted in the complex.

There are conflicting reports about conditions at Jonestown. Some survivors claimed that this was without doubt the best period of their lives, while others described conditions as severe. One survivor swore an affidavit in which she claimed that there were long hours of work, from seven o'clock in the morning until six in the evening. Food was inadequate, she stated, with only 'rice for breakfast, rice water soup for lunch, and rice and beans for dinner', with vegetables only two or three times in the week. Jones, by contrast, had his own provisions from his own refrigerator, the ostensible reason being that he had problems with his blood sugar level. On the few occasions when visitors arrived, standards of cuisine were markedly better, and they were never permitted to see the Jonestown community as it really was. Jones carefully rehearsed the members about the questions they might expect and how to answer them. (Critics will regard this as sinister, while more sympathetic commentators suggest that Jones was simply being astute: after all, visitors from the media were not on Jones's side, and could do much to give the community negative publicity.)

Jones used to broadcast to the community over a loudspeaker system for about six hours a day, and frequently sounded hectic in tone. Death was a dominant theme, and Jones frequently talked of 'suicide for socialism'. Such instruction was not confined to the realm of belief: appropriate preparation was needed. Accordingly, Jones instituted 'white nights' – practices which occurred at approximately weekly intervals in the middle of the night. The community would be awakened by the sound of sirens, and everyone was expected to vacate their living quarters. Fifty selected members would go round the compound with rifles to ensure that everyone had come out. Jones then informed his followers that there were mercenaries in the jungle, posing an imminent threat of death. There would then be a general meeting, in which members were instructed about appropriate preparation. During one 'white night' Jones informed the community that the situation was hopeless and that they would be tortured by the mercenaries if they were captured alive; the only viable course of action, he declared, was mass suicide. Everyone was then made to line up, including the children, and small glasses containing a red liquid were passed around and drunk. Jones informed the assembly that the liquid was poison, and that death would occur within 45 minutes. They obeyed, only to find that they remained alive. Jones then informed them that the liquid was not poisonous after all and that this was merely a test of their loyalty. However, he added, a time would soon come when they would be asked to do this in reality.

There can be little doubt that Jones exercised an iron grip over his followers. He dealt firmly with any dissent, meting out punishments which could include extra physical labour, making dissenters chew and swallow hot peppers, and confining them within small coffin-like boxes. He could also exercise psychological manipulation, staging heart attacks or assassination attempts upon himself.

During the last year of his life, Jones' behaviour became increasingly idiosyncratic. The reasons are not clear. His physical condition deteriorated: he complained of having some serious illness, his speech became slurred, and at times he was unable to walk without support; followers even witnessed him urinating in public on occasion. Some critics say he became manic-depressive; others believe he was on drugs, and it is difficult to be sure how much of his behaviour could be attributed to drug addiction, medication, genuine illness or attempts to manipulate his followers. A doctor was brought in from California, but found little amiss with him apart from an ear infection.

In the meantime, other problems were building up for Jones. The Peoples Temple was being sued by various plaintiffs, who sought a total of 56 million dollars in damages. Private detectives had been commissioned to investigate the church, and a public relations firm in San Francisco had been employed to co-ordinate a campaign of negative publicity against the Temple. There were allegations that the Peoples Temple was stockpiling weapons, which caused the US Customs Service to initiate an investigation, and Interpol became involved. Jones had experienced various sexual encounters with women – and possibly men – in the community, and a number of children were born as a consequence. Grace Stoen (Timothy Stoen's ex-wife) left Jonestown after giving birth to a son, John Victor; Jones refused to return her son to her and a legal battle ensued.

In the face of this mounting pressure Congressman Leo Ryan was sent to Jonestown to investigate the alleged malpractices. Amongst Ryan's constituents were Patty Hearst's family: Ryan was therefore familiar with the notions of 'brainwashing'. He spent a day at the compound, and returned to the airport to depart with 16 members of the Peoples Temple who had expressed a desire to leave. One of Jones' followers pursued him to the airport, and shot Ryan, three newspaper reporters and one of the defectors, all of whom died. Eleven defecting members were injured. On hearing the news Jim Jones called his people together, and after a lengthy discussion the community was persuaded to commit mass suicide. Some 85 members survived: a handful managed to hide in the jungle, and a few were away at the time on other business. Of the rest, anyone who attempted to escape was shot, and Jones himself was found dead with a bullet wound in his head: it is unclear whether he killed himself or whether someone else shot him.

Many of the bodies could not be identified. They were flown back to the United States for burial or cremation. Many cemeteries refused to accommodate the victims until the Evergreen Cemetery in Oakland offered to accommodate 409 of the bodies. The rest were interred in family graves. The survivors of the massacre returned home, but had no wish to ensure the survival of the Peoples Temple. Because of the scale of public outrage at the massacre, they found themselves the victims of much hostility, accused of being responsible for the murders, and particularly for the deaths of children. They found it difficult to gain employment, and were subjected to considerable harassment. As for the physical remains of the community, a fire in the early 1980s finally consumed the complex, and the 1989 earthquake destroyed the headquarters in Geary Street, San Francisco.

Analysis and assessment

The anti-cult movement continues to portray Jonestown as a 'bizarre cult' that serves as a warning of the dangers of joining 'fringe' religious groups. However, an analysis of the events leading up to the massacre does not bear this out. The Peoples Temple, as we have seen, belonged to the Disciples of Christ – a mainstream Christian denomination affiliated to local and national councils of churches.

The formation of a separate residential community, although unusual, has its precedents in mainstream denominations, the best-known examples being the Iona Community in Scotland, and the Taizé community in France.

The Jonestown tragedy was the result of quite a complex interaction between the Peoples Temple, the anti-cult movement, politicians and the racist elements in American society. If the Peoples Temple had not been the victim of racist attacks and smear campaigns, the incentive for Jones' followers to emigrate to Guyana would have been considerably less. Once there, their hopes of a perfect society, free of external interference, were dashed by the continued campaigning of Concerned Relatives and the intervention of Congressman Ryan.

I am not suggesting that all was well with the Peoples Temple – far from it! Concerned Relatives certainly had cause for concern about a congregation whose leader performed fake miracles, solicited such large proportions of its members' money, displayed sexual habits that are normally considered unacceptable, and who meted out punishments to deviant members. However, it was the interaction between the Peoples Temple and the rest of society that led to its final downfall.

Realizing the enormous problems of achieving racial integration in his community, the prospect of establishing one's own prejudice-free society, and founding it upon the principles of early Christian communism must have had its appeal. However, the sheer isolation of the community brought about its own problems. The proximity of other people and other religious communities would have provided a touchstone by which members of the Peoples Temple could have assessed their living conditions, their ideals, and the teachings and competence of their leader. A surrounding community provides an alternative for doubting or dissatisfied members – a feature that was singularly lacking in the middle of a Guyana jungle. Isolated from other member churches within the Disciples of Christ, there were no checks on the reliability or orthodoxy of Jones' teaching, and, with the exception of the few visitors, no outsiders to make comment on the degree of Jones' moral integrity. The move from an urban to a farming community brought its problems too: as Maaga (1996) points out, Jones was not without merit as an urban leader, but he was not a competent leader of an agricultural community.

Rather than being a bizarre cult that led to tragedy, it would be more accurate to suggest that it was the tragedy that led to the Peoples Temple being portrayed as a 'cult'. After the mass suicide the group was disowned, not only by the Disciples of Christ, but those who claimed to speak for Christianity as a whole. Thus the evangelist Billy Graham described Jim Jones as 'Satan's slave' and proclaimed that his community had 'no relationship to the views and teachings of any legitimate form of Christianity' (Chidester, 1988; quoted in Robbins, in 1989, p. 119). Chidester argues that there were three ways in which American culture displayed 'cognitive distancing' from the Jonestown phenomenon. First, there was 'psychological distancing' whereby conventional society attempted to portray Temple members as mentally ill, victims of brainwashing, or religious fanatics. Second, there was 'political distancing', in which the authorities in Guyana and San Francisco absolved themselves of any responsibility for the development of the Peoples Temple and its tragic end. Third, there was 'religious distancing' whereby mainstream religion disowned the Jonestown community. The Peoples Temple *became* a cult as a result of public perception of it.

The Jonestown tragedy gave further impetus to the anti-cult movement's subsequent development. Jonestown became a kind of icon. The fact that a mass suicide had actually happened within a religious group provided a salutary warning that 'extreme religious groups' were dangerous. Jonestown became grist to the anti-cultists' mill, and continues to receive frequent mention in anti-cult literature, even 20 years on. The scale of the tragedy appeared to vindicate those who had argued that much firmer measures were needed to cope with 'the cult problem', such as political control of religious groups or deprogramming. Deprogrammers not infrequently forced their abductees to watch videos of Jonestown as a warning of what might happen if they ever returned to their 'cult'. As Ted Patrick said in an interview for *Playboy*:

> Those organizations are multimillion-dollar rackets, and if Congress is not forced by the public to do something, the cults are not just going to give up their paradises without a fight ... The Jonestown suicides and murders weren't anything compared with what's going to happen. There's going to come a time when *thousands* of people are going to get killed right here in the United States. (Patrick; in Moore and McGehee, 1989, p. 165)

Presuming Jonestown to be the harbinger of a wave of mass suicides in NRMs, anti-cultists used the Peoples Temple in two ways. First,

45

they claimed to find similarities between the Temple and other NRMs: charismatic authoritarian leadership, a 'false messiah' figure, community living, total commitment, high financial contributions and so on. Second, it was alleged that other NRMs were preparing their members for similar suicides. The Unification Church, which was typically regarded as the most sinister of the extant NRMs, was alleged to be preparing its members for suicide. Some UC ex-members alleged that they were instructed on how to slash their wrists if they were subjected to deprogramming, and anti-cultists scoured the UC's writings to find support for such allegations. One piece of putative evidence that was frequently cited was the line of the UC's daily 'Pledge Service', 'I will fight with my life', although, as I have elsewhere argued, this statement does not entail preparedness for suicide (Chryssides, 1991, pp. 151–2).

The anti-cult prediction of a wave of suicide cults simply did not materialize. Years passed without any similar incident, and no NRM has ever led to a mass suicide on that scale since Jonestown. It was not until 1993 – fifteen years later – that 82 Branch Davidians died at Waco, Texas.

Waco

Unlike the Peoples Temple, Waco was a fundamentalist Christian group. As with the Peoples Temple, David Koresh's group was not an independent 'cult' (in Troeltsch's sense of the word), but originated as part of a well-accredited sector of Christianity, the Seventh-day Adventists. In its earlier years the SDA were regarded as sectarian by many mainstream Christians: Horton Davies discusses them as one of his 'Christian deviations', and they also feature in other examples of anti-cult literature, such as Walter Martin's *The Kingdom of the Cults*. In more recent times, however, they have come to be regarded as a form of mainstream Christianity, currently enjoying observer status in the Council of Churches for Britain and Ireland.

The name 'Seventh-day Adventism' highlights the two principal features of the movement, namely the practice of observing the seventh day – the Jewish sabbath – as the day of worship and rest, and the expectation of the imminent return ('advent') of Jesus Christ. The movement originated with William Miller (1782–1849), who proclaimed in 1831, at Dresden, New York, that humankind could expect the Second Coming in the year 1843. When the year 1843 passed without Christ's appearance, Miller revised his calculations, and concluded that they were adrift by one year: what he had failed to take into account was that there was no year zero between BCE and CE. Accordingly, the Second Advent should be expected in 1844.

As one might expect, Miller's movement practically collapsed when his second prophecy failed. However, one of his principal followers, Hiram Edson, claimed to have received a vision in a corn field one day. God, he believed, had revealed to him that Miller's calculations were quite correct, but that the event that he had expected was the wrong one. It was not the Second Coming that would take place in 1844, but a new stage of Christ's ministry. Christ had now assumed his rule in heaven, and was beginning 'the investigative judgement'. What this meant was that the final judgement was beginning, and that God had opened the heavenly books in which the deeds of those who had died were recorded. God, with Christ's help, had started the task of determining which of those among the dead were fit for entry to the kingdom of God and which were not.

Edson's revelation was confirmed by Ellen Gould Harmon, better known by her married name of Ellen G. White (1827–1915), an accredited prophet within the Adventist movement. White had a series of visions concerning the events leading up to the end. One important teaching was that of 'progressive truth': God allows his prophets and messengers to fall into error as a means of testing his people. At a later stage, he enables other prophets to discover such mistakes. The light dawns gradually, rather than shines all at once, and God's messengers teach according to the amount of light they possess at the time.

Miller himself was unable to accept the notions of progressive truth and investigative judgement, and thus he and White had their separate followings. The 'Seventh-day Adventists' became the name of the organization led by White, and which formally came into being in 1861. Amongst the beliefs of the Adventists were a firm conviction of the inerrancy of scripture, an expectation of an imminent Second Coming of Christ, salvation through grace, adult baptism by total immersion, and abstinence from alcohol, tobacco, tea, coffee and meat, since the Bible teaches that one's body is the

Holy Spirit's 'temple' (1 Corinthians 6:19). Members also adopted the Old Testament practice of 'tithing', donating one tenth of their income for the Church's work.

The Branch Davidians

When Ellen G. White died in 1915, Victor T. Houteff (1885–1955) claimed the prophetic office in the SDA. However, he was later accused of distorting White's teachings, and he and his followers were disfellowshipped. Houteff bought property at Waco in Texas, and called it the Mount Carmel Center. He ran various business ventures at Mount Carmel, and the community used its own currency for buying and selling.

Houteff drew extensively on White's writings, despite his expulsion. His best-known book was *The Shepherd's Rod,* in two volumes, and he published various tracts and sermons. His movement was known as 'The Shepherd's Rod' or simply 'The Rod'. The allusion was to Isaiah 11:

> And there shall come forth a rod out of the stem of Jesse, and a Branch shall grow out of his roots: and the spirit of the LORD shall rest upon him, the spirit of wisdom and understanding, the spirit of counsel and might, the spirit of knowledge and of the fear of the LORD ... (Isaiah 11:1–2)

The verse also is the occasion of the name 'Davidian Seventh-day Adventists', by which Houteff's followers were known, since King David was the son of Jesse.

Houteff taught that a latter-day King David would arise and lead Israel (that is, the Church) to the Kingdom of God. This new David would be a prophet – a religious and temporal king. The wicked would be purged from the SDA and those who remained would attain the promised kingdom under this modern David's leadership. Those who refused to accept this message of the 'Rod' would be slaughtered, as described in the ninth chapter of Ezekiel: Ezekiel receives a vision in which God sends a man with an 'inkhorn' amongst his people, instructing him to put a mark on the foreheads of those who deplore the 'abominations' that are perpetrated within Jerusalem – this mark ensured that they would escape God's destruction.

The notion of a latter-day King David was reinforced by Houteff's 'typological' interpretation of scripture, a supremely important feature of Branch Davidian theology. Typology is a method of reading scripture that assumes that certain biblical events (mainly those of the Old Testament) foreshadow or prefigure events in the Christian era. This method of interpretation can be found in some of the New Testament and early Christian writers: for example, St Paul refers to Moses striking the rock at Rephidim while leading the Israelites through the desert, and adds, 'and the rock was Christ' (1 Corinthians 10:4). Critics of this hermeneutical method regard it as contrived and far-fetched, but Houteff not only took it seriously as a component of scripture, but went further by suggesting that certain biblical passages prefigure present-day happenings. As Houteff stated, 'where there is no type there is no truth' (quoted in King and Breault, 1993, p. 362). For example, Assyria is the 'type' of the USA (the 'anti-type'), Syria the 'type' of the USA's government; the ten tribes were the SDA, and the two tribes the Branch Davidians; 'butter and honey' meant truth, the two sheep were the Old and New Testaments, and references to Immanuel were to an anti-typical David. (The import of the last of these type and anti-type pairings will become obvious later.)

In 1955 Victor Houteff died and was succeeded by his wife Florence. This proved problematical for the Rod movement. The office of president, constitutionally, had to be filled by a prophet. The movement probably believed that Houteff would be their final leader before the end came; indeed its constitution stated that the President would hand over his leadership to Christ when the Second Advent arrived. The Davidian Seventh-day Adventists decided, therefore, to leave the President's office vacant, and to make their new leader Florence Houteff merely the Vice-President.

The Davidians did not abandon the belief that Victor Houteff would directly hand over his leadership to Christ. Florence taught that Victor would rise from the dead and once more assume the office of President. Three and a half years would elapse, then in 1959 God would take vengeance on the unbelieving SDAs. Their envisaged programme of end-time events was as follows. In three and a half years (a time span suggested by the Book of Daniel), the slaughter predicted in Ezekiel 9 would be carried out. In some circles it was believed that the Rod members themselves would carry out this slaughter. (This event was identical with the event described in

Matthew 13, where the 'tares' – weeds – are separated from the good corn, and are destroyed.) After the destruction of the wicked, members of the Rod would be exalted, and the faithful miraculously transported to Israel, where they would enjoy a reign of peace and prosperity. Victor Houteff would then rise again, together with a few of the faithful, whereupon he would be crowned King, with his headquarters in Jerusalem, from whence the 'third angel's cry' would go out to the rest of the world.

In 1955 Florence Houteff sold off the Old Mount Carmel site and bought New Mount Carmel, a site of 400 acres, also situated in Waco. Parts of the property were progressively sold off, leaving only 77 acres, which was known as 'the compound'. (This was the site on which the events of 1993 were to take place.) In 1959, after the 'three times and half a time' had elapsed, over a thousand Davidians came to New Mount Carmel, anticipating the fulfilment of Ezekiel 9, followed by their deliverance and admission to the kingdom of God. Many had given up their homes and their jobs in order to see this cataclysmic event take place.

There were other Adventists, too, who did not endorse Florence Houteff's end-time prophecies, and arrived on the site with the purpose of dissuading the Davidians. Among them was Ben L. Roden (d. 1978), a former bricklayer who had acquired a small piece of land in Israel, convinced that the end-time events would take place there in 1960. He then saw a vision of a large map of the world spread out on a floor; just as he was about to walk across it to Israel, he heard a voice saying, 'No, Waco!'

When the expected events did not take place in 1959, Florence Houteff's prophecy was of course discredited. A number of splinter groups then arose, each claiming its own prophet. Ben Roden founded the Branch Davidian Seventh-day Adventists, the largest of these groups. Meanwhile, the New Mount Carmel complex was declared bankrupt, and this provided Roden with his opportunity to take it over. He appealed to his followers for funds, and raised $75,000 – enough to make the purchase.

Ellen G. White had prophesied the return of Elijah, and Roden claimed this office for himself. He also asserted himself to be 'the man whose name is The BRANCH' (Zechariah 6:12). This verse continues:

> and he shall build the temple of the LORD ... and he shall bear the glory, and shall sit and rule upon his throne ... (verses 12–13)

Accordingly, Roden was crowned king at a specially devised coronation ceremony at Mount Carmel, and assumed absolute authority over the community – an authority which was also embedded in the group's constitution.

The institution of the Jewish sabbath as the day of rest and worship was part of an attempt to recognize the authority of the whole Bible, the Old Testament as well as the New. However, if the institution of the sabbath was an obligation, then what about the Jewish pilgrim festivals that are prescribed in the Mosaic law? This question seriously engaged Roden, and in 1964 he reinstituted the Jewish festivals: Passover, Pentecost ('Weeks'), the Day of Atonement and the Feast of Tabernacles. Roden stopped short of requiring the accompanying animal sacrifices that the Jewish law prescribed, stipulating that these festivals should be celebrated in a 'Christian' way. Additionally, Rodin introduced a last 'feast' which was called 'the daily', consisting of two one-hour services each day.

Roden's identification of himself as Elijah was an indication that he expected an imminent end to earthly affairs, since the Bible taught the return of Elijah would herald the last days (Malachi 4:5–6). After Roden's death, his wife Lois led the movement until 1983. It was during Lois Roden's leadership that David Koresh – then known by his given name of Vernon Howell – came on the scene.

Vernon Wayne Howell (1959-93) was the son of a carpenter, whose sexual relationship with Bonnie, then only 14, left her pregnant, with the task of bringing up Vernon as a single parent. This was somewhat of a scandal in the middle of America's Bible Belt, and Vernon was entrusted to the care of an elder sister. Howell described his childhood as deprived; he was academically weak, possibly dyslexic, although he was good at sports, and left school in the ninth grade. He had difficulty holding down jobs: he was variously employed in Dallas as a roofer, a tiler and a mechanic, but was accused of being arrogant and sanctimonious.

Howell became a fundamentalist Christian, and joined the Southern Baptist Church. Perturbed by the problem of frequent masturbation, he sought advice from the pastor, Billy Harris. Harris advised him to pray, but this proved ineffectual, and Howell severed his connection with the Southern Baptists, turning to a local Seventh-day Adventist Church into which he was baptized in 1979. Howell frequently preached, but offended most of the congregation by his constant references to sex: in fact, George Roden (the son of Ben and

Lois Roden) later referred to him as the 'masturbating messiah'. He was disfellowshipped from the congregation in 1981.

Howell decided to seek his fortune at the Mount Carmel Center, under Lois Roden's leadership. He secured employment there as a vehicle mechanic, and was given responsibility for other maintenance jobs. Around this time there was controversy between Lois and George regarding the leadership of the Waco community, and Howell decided he would stake a claim for the leadership himself. He did this by claiming divine instruction to have a sexual relationship with Lois. His claim was based on a verse in Isaiah:

> And I went unto the prophetess; and she conceived, and bare a son. Then said the LORD to me, Call his name Maher-shalal-hash-baz. (Isaiah 8:3)

The name 'Maher-shalal-hash-baz' means 'a remnant shall return': the notion that a small number of people would remain faithful to God was later applied by Adventists (and subsequently, the Jehovah's Witnesses), to refer to those who remained faithful during the Great Tribulation. Howell later claimed that Lois Roden became pregnant as a consequence, but no baby was ever produced. The claim seems unlikely, since Lois was 69 at the time, and fortunately no child at Waco ever received this somewhat cumbersome forename!

Unsurprisingly, when George Roden discovered Howell's sexual relationship with his mother, he was furious. In the meantime, Howell, having claimed divine revelation to do so, had married Rachel Jones, the daughter of Perry Jones, Ben Roden's chief assistant; she was only fourteen at the time. A meeting was convened in 1984 to try to resolve matters, but it proved to be fruitless. In the end George Roden ordered Howell off the compound at gunpoint. He fled, but not without claiming that he regarded George as the Antichrist.

The following year Howell went to Israel. There he claimed to have received another divine revelation, this time of the anti-typical Cyrus and anti-typical David. This revelation is important in the story of the Branch Davidians, since Howell himself claimed to be the new Cyrus and David; indeed the name 'David Koresh', which Howell formally assumed in 1990, was a compound of the names 'David' and 'Cyrus', 'Koresh' being the Hebrew form of the latter. What David and Cyrus have in common is that they are both described as 'anointed' in Hebrew Scripture: to be thus described meant that the bearer of the title (either a priest or a king) had been divinely chosen and formally appointed to that office. David is to the Jew the epitome of the successful chosen ruler; King Cyrus, by contrast, is a somewhat surprising holder of such a title, being a foreign and not a Jewish king, but the fact that Isaiah describes him as 'anointed' (Isaiah 45:1) is presumably because Cyrus allowed the Jews to return from exile in Babylon to their home territory. The Hebrew word for 'anointed' is *mashiach;* thus, by assuming the new name of 'David Koresh', Howell was indicating that he was the anti-typical king or messiah of both the Jews and the Gentiles.

Howell attended the General Conference of the SDAs in New Orleans later that year, and attempted to present this new revelation to them, only to find that it was rejected. Undaunted, Howell now attempted two thrusts towards gaining recognition as the new messiah. In 1986 he visited Australia, where he successfully attracted members of the former Branch Davidians who had been under the leadership of Ben and Lois Roden. In 1988 Howell targeted Britain. His principal supporter, Steve Schneider, went back to Newbold College in Bracknell, Berkshire, where he had been a student in the 1970s before being expelled. Barred from addressing the students there, Schneider proceeded to lecture to the small group in a local Adventist's home, where he proclaimed that he was heralding the arrival of another leader. Howell arrived a few weeks later, and was introduced to members. Staff of the college infiltrated one of Howell's meetings and were disgusted by Howell's many sexual allusions. The preaching sessions were long: apparently they could last for up to 17 hours at a stretch, and both Howell and Schneider could talk continuously for as long as six hours on end. Attendees were invited to come back to the USA to receive Howell's full message.

Back in the US, Howell had set up his community at Waco. He was not only the leader, but the anti-typical messiah, the Lamb of God, whose authority was not to be questioned. Belonging to the community meant breaking one's earthly ties, including those of one's family and friends. One had to forsake all for the sake of the coming kingdom:

> If any man come to me, and hate not his father, and mother, and wife, and children, and brethren, and sisters, yea, and his own life also, he cannot be my disciple. (Luke 14:26)

Koresh later taught that Jesus did not die for the sins of the entire world, but only for those who stood before him when he was on the cross. Thus there remained important saving work to be done, which could only be carried out by the present-day anti-typical messiah – Koresh. As the anti-typical messiah, he regarded himself as not having to assume all the characteristics of Jesus, the earlier messianic 'type'; if Jesus was perfect, this messiah was sinful. One way in which Koresh's messianic authority was supposedly vindicated was by his practice of polygamy. As the Song of Solomon stated:

> There are threescore queens, and fourscore concubines, and virgins without number. (Song of Solomon 6:8)

Koresh noted that many of the Old Testament leaders had plural wives, such as Abraham, David and Solomon. As Koresh said:

> The people of the world, Christianity, worship the Bible. They idolize these men who lived 2000, 3000 years ago. Yet look at the Bible. Look at what it's saying. Abraham had more than one wife. David had more than one wife. Solomon had a thousand. Can you imagine a thousand wives? ...
>
> Yet these stupid Christians, with their stupid scholars, will condemn me one day for having more than one wife. They don't even know the damn book they say they believe. (King and Breault, 1993, p. 73)

Accordingly, from 1989 onwards he taught that all the community's women belonged to him and that only he was permitted by God to have children. Some of the women became wives, while others (some may have been minors) were commanded as a special privilege to enter his bedroom and have sexual intercourse with the messianic leader. Later, Koresh taught that no other male member of the community was permitted to have sex with any of the women.

Koresh attempted to claim that this was not sexual licentiousness on his part. There were serious disadvantages, he argued, in such arrangements, such as ensuring that his sexual partners were free from AIDS and other sexually transmitted diseases (King and Breault, 1993, p. 81). Since contraception was not permitted, even by the messiah, there was the responsibility of bringing new children into the community. Koresh may have been trying to raise a new master race of children, sons and daughters of the messiah, who would serve as 'righteous judges' who would destroy the Babylonian children (King and Breault, 1993, p. 25).

Much of Koresh's preaching was apocalyptic. He had a

fascination for the 'seven seals' described in the Book of Revelation, believing that it was his mission to open the 'seventh seal' mentioned there. The seal could only be opened by 'the Lamb that was slain' (Revelation 5:6–10); thus Koresh's promise to open the seal was not only a further claim to messianic status, but a possible reference to Koresh's death.

Several events led up to the final holocaust at Waco. In 1989 Marc Breault, one of Howell's principal supporters, left the group, departing for Australia, and subsequently New Zealand, to alert the Branch Davidians there of the Waco situation. Most of the Australians were shocked at what they were told, and made efforts to contact the authorities in the USA. The authorities were somewhat slow to take notice of the complaints, but their hiring of a private investigator, and the apostasy of Robyn Bunds – one of Koresh's 'wives' – in 1990, provided further evidence to present to the Waco police. The Waco premises were raided, and warrants were served on Koresh for statutory rape.

From October 1991 the Waco community began to arm itself more heavily. Koresh obtained a number of semi-automatic machine guns and grenades. From then on, death appears to have been quite a prominent theme in his preaching. The community might be called upon to die in the coming battle of Armageddon, as a means to attaining salvation.

In January 1993 the first official reports of child abuse were noted. On 28 February, ATF (Alcohol, Tobacco and Firearms) agents served a search warrant on Koresh. This led to a confrontation in which four agents died and 16 members of the community were injured. The Waco siege had begun. Koresh himself may have been convinced that, as the 'lamb who was slain', he was called upon to die and that the Battle of Armageddon was commencing. Easter was approaching, and it was suggested that Koresh felt it would be appropriate for the new messiah to die at the same time of year as Jesus of Nazareth and also at the same age (*Independent on Sunday*, 25 April 1993).

Whether the confrontation that followed was inevitable is a matter of speculation. With a less confrontational approach it may have been possible for the authorities simply to wait until Koresh next left the compound, and then arrest him. The confrontation was no doubt exacerbated by the fact that the FBI allowed Rick Ross of the Cult Awareness Network to advise them. Apparently Ross had already been approached by relatives of Waco members and paid to carry out their deprogramming. Ross had already carried out some 200 deprogrammings, for which he had been arrested, although not convicted. Trained to confront NRMs, Ross endorsed the FBI's confrontational stance. Had the authorities chosen an academic adviser, who might have been more familiar with the kinds of ideas that were being preached at Waco, it is possible that negotiation could have been accomplished with a happier outcome. Ross endorsed the view that another Jonestown was about to occur, and that the Waco community was ready for a mass suicide.

Whether the 93 deaths were suicides or whether the FBI started the fire at the compound is unclear. While it is possible that Koresh's followers preferred death to having to face criminal charges and the end of their religious community, it is equally possible that the FBI started the fire in the hopes that it would flush out the occupants and thus achieve the authorities' strategic goal.

Whatever really happened, only a small handful of members survived, without their leader. Koresh was discredited in the eyes of the public. Whether it was intentional that he should die as a carpenter's son, at Easter, and – like Jesus of Nazareth – at 33 years of age, or whether these facts are coincidental can never be known for certain.

Solar Temple

At the beginning of October 1994 international news headlines announced more multiple deaths in a 'killer cult'. Few had heard of the Solar Temple (Ordre du Temple Solaire, or OTS), a group that had no more than 200-300 members in its heyday, and whose beliefs and practices still remain obscure. Although the Solar Temple tragedy may have looked to many like 'another Waco', the incident was significantly different in several respects.

Although the deaths were roughly simultaneous, they occurred at several different locations: on 4 October five were found burned to death (including a child) at the house of OTS leader Joseph di Mambro at Morin Heights in Canada. Just after midnight on the morning of 5 October a fire had been started at the Ferme de Rochettes, in Cheiry, Switzerland, and fire fighters discovered 23 bodies. At 3 a.m. at Les Granges sur Salvan, in Vilasi Canton in

Switzerland, three chalets occupied by OTS members experienced similar fires, this time revealing 25 dead on investigation. The fires had been started by means of incendiary devices, timed to activate simultaneously.

Unlike Waco, the victims appeared to have died in different ways. At Morin Heights, three of the dead had been stabbed before the fire began. At Cheiry twenty out of the 23 dead had bullet wounds in the head, and showed signs of having been drugged. They were found in an underground room that had been converted into a temple, with mirrors on each side, and the bodies were arranged in a circle, with their heads to the outside and feet touching. The victims were dressed in ceremonial robes – black, red, white and gold – and some had black plastic bags over their heads. Twenty out of 23 had been shot in the head, some with as many as eight bullet wounds, a sure sign that they had not committed suicide. At Salvan, ten of the 25 victims had also been shot in the head. All in all, 53 people were dead. Were these murders or suicides, and what possible motive could trigger off such bizarre incidents? The group's leader was named as a doctor by the name of Luc Jouret (1947–94), who could not be found. It was later established that he was one of the casualties.

By way of a postscript to these incidents, mention should be made of two similar incidents. In 1995, 16 OTS members were found dead near Grenoble in the French Alps, in similar circumstances. They had been drugged and shot, placed in a ritual star formation and then burned. It is unclear whether this event was a continuation of the murders/suicides of the previous year, or whether it was a copycat event staged by someone else. The Cult Awareness Network suggested that the episode was linked with the Temple's seasonal rites, being near the winter solstice, but in fact this event occurred between 15 and 16 November. The second incident occurred in 1997, when five more Solar Temple members appeared to have burned themselves to death. This event was eclipsed by the Heaven's Gate affair, however, and passed relatively unnoticed by the public.

The Solar Temple was mainly based in Switzerland, but also attracted a following in France and in French-speaking parts of Canada. There was no British branch, although some of the members, possibly including Jouret, may have visited Stonehenge in England in 1992 at the summer solstice.

Before the 1994 deaths occurred, Jouret had sent out 300 packages to various organizations and individuals throughout the world, including Dr Jean-François Mayer, a historian of religion in Switzerland, and who is now probably the world's leading authority on the Solar Temple (see Mayer 1996). The packages set out OTS's beliefs and practices, together with a departure message from Jouret. Yet despite the wide dissemination of these packages, little information about OTS is extant at the time of writing. There are two principal reasons for this: first, the Solar Temple's teachings were highly esoteric, and could only be fully revealed to members after two degrees of initiation after admission; second, the legal inquiry that followed required confidentiality on the part of expert witnesses. Additionally, as Susan Palmer (1996) points out, ex-members are reluctant to identify themselves because of the stigma attached to belonging, and many of them are unlikely to have been privy to the Temple's secrets, which were only revealed to the inner core of highest initiates. Apparently a number of books are currently in preparation, but it seems that these are likely to be sensationalist rather than objectively informative, invoking conspiracy theories. According to Palmer, one such publication reveals that Jouret lives on, perhaps having faked his death to avoid impending legal inquiries, while another alleges that events at the Solar Temple were a CIA conspiracy, to cover up a deal between President Jimmy Carter and some extra-terrestrials who had settled in Nevada, where they built an underground laboratory!

There are therefore few reliable sources on the Solar Temple. Newspaper reports describe the events in some detail but are singularly lacking in solid information about the Solar Temple's origins, beliefs and practices, and counter-cultist material has been largely culled from press reports. Massimo Introvigne (1995) provides a very detailed analysis of the relationship between the Solar Temple and various Templar organizations that have arisen since the late eighteenth century. Susan Palmer (1996) has collated material from Bill Marsden, a Canadian journalist who interviewed several OTS members. Finally, and most significantly, Jean-François Mayer conducted an extensive interview with Luc Jouret in 1987, and has continued to follow the organization's progress.

The Knights Templar

Since the Solar Temple's background lies in the Templar movement, it is necessary to say something about Templarism. The Templars were a military monastic order, and were associated with the Crusades which occurred between 1095 and 1270. They were supported by the Cistercian Abbot Bernard of Clairvaux (1090–1153), who was instrumental in the founding of the order. The Templars protected pilgrims who were travelling from Europe to Jerusalem, which the Christians had recently captured. Not only did they offer protection against physical attack, but they undertook to safeguard pilgrims' monies, either by transporting them to their intended destination or by concealing them in secret places for security. It is said that the Templars could transport money either in place or in time, retrieving monies on their owners' behalf when their value was high. Thus the Templars became the Church's first bankers – an innovation, since usury was contrary to the Church's teaching.

Despite being described as 'the poor fellow soldiers of Christ and the Temple of Solomon', the Templars' money-handling enabled them to gain wealth, and this wealth, combined with their physical strength and their piety, was instrumental in their gaining power. Pope Innocent II gave them exemption from all earthly authority apart from papal authority, thus making their power second only to that of the papacy.

After the Crusades, the Templars returned to their chapters, where many of their secret meetings and rites arose. Holy relics were associated with the orders, particularly the Holy Grail, the true cross, the crown of thorns and the spear that pierced Jesus' side. However, the orders were becoming unduly powerful, and in 1307 Philip IV of France ('Philip the Fair'), desiring the Templars' wealth for his own use, conspired with the Pope to defeat them. They were arrested for heresy, and tortured in an attempt to extract confessions. Whether their confessions were true is doubtful, but they admitted trampling and spitting on crucifixes, worshipping Baphomet (the devil) and practising homosexuality. (The Templar Seal, which depicts two riders on one horse, has sometimes been cited in support of the homosexuality accusation, but this is a highly improbable interpretation.) In 1312 the Knights Templar were formally disbanded by Pope Clement V, in the papal bull *Vox in*

Excelso. A few Templars moved on to Portugal, where they founded the Order of Christ. It has been speculated that the famous Shroud of Turin bears the image of Jacques de Molay, the Templars' last Grand Master: it seems to have become known from around this period, or perhaps some 50 years later.

It was not until the late eighteenth century that the Templar movement experienced a revival, facilitated by the French Revolution. The abolition of monarchy meant the demise of a powerful source of opposition to aspiring Templars, and as a consequence a variety of Templar groups gained momentum. One key figure in the rise of the neo-Templars was Bernard-Raymond Fabré-Palaprat (1773–1838), a Parisian medical doctor. Fabré-Palaprat claimed to have discovered an unbroken lineage of Grand Masters, ending with himself. The Roman Catholic Church was still opposed to Templarism; Fabré-Palaprat's response was that Roman Catholicism was a 'fallen church'. He therefore established a rival 'Johannite' church, an esoteric movement with its own lineage of bishops, the first of whom he consecrated himself, by virtue of his status as Grand Master. As Introvigne points out, the Templar movement therefore becomes intertwined with various independent churches governed by 'irregular bishops' – that is to say, bishops who are ordained in a 'valid' but not a 'legal' manner in the eyes of Roman Catholicism. Introvigne believes that Luc Jouret was not consecrated as an irregular bishop, but merely as a priest in one of these schismatical churches in France. One of Jouret's ceremonies in the Solar Temple was based on the Roman Catholic Mass, although he referred to it as an 'Essene ritual'. Not all the neo-Templar groups claimed an unbroken lineage that could be traced back to mediaeval Grand Masters, however. Some claimed that the spirits of medieval Templars channelled messages to more recent followers; others contended that Templarism survived through the Freemasons, whose rites were perpetuated in the various Masonic rituals. As Introvigne convincingly argues, however, it is unlikely that the practices of monastic orders would survive in unbroken form into a movement that was founded by guilds people.

One key figure in the neo-Templar movement is Julien Origas (1920-83), who founded the Renewed Order of the Temple (ORT). Origas was simultaneously a member of AMORC ('Ancient Mystical Order Rosae Crucis', a Rosicrucian order), and in 1970 persuaded its (then) French 'Legate', Raymond Bernard, to support its inception.

The idea of creating the ORT is said to have been legitimated by Bernard seeing an apparition of a 'white cardinal' – an experience which resulted in a coronation ceremony, in which Origas was enthroned as 'King of Jerusalem'. The close association between AMORC and ORT was important to Bernard, since AMORC wished to hold on to a monopoly of occultism; this association helped to ensure that existing AMORC members did not view ORT as a rival organization and transfer their allegiance. Despite this 'coronation', Origas's reputation was not enhanced by his support for neo-Nazi and white supremacist organizations, for which he received bad publicity in the press. Although Luc Jouret's political sympathies lay at the opposite end of the political spectrum (he was a communist), he first came into contact with ORT in 1981 and joined in 1983.

Luc Jouret

Luc Jouret was born in the Belgian Congo (now Democratic Republic of Congo) in 1947. He became a medical student at the Free University of Brussels, qualifying as a doctor in 1974. After graduating, he entered the Army as a paratrooper, apparently with the intention of spreading communist ideas within the armed forces. Jouret's military career was short-lived: within a year he had left, and was pursuing an interest in alternative medicine, particularly natural remedies and homeopathy, and in 1977 he visited the Philippines in order to study the techniques of spiritual healers there. In his interview with Mayer, he also claimed to have visited China, Peru and India to study their native therapeutic techniques. In 1980 Jouret set up a homeopathic practice in Annmasse in France; this was near the Swiss border, and hence he attracted a number of Swiss clients. As his reputation as an alternative therapist grew, Jouret attracted a Canadian as well as a French and Swiss clientele.

Jouret obtained various invitations to lecture on natural medicine and on ecology, securing engagements in a number of New Age bookshops and esoteric groups on both sides of the Atlantic. One such group was the Golden Way Foundation of Geneva, previously known as La Pyramide: it was there that Jouret came to know its leader, Joseph Di Mambro (1924–94). Jouret also obtained contracts as a speaker from Hydro-Québec, from whence he successfully recruited fifteen of its executive and managerial staff for the Solar Temple. (It is important to note that the Solar Temple was by no means a 'youth cult' or an organization that attracted the disadvantaged. Members tended to be professional people, normally middle-aged or older.) French-speaking Canada – particularly Montreal – and Geneva had an abundance of esoteric groups, for which Jouret came to have a fascination.

Introvigne has described the Solar Temple's organizational structure as a 'Chinese box' system. Members were initially admitted to the Amenta Club (subsequently called Amenta), which formed the outer layer of two more esoteric organizations. Membership of Amenta could lead to ritual initiation into the Archédia Club, and from thence to the International Order of Chivalry Solar Tradition (OICST). Jouret founded OICST in 1984, following an unsuccessful bid for the leadership of ORT after Origas's death the previous year. Having been obstructed by Origas's daughter Catherine, Jouret withdrew, together with 30 others, to form his own schismatic group, the International Order of Chivalry Solar Tradition, which was the precursor of the Ordre du Temple Solaire.

Joseph Di Mambro

The general public is probably more familiar with Jouret's name than that of Joseph Di Mambro. Jouret was the more charismatic of the two Solar Temple leaders, and it was Jouret who was their principal speaker, both inside and outside the organization. Di Mambro was the more senior, and arguably the one whose ideas more readily found expression within the Temple, and who exercised the greater control over its members.

Di Mambro had studied Egyptian mythology, and had a general interest in the occult, becoming a Grand Master in AMORC and leader of La Pyramide (later to become the Golden Way in 1974). Reincarnation loomed large in Di Mambro's thinking, as well as the Solar Temple's, and he claimed variously to be the reincarnation of a Pharaoh, one of Jesus' apostles, and the soldier at the crucifixion who pierced Jesus' side. Di Mambro had a particular interest in 'sex magic', which became a dominant Solar Temple theme, the importance of which will become apparent.

Di Mambro had reached the age of 70 in the Temple's final year, and by that time his health had deteriorated considerably. He was suffering from kidney failure and had to wear incontinence pads; he had contracted diabetes, and began to experience diabetic fits; moreover, he had been diagnosed as having cancer. Unable to continue to exercise authority over the group in this condition, it is possible that Jouret attempted to assume control, and that this led to rivalry between the two leaders.

Beliefs and practices in the Solar Temple

The Solar Temple had no agreed monolithic belief system. Palmer (1996) describes it as an example of 'strong group, weak grid'. Being a relatively small organization, it was closely knit, with strong personal bonding among its members. At the same time, there was no definite ideology or set of goals that united its members. It is possible to identify a number of dominant themes in its world-view: an interest in, and intertwining with, Rosicrucianism; an interest in ancient Egypt, particularly Egyptian death rituals; oriental and alternative medicine; reincarnation; and a belief in a Great White Brotherhood, consisting of Ascended Masters, who presided over humanity from a subterranean spiritual realm (Agartha), from whence they appeared occasionally. Jouret's New Age ideas entailed a typical belief that a new astrological age was dawning, and that the earth was 'on the cusp' between the Age of Pisces and the Age of Aquarius. The coming of the New Age heralded an apocalypse, in which the earth would be consumed by fire.

The group's emphasis on a subterranean realm was symbolized by several underground sanctuaries at the Cheiry headquarters. Members would make ritual descents to these shrines, when they were afforded various 'visions' in which Ascended Masters, the holy grail or some other sacred object appeared to materialize in front of the assembled gathering. At other times the sanctuary appeared to be subjected to violent thunder and lightning storms. Jouret averred that these visions were from the ascended Grand Masters, but in reality they were special effects created by Antonio Dutoit, an electrical technician who had considerable expertise in creating lighting effects, especially through holograms. They were nonetheless impressive, and members regarded it as a special privilege when Di Mambro selected them to witness them. The members' perception of these appearances was enhanced by means of stimulants and by hallucinogenic drugs; often a visit to the subterranean sanctuary was preceded by coffee, which some of the survivors claim had been laced with a mind-altering substance.

Among the ceremonies conducted by the Solar Temple were 'cosmic marriages'. Jouret and Di Mambro firmly believed in reincarnation. Individuals, they held, were essentially spirit, rather than body; qualities such as gender belonged to the physical body, and were shed at death. Solar Temple beliefs have been described as 'gnostic', implying that the seeker had embarked on a spiritual journey, with successively higher levels of initiation, the final one being the abandonment of one's body at death. The three levels of initiation within the Solar Temple created three categories of follower: initiates, 'awakened souls' and 'immortals'. Jouret was held to be a reincarnation of St Bernard of Clairvaux, and Di Mambro's previous incarnations have already been mentioned. The cosmic wedding ceremony sought to bond the spirits of the Ascended Masters. Di Mambro, regarded as a reincarnation of Manatanus (an Ascended Master), underwent a ceremony in which he was bonded with Dominique Bellaton, who was believed to be the reincarnation of the ancient Egyptian queen Hapsetphout. (I make no pretence that the enactment of such ceremonies made good sense. The 'cosmic weddings' seemed to presuppose that the spirits of the Ascended Masters still existed apart from their most recent reincarnation, and such weddings seem to militate against the Temple's belief that spirit gender did not exist. Such observations may illustrate Palmer's point that the group was weak on doctrine: certainly Jouret and Di Mambro were neither philosophers nor theologians. Unfortunately it is no longer possible to seek elucidation of their thinking on such matters.)

Dominique Bellaton was a prominent member of the Solar Temple, having joined at the age of 19, and officiated as a priestess; she was also Di Mambro's principal mistress. Di Mambro supposedly engaged in a ritual with her in the subterranean temple, at which Manatanus appeared (by means, presumably, of the sophisticated lighting effects). It was believed that, as a consequence, Dominique, whom Di Mambro called the 'perfect vessel', miraculously became pregnant, since the ritual did not involve copulation. On the night of 20–1 March 1981 she gave birth to a daughter who was named Emmanuelle. The choice of name was of course significant: this child, to whom Di Mambro always referred as 'he', was said to be the 'cosmic child', the avatar, who would be the harbinger of the New Age. She was regarded as so sacred that, for the first three months of her life, no one was even allowed to look at her. A ceremony was arranged, in which she was baptized in water brought from the River Jordan, and anointed with oils from Jerusalem. Even her excreta were regarded as sacred, and were placed in the vegetable garden at Cheiry.

Emmanuelle's conception was part of the 'sex magic' in which Di Mambro is said to have believed. Just as it could be deemed important for a birth such as Emmanuelle's to take place within the community, Jouret and Di Mambro could equally demand that Temple members did not conceive. One such example was Nicki Dutoit, wife of the lighting engineer: Di Mambro forbade her to bear children, following a miscarriage. The Dutoit couple disregarded this instruction, however, and a son was born for whom the Dutoits chose the middle name 'Emmanuel'. This apparently was an affront to Di Mambro, who declared the child to be the reincarnation of the Antichrist. The Dutoits were declared 'polluted', and Di Mambro gave strict instructions that none of the community should look at the baby, that they should sever all contact with Nicki, and that all the rooms at Cheiry should be disinfected. The family left the Temple in 1991, departing for Quebec, although it would seem that Antonio Dutoit continued to be employed by the Temple. Later, the couple and the child were found murdered, as part of the Quebec killings, possibly at Jouret's instruction.

Despite the nebulous nature of the Solar Temple's beliefs, notions of orthodoxy and heresy loomed large in Di Mambro's thinking. At times there could be severe sanctions for dissent, and a number of 'witch-hunts' were directed at deviant members. In May 1993 Jouret and two senior members – Pierre Vinet and Herman Delorme – were arrested, following an attempt to buy hand guns, at Jouret's instruction. They all received a 'suspended acquittal'.

It is evident that by 1994 there were a number of serious problems within the Temple. Jouret and Di Mambro were having some difficulties in keeping several of the Solar Temple members in line (the Dutoits were but one example), and Jouret had already begun to wreak revenge on a number of them. Avoiding schism was therefore a problem, and it appears that Jouret and Di Mambro themselves had their own quarrels; as already indicated, Di Mambro's serious medical condition may have provided a good opportunity for Jouret to stake a claim to be leader. Furthermore, several law suits were imminent, brought by ex-members who believed that they had been damaged by their experiences at the Temple. It has also been suggested that Jouret was guilty of financial irregularities, and that he was about to be exposed for laundering monies that had been donated to the Solar Temple.

While it was expedient for Jouret to want to fend off the various problems surrounding the Temple, the Solar Temple offered a future that transcended all worldly concerns. The cosmic weddings were a prelude to the achievement of a communion of souls of those who survived the coming fiery apocalypse. This could be achieved by making a 'transit', and members had learned that one could survive apocalypse by being transported to the star Sirius. Although the motives for the Solar Temple deaths cannot be known for certain, it is known that of the 53 dead, fifteen were 'awakened ones', and appear to have been true suicides; thirty were 'immortals'; and seven were 'traitors'. Palmer speculates that Di Mambro failed to persuade the 'immortals' at Cheiry to relinquish their own bodies, and therefore shot them himself. The black garbage bags that covered the heads of several of the victims may have been a form of protection against pollution: we know that such bags were not infrequently used at Temple ceremonies for this purpose. If this is correct, then the multiple deaths were part of a final ceremony, the fires being for magical purposes, to purify the spirit and to send the released soul into transit to its final destination, possibly Sirius. The destruction of the bodies served to ensure that the soul could not return to them, but would complete its journey. Palmer quotes one survivor, who stated:

> I knew all these people they found in Switzerland – and each one of them, to my knowledge, was perfectly capable of de-corporealizing at will. But some of [them] were worried they might not make it all the way to Sirius – that they might lose their way and wake up back in their bodies. So, an obvious way to prevent that was to *destroy* the bodies so they would not come back! (Palmer, 1996, p. 315; square brackets and italics original)

Palmer suggests that Di Mambro would have preferred a more dignified end to the Templars. Being thoroughly acquainted with Egyptian rituals, he may have wanted a Pharaoh's funeral, in which he would die, together with his retinue. Palmer observes that a note accompanied some copies of the 'Testament', accusing Jouret of a 'veritable carnage', in contrast to Di Mambro's desire for 'honour, peace and light'. Palmer writes:

Does this signal a rivalry between the two leaders? Was Di Mambro, the fastidious opera *aficionado,* deploring Jouret's violent means when, failing in his mission to inspire the 'Immortals' assembled at Cheiry to nobly opt for self-destruction, he lost his temper and shot them, leaving 22 bodies riddled with bullets as he drove to Salvan? Was Di Mambro, the aesthete, concerned lest this distressing carnage would undermine the dignity and moral high ground of the final act of his Templars? (Palmer, 1996, p. 315)

Heaven's Gate

Waco and the Solar Temple were still prominent in the public mind when the news broke of yet another 'suicide cult' in the spring of 1997. Thirty-nine bodies had been found in San Diego, California, laid out on their backs, having died from imbibing a cocktail of phenobarbitone, vodka and a small amount of a pudding-like substance. All but the two who were last to die were discovered underneath a purple shroud, with black trousers and new Nike training shoes. The members of the Heaven's Gate community had spent most of their time in seclusion, working with computers and placing their materials on the Internet. Before the suicide, the leaders had made and circulated farewell videos.

The name 'Heaven's Gate' was largely unfamiliar to the general public. The group had sought publicity in the mid-1970s, but the media tended to dismiss them as a somewhat eccentric 'UFO cult'. They had generated little discussion amongst scholars, although Beit-Hallahmi considered it worthy of inclusion in his *Illustrated Encyclopedia of Active New Religions, Sects and Cults* (1993), considerably before the suicides.

The group arose in the 1970s, amidst general public interest in extra-terrestrial life forms. The year 1969 had seen the first landing on the moon, described by some as an 'evolutionary leap'. Interest in space travel was widespread. Films like *E.T.* and *Close Encounters of the Third Kind* were immensely popular, and Marshall Applewhite, one of the Heaven's Gate founder-leaders, made occasional reference to them. Although there is no evidence that either Applewhite or his 'Older Member' Bonnie Nettles were familiar with Erich von Daniken's writings, the latter's best-seller, *Chariots of the Gods,* was widely read and convinced many, often highly intelligent, people that the Bible's account of God and his dealings with the world arose from visits of other life forms from outer space. For example, when Elijah and Ezekiel saw the divine chariot descending from the heavens, what else were they witnessing but beings from some other planet alighting on earth? On such matters, Applewhite, Nettles and von Daniken were certainly in accord.

An extensive Internet site created by the Heaven's Gate community is immensely valuable in tracking the group's history and its teachings. The two founder-leaders, Marshall Applewhite (1931–97) and Bonnie Nettles (1927–85), did not meet each other until 1974, but on acquaintance discovered how much they had in common, despite their different backgrounds. Applewhite had been a music professor and, following a marriage that ended in divorce, came to regard himself as a homosexual and was living with a male partner. Nettles was a nursery nurse who was working in a local hospital, and was married with four children; she also spent part of her time practising as an astrologer. Shortly before they met, both Applewhite and Nettles experienced serious upheavals in their personal lives, and came to attribute this to their bodies being taken over by 'Next Level' minds. They had also recently given up smoking, alcohol and sex.

Initially they spent six weeks in a Texas ranch, becoming increasing acquainted with each other. The relationship was not a sexual one: they were attempting to come to terms with their recent experiences, and both regarded themselves as having an important mission. This mission, they believed, had something to do with the Bible and fulfilling biblical prophecies, and it involved 'an update in understanding'.

The pair left the Texas ranch in a small convertible sports car, driving off with no particular destination in mind. By chance, the car broke down outside an Ananda Marga residence in Portland, Oregon. They stayed there for a short time, but disliked the claims made by certain group members to have been famous people in previous existences. At the end of their stay, Applewhite and Nettles became convinced that they were the 'two witnesses' of whom the Book of Revelation spoke (Revelation 11:1–12).

The couple received some insurance money for the car, after which a woman had presented Nettles with her husband's credit card, which she said she could use. The 'witnesses' then hired a car, in which they travelled through Canada, leaving anonymous notes on church pulpits, stating, 'The two witnesses are here.' At one point they arrived at a New Age centre. Thinking that this might be an appropriate place to reveal their new-found identity, they went in, only to discover that the centre's two leaders had already made identical claims for themselves!

Their next move was to inform the media of their mission. They contacted a reporter, telling him that they were about to provide him with 'his biggest story ever'. Thinking that he was about to receive information about drug trafficking, the reporter brought the police with him, much to the alarm of Nettles and Applewhite. The two of them fled, with the police in hot pursuit. The authorities found no drugs, of course, but the car hire company had reported their vehicle as stolen, and discovered the credit card that Nettles had. The two were arrested; Nettles was detained for 30 days, and Applewhite for six months.

Convinced that their mission was connected with extra-terrestrial travel, Nettles and Applewhite organized a series of public meetings in 1975 and 1976, aimed at bringing their 'crew' together. Their first poster read:

UFO'S

Why they are here.

Who they have come for.

When they will leave.

NOT a discussion of UFO sightings or phenomena.

Two individuals say they were sent from the level above human, and are about to leave the human level and literally (physically) return to that next evolutionary level in a spacecraft (UFO) within months! 'The Two' will discuss how the transition from the human level to the next level is accomplished, and when this may be done.

This is not a religious or philosophical organization recruiting membership. However, the information has already prompted many individuals to devote their total energy to the transitional process. If you have ever entertained the idea that there may be a real, PHYSICAL level beyond the Earth's confines, you will want to attend this meeting.

The first meeting took place on 14 September 1975, and was reported by the press. Nettles and Applewhite assumed the names of Bo and Peep, and organized a total of 130 such meetings in the USA and Canada. Their message was that the 'two witnesses', Bo and

Peep, were here to continue the message of Jesus, restating the truth that he had taught, but this time – 2000 years later – as a male and female couple. Nettles died in 1985, having contracted liver cancer. This left Applewhite to lead the group during its 12 remaining years, and the group's teachings that remained on the Internet after the suicides largely reflect Applewhite's thinking. However, Applewhite claimed to experience a close relationship with Nettles after her death, frequently seeking her guidance and claiming that they could telepathically communicate with each other and that she continued to speak through him.

Applewhite's teachings were essentially a blend of Christianity and UFOlogy. His frequent references to a 'Next Level Evolutionary Kingdom Above Human' have caused some commentators to label their teachings as 'gnostic', but the Heaven's Gate community does not appear to have used the term. While it is true that attainment of this next level required special preparation and teaching, there is no evidence that the community believed in any further hierarchy of heavens, as the Gnostics did. Likewise, there is little to indicate that Heaven's Gate was influenced by eastern traditions: although Applewhite appears to have been vaguely aware of concepts of karma and reincarnation, the group's understanding of successive births is markedly different from that of the Hindu and Buddhist tradition, as I shall show. Heaven's Gate's world-view seems to consist of little more than Applewhite's home-spun biblical exegesis, undertaken in the light of UFOlogy.

The ideas of Heaven's Gate stem from a firm belief in extra-terrestrial life forms and their interaction with beings on earth. Applewhite was convinced that there was ample evidence of these, and that various world governments have conspired to conceal such information from the public. The 1947 Roswell incident was one such example: debris from a large metal object was found in a field outside Roswell in New Mexico. Five bodies were supposedly recovered, allegedly space aliens, one of whom was still alive and who communicated telepathically with its captors. Military intelligence denied such rumours, claiming that the wreckage was the remains of a weather balloon that was being tested.

The media have attempted to demonize space aliens, portraying them as abductors of human beings, with malevolent intent. These portrayals embody serious misunderstandings, Applewhite contended: the beings from the 'Next Level Above Human' have an important purpose for humankind. Their crafts are wrongly called UFOs or flying saucers: they are vehicles or laboratories from the heavens. According to the Heaven's Gate world-view, there are three kinds of living being: those on earth, those on the 'Next Evolutionary Kingdom Level Above Human', and the 'Luciferians'. (In his teachings to the community, Applewhite says there may be living beings on other planets, but that he does not know this for certain.)

Human beings are inherently souls attached to bodies. In the human level these bodies are perishable and cannot survive death. They are also gender-specific, being either male or female, and are subject to earthly attachments, particularly the desire for material things and for sex. Those who belong to the Next Evolutionary Kingdom Level Above Humans still have physical bodies, although these are significantly different from those of the human level. In particular, such bodies are genderless and have overcome earthly attachments.

> That Next Level body is a creature that looks very attractive, has two eyes, some remnant of a nose, some remnant of ears – what you would call remnants – even though they function very well as nose, as ears. They have a voice box, but don't really need to use it, for they can communicate by thought – communicate with their minds. And that's an extraterrestrial – that is the 'body' belonging to a member of the Evolutionary Level Above Human, the Kingdom of Heaven, the Kingdom of God. (Heaven's Gate, 1997)

Members of the Next Level are able to prepare appropriate individuals on earth to make the transition from the human realm to this higher plane. To achieve this, Next Level members use a process of 'tagging' earthlings with 'deposit chips' or souls. Not everyone has this privilege: many members of the human race are no more likely to experience immortality than plants, which wither and fade when their physical existence is finished. Of those who have been implanted with souls, there are those who are progressing, with the assistance of Next Level representatives' ('Reps') teaching, towards 'metamorphic completion'. Then there are those who have been given deposits, but who are not currently in a classroom preparing for this transition, either because they have not yet received the Representative's information or because they have decided 'not to pursue'. Those who decide not to pursue become part of Lucifer's kingdom, and are in opposition to the Next Level. Souls who have not fully progressed to metamorphosis are 'put on ice' in the Next Level; at the next Representatives' visitation of earth, they will be re-implanted in a physical body and given the opportunity to pursue.

The Next Evolutionary Kingdom Level Above Human is governed by Older Members, one of whom was elected some 2000 years ago to send a representative ('his son') to earth. This Representative – the 'Captain' – brought with him an 'away team', and came to earth with the mission of telling humans how to enter the kingdom of God. This was Jesus, who proclaimed that the kingdom of God was at hand, and that the human race should prepare itself by renouncing worldly possessions and following him.

However, the human race, under the control of 'adversarial space races' (the Luciferians), put the Captain and his crew to death. Not content with killing the leader, the Luciferians diluted Jesus' teachings 'into watered-down Country Club religion', distorting and obscuring his message. Far from showing men and women the truth, Applewhite taught, religions are the work of Lucifer, especially Christianity in its charismatic form. The idea that one can be saved by faith is totally false: to enter the Next Level, meticulous preparation and an appropriate lifestyle are necessary.

Something should be said about the Luciferians. Their ancestors fell away many generations ago, after creating a technologically advanced civilization. Despite their fallen nature, they still retain some of the knowledge that is needed by members of the true kingdom: they are able to build spacecrafts, to travel in space and time, to communicate telepathically, to undertake genetic engineering and to increase their life expectancy. The Luciferian space races are the greatest enemy of humanity: they perpetrate misinformation, and encourage the promotion of worldly values. They abduct humans for genetic experimentation, steal their bodies and induct human beings into their service.

It is Lucifer who is responsible for the proliferation of religions in the world. Humans have sometimes been confused into thinking that space aliens are gods, and such false views have given rise to polytheism. Eastern religions, especially those which posit a plurality of gods or spiritual beings, are thus the work of Lucifer. So are religions which equate God with the self, since this is quite an erroneous understanding of reality. Accordingly, Applewhite disapproved of the New Age, in which one finds the view expressed that

'Ye are gods', that there is a Christ-consciousness within oneself, that Jesus Christ was an 'Ascended Master' or that he once lived in India. New Age activities, such as channelling, he regarded as dangerous, since it could cause one's body to be taken over by a plurality of spirits, thus leading to psychiatric disorders such as schizophrenia.

Amongst the distorted teachings propagated by Christianity is the idea that God became human in the form of a newly born infant. The Older Member 'tagged' Jesus' body, and allowed it to mature until his baptism, which signalled the beginning of his mission. His transfiguration was the final event that completed Jesus' 'christening'. (According to Heaven's Gate, only adults are capable of being used by members of the Next Level.) Finally, Jesus' resurrection equipped him with a new Next Level body, and his ascension into heaven in a cloud of light was his assumption to this Next Level by a heavenly vehicle (UFO).

Two thousand years on, another 'away team' incarnated into carefully selected human bodies which they had been preparing from the 1920s until the 1950s. The 'Admiral' (or 'Father') this time assumed a female form, taking over the body of Bonnie Nettles, and was accompanied by the 'Captain', who worked through Marshall Applewhite. Nettles and Applewhite therefore claimed to be continuing the work of Jesus, proclaiming exactly the same message. The only significant differences from Jesus were that they were a male and female couple, and that they did not claim to be as 'pure' as Jesus was: their awakening occurred somewhat later in their lifetimes. To emphasize the fact that they were working, not separately, but as an awakened couple, Applewhite and Nettles assumed the respective names of Bo and Peep (possibly to indicate that they were shepherds of their flock), and later Ti and Do. (This second pair of titles perhaps related to the tonic solfa scale in music, ti and do – or te and doh – being the final two notes in the completion of a scale.)

The 'classroom' in which those with implants undertook their training was Do's closed secluded community. To live in the community one had to renounce the world and its material wealth, assigning over one's material assets to Heaven's Gate. For new members there was a trial period, in which one's assets were set aside and could taken by the novice if he or she decided to leave. All other goods were communally owned by the fully fledged members, or 'candidates' as they were called. Members were expected to live a simple lifestyle, to have given up drugs, alcohol, tobacco and sex.

Other expectations include honesty, self-control and avoiding vanity. Even habits such as addiction to caffeine were discouraged: tea and coffee were not made available on a regular basis; Applewhite even taught that one should not become attached to particular brands of product, such as one's favourite toothpaste. At one point the community experimented with vegetarianism, but this was discontinued. In order to encourage such abstinence in the early years, Nettles and Applewhite established the 'Anonymous Sexaholics Celibate Church', but this lasted for a short period only. From 1991 to 1992 Applewhite instituted 'Total Overcomers Anonymous', a self-help group with somewhat wider aims.

The community cut itself off from all earthly ties, including one's family. After all, had not Jesus said: 'If any man comes to me and hate not his father, and mother, and wife, and children, and brethren, and sisters, yea and his own life also, he cannot be my disciple'? (Luke 14:26). Originally, about 100 seekers joined Ti and Do in 1976, when the training began in earnest. On 21 April of that year, it was declared that the 'harvest' was 'closed': there were no further public meetings and no further overt attempts to persuade people to join the community. However, because of the stringency of the community's demands, numbers dwindled. In the group's early days the leaders challenged those who were still smoking cannabis or continuing to be sexually active, questioning whether they were serious students. Some of them refused to mend their ways and left; others simply lost interest, and by 1988 there remained somewhere between 40 and 50 people who were prepared to persevere.

According to Applewhite, time can be divided into three ages: past, present and future, each period being some 6000 years in duration. By 1997 the present age had attained its 6000-year duration, and was suffering the effects of pollution, decay and overuse of the earth's resources. It had therefore to be 'spaded over', to make it ready for recycling for the next era. Jesus had been born 2000 years previously: in accordance with many historians, Applewhite concluded that his birth did not take place in the year 1 CE, but probably in the year 4 BCE. Thus the year 1996 signalled the end of the millennium.

The end of Heaven's Gate was finally heralded by the coming of the Hale–Bopp comet. Given these end-time calculations, however, the group suspected there might be rather more than an astronomical phenomenon that could be scientifically predicted. Although the group were able to recognize it as a comet, they suspected that its presence masked a spacecraft that lay behind it, and which had come to collect the Heaven's Gate community to take them to this Next Evolutionary Level Above Human. Applewhite stated:

> Whether Hale–Bopp has a 'companion' or not is irrelevant from our perspective. However, its arrival is joyously very significant to us at 'Heaven's Gate.' The joy is that our Older Member in the Evolutionary Level Above Human (the 'Kingdom of Heaven') has made it clear to us that Hale–Bopp's approach is the 'marker' we've been waiting for – the time for the arrival of the spacecraft from the Level Above Human to take us home to 'Their World' – in the literal Heavens. Our 22 years of classroom here on planet Earth is finally coming to conclusion – 'graduation' from the Human Evolutionary Level. We are happily prepared to leave 'this world' and go with Ti's crew.
>
> If you study the material on this website you will hopefully understand our joy and what our purpose here on Earth has been. You may even find your 'boarding pass' to leave with us during this brief 'window.'

In order to board, one had to leave one's earthly physical body behind – something that could only be done through taking one's own life. Applewhite had considered the possibility, and indeed one of his lectures to his 'crew' refers to the mass suicide of the Jews at Masada in 70 CE, although he expresses the hope that this will not prove necessary. Yet the group had to be prepared for such an eventuality, for, as he said:

> The true meaning of 'suicide' is to turn against the Next Level when it is being offered. In these last days, we are focused on two primary tasks: one – of making a last attempt at telling the truth about how the Next Level may be entered (our last effort at offering to individuals of this civilization the way to avoid 'suicide'); and two – taking advantage of the rare opportunity we have each day – to work individually on our personal overcoming and change, in preparation for entering the Kingdom of Heaven.

Applewhite would of course have been familiar with the Bible's description of how the 'two witnesses' meet their end:

> Then they heard a loud voice from heaven saying to them, 'Come up here.' And they went up to heaven in a cloud, while their enemies looked on. (Revelation 11:12)

Presumably he viewed his death and those of his followers as a fulfilment of this prophecy.

Some observations

These 'suicide cults' have provided excellent material for the media, providing corroborative evidence for the counter-cult view that 'cults' are dangerous and destructive, and that the public might expect to hear of further similar events perpetrated by NRMs. Words like 'victim', although justifiably used of the dead, readily become transferred to members of other NRMs, who in all probability are not under any similar risk. Of course the fact that such events make sensational news is precisely because they are the exception rather than the norm. Whatever the lot of NRM members, the vast majority can expect at least to experience continued physical survival. To put these incidents in perspective, there are four times as many people killed in accidents on British roads in any one year than died at Jonestown, yet traffic accidents seldom make news headlines, and few would try to dissuade others from driving because of the dangers involved. This is not to say of course that what happened in Jonestown, Waco, the Solar Temple and Heaven's Gate is acceptable, only that one should resist falling prey to scaremongering.

Mass suicide is not something to which people in everyday life normally succumb, and one cannot help wondering what the factors were that persuaded the followers of these four groups to terminate their lives. The groups were substantially different in character: although each contained Christian components, there is little common ground between the social gospel, fundamentalism, Templarism and UFOlogy. Two common elements are significant, however. Firstly, both groups had their own communities, separated off and remote from everyday society. Those who follow a religion in conjunction with a working life and unbelieving friends inevitably find their beliefs challenged from time to time, and encounter concrete confirmation that not everyone shares their chosen religion's world-view. Secondly, all four groups seem to have believed in an imminent end to human affairs, and it is commonly suggested that the end of a millennium is a time when one expects certain religious groups to anticipate a final cataclysm. However, while there are some groups who are expecting an imminent end to the present world system, there is little evidence to indicate that a wave of similar suicides is to be expected.

3. The old new religions

A previous chapter has dealt with the question of how new a minority religion has to be in order to count as an NRM. In this chapter I shall explore some of the earlier NRMs whose claims to novelty may now be waning. Like everything else, religions become old, and claims that organizations like the Mormons (Latter-day Saints), Jehovah's Witnesses and Theosophists – the case studies of this particular chapter – are new religions may now be waning in plausibility. Nevertheless these groups still remain controversial, and particularly the Mormons and Jehovah's Witnesses continue to attract the description 'cult' and remain the subject of Christian evangelical attack.

These older NRMs can be arranged in three broad groups, in accordance with Melton's classification scheme. First, there are those which are influenced by Mesmer, and which may be labelled by evangelical Christians as 'occultist' or 'spiritualistic'; alternatively, they can be described as New Thought. Second, there are those groups which purport to be basically Christian in character, believing in the inerrancy of Christian scripture, and offering definitive, or even innovative, interpretations for the present times. Third, there are those groups which have been largely influenced by the Theosophical ideas of Helena P. Blavatsky and Henry Steel Olcott.

New Thought

Mesmerism

As Melton suggests, the fountainhead of New Thought can be traced back to Anton Franz (Friedrich) Mesmer (1734–1815). Mesmer, of course, is popularly associated with mesmerism and with its development into hypnotism – particularly its stage versions. However, Mesmer brought together a number of ideas that were gaining momentum in his time, both scientific and religious. He drew on the new discoveries in electricity and magnetism by Galvani and Volta, developments in medicine, astrology, and various occultist ideas that were rife.

Mesmer championed the idea that one's body was surrounded by a magnetic field or 'fluid' (Mesmer used the terms 'field' and 'fluid' quite interchangeably), which transmits 'universal forces'. The magnetic fluid can be impeded by certain obstacles, resulting in various forms of illness. This idea came to be known as 'animal magnetism', or sometimes 'electro-biology'. Mesmer developed a number of means of treating imbalances in one's bodily magnetic fields. Some of his therapy sessions were arranged somewhat like seances, in which participants sat around a vat of sulphuric acid (widely used until recently for the generation of electricity in laboratories), and held either hands in a circle or iron rods which were partly immersed in the vat. This supposedly altered the electrical currents that circulated in one's body. Alternatively, healing could be mediated by a 'sensitive': this was a person of high moral integrity, skilled in concentration, who could either pass an iron magnet over the patient's body or work directly on the body with his or her hands or nose. Another therapeutic technique involved putting the patient into a trance, in which he or she was sometimes held to 'prophesy': thus mesmerism became associated with clairvoyance. Mesmerism also enjoyed a good symbiotic relationship with phrenology ('cerebral physiology'), which was much in vogue in the early nineteenth century. In 1824 John Elliotson, who led a revival of mesmerism in England, established the British Phrenological Society.

Inevitably, Mesmer's ideas attracted much adverse criticism from other physicians, and he was forced to leave Austria for Paris. Once in Paris he proved equally controversial, being accused of practising magic. In 1784 King Louis XVI set up a commission to investigate Mesmer, which included Benjamin Franklin and Lavoisier. The French Revolution caused Mesmer finally to flee to London, throwing mesmerism into neglect in France. In the 1820s, however, it experienced a revival, and entered Britain in 1837. After Mesmer's death in 1815, some of his disciples claimed to maintain a psychic relationship with him, thus giving further impetus to associations between mesmerism and the occult.

Mesmer was an important influence on Freud, who is renowned for psychoanalysis, and who developed hypnotism from Mesmer's techniques. Hanegraaff claims that clairvoyance, phrenology and mesmerism were factors in the development of psychoanalysis, which he describes as 'a twentieth-century "science" in which the analyst plays the role of sensitive' (Wessinger, 1998, p. 16). For our present purposes, Mesmer is particularly significant for the development of 'New Thought', which laid important emphasis on the powers of the mind, and in particular their role in effecting healing – an idea which finds expression most notably in Christian Science as well as in Spiritualism.

In order to understand New Thought adequately, two related bodies of thought are important: Swedenborgianism and Transcendentalism.

Swedenborgianism

Emanuel Swedenborg (1688–1722) was the son of Jesper Swedenborg, a Lutheran professor of theology at Uppsala University and Bishop of Skara. He studied mathematics and science, and pursued a distinguished career in mining engineering and metallurgy. Although in secular employment, Swedenborg was particularly interested in the nature of the soul and how it related to the body, concluding that the life force resided in the brain's cortex and circulated through the body by means of the blood.

During the years 1743–5 Swedenborg's thought took on quite a new aspect. A series of visions, the first of which was of Jesus Christ, began in 1744, and this was followed by further appearances of angels and spirits, glimpses of heaven and hell, and even a vision of God. Swedenborg recorded his visions and dreams in a *Journal of Dreams,* and in 1745 he abandoned secular study in favour of close contemplation of scripture, and finally relinquished his post in the Swedish Board of Mines in 1747. For nearly 30 years of his life Swedenborg claimed to have been in communication with spirits and angels, and with God himself.

By mainstream Christian standards, Swedenborg's theology was unorthodox in several respects. He taught that Christ was not the

Son of God, but God himself, manifested in human form: Jesus was therefore to be worshipped directly as God, rather than as a mediator between God and humanity. Jesus was not someone who vicariously atoned for sin, but rather one who offers deliverance from sinning. Responsibility and love in practice are the conditions for gaining entry to heaven: the final judgement of humankind would therefore be an assessment of men's and women's character.

One particularly noteworthy vision of Swedenborg's was that in which he saw the New Jerusalem descending from heaven to earth, as described by John in the Book of Revelation (Revelation 21). Swedenborg interpreted this vision not as a portent of some future parousia, but rather as an event which actually took in 1757. The second coming of Christ had actually occurred, paving the way for a new dispensation, a new evolutionary step in humankind's spiritual development.

Swedenborg published a total of 30 theological works, including his biblical commentaries. He did not hold that the Bible was to be believed literally in its entirety: its importance lay, he taught, in its spiritual teachings. Not all the books of the Bible afforded the same degree of spiritual insights, and particular emphasis was given to the gospels and the Book of Revelation. In his later writings he attached greater weight to the New Testament epistles, particularly 1 John. Of special importance is Swedenborg's theory of 'correspondences', set out in his *Clavis Hieroglyphica,* published in English in 1784 under the title *A Spiritual Key.* In this work, Swedenborg claimed that everything in the universe bore three levels of meaning: natural, spiritual and divine. Natural meaning is what is derived from human observation, the sciences and history; spiritual meaning comes from the mind and its imagination; and divine meaning relates to the apprehension of God. The material world, then, has a spiritual structure, and everything in the material world is therefore capable of pointing towards these two higher levels and of being understood accordingly.

Peter Washington identifies four key points in Swedenborg's thought: the theory of 'correspondences' between the material and the spiritual; communication with the world of spirits; the notion of a new politico-religious dispensation; and the reconciliation of science and religion, imagination and reason (Washington, 1993, p. 15). To these one might add a fifth: the notions of responsibility and practical morality. Swedenborg was concerned that his ideas should be propagated, but within the Christian Church rather than in a separate religious organization. After his death, however, five former Wesleyan pastors established the Church of the New Jerusalem (also known as the 'New Church') in 1787. The first American congregation was founded in 1792, and in 1810 the Swedenborg Society – created for the publication and dissemination of Swedenborg's teachings – began in England. In 1897 the General Church of the New Jerusalem was established at Bryn Athyn in the USA.

Although the Church of the New Jerusalem has experienced serious decline, and Swedenborg's writings now tend to be read only by a small handful of followers, Swedenborgianism made an important impact on a number of forms of spirituality. The New Church attracted no less a figure than William James's father, and had an important bearing on James's interest in and treatment of religious experience. Swedenborg's interest in the world of spirits had an important bearing on the rise of Spiritualism, even though Spiritualists had their own criticisms of Swedenborg, variously accusing him of undue emphasis on the material world, denying Christ's divinity, and setting himself as a unique channel of supernatural revelation. Swedenborg, reciprocally, had warned against casual contact with spirits.

Swedenborg's interest in spirits also paved the way for subsequent interest in the development of New Thought and in psychical research. Although today's New Agers may not directly relate their interest in dream work, the paranormal and psychic phenomena to Swedenborg, his ideas gave momentum to these areas. Of particular importance is Swedenborg's influence on Ralph Waldo Emerson and the Transcendentalist movement. Emerson identified Swedenborg as one of his 'representative men' – that is to say, figures in humankind's history who have had special insights that have marked them out from other individuals. Emerson was prepared to put Swedenborg on a level with Plato, Shakespeare and Goethe (Chryssides, 1998, p. 98).

Transcendentalism

Ralph Waldo Emerson (1803–82) was one of the key founders of the Transcendentalist movement. At first a Unitarian minister in Boston,

Emerson resigned his post because he could no longer accept the sacraments and had serious concerns about practising a religion that was based on a book such as the Bible. On Christmas Day 1832 he departed for England, where he met several of the English Romantics, principally Thomas Carlyle, Samuel Taylor Coleridge and William Wordsworth. On returning to America in 1834, Emerson gathered a group of like-minded friends together to form the Transcendentalist Club.

Transcendentalism presented an alternative way of looking at the world from that of the Enlightenment, emphasizing experience, intuition and oneness with nature as an alternative to rationalism, book learning and institutional teaching such as that carried out by the Church or within universities. Nature, Emerson taught, was the true teacher, to be preferred by far to the scholarship and pedantry of academics. Oneness with nature entailed that there was no separate self that stood apart from creation.

This was based on an experience which Emerson had on 19 March 1835, while walking in the woods. Emerson writes:

> In the woods, we return to reason and faith. There I feel that nothing can befall me in life, – no disgrace, no calamity (leaving me my eyes,) which nature cannot repair. Standing on the bare ground, – my head bathed by the blithe air, and uplifted into infinite space, – all mean egotism vanishes. I become a transparent eye-ball; I am nothing; I see all; the currents of the Universal Being circulate through me; I am part or particle of God. The name of the nearest friend sounds then foreign and accidental: to be brothers, to be acquaintances, – master or servant, is than a trifle and a disturbance. I am the lover of uncontained and immortal beauty. (quoted in Geldard, 1995, pp. 13–14)

The import of this somewhat strange reported experience is that there is no self that exists apart from the cosmic self, or – as Emerson called it – the Over-Soul. What my eyeball perceives, in the form of either the world or my body, is not me. Equally, there is no 'me' on the 'other side' of my eyeball, but only God. The eyeball itself, being transparent, has no being which is independent of either the world or the Over-Soul. What Emerson is propounding, in short, is nothing other than the Upanishadic idea that *atman* and *brahman* are one. Emerson was one of the few intellectuals of his time who acquainted himself with eastern philosophy, particularly the Upanishads and the Bhagavad Gita, and drew on them as a source of inspiration. Emerson was one of the first westerners to possess a copy of the Upanishads.

Additionally, Emerson, in common with both the Upanishads and the Idealists of his time, was affirming the essential reality of the mind. Nature does not exist independently of the mind, but as a set of ideas within it. Just as the eye is not something which forms a barrier between oneself and the world, but rather unifies them, so any division which appears to exist between the self and the world is a false one. As Emerson said, 'The simplest person, who in his integrity worships God, becomes God' (quoted in Lash, 1990, pp. 385–6).

The basic principle of Transcendentalism was the essential unity of all things. The individual was essentially one with nature, and nature was ultimately one with God. The world, being one with the self, is thus God's 'logos', or 'word'. It is our mother and also the school at which we learn. Internal growth is therefore much superior to external teaching. As one lives one's life, one experiences a 'procession of a soul in matter', learning from nature's character- istics, one's everyday experiences of ordinary work, one's joys and sorrows. Sorrows and disappointments are themselves part of this intimacy with nature: Emerson characteristically avoided the use of terms like 'fortunate' and 'unfortunate'; he believed that these terms implied that we are beyond the laws of nature, which reward and compensate us in the way we deserve. Emerson believed in a principle of 'compensation' or 'retribution' that pervaded the universe.

It is sometimes said that Emerson is a herald of the New Age, or even the 'father of the New Age'. A number of points in common will no doubt be instantly recognizable. First, the world-affirming nature of Emerson's philosophy, and its emphasis on enjoying and learning from the natural world has filtered down into New Age thought. Emerson would no doubt have been attracted by those New Agers in the South-West of England who once invited me in an early morning walk on a deserted Cornish beach to learn from the dolphins! Like the present-day New Agers, Emerson exudes an optimism, not only about nature itself, but about the human beings who inhabit the physical world. Human disasters are not inherently bad, and men and women are 'part or particle of God'.

In common with the late-twentieth-century New Age movement, Emerson uses what would now be called the right-hand side of the brain, and radically questions the ability of reason to enable the seeker to arrive at truth – particularly spiritual truth. Emerson is anti-intellectual and anti-establishment, radically questioning the role of traditional institutions such as universities and churches to mediate knowledge of the divine.

Like the present-day New Ager, Emerson was eclectic, not confining himself to the scriptures of any one religious tradition such as Christianity, but combining the insights of the Judaeo-Christian Bible with the Upanishads, the Bhagavad Gita, his experiences of nature and some of his dreams. No doubt if a wider variety of religious writings had been available to him, Emerson would have drawn on them also.

Having said this, Emerson's eclecticism and emphasis on learning from nature did not entail that 'anything goes' in the name of experience. Indeed, Emerson was critical of several innovatory 'alternative' ideas of some of his contemporaries. In an essay entitled 'Demonology', as well as elsewhere, he comes down very heavily on proponents of 'mind cure', 'animal magnetism', omens, spiritism and mesmerism.

> Animal magnetism, omens, spiritism, mesmerism have great interest for some minds. They run into this twilight and say, 'There's more than is dreamed of in your philosophy.' Certainly these facts are interesting and deserve to be considered. But they are entitled only to a share of attention, and not a large share. It is a low curiosity or lust of structure, and it is separated by celestial diameters from the love of spiritual truths. It is wholly a false view to couple these things in any manner with the religious nature and sentiment, and a most dangerous superstition to raise them to the lofty place of motives and sanctions. This is to prefer halos and rainbows to the sun and moon. These adepts have mistaken flatulency for inspiration. Were this drivel which they report as the voice of spirits really such, we must find out a more decisive suicide. The whole world is an omen and a sign. Why look so wistfully in a corner? Man is the image of God. Why run after a ghost or a dream? (quoted in Geldard, 1993, pp. 115–16)

Although Emerson had an undoubted influence on New Age ideas, New Agers who wish to claim Emerson as their own would do well to note remarks like these.

The mind's role in healing

Mesmer's influence gained momentum in the USA as a result of Charles Poyen's work. Poyen was a French hypnotist who undertook a lecture tour in America in 1836, returning to France three years later. Like Mesmer, Poyen believed in 'animal magnetism' and he did much to popularize mesmerism in New England and on the American East Coast. Animal magnetism achieved a further impact as a result of J. P. F. Deleuze's book on the subject, which was translated by Thomas C. Harthorn under the title *Practical Instructions in Animal Magnetism,* and the celebrated writer, Edgar Allan Poe, wrote a short horror story, 'The Facts in the Case of M. Valdemar', which was originally entitled 'Mesmerism in Articulo Mortis' ('Mesmerism at the moment of death'). The plot concerned a decomposing corpse which was miraculously kept alive by means of 'trance induction', and the story appeared in various magazines in the 1840s. Despite its fictional character, it provoked popular discussion as to whether such phenomena might really be possible.

In 1838 one important member of Poyen's audience was Phineas Parker Quimby (1802-66), who is said to have laid the foundations of the New Thought movement. Impressed by what he heard, Quimby went on to become a 'mesmeric healer'. Although Quimby would sometimes employ his own independent psychic powers, he was usually assisted by one Lucius Burkmar, who assumed the role of a medium, and went into trance states, using clairvoyance and telepathy to offer diagnoses and cures which 'harmonized the vital fluids' of the body.

Ostensibly, the electrical-magnetic phenomena were identified as the cause of ill health and the means of effecting a cure. However, Quimby came to note that the patients' own belief appeared to be an important contributory factor in making a recovery, and Quimby came to hold that the source of ill health was the mind. This observation did not cause Quimby to abandon his belief in the body's 'vital forces': these still played an important role in one's state of health, but the patient's beliefs acted as a set of 'control valves' that affected the flow of these vital forces. Quimby thus became one of the earliest exponents of 'mind cure', which led to New Thought. As Hanegraaff (1996) points out, Quimby's philosophy of health had two important components: he believed that health had an important spiritual dimension to it; and he regarded his brand of

85

religion as 'scientific'. Hanegraaff describes his theories as a blend of occultism and Transcendentalism, although it should be remembered that Emerson himself was extremely scathing of 'mind cure' and 'animal magnetism'.

Quimby's successors

Quimby's teachings were disseminated by Julius and Anetta Dresser, and especially by Warren Felt Evans, all of whom were Quimby's pupils. This heralded a proliferation of 'positive thinking' or 'self-help' books: titles included *Thought is Power, How to Use New Thought in Home Life, How to Get What You Want,* and *Making Money: How to Grow Success.* These are quite similar to many of the more recent New Age self-help books that are currently in vogue. Evans developed the idea of using 'affirmations' – brief ego-boosting statements to be recited at regular intervals (Hanegraaff, 1996, p. 488). (Again, one can recognize the affinities with some of the 'self-help' ideas of the present-day New Age.)

New Thought's main themes can thus be seen as these. First, there is a belief in the powers of the mind, which are held to be much greater than previously recognized, and particularly influential on one's state of health. Second, there is an emphasis on personal responsibility: if the mind is responsible for one's state of well-being, then individuals have it in their power to determine how well or ill they fare. Self-help is thus a corollary of a belief in the powers of the mind and personal responsibility. Furthermore, exponents of New Thought often held a belief in a harmonious perfection of a cosmic whole: this perfection needed to be replicated in one's own mind; thus New Thought is sometimes described as 'harmonial religion'. Hanegraaff describes it as a 'sacralization of psychology' (Hanegraaff, 1996, p. 500).

Possibly the most important, and certainly the best known, of Phineas Quimby's followers was Mary Baker Eddy (1821–1910), the founder of Christian Science. Eddy had been ill, and, having tried homeopathy without success, turned to Quimby for treatment. She experienced some improvement, but relapsed into illness after Quimby died. After reading the accounts of Jesus' healing miracles in St Matthew's gospel, she then effected a self-cure, by the powers of the mind. This led to her discovery of Christian Science.

In the early years of Christian Science, Eddy's co-worker was Emma Curtis Hopkins, who assumed responsibility for editing the *Christian Science Journal*. Eddy and Hopkins split, however, and Hopkins rivalled Eddy's work, at first in Chicago, but eventually country-wide, establishing the Hopkins Metaphysical Association in 1887. A number of important founders of New Thought groups studied under Hopkins, including Melinda Cramer (founder of Divine Science), Annie Rix Militz (Homes of Truth), Charles and Myrtle Fillmore (Unity School of Christianity), Ernest Holmes (Religious Science) and Frances Lord, who took New Thought to England in 1880s. The International New Thought Alliance was formed in 1914, and brought various New Thought groups together.

Theosophy

Another fountainhead of ideas and movements that have become part of the current NRM scene is Theosophy. Founded by Helena Petrovna Blavatsky (1831–91) (often referred to as 'Madame Blavatsky' or 'HPB' within the movement) and Colonel Henry Steel Olcott (1832–1907), Theosophy is particularly important for understanding several other religious groups that are still extant. Rudolf Steiner's Anthroposophy, Krishnamurti, J.I. Gurdjieff and P.D. Ouspensky all stem directly from the activities of the Theosophical Society, and the development of modern Buddhism, both in its western forms and especially in its indigenous form in present-day Sri Lanka, is largely due to Olcott's work.

Helena Blavatsky was born into an aristocratic family in Russia; her father was Baron von Hahn. Even as a child, she apparently claimed psychic abilities: she is said to have been proficient at 'table tapping', clairvoyance, levitation and materializing objects, such as bunches of flowers, out of thin air. In 1848 she married Nikifor Blavatsky, who was Vice-Governor of Yerevan, and almost 20 years her senior. The marriage was unsuccessful, with Helena leaving Nikifor after only a few weeks. According to some accounts, the marriage was unconsummated. However, she continued to use his surname throughout the rest of her life.

The same year marks the beginning of Blavatsky's travels. This decade in her life (1848–58) is often referred to as 'the veiled time', since it is impossible to verify with any certainty the places to which she travelled. According to her own version of events, she journeyed to the Far East, and into Tibet, where she studied under its 'Secret Masters'. Peter Washington (1993), in his account of the life and influence of Madame Blavatsky, thinks that this is highly unlikely, since Tibet was closed to the outside world until the Younghusband expedition of 1903. Other alleged episodes during this period include meeting Red Indians in Canada and the USA, travelling across the Middle West by wagon, and speaking with Egyptian cabbalists, voodoo magicians and bandits, amongst others. Washington writes:

> Quite how she supported herself is not clear, though she may have had an allowance from her father and seems to have set up as an itinerant spirit medium. She also claimed to have ridden bareback in a circus, toured Serbia as a concert pianist, opened an ink factory in Odessa, traded as an importer of ostrich feathers in Paris, and worked as interior decorator to the Empress Eugénie. (Washington, 1993, p. 31)

Certainly, Blavatsky visited Europe, the Americas and part of Asia. However, her most decisive encounter was with the Tibetan Master Morya, a somewhat mysterious being who apparently could materialize and de-materialize at will. Blavatsky's first meeting with Master Morya was not in Tibet, as one might have expected, but at the Great Exhibition at Crystal Palace in London in 1851.

According to Blavatsky's teaching, Morya is one of the so-called Great White Brotherhood, a group of spiritual beings who have passed beyond or exist outside the physical world in which we live. This Great White Brotherhood is headed by the 'Lord of the World', who presides over a hierarchy of beings, including the Buddha, Mahachohan, Manu and Maitreya. Manu and Maitreya have assistants, the former being aided by Master Morya, and the latter by Master Koot Hoomi. (Some of these beings are deceased historical figures, while others, such as Maitreya, belong to religious mythology. Morya and Koot Hoomi fall into neither category, and critics have attributed them to Blavatsky's fertile imagination.) Also among this Brotherhood of Masters belonged all the world's great religious leaders and all past teachers of the occult. They included Abraham, Moses, Solomon, Confucius, Lao Tzu, Plato, Boehme, Roger Bacon, Francis Bacon, Cagliostro and, interestingly, Mesmer. Below such figures are the 'arhats': these are enlightened beings who seek full Mastership, and they in turn have their disciples, called 'chelas' (Washington, 1993, p. 35). This Brotherhood is usually hidden from humanity's view, but on occasions members appear to divulge their teachings to selected individuals – 'initiated seers' of whom Blavatsky considered herself to be one. Such agents are typically disbelieved by their fellow humans, who are influenced by Dark Forces ('Lords of the Dark Face') who oppose them. Jesus' crucifixion was one striking example of Dark Forces annihilating one initiated seer.

Blavatsky moved to the USA in 1873, where she continued to propound these teachings. In 1874 she met Colonel Henry Steel Olcott, who was become her mentor, ally and co-founder of the Theosophical Society, which they established in New York in 1875, together with William Q. Judge (1851–96). The Theosophical Society had three principal stated aims:

1. 'To form a nucleus of the universal brotherhood of humanity without distinction of race, creed, sex, caste or colour.'
2. 'To investigate unexplained laws of nature and the powers latent in man.'
3. 'To encourage the study of comparative religion, philosophy and science.' (quoted in Annett, 1976, pp. 110–11)

Various commentators have perceived a number of problems with the inception of Theosophy and these stated aims. The very name 'Theosophy' literally means 'divine wisdom', yet Blavatsky and Olcott placed little emphasis on God, preferring instead the wisdom of the co-called Masters, many of whom indeed (such as the Buddha, Confucius and Lao Tzu) belong to non-theistic religions. Blavatsky's ideas, which she published in 1877 under the title *Isis Unveiled*, tended to draw most heavily on ancient Egyptian religion, rather than other major world religions, and she was herself quite hostile to traditional Christianity. The Theosophical Society's aim of fostering the study of comparative religion was therefore carried out only in a very piecemeal and selective way. There were no invitations extended to major scholars to deliver lectures on world religions, and most of the teaching came either from Madame Blavatsky's writings or from sympathizers who could boast no formal qualifications in such areas. Teachings largely purported to come from those initiated seers who had access to the Masters. It is therefore very doubtful whether the early Theosophists really engaged in any 'investigation' of the 'unexplained laws of nature' in any scientific or objective way: the society appears to have consisted of those who already believed in the veracity of such phenomena. The reference in the first aim to the forming of a 'universal brotherhood of humanity' was certainly not pursued by any programme of societal reform or even consciousness-raising, but rather seemed to serve as an inducement to attract those who might be favourably disposed to such sentiments.

As far as religion, philosophy and science were concerned, Blavatsky taught that existence was a unity, governed by universal laws. This applied equally to the physical and the spiritual worlds: natural laws govern human (and all physical) existence, while the laws of 'rhythm' and karma govern the spirit (Annett, 1976, p. 111). The spirit is eternal, although humans who are subject to these laws are transient. One's spirit continues, being transported through various physical bodies, as one's spiritual powers progressively unfold. We have the power to become free from human limitations: when we do this, we experience God without any intermediaries (such as 'initiated seers') and know reality directly.

Humanity is therefore evolving. Blavatsky could accept the theories of evolution which had recently been propounded by Darwin and others, but she believed that the evolutionary process which transformed monkeys into humans was no astonishing feat. Any such evolutionary progression was only a minute part of the entire evolution of human beings, who are still in the process of an evolutionary journey through many successive reincarnations. It is significant that Theosophists have tended to talk about reincarnation, not as a range of possibilities for future births in which one might either enhance or worsen one's status, but rather as a constant progression in an upward direction, where there is no 'falling back'. Although the Theosophists did not conceive of future rebirths as possibly being in the animal, ghost or hell realm (as in traditional Buddhism), one's present life could either accelerate or retard one's upward progression. The 'secret knowledge' could achieve the former, as could meditation. While the secret knowledge could be found latent in all religions, it had been passed on only to a few individuals in small degrees; it was through those who had access to the Masters that it could be revealed and disseminated in its fullness.

These problems of Theosophy's internal coherence may well have contributed to its relative lack of popularity. Whatever the cause, in 1878 the Theosophical Society was foundering. At this point Blavatsky and Olcott decided to make their journey to India and Ceylon (now Sri Lanka) – a journey which is well authenticated – in the hope that the society might experience some revival as a result of contacts with Hinduism and Buddhism. Blavatsky firmly believed that a great revival of spirituality would come from India, and the headquarters of the Society were therefore moved to Adyar, near Madras, in that year.

The Indian visit, Rawlinson argues, effected an easternization of Theosophy, as a result of which 'Theosophy can be said to be complete' (Rawlinson, 1997, p. 195). As a result of the Indian visit, Blavatsky was able to draw together elements of Hinduism and Buddhism in her second major work *The Secret Doctrine*. As Rawlinson comments, 'Unlike *Isis Unveiled*, which was essentially Western, *The Secret Doctrine* is predominantly Hindu with some admixture of Mahayana and Vajrayana Buddhism' (Rawlinson, 1997, p. 195).

Brief mention needs to be made of several other figures who were associated with Theosophy and affected the way in which the organization developed. Annie Wood Besant (1847–1933) assumed control of the Society after Blavatsky. The separated wife of an Anglican clergyman, she was a radical both in religion and in politics, being a member of the Fabian Society, an ardent champion of women's rights, and someone who did much to secure social and educational improvements in India. She established the Indian Home Rule League, and founded several schools in the subcontinent, one of which became the University of Benares. She was thus more of an intellectual than a psychic. She was involved in Co-Masonry – a form of Freemasonry that granted equality to women. Her principal writings were *Esoteric Christianity, Introduction to Yoga* and a translation of the Bhagavad Gita.

Closely allied with Annie Besant was Charles W. Leadbeater (1854–1934). Leadbeater was a mainstream Christian clergyman until his bishop denounced Theosophy, claiming it to be incompatible with the Christian faith. In 1916 Leadbeater broke away from the Church of England to become the founder and 'bishop' of the Liberal Catholic Church, a breakaway group of the Dutch Old Catholic Church. The Christian background of Besant and Leadbeater injected more of a Christian element into Theosophy, which, under Blavatsky and Olcott, had focused principally on ancient Egyptian religion, and on Hinduism and Buddhism.

Leadbeater's role in NRMs is particularly important for his 'discovery' in 1908 of Jiddhu Krishnamurti (1895–1986), then a 14-

year-old boy. Leadbeater and Besant met him in India, and determined, by examining his 'aura', that he was the coming Maitreya, the buddha of the next aeon. In 1910 Krishnamurti was initiated into the Great White Brotherhood, and the following year Leadbeater and Besant established Krishnamurti's own organization, the Order of the Star in the East. This lasted until 1929, when Krishnamurti disbanded it. *At the Feet of the Master* was Krishnamurti's first book, although some believe that it was really written by Leadbeater: it attempts to show how other masters accepted the Great White Brotherhood. Krishnamurti taught throughout his life, and his teachings continue to attract an interest. His main themes are the individual and personal nature of truth and the importance of self-knowledge; neither of these can be transmitted through any formal religion or religious organization.

Although Krishnamurti has been much acclaimed by some, Besant's promotion of him alienated others. Rudolf Steiner, for example, who was once a Theosophist, and who is renowned for his innovatory educational techniques, left the movement because of Krishnamurti.

Other new religious leaders whose spiritual cradle was Theosophy were J.I. Gurdjieff (*c*. 1874–1949) and P.D. Ouspensky (1878–1947). George Ivanovich Gurdjieff was born in Armenia, of Greek parents. During the first 40 years of his life he travelled widely, as far afield as Tibet where he claims to have learned ancient wisdom. Gurdjieff founded the Institute for the Harmonious Development of Man in 1922 in France: this organization demanded relentless physical labour with little relaxation, but also taught a kind of esoteric Christianity, combined with spiritual dancing, influenced by Dervishes whom Gurdjieff had encountered. Ouspensky sought to clarify Gurdjieff's teachings in his book *In Search of the Miraculous:* being a mathematician, he was able to combine a more rational and systematic approach with Gurdjieff's intuition and exuberance. Ouspensky taught that for most of the time we live only in the basement of a larger house: we are observers, rather than participants. He identified three spiritual paths that sages had recommended: the fakir (physical austerity), the monk (who sought to develop the emotions), and the yogi (who favoured intellectual progress). Ouspensky offered a 'Fourth Way School' which taught the mystical, and much of Gurdjieff–Ouspensky incorporated esoteric study, including the Kabbalah and the Tarot (on which

Ouspensky wrote a book). Gurdjieff-Ouspensky teachings included the notion of three 'centres' within the human self – the emotional, the intellectual and the physical – an idea that forms the basis of biorhythms. Ouspensky is also said to have been the originator of the enneagram. Gurdjieff and Ouspensky are pivotal figures in the develop of alternative spirituality. A number of Gurdjieff groups still exist, the largest of which is the Gurdjieff Society. J.G. Bennett (1897–1974), who also became associated with Subud, was a follower of Gurdjieff.

The Theosophical Society, which was the breeding ground of these emergent spiritualities, continues today with a worldwide membership of 34,000, consisting of national societies with various branches called 'lodges'. Each group is autonomous. Although many of its supporters are drawn to the original ideas of a secret core of all religions and an interest in the occult, there is no required body of belief that is demanded of Theosophists. Any views of its founders, members or anyone else are 'hypotheses' and should be examined by all seekers. The value that is placed on freedom of thought is indicated by a Resolution passed by the General Council:

> there is no doctrine, no opinion by whomsoever taught or held that is any way binding on any member of the society ... Approval of its three objects is the sole condition of membership. No teacher or writer, from H. P. Blavatsky downwards, has any authority to impose his teachings or opinions on members. (quoted in Annett, 1976, p. 112)

It is the power to examine beliefs for oneself that enables one to become a 'knower'. True knowledge, however, goes beyond 'hypotheses' or any kind of factual knowledge: the goal is knowing the Truth, not merely knowing *about* the Truth. Spiritual practice is therefore important, and Theosophists typically engage in meditation, as well as attend lectures, seminars and discussions.

New Christian NRMs

The effects of New Thought, Transcendentalism and Theosophy were to create an interest in forms of spirituality that lay beyond the western Christian tradition. By contrast, there were other groups that reaffirmed the Christian faith. Not content with its mainstream forms of expression, two groups in particular came to regard Christianity as having lost its authenticity and in need of a restoration to its true primordial form. The remainder of this chapter is therefore devoted to an examination of the Jehovah's Witnesses and the Church of Jesus Christ of Latter-day Saints (the Mormons), both of which are 'restorationist', seeking to revive the Church's original lost identity. Clearly, any attempt at reviving a primordial form of the original Church assumes that it is possible to establish what a truly authentic form of that Church was like. The fact that the Jehovah's Witnesses and the Mormons arrived at radically different answers to this question indicates the difficulty and complexity of such a quest, and the problems are partly historical and partly doctrinal.

The Jehovah's Witnesses

Charles Taze Russell (1852–1916) was the founder-leader of the organization that came to be called the Jehovah's Witnesses. Russell came from a Congregationalist-Presbyterian background in the United States. He was religious, but particularly disliked the doctrines of predestination and eternal punishment that were taught by mainstream Protestantism. Russell also found the doctrine of the Trinity problematic, and could not find scriptural support for it. He taught that the Second Advent of Christ was near, and that it would happen in 1874. (JWs are frequently accused of changing dates of the Second Coming, but they insist that Russell taught that the Second Coming would be 'secret', and that the end would occur in 1914.)

Russell studied the Bible carefully, together with a number of like-minded young men. His movement gained momentum, and in 1874 Zion's Watchtower Society was formed. The movement spread internationally: an office in London was established in 1900. Zion's Watchtower Society later became the Watchtower Bible and Tract Society (1884), the name by which it is known today. Three years later, Russell gave up his secular work as a haberdasher, sold off the five shops he had inherited from his father, and embarked on a full-time preaching career. In 1878 he assumed the title 'Pastor'. The year 1879 saw the publication of the first *Watchtower,* and in 1880 missionaries were sent from the USA to England.

When Russell died in 1916, he was succeeded by Joseph Franklin Rutherford (1869–1941). He was often known as 'Judge Rutherford', having obtained an attorney's licence in 1892, and acted as a special judge in the Eighth Judicial Circuit Court of Missouri. According to Watchtower sources, Rutherford once secured employment as a doorstep encyclopedia salesman, in order to pay for his law tuition, and hence encountered the problems of door-to-door work, having the door shut in his face on many occasions. On one occasion, he fell into an icy stream, and nearly died as a result. He then resolved that, if he ever encountered anyone selling books, he would buy them. Two colporteurs appeared at his law office one day, distributing copies of Russell's *Millennial Dawn*. He accepted them, and was persuaded by them. He was baptized in 1906, and in the following year became legal adviser to the Watchtower Society.

Under Rutherford's leadership a number of important developments took place. It was in Rutherford's period of office that the Witnesses' door-to-door work commenced. Rutherford encouraged Witnesses to use the latest technology: he broadcast on the radio network and between 1934 and 1944 a number of 'publishers' brought a gramophone to people's homes to play them some of Rutherford's sermons. However, after 1944, personal presentation from publishers was preferred, which is the style that continues today.

Important too was a convention in Columbus, Ohio, which Rutherford chaired in 1931, at which attendees adopted the resolution giving themselves the new name 'Jehovah's Witnesses' (Isaiah 43:10). Formerly, they had been called 'Bible Students' or the 'International Bible Students' Association', a name which they still continued to be called in certain circles, by force of habit.

During Rutherford's period of office, some of the more 'revolutionary' elements of Witnesses' teaching developed. In 1917 Russell's book *The Finished Mystery* was published posthumously. It was a commentary on the books of Revelation and Ezekiel, but its sharp criticism of the Christian churches made it highly controversial: amongst other things it was anti-war – a dangerous stance when the world was in the midst of armed conflict. It was banned in many countries, where one could be imprisoned for possessing a copy.

The Bible teaches that Christ's followers are 'no part of the world' (John 17:16), and JWs have taken this to mean that their members should not involve themselves in worldly political affairs, since the world is ruled by Satan, and God's kingdom by God's theocratic rule. Consequently, Witnesses do not vote. They do not belong to political parties, and hence *a fortiori* Witnesses in Germany would not join the Nazi party. They have consistently refused to take up arms in military conflict:

> They will have to beat their swords into plowshares
> and their spears into pruning shears.
> Nation will not lift up sword against nation,
> nor will they learn war any more. (Isaiah 2:4)

> My kingdom is no part of this world. If my kingdom were part
> of this world, my attendants would have fought ... (John 18:36)

Strictly speaking, Jehovah's Witnesses are not pacifist: they acknowledge that there are wars described in the Old Testament, which appear to be sanctioned by God. Hence, if they believed that God called them to fight, then they would do so. However, the Old Testament reflects the old order of things, which is superseded by the New.

Other examples of belonging to the world included 'worldly celebrations and holidays' (Watchtower, 1993, p. 79). During the 1920s and 1930s, Witnesses were progressively coming to the conclusion that festivals such as Christmas, saints' days and other national festivals were inappropriate. Part of their objection was that such festivals evidenced worldly or apostate allegiance, either sanctioning selfishness and greed (as in the case of birthdays and Christmas) or incorporating accretions added by mainstream Christianity that are not scripturally sanctioned. For example, there is no scriptural evidence that the earliest Christians celebrated Christmas, and the festival, arguably, incorporates various pagan elements; even the Magi themselves, who brought gifts to Jesus, were oriental astrologers and not followers of Jehovah. One member of Watchtower Society's staff at its Brooklyn, New York headquarters had researched the origins of Christmas customs, and broadcast his conclusions over the radio in 1928. This helped to define the Witnesses' stance, which prevails today, and brought their position into the public arena.

In 1920 Rutherford wrote his famous work *Millions Now Living Will Never Die!* It is no doubt this book which helps to convey the impression that Witnesses are first and foremost concerned with biblical prophecies and fixing dates for the last things. In the Book of Revelation the author describes a vision in which he sees a scarlet-coloured seven-headed beast. The seer is informed that the seven heads represent seven hills, and also seven kings, of whom 'Five have fallen, one is, [and] the other has not yet come; but when he does come, he must remain for a little while. The beast who once was, and now is not, is an eighth king. He belongs to the seven and is going to his destruction' (Revelation 17:3–11).

If five kings have fallen, then, if we are to ascertain the meaning of the passage, their identity should be ascertainable by looking into human history. According to the Witnesses, they are the kings of five world powers: Egypt, Assyria, Babylon, Medo-Persia and Greece. Rome is the sixth, with the seventh still to appear. The seventh is said to be jointly the USA and the UK, which have dominated the world in recent times (Watchtower, 1988, pp. 251–4). If this is so, then this means that biblical prophecies are being fulfilled in the twentieth century, as indeed Jehovah's Witnesses hold. According to the Witnesses, we are living in the end times: these two world powers will only dominate human affairs for a short time, and then the final battle of Armageddon will take place, bringing the world to an end in its present form.

Rutherford mentioned a number of key dates, principally 1914, 1918 and 1925. The date of 1914 marked the commencement of Christ's invisible rule, with the other two dates being significant for the Jews' return to God's favour. Thus 1918 relates to the Balfour Declaration (2 November 1917), and 1925 was the end of the 70 'jubilees', at which time 'the earthly phase of the kingdom shall be recognized' (Rutherford, 1920, p. 89). Until 1932 the Witnesses understood biblical prophecies as referring to the Jewish nation finding favour with God once more, but they came to the view, however, that the Jews were showing no signs of repentance, and from 1932 onwards biblical prophecy was reappraised. Prophecies which purported to refer to modern-day Jews really referred to God's 'spiritual Israel', those he had chosen under his new covenant. The political state of Israel, according to the Witnesses, made the fatal mistake of joining the United Nations in 1949, that organization being part of Satan's empire, which was controlling the world. After this event, the Witnesses reappraised their teachings, concluding that the biblical prophecies referred to the 'spiritual Israel', that is to say, those who have accepted the truth of the gospel message (Watchtower, 1993, p. 141).

Critics will usually allege that the Witnesses have named specific years in which they expected the world to end, and, when this failed to happen, changed their calendar of events, naming first 1874, then 1914, 1918, 1925 and, most recently, 1975. Three points should be made about this image of the Jehovah's Witness as the failed clairvoyant. First, Witnesses will point out that they are not committed to affirming the infallibility of Russell and Rutherford: they were not special prophets or messiahs, but ordinary human beings who sought to interpret scripture to the best of their ability. Being human, they were subject to error, like everyone else.

Second, although Witnesses are characteristically associated with prophecies relating to the future, they also make comments on past and present affairs. When Rutherford wrote *Millions Now Living,* he was writing in 1920, six years past the date which had been set for Christ's second presence. It must have been obvious to Rutherford, of course, that the world had not ended in 1914, but yet he continued to endorse the 1914 date. What Rutherford was doing was offering an analysis of human history, which incorporated past, present and future events. As far as Rutherford was concerned, Jesus Christ's rule had begun in 1914. Mainstream evangelical Christians are confused on this point, because they expect Jesus to return, descending on the clouds of heaven (the 'Rapture', as American Protestants call it). As Witnesses point out, the Greek word used for 'coming' is *parousia,* which literally means 'being with' or 'presence with', rather than implying any physical motion such as descent from heaven. Consequently, it was possible for Rutherford, and continues to be possible for all Jehovah's Witnesses, to believe in Christ's second presence without any cataclysmic event having taken place. The presence of Christ is carefully distinguished from the rule of Christ, which has not yet begun.

Third, the other dates that Rutherford talks about refer to quite different events in human history. That of 1918 was the year of the Jews' return to God's favour, being the year following the Balfour Declaration. The date of 1925 marked the end of the 70 'jubilees' – a procession of 50-year periods, after which 'the earthly phase of the kingdom shall be recognized' (Rutherford, 1920, p. 89).

What about 1975? In actual fact Jehovah's Witnesses' literature says little about this date, although it does bear significance. Unofficially, some Witnesses expected something of cosmic importance to take place in that year, and there were some who, disenchanted by the fact that it passed unmarked, left the movement. The significance of the date lies in its being 6000 years after the creation of Adam (4026 BCE by the Watchtower's reckoning: as Witnesses will point out, incidentally, there was no year zero, hence 1975, not 1976). This date thus heralds the beginning of the seventh millennium, God's sabbatical day. To quote *Watchtower:*

> Are we to assume from this study that the battle of Armageddon will be all over by the autumn of 1975, and the long-looked-for thousand-year reign of Christ will begin by then? Possibly, but we wait to see how closely the seventh thousand-year period of man's existence coincides with the sabbathlike thousand-year reign of Christ. If these two periods run parallel with each other as to the calendar year, it will not be by mere chance or accident but will be according to Jehovah's loving and timely purposes. Our chronology, however, which is reasonably accurate (but admittedly not infallible), at the best only points to the autumn of 1975 as the end of 6,000 years of man's existence on earth. It does not necessarily mean that 1975 marks the end of the first 6,000 years of Jehovah's seventh creative 'day'. (*Watchtower*, 15 August 1968, para. 30)

It is important to remember that this article was written before 1975 and not after, otherwise it could be construed as a rationalization of failed prophecy. It is also significant that the Society is making a distinction between the creation of humanity and the completion of creation, two separate events. Although it is apparently possible to ascribe a date to Adam's creation, there is no exact indication of when creation as a whole ended; hence, if it is the case that the beginning of Christ's rule and the Battle of Armageddon commence at the end of the thousand-year period, all one can say is that it is soon to be expected, and that is all.

LEADERSHIP AFTER RUTHERFORD

Subsequent leaders were Nathan H. Knorr (1905–77), who took up office in 1942, F. W. Franz (1899–1992) and currently Milton G. Henschel (b. 1920). Knorr improved the Society's training programme, establishing the Gilead Watchtower Bible School in South Lansing, New York, and organizing the 'theocratic ministry schools' in each congregation. Knorr expanded the work of the Witnesses abroad; in 1942 the organization had reached 54 countries; by 1961 this had increased to 185. It was in Knorr's period of office that textbooks giving information about the Bible, witnessing and history appeared (Hoekema, 1963, p. 232). From 1942 onwards, the

Watchtower policy was to publish these works, as well as articles in *Watchtower* and *Awake!* anonymously, the reason being that 'man' should not receive the glory for these, but only Jehovah. One major publishing undertaking was the translation of the Bible into modern English. This began in 1950, and culminated in the completion of the New World Translation in 1961. Predictably, mainstream Christians accuse the New World Translation of inaccuracy, as if their own translations were thoroughly reliable. Jehovah's Witnesses will engage in discussion with others, using whatever translation is available; indeed, there are many countries that do not have a Watchtower translation in the vernacular. The New World Translation is characterized by its literalness rather than its elegance, and deliberately so: it is important that Bible students should know Jehovah's teaching as accurately as possible.

Witnesses have gained a reputation for end-time calculations, although they lay less emphasis on this aspect of their doctrines today than in the time of Russell and Rutherford. The Witnesses expect the Battle of Armageddon, when Christ will destroy Satan and establish his final rule over the earth. The exact date for this is unspecified, although Rutherford made it clear that at least some ('millions') who were living at that time would not die, but see this day come. This certainly means that, if the Witnesses are right, this event cannot be far off, and all Witnesses have the firm conviction that humankind is living in the last days.

When Armageddon takes place, 144,000 of Christ's followers will be taken up into heaven. Affairs in heaven have not yet begun: the dead are still sleeping and await this final occurrence. The idea that there are 144,000 who are 'sealed', and will 'rule with Christ in heaven' is based on a verse in the Book of Revelation, where St John writes: 'And I saw, and, look! the Lamb standing upon the Mount Zion, and with him a hundred and forty-four thousand having his name and the name of his Father written on their foreheads' (Revelation 14:1).

Critics who do not understand the Witnesses particularly well will point out that the number of Jehovah's Witnesses far exceeds 144,000. (In 1998 the total worldwide attendance at the annual Memorial was 13,896,312.) The 144,000, however, merely constitute one class of those who are 'in the truth' – as the Witnesses put it – and who will attain everlasting life. The remainder will live under Christ's kingly rule on earth, in a world which will be fully restored and perfect. They will not feel in any way that they are second-class spiritual citizens.

I mentioned earlier that Russell and Rutherford could not accept the mainstream Christian doctrine of the eternal punishment of the wicked. Jehovah's Witnesses have consistently followed their founder-leaders on this matter: those who have failed to accept the truth will not be punished, but will simply enter into a state of non-being, experiencing nothing whatsoever of the joys, either of reigning with Christ in heaven or of living in the Paradise on the renewed earth. Faced with sayings of Jesus which might be taken to imply that there is eternal punishment – for example, the description of hell as a place where 'their maggot does not die and the fire is not put out' (Mark 9: 47–8) – Witnesses will point out that the Greek New Testament has two words which are translated as 'hell' in most standard editions of the Bible: *gehenna* and *hades. Gehenna,* they explain, refers to the refuse heap outside the city, where there was constant burning, but of course it was not expected that the fires would continue eternally.

Just as Witnesses cannot support the rule of secular states, neither can they support the Church, which is equated with 'Babylon the Great' referred to in Revelation. It is their firm belief that, at a very early stage in its history, the Christian Church became apostate, and developed teachings and practices that diverged from those laid down in scripture. The Witnesses are thus a 'restorationist' movement, attempting to rid themselves of the accretions that centuries of tradition have superimposed over the Bible's plain message. For example, the doctrines of the Trinity and of the deity of Christ are not to be found in scripture.

As far as Jesus of Nazareth is concerned, he is not regarded as merely a teacher. Although not divine, he was the first direct creation of God. There was therefore a time when he did not exist: thus the Jehovah's Witnesses' position might roughly be described as 'Arian'. Jesus' pre-existent form is equated with the Archangel Michael (Daniel 12:1), and he is regarded as the redeemer of humanity, having paid the 'ransom sacrifice' for sin. However, the atonement remains incomplete, awaiting the Millennial Age. Jesus, they believe, rose from the dead, but with a new spiritual body, not a physical one.

Since the Witnesses are endeavouring to restore Christianity to its original form, it is important to restore its original rites and remove others that have become added through the passage of time. Herein lies the reason for the Witnesses's refusal to celebrate Christmas. There is no evidence, they claim, that Jesus was born on 25 December, and, although the exact day of his birth cannot be established, the evidence that does exist points away from a December date (for example, the shepherds keeping flocks in fields at night). More importantly, the 25th of December was chosen in the early centuries of Christianity to coincide with the Roman Saturnalia festival, which is one example of how paganism has infiltrated the Christian faith. A similar problem exists with Easter, which originates from the pagan festival of Eostre, a spring fertility festival. Such intrusions on the Christian faith must be removed if a pure form of Christianity is to be revived.

The two rites that can be traced back to the Bible are baptism and the Last Supper. Jehovah's Witnesses practise baptism by total immersion as a means to membership, and this is normally carried out in the local Assembly Hall. (The Assembly Hall is used for the meetings of the Circuit, a wider body than the local congregation which regularly meets in a Kingdom Hall.)

The second rite is the Memorial, which is the Witnesses' name for the Last Supper. This occurs annually, and is the most important day of the Witnesses' calendar. Since Witnesses hold, in common with some mainstream Christians, that the Last Supper was a Passover meal, the date of the Memorial is calculated according to the instructions given in the Bible for celebrating the Passover. (This usually, but not always, coincides with the Jewish Passover.) At this service, the 'emblems' of unleavened bread (prepared according to a special recipe) and wine are passed around, but they are not consumed by the congregation, only handled. Only those who belong to the 144,000 may actually partake of the emblems.

It is no light matter to claim to expect to rule with Christ in heaven, and, as time passes, this quota is filling up. It is uncommon to see anyone partaking of the emblems at a Memorial service today, although, as the Witnesses move into Eastern Europe (in common with several other new religious groups) the number of partakers has increased in recent years. Although partaking is an individual decision, any member who thinks he or she may belong can be encouraged or discouraged by the comments of peers. There have been cases of members who have partaken of the emblems, believing themselves to have belonged to the 144,000, but who have subsequently reconsidered this, and at the next Memorial have merely handled the emblems, like the vast majority of the congregation.

While on the theme of festivals, it is worth mentioning the JW position on birthdays. The reasons for not celebrating birthdays partly consist of a belief that it is inappropriate to celebrate one's own birth. More especially, Witnesses will point out that only two birthdays are mentioned in scripture, and both had unfortunate repercussions: Pharaoh, on his birthday, hangs his chief baker (Genesis 40:20–2), and when King Herod celebrates his, John the Baptist is beheaded (Mark 6:21–9). In place of birthdays, some (not all) Witnesses celebrate 'present days', when members of a family will select a date of their own choice on which they agree to exchange presents: this enables them still to have a celebration, but without the Christmas commercialism and without the self-centredness that they believe is associated with birthdays.

Weddings, engagements and wedding anniversaries are other important causes for celebration, underlining the value that Jehovah's Witnesses place on marriage and on family life. Weddings are occasions which involve not merely the two families involved, but also the whole of a congregation, who will attend the ceremony and join in the festivities. Jehovah's Witnesses tend not to be wealthy, and normally find conventional weddings financially prohibitive; the do-it-yourself approach to such celebrations not only reduces costs substantially, but helps to bond the community together. Those who have only seen Jehovah's Witnesses at their front doors with their copies of *Watchtower* and *Awake!* might be surprised to see the exuberance of weddings. JWs are not teetotal, and alcoholic drinks are available, although they do not drink to excess. At a wedding I recently attended, the meal was followed by a variety of cabaret acts which were devised and performed by their own members, some of which even poked fun at expressions of their own faith!

On matters of lifestyle, Witnesses believe in traditional Christian values. Chastity is to be prized, and sexual relations are solely to be practised within marriage. Fornication and adultery are matters for which discipline is exercised within the movement, and these can be grounds for 'disfellowshipping' a member. Disfellowshipping is no light matter: members who do not live up to the movement's ideals will first of all be approached by elders and given an opportunity to repent; but, if this fails, then disfellowshipping is the ultimate remedy. Disfellowshipping puts the former member beyond the pale in a very real sense, since members may not engage in contact with an 'apostate', lest their own faith be damaged.

Tobacco and recreational drugs are not allowed. Until 1973 some Witnesses still smoked, but the concern for health prevailed, particularly in the light of the biblical statement that the human body is the temple of the Holy Spirit and therefore should be respected. In 1973 it was announced that being a non-smoker was an accompanying obligation to being a Witness, and Witnesses were given a period of time in which to give up. The only remaining choice was to leave the movement.

Something should be said about attitudes to education. British schoolteachers in particular often perceive Jehovah's Witness children as having problems about undertaking Religious Education. This is not strictly the case. Religious Education in Britain is often popularly confused with collective worship, which British schools have an obligation to provide: it is the latter that is unacceptable to Witnesses, who have no objection to RE, so long as it is taught in an objective and non-proselytizing way. Having said this, the distinctive religious beliefs of Witnesses can cause conflicts in other areas; one notable example is when science teachers propound theories about evolution and origins of species, when Witnesses take literally the biblical account of creation and view humanity as a separate and distinct creation.

In general, Witnesses are less likely to aspire to higher education than their peers, no doubt for a cluster of reasons. They typically disapprove of the rat race that is rife in contemporary society, and view earthly aspirations as being of much less importance than spiritual concerns: it is far preferable to work for Jehovah's kingdom than for material gain. They are encouraged to have few financial investments: if these are indeed the end times, there is little point in saving for an earthly future that will shortly come to an end. Although Witnesses are to be found in many walks of life, they are more likely to follow trades than professions. If they need to learn skills for Jehovah's work, they are taught them within the organization, where Witnesses are trained in undertaking door-to-door work, presentation skills, biblical knowledge and so on. Even those who work in a Bethel (a residential publication house) are trained on the job, learning writing skills, editing, printing and whatever else is needed to bring out the movement's various magazines and other publications.

Something remains to be said about blood transfusion. This is an issue which most people associate with the Witnesses, although it entered into their beliefs and practices relatively late on: it was during the Second World War that blood transfusions became widely available, and raised the 'blood' issue for JWs. Russell and Rutherford, for example, do not mention it at all, for the simple reason that it was not widely used in medical practice at the time. The underlying reason for the prohibition is their understanding of the early Church's dietary laws. As the Bible makes clear, there was a dispute between followers of Peter – who wanted to insist on Christians accepting the Jewish law as a precondition for conversion to Christianity – and followers of Paul, who saw Christianity as an independent faith, not a form of Judaism which needed to be approached through the Jewish religion. The decision of the first Council at Jerusalem is recorded in Acts 15, and gives the outcome of this dispute: Christians are 'to abstain from things polluted by idols and from fornication and from what is strangled and from blood' (Acts 15:20).

It should be noted that the Council's ruling was that one should 'abstain ... from blood', not merely that one should not consume it. In accordance with this scripture, Witnesses will not eat meat that has not been drained of blood (black pudding, for example, is unacceptable), but, as is well known, the prohibition is also extended to ingesting blood through modern medical methods. Witnesses see (what they take to be) the scriptural prohibition as the paramount reason for their stance; the rise of the AIDS epidemic in recent times is merely seen as corroborative evidence of their position.

Jehovah's Witnesses do agree that there are occasions on which members have lost their lives through the denial of a blood transfusion, and that they can see no reason for the prohibition other than that God commands it. Equally, of course, there are people who have died precisely because they were given a blood transfusion, for example, when blood used by a hospital has been contaminated. However, when medical staff recommend blood transfusion for a Jehovah's Witness patient, the dilemma need not be between blood transfusion or death: Witnesses have been instrumental in advocating the case for alternative 'no blood' forms of treatment, such as saline blood expanders, which have proven effective in some cases.

Witnesses have also established a number of 'hospital liaison committees' in western countries, where leaders meet with medical staff and discuss how treatment can be provided to optimize patient care without compromising Witnesses' convictions.

Critics of Jehovah's Witnesses tend to alight on legal, medical and even ethical questions, overlooking the theological issue that is at stake here. However one evaluates the Witnesses' solution, the 'blood' issue is an attempt to answer the question of how those who claim to accept the inerrancy of scripture deal with the so-called Old Testament. Christian fundamentalists might claim to accept that all scripture is inspired, indeed authoritative, but yet they rarely, if ever, attempt to follow all the dietary laws that are prescribed in Leviticus and Deuteronomy, which prohibit pork, shellfish, the mixing of milk and meat, and of course meat from which the blood has not been drained.

Some of the New Christian groups have addressed this issue: for example Herbert Armstrong's Worldwide Church of God commits itself to the full observance of Jewish dietary law. The Jehovah's Witnesses adopt a different solution: the first Council of Jerusalem (Acts 15) suggested a compromise between the Judaizers and the innovators, and thus concluded that substantial components of the Jewish law, such as circumcision, belonged to the 'old covenant', which no longer applies. Unlike the Worldwide Church of God, then, the Jehovah's Witnesses do not strive to fulfil the injunctions of a law code which they regard as superseded. Sabbath – or Sunday – observance, for instance, is not required by the Witnesses, who are quite happy to undertake their 'quick build' programmes, in which they erect an entire Kingdom Hall from its foundations in a single weekend, which spans Saturday and Sunday. This is not law breaking, since keeping the sabbath day holy belongs to the former dispensation.

RECENT DEVELOPMENTS

From the above discussion it should be obvious that the Jehovah's Witnesses' thinking has moved with the passage of time, and that the Witnesses are not committed to the views of founder-leaders Russell and Rutherford, however much they hold them in high regard. While the general public (also some writers such as Richard Crompton) often associate the Witnesses with end-time calculations, even a casual glance at copies of *Watchtower* and *Awake!* today will reveal that these themes do not loom as large as they did in earlier years. As the years have gone by, Rutherford's claim that 'millions now living will never die' has become increasingly implausible, if taken as a statement of literal truth about the last days. There are now few Witnesses who were alive in 1920 who have not met with death.

In more recent times the Witnesses' Governing Body debated this problem, and in November 1995 an article appeared in *Watchtower* giving a 'new understanding' of biblical texts such as 'This generation will by no means pass away until all these things occur' (Matthew 24:34). The article points out that the Greek word *genea* means a race of people who share a common ancestor, or a society of people who co-exist. In Jesus' teaching the expression takes on negative connotations, since 'this generation' is variously described as 'wicked and adulterous' (Matthew 12:38), 'serpents, offspring of vipers' (Matthew 23:33, 36), 'sinful' (Mark 8: 38) and 'faithless and twisted' (Matthew 17:14–17; Luke 9:37–41). This 'faithless genera-tion' was the Jewish nation, responsible for bringing about Jesus' death. That generation experienced the afflictions and calamities that Jesus described, culminating in the fall of Jerusalem – the 'great tribulation' – in 70 CE. That generation indeed did not pass away before Jesus' prophecies were fulfilled.

However, this does not mean that men and women of today's generation can dismiss Jesus' prophecies, which still have their 'major fulfilment' in the times in which we are living. Even though it remains possible that every Witness who was alive in 1920 may die before the beginning of Armageddon, nevertheless the Witnesses still retain a very firm belief that these are the last days and that it will not be long before the end of Satan's earthly rule.

The Latter-day Saints

Like the Jehovah's Witnesses, the Latter-day Saints (more commonly known as the Mormons) represent an attempt to revive the practices of primordial Christianity, albeit in a different way. One striking point of contrast between Mormons and Witnesses is that, whereas the latter use the Protestant principle of *sola scripura*, Mormonism is based on new revelations and new scriptures. In addition to the Judaeo-Christian Bible, there are three other scriptures: the Book of Mormon, the Doctrines and Covenants, and the Pearl of Great Price.

(The last of these consists of revelations to Joseph Smith, and writings attributed to Abraham, which Smith is believed to have translated.) Indeed, the expression 'Latter-day saints' should be construed not so much in an apocalyptic sense, but rather as indicating that the tradition of prophets ('saints') has now been revived in recent times.

Most people who have a superficial acquaintance with Mormonism are familiar with the story of how its founder-leader Joseph Smith (1805–44) was undecided as to which of several Protestant denominations to join, prayed for guidance and then in 1820 received his first vision in a grove in Palmyra, New York. Three years later the angel Moroni directed him to Cumorah Hill, where gold plates were buried, and which Smith, together with Oliver Cowdery, his amanuensis and principal disciple, translated from 'Reformed Egyptian' into what is now the Book of Mormon, and which first became available publicly in 1830.

The transition from Mormonism's Palmyra period to its establishment in Salt Lake City is somewhat more complex. Faced with local opposition and limited acceptance of his message, Smith moved to Kirkland, Ohio in 1831, at the suggestion of Sidney Rigdon, a Campbellite whom Smith had impressed, and who had accepted early Mormon teachings. In 1836 the first Mormon Temple was consecrated at Kirkland: it still remains there, although it is owned today by the Reorganized Church of Jesus Christ of Latter Day Saints. Faced with more opposition, Smith fled to Missouri, where another Mormon community had already established itself. Hostility to the Mormons continued, and Smith found himself imprisoned. Released in 1839, he decided to establish his own Mormon community, this time in Nauvoo, Illinois. Although self-contained, the community was still subject to the state laws of Illinois, and state troopers visited the town periodically for enforcement purposes. Matters came to a head when some non-Mormons attempted to print a newspaper, the first edition of which contained trenchant anti-Mormon criticism. Smith did not merely prohibit further publication, but sent in some of his officials to smash up the printing works. The Governor of Illinois viewed this matter very seriously, regarding a free press as one of the supreme civil liberties required by the American Constitution. Smith was arrested and imprisoned in the adjacent town of Carthage, where a mob broke into the gaol and killed him, together with his brother Hyrum.

The leadership of the Mormons was then taken over by Brigham Young, who led over 30,000 Mormons out from Nauvoo to seek their fortune further west. Young aimed to settle on the Pacific Coast, but the community mistook the Great Salt Lake for the Pacific Ocean, after travelling 1400 miles. Salt Lake City, and the wider state of Utah, became predominantly Mormon territory, and Mormons are still the majority there today, constituting 51 per cent of the population.

The Book of Mormon is somewhat of an enigma. If it was indeed written in the circumstances described by the Mormon tradition, the work is certainly a remarkable achievement, and it is not surprising that an LDS leaflet faces doubters with the challenge to try to write a book of similar length and content without divine help. It must span a historical period from 2200 BCE to 421 CE; it must be perfectly consistent with the history of Israel and America, and demonstrate the fulfilment of biblical prophecies; it must be around 80,000 words long, and written in only 80 days. The Book of Mormon, the challenger points out, was written by a young man of 23 or 24, who had only three years' schooling, and no access to external sources (Church of Jesus Christ, n.d.).

Those who cannot accept the Mormon account of its supernatural origins have devised various theories about how it came into existence. Thus early Palmyra critics claimed that it was plagiarized, stating in a letter to the *Telegraph*, that it was 'chiefly garbled from the Old and New Testaments, the Apocryphy [*sic*] having contributed its share' (Bushman, 1984, p. 125). D.E. Howe and Philastus Hurlbut have therefore proposed a theory ('the Howe–Hurlbut hypothesis') that contends that the book is a composite work, being derived from two authors, one of whom was a theologian (named as Sidney Rigdon) and the other a novelist (Solomon Spalding). Rigdon, they claim, transformed Spalding's story into the Book of Mormon by adding specifically religious material. I cannot pretend to settle the question of how the book came into being. However, even if Smith completed it in 80 days, this would only require him to achieve a daily rate of 1000 words – certainly good going, but not at all impossible, as most experienced authors will testify – particularly since he is said not to have had to invest time in researching source material. It is also possible that Smith took somewhat more than 80 days to complete the work.

Whatever the pedigree of the Book of Mormon, it is its

contribution to Mormon doctrine that is of supreme importance. Although the Bible provides a true record of the history of the Jewish people, it cannot be taken as a blueprint for the Church's doctrine and practice. While it refers to the key institutions, such as the priesthood and the Temple, these can only be viewed as departures from a long-lost archetype. The Pearl of Great Price shows how Joseph Smith restored these institutions, and Doctrine and Covenants sets out Smith's revelations. While the Bible tells of the history of the Israelites and the advent of Jesus Christ, the Book of Mormon deals with the history leading to Christ's appearance in America.

According to Mormon teaching, the origin of the Church does not stem from the coming of Christ or from the Day of Pentecost, which mainstream Christians often identify as the birth of the Christian Church. The original Church, being eternal, existed from the very moment of creation, and was given by God to Adam, four thousand years before Jesus' appearance on earth. Adam was given the gospel and baptized by Jesus in the latter's pre-existent form. (Mormons believe that all souls have existed in spirit form before being born into human bodies.) Within a short period of time, the Church became corrupted, and people either rejected or distorted the gospel. God sent various prophets at intervals throughout ancient Hebrew history; they were given insights into the nature of the true Church, and attempted to persuade God's people to re-establish the true authentic Church. Such prophets included Enoch, Jared, Noah and Moses.

Of these four names Jared is no doubt the least familiar to those in the mainstream Judaeo-Christian tradition, and indeed all the Bible tells of him is that he was fathered by an equally obscure figure called Mahaleel (Genesis 5:15). Within the Mormon tradition, however, Jared has great significance, partly because he features jointly in the ancient Israelite and ancient American Mormon traditions. Jared and his family were a small group of people who had faith in God and whose language therefore did not become 'confounded' at the Tower of Babel. The Jaredites (the name given to Jared's followers) built several barges, and set sail to America – a journey which took them almost a year. They settled there, establishing an agrarian economy and a government with laws that pre-dated those of Moses. They also had foreknowledge of the gospel, which told of Jesus' coming and his atonement for humankind's sins. With the passage of time, however, the Jaredites became increasingly disobedient to God, and failed to heed the words of Ether, his prophet. After a series of internal wars, the Jaredites finally became extinct.

The next chapter of the story takes place over 500 years later, with the Mormon prophet Lehi, whose story is told in the Book of Mormon by his son Nephi. We are told that Lehi lived towards the end of the sixth century BCE. He is not mentioned in Jewish scripture, but is held to have been a contemporary of Jeremiah in the city of Jerusalem. God commanded Lehi to leave, and he departed into the desert, eventually arriving at the sea, from whence, like Jared, he sailed to America. The story continues with Nephi's elder brothers Laman and Lemuel, who apparently resented Nephi's piety. Conflict occurred, and thereafter there was a long period of conflict between the Lamanities and the Nephites.

By the time of Jesus Christ, peace and integrity were restored. After his ascension Jesus Christ appeared to the Nephites, and preached to them; among his sermons was a version of the Sermon on the Mount, 'but with certain vital clarifications and additions' (Ludlow, 1992, vol. 1, p. 140). This was followed by a further 160 years of peace, but then conflicts arose once more between the Nephites and a group of rebels who adopted the name of 'Lamanites'. Mormon (c. 310–85 CE) was the Nephites' military leader, as well as a historian. He collected together a set of metal plates that had been used to record ancient American history from the time of Jared onwards, and abridged them on to a single set of gold plates, which he hid in Cumorah Hill, at Palmyra. He gave the angel Moroni a few plates on which to complete the history of the Nephites' final days. Mormon had tried hard to persuade his people that if they repented and obeyed Christ's gospel they would be spared from the Lamanites' onslaught. They refused to listen, and in 385 CE Mormon led them into their final battle, in full knowledge that they would be defeated. Moroni was one of the few survivors, and managed to complete the Nephites' records.

The Latter-day Saints claim that Joseph Smith experienced visions and revelations. First, the Book of Mormon, to which he is believed to have been led, is the rediscovery of the history of this group of Americans, going back to ancient times, and demonstrating their varying relationships with God and God's dealings with them. Second, Smith's revelations concern the nature of the authentic Church which existed eternally, but which became corrupted throughout human history. Instructed to avoid all of the corrupt Christian denominations in the Palmyra area, Smith was called upon to re-establish the authentic Church which God gave to Adam. The Mormon quest for authenticity therefore differs significantly from that of the Jehovah's Witnesses: the true Church is not that of the first century common era, for that in itself was a corruption of the eternal Church; the true Church is not what is described in the New Testament, for the Bible is a record of human corruption of God's institutions; finally, the nature of the true Church is established through God's continuing revelation to humanity, and in particular by the restoration of its lost prophetic tradition.

THE MORMON RESTORATION

Like the Jehovah's Witnesses, the LDS believe that there is an important need to revive the original institutions of the Christian Church, which, they declare, have been lost as the centuries have progressed. These institutions, however, do not merely include those that are explicitly enjoined in the New Testament (such as elder, deacon and overseer), but also the environment of the ancient Hebrew religion that was in operation at the time of Jesus. This included temple worship, in which Jesus participated, and a lineage of priests.

CONTINUING REVELATION

We have noted that the Church of Jesus Christ of Latter-day Saints has a firm belief in continuing revelation. This continuing revelation, however, has to be reconciled with the notion that it is a restorationist group – that is to say, it is endeavouring to restore Christianity to its primordial form, rather than use continuing revelation as a means of doctrinal and institutional innovation. Unlike the Unification Church, which unashamedly takes its version of Christianity significantly beyond that of Jesus and the early Church, Mormonism is committed to reviving what it takes to be the Church's ancient institutions.

Restoration of institutions and continuing revelation are not easily reconciled, and indeed the prophets of Hebrew scriptures are frequently portrayed as being in opposition to the institutionalized religion of their times. Institutions tend to be reactionary and rule-governed, whereas the prophet tends to be spontaneous and innovative. The Mormon Church therefore displays an interesting attempt to reconcile prophetic and institutional features.

This apparent tension is reconciled in two complementary ways. First, prophecy is embedded within the Mormon Church's institutions themselves. Second, one important function of latter-day prophecy is to reveal the nature of the Church's institutions that have been lost or corrupted through the centuries. I shall deal with these points in turn.

Prophecy in Mormonism is not spontaneous or particularly innovative, and it certainly does not offer a critique of the Church's institutions. While it is acknowledged that individual members can be afforded revelations from God and from angels – for example, in feelings of intense conviction, in dreams, in answered prayer, and even in more striking forms of revelation such as face-to-face visitations and visions – it is important that revelation is strictly controlled. Included in the criteria for assessing the authenticity of a revelation is its consistency with one's role within the LDS hierarchy. Thus individuals may receive divine guidance for their own lives, parents for their families and bishops for their stakes, but only the President (also known as the Prophet) may receive revelations on behalf of the entire Church (Ludlow, 1992, vol. 3, p. 1226). Any such revelations, of course, must be consistent too with the fundamental sources of authority within the LDS, namely the four sets of scriptures.

THE CHURCH

Joseph Smith is believed to have restored the priesthood and the 'keys of the kingdom'. This latter expression refers to Jesus' statement to the apostle Peter that his (Jesus') messiahship is the rock on which he will build his church (Matthew 16:18). (The Roman Catholic Church claims that its papacy is based on the apostolic succession which can be traced back to St Peter, but the LDS contend that Roman Catholicism lacks the key 'ordinances' which they, the LDS, have restored.) The two key aspects of the restoration of the Church's institutions are priesthood and 'ordinances'.

THE PRIESTHOOD

The Jerusalem Temple which Jesus knew was presided over by a priesthood whose lineage stemmed from Aaron, the brother of

Moses. After Joseph Smith had completed the translation of the Book of Mormon, it was revealed to him that this priesthood was now restored. This enabled the possibility of baptism and the 'everlasting covenant'. Although baptism was of course practised in the Protestant churches that Smith abandoned, Mormons would regard such baptisms as being invalid, since they are not carried out within the context of the proper church institutions. For a long time Smith had been concerned about the question of his baptism, and so, on receiving the revelation concerning the restoration of the priesthood, he went with Oliver Cowdery to the nearby river, where John the Baptist is said to have appeared to them. Smith and Cowdery then baptized each other, and ordained each other as priests.

Baptism is administered to boys and girls, normally when they reach the age of 8, after which boys may also receive the Aaronic priesthood at age 12. Baptism is by total immersion, which is the authentic method by which Jesus was baptized by John in the River Jordan, and the method that Joseph Smith and Oliver Cowdery used to baptize each other.

Beyond the Aaronic priesthood lies another important order of priesthood within the Church of Jesus Christ of Latter-day Saints, the Melchizedek priesthood. The Bible refers to a priestly order of Melchizedek (Psalms 110:4; Hebrews 6:20); although mainstream biblical scholars regarded these references as metaphorical, the Mormon Church takes them literally, and hence claims to revive an ancient priestly lineage which became lost. Joseph Smith is regarded as having restored this priesthood, and this higher ordination to the Melchizedek priesthood is administered to young men of 18 or 19 years of age. It is not an automatic right: it is only received if a young Mormon man is considered to be worthy of it. The Melchizedek priesthood subsumes the offices of deacon and teacher, both of which are mentioned in the New Testament as key functions within the early Church (1 Timothy 3:8–10). The young male Mormon missionaries who devote two years of their lives to this work have normally been recently ordained in the order of Melchizedek. Women are not eligible for priesthood, which was exclusively a male office; instead they may belong to the Relief Society, a charitable association which was founded in 1842, with Emma Smith (Joseph's wife) as its first president.

THE ROLE OF THE TEMPLE

The Mormon Temple is important for carrying out the restored 'ordinances'. These are three in number: endowment, the sealing of marriage and the sealing of ancestors. In order to be able to enter the Temple at all, one must not only be an LDS member, but secure the recommendation of one's bishop. To do this, one must be in good standing, which entails being upright in character and having paid one's tithes (a tenth of one's income) to the church. King Solomon's instruction from God to commission the building of the Jerusalem Temple indicates that Temple worship was indeed an important part of God's plan for the authentic Church. Mormon Temples today have sometimes been criticized for failing to be exact replicas of Solomon's Temple, but the LDS hold that God's instructions to Solomon related specifically to that Temple, without any implication that they should be followed in every other such building. Accordingly, modern Mormon Temples incorporate some of the features of Solomon's Temple, but not all. Each Mormon Temple has its own distinctive design, and does not slavishly follow a uniform formula.

The Temple is a working building, with offices and facilities, such as computers for tracing one's ancestors, a cafeteria in the basement for refreshments, waiting rooms, changing rooms and even a laundry room. A number of the rooms are specially designed for the ordinances: there is always a baptismal font, supported by 12 metal or marble oxen, a number of chapels for worship, an Endowment Room, some Sealing Rooms, and, most importantly, a Celestial Room.

The first ordinance one performs in the course of one's lifetime is normally Endowment, which should be undergone at least once. This involves going through the various rooms of the Temple, contemplating God's purpose for humankind in general and for oneself as an individual. To achieve this, the member is shown in dramatic form the events described in the Bible from the story of Adam and Eve onwards. Today this is normally shown by film, but there are still some Temples that use the older practice of having actors and actresses act out the scenes, rather in the style of medieval mystery plays. The Endowment culminates in the Celestial Room: this room is usually situated at the top of the Temple, and is undoubtedly the most opulent, as well as the most peaceful. In order to reach it, the member has to pass through a veil in an antechamber: this is reminiscent of the High Priest's practice in Jerusalem during the Day of Atonement, in which he passed through the Temple veil into the Holy of Holies to make atonement for the people's sins. Unlike the practice in Jerusalem, however, all members in good standing may pass through this veil, and not merely a single spiritual leader.

MARRIAGE

A further important ordinance is the 'sealing' of one's marriage. Marriage and family life are supremely important to Latter-day Saints. The marriage ceremony is normally conducted at one's local LDS church, where in most countries the ceremony has legal validity, making the couple 'man and wife'. After the reception the couple usually proceed to the nearest Mormon Temple, where their marriage is 'sealed'. This must be done within 24 hours, otherwise a waiting period (normally a year) must elapse before sealing is permitted. (This is because it is assumed that the couple must have reasons for not going to the Temple – perhaps they are not spiritually pure enough.) The sealing room has an altar, and the couple face each other, in front of two facing mirrors. The facing mirrors (theoretically) generate an infinite number of images, going back for ever, and thus the setting symbolizes eternity, since LDS marriages are eternal, not merely 'till death us do part'. It is expected that, after one has died, one's marriage will continue in the spiritual realm to which the couple have earned entry. For those who have died before their marriage has been sealed, those who remain alive on earth can undergo an ordinance at a Mormon Temple which secures the sealing of a couple to whom one is related.

Family life is very important to Mormons, and it is expected that the married couple will have children, preferably a large family. Contraception is discouraged, since it is believed that a predetermined number of souls already exist, and are merely awaiting birth in human form. Once children are born, it is the parents' duty to provide a loving environment for them, and the institution of the 'family home evening', which usually occurs every Monday, is generally regarded as sacrosanct by LDS members. Other commitments, whatever their nature, are seldom allowed to take precedence over the Mormon family home evening, at which a nuclear family undertakes to be together for a common meal, to read and discuss scriptures, to converse and socialize, and perhaps even to play games together, especially where there are young children in the family.

Because marriage is eternal, it cannot be dissolved at will. Of course, it is as possible for Mormons as it is for non-Mormons to undergo a civil divorce, but, unless one's partner has committed adultery, such divorces would not be recognized by the Mormon Church, and a member in this situation would not be entitled to undergo any subsequent LDS marriage ceremony.

The popular mind often associates Mormonism with polygamy, and brief mention must therefore be made of this topic. It was originally practised in Utah in the early days of the Mormon pioneers. However, there were problems with the Federal Government on this matter, until 1890, when the Church finally decided to conform to the law of the land. Polygamy is sanctioned in Doctrines and Covenants, but monogamy is required in its original version. In a situation where a wife has died and the husband remarries (which Mormonism permits), it would be possible to have more than one wife on the other side of death.

SEALING OF ANCESTORS

We have already remarked on the institution of baptism. It is important to add, however, that baptism can be afforded to the dead as well as to the living. That Jesus was concerned to secure the spiritual well-being of the dead is evidenced by his words to the dying thief on the cross, 'Today thou shalt be with me in Paradise' (Luke 23:43), and the statement in 1 Peter that Jesus descended into the spirit world to preach to the spirits of the departed – a doctrine which appears in the Apostle's Creed as the descent into hell. The problem that Mormonism seeks to address here is the same problem with which mainstream Christians have wrestled: how can one be saved if, through no fault of one's own, one happens to have been born in a time or place which the gospel message has not reached?

The LDS deal with this problem by the practice of baptism by proxy. In one of his letters, St Paul talks about baptism for the dead (1 Corinthians 15:29). Again, mainstream Christian commentators have made various suggestions about what the practice might have been, and whether Paul is criticizing or accepting it, but the Latter-day Saints claim to have revived a first-century practice. In order to 'seal' an ancestor, and thus ensure that he or she obtains eternal salvation, a genealogical search is carried out and checks are made to determine whether the ancestor has already been sealed. Assuming he or she has not, the LDS member goes down into the Temple baptismal pool and undergoes a proxy baptism. This vicarious baptism is generally undertaken on behalf of one's ancestors: a Mormon would certainly not pick names randomly from a history book and attempt to secure their salvation. The great Mormon interest in genealogy enables members to ascertain the identities of departed family members.

Once a member has identified deceased relatives, and ascertained that they have not previously been offered proxy baptism, he or she then arranges to undergo a ceremony at a Mormon Temple on those relatives' behalf. The spirits, who are waiting in a 'spirit prison', pending such baptism, are then enabled to have the opportunity of salvation. It is an opportunity, not a compulsion, and the spirit may decide to accept or to reject the consequences that one's proxy baptism affords. There is no hell following rejection, only the 'cessation of progress' in the spirit world.

This may be a convenient point at which to outline the LDS doctrines on life after death. Pending the final judgement, the dead either go to paradise or to the 'spirit prison'. Those in paradise can influence those in prison and enable them to make progress there. At the final judgement people will be consigned, according to their deeds, to one of three realms of glory – the terrestrial, the telestial or the celestial – or, if they have rejected the gospel, to outer darkness. Mormons will point out that Paul spoke about three different 'glories' – the glory of the sun, of the moon and of the stars (1 Corinthians 15:41). Although the celestial realm is the highest, unsurpassable state of exaltation, the telestial glory is nonetheless highly desirable, and, as the *Encyclopedia of Mormonism* states, 'Even the lowest glory surpasses all mortal understanding' (Ludlow, 1992, vol. 1, p. 369). Also worth mentioning, too, is the point that Mormons do not believe in predestination: all the various after-death states are achievable through human effort; unlike Calvinism, Mormons do not believe that there are limited number of spaces reserved for a predetermined elect whose salvation is secured through divine grace alone.

In addition to sealing one's ancestors in baptism, one can also seal their marriages, and since it is firmly held that bondings of husband and wife endure eternally, it is important that one's spouse attains the relevant glory also. Ancestors can also receive vicarious endowment, where a member undertakes the Endowment Ceremony yet again on behalf of an ancestor. Not only is this of benefit to the deceased, but it affords an opportunity to the member to reflect once again on the meaning of creation and one's place in it, on life, on death and what lies beyond.

In conclusion, many features of the Mormon Church may appear to be novel and innovative. If they seem innovative, however, such a judgement is probably made from the standpoint of mainstream Christianity, which, as I have shown, is an apostate form of the authentic Church. True, the Church of Jesus Christ of Latter-day Saints has a different concept of authenticity from that of the Jehovah's Witnesses, but there are different ways in which one can endeavour to be authentic, and different points at which one can identify God's true Church.

4. The 'New Christian' movements

During the years surrounding the formation of the International Bible Students' Association (subsequently the Jehovah's Witnesses) and the Church of Jesus Christ of Latter-day Saints, a number of important issues had their impact on Christianity. The mid-nineteenth century had seen the rise of Darwinism and the challenge this posed to traditional understandings of the Christian faith. Christianity, however, was not only challenged from outside, but from within, when a number of liberal scholars, first in Germany, but subsequently in Britain, under the influence of Benjamin Jowett, Frederick Temple, Rowland Williams and others, had attempted to subject the Bible to 'higher criticism'. Following hard on the heels of Darwin, the year 1860 saw the publication of *Essays and Reviews*, edited by Jowett, in which seven liberal scholars argued the case for identifying different sources which comprised the Bible, and for applying historical and scientific methods of criticism to it. In a scientific age, they argued, the miracle stories lacked credibility, and must therefore have been later embellishments.

Christian fundamentalism was a response to both sets of challenges. The term 'fundamentalism' is often applied loosely by the media, to refer to uncompromising extremist groups, spanning Muslims, Hindus and even Sikhs. It is in Christianity that fundamentalism has a precise technical meaning, without pejorative connotations, and many Christians are happy to accept the label. Christian fundamentalism dates back to a conference in Niagara in 1895, when a statement reaffirming the basic principles of the Christian faith was defined. The five principles, which came to be known as the 'five points of fundamentalism', were these: (1) the verbal inerrancy of scripture; (2) the divinity of Jesus Christ; (3) the

Virgin Birth; (4) the substitutionary theory of Atonement (that is to say, the doctrine that Jesus died in place of sinful humanity); and (5) the physical resurrection and bodily return of Jesus Christ. These doctrines were further expounded in a series of tracts, the first of which appeared in 1909, entitled 'The Fundamentals', and the World's Christian Fundamentals Association was founded in 1919.

For Christians who were persuaded by Darwinism and liberal scholarship, the obvious question was what was left of the Christian faith. Were there any core truths remaining that were immune from the criticism of the scientist and the biblical scholar? Which parts of the Bible should one accept, and which should one reject? Fundamentalism, on the other hand, rebutted modern scholarship and purported to offer certainties, but it generated problems of its own, which its mainstream supporters never satisfactorily appear to have solved. For example, what should the fundamentalist believe about the Old Testament? If all the Bible is inerrant, then should Christians still be observing the Jewish law, avoiding pork and shellfish, celebrating the Jewish festivals, and worshipping on the sabbath – the seventh day of the week – rather than on the traditional Christian Sunday? Another logical implication of fundamentalism is that, if all the Bible is true, then all parts are equally true. Why, then, do Christians tend to focus on a number of 'favourite' passages, reading them in worship and for private devotion, to the exclusion of others? The Bible contains many passages which are obscure (such as the Book of Revelation), uninspiring (for example, long genealogies), lacking in obvious purpose (for example, Gershom's circumcision or Noah being found naked by his three sons), or even quite unacceptable by modern standards, such as its condonement of polygamy or its prescriptions of barbaric punishments like stoning.

Mainstream Christians will often express surprise, even indignation, at the interpretations of the Christian faith that are offered by the New Christian groups. Yet in most cases the New Christian groups represent an attempt not only to propagate the Christian message in a radical way, but to get to grips with a number of fundamental problems which mainstream Christianity often ignores. Thus the Adventist Churches with justification point out that the Ten Commandments enjoin keeping the seventh day holy, and that there is no scriptural warrant for Sunday observance; the Worldwide Church of God makes a point of keeping the Jewish festivals and dietary laws; and the Jehovah's Witnesses, as we have seen, point out that the doctrine of the Trinity is to be found nowhere in the Bible.

A second phenomenon that has influenced not only the New Christian NRMs, but mainstream Christianity too, has been a renewed emphasis on the Holy Spirit. It was the coming of the Holy Spirit, as recorded in the Book of Acts (chapter 2) that afforded the Pentecost experience, empowering the disciples to proclaim their message with confidence, and, it has been claimed, affording them the gift of 'speaking in tongues' or 'glossolaliation'. The precise meaning of the Pentecost story is unclear: on the one hand the Book of Acts suggests that an amazing miracle happened, whereby visitors from all parts of the world heard the disciples speak in their mother tongue, while on the other, the same speakers were accused of acting as if they were drunk – perhaps more reminiscent of the euphoric unintelligible utterances which are more characteristic of the present-day Pentecostalist meeting.

If speaking in tongues is a gift that is promised in scripture, and if it is important to emulate the early Church's practices, then it is understandable that some Christians should want to revive the practice of glossolaliation. The Pentecostalist phenomenon is, perhaps surprisingly, relatively recent, first gaining attention in 1906 at a revivalist meeting in Los Angeles, where believers sought to be 'baptized in the Holy Spirit'. The Pentecostal movement gradually became institutionalized, with the formation of the Elim Foursquare Gospel Alliance in Monaghan, Ireland, in 1915, the formation of the Apostolic Church (still a relatively small group) in 1920, and the Assemblies of God in Great Britain and Ireland in 1924. Pentecostalists have not merely stressed the phenomenon of speaking in tongues: Christ's followers should expect to receive all the 'gifts of the Spirit', defined by Paul as wisdom, knowledge, faith, healing, miraculous powers, prophecy, discerning the spirits, speaking in tongues and interpreting tongues. In Pentecostalist churches, spiritual healing is particularly emphasized.

The phenomenon of speaking in tongues gained further momentum in the 1960s, when the charismatic movement swept across many of the mainstream Protestant denominations. More recently, the 'Toronto Blessing' gave a further impetus to the power of the Spirit, when in 1994 members of the Airport Vineyard Church in Toronto were visited by Randy Clark, the founder of the Vineyard movement. Members of the congregation spoke in tongues, shook, fell to the ground, wept, laughed uncontrollably, and even in a couple of cases barked like dogs. Such phenomena were decisively attributed to the power of the Holy Spirit.

Such manifestations attributed to the Spirit are important to charismatics in a number of ways. They are held to vindicate the truth of the gospel; they confer various 'gifts of the Spirit', particularly healing; and – importantly – they enable 'deliverance' from evil spirits, which can often be found inhabiting even those who are within the Christian fold. While liberal Christians contend that evil spirits belong to an outmoded world-view, fundamentalists today often insist on their literal reality, since their existence was plainly acknowledged by Jesus himself, and is clearly found in the Bible. 'Deliverance' is the word popularly used in such circles for casting out demons, in preference to the more traditional word 'exorcism' – a practice which has more normally been the province of an ordained priest. Deliverance need not be carried out exclusively by ordained clergy, and is practised much more widely than old-style exorcism.

The charismatic movement therefore jointly contains conservative and radical components. It is conservative in accepting the principles of fundamentalism: a belief not only in the inerrancy of scripture, but in its accompanying world-view, complete with a personal devil and evil spirits. It is radical in that it holds that revelation is continuing and hence that believers might expect new manifestations of God's power, manifested through the Spirit. In the New Christian movements, both these factors are apparent: there is a firm belief in the authority of scripture, but yet in many cases an acknowledgement of continuing revelation.

In many cases, keeping the activities attributed to the Holy Spirit under due control has proved to be a problem within Christianity. At times Spirit-inspiration can appear to go too far. To claim that there are new scriptures or that there is a new messiah destined to complete Jesus' atoning work are two respects in which an NRM can go over the limit and be judged unacceptable by mainstream Christianity, however compelling the revelatory claims of its leader or its followers may seem. The Unification Church appears to add to scripture with its *Divine Principle,* although some Unificationists would regard their principal text simply as an important theological work, rather than part of an official canon; there can be no doubt however that the UC teaches that its founder-leader has come to

123

complete Jesus' unfinished mission. In the case of The Family (formerly the Children of God), the main barrier to acceptability by Christians is its teaching on sexual relationships: founder-leader Moses David is also perceived as being endowed with too much authority, by being treated as a modern-day prophet. Mainstream Christians certainly become uncomfortable when a 'prophetic' leader is treated with veneration. The case of the Jesus Army is an interesting one, for it has never added to scripture or appeared to give undue veneration to its founder-leader, while its morality is very conservative and its theological position thoroughly orthodox. It is the sheer zeal of the movement that its critics find disturbing.

The Unification Church

Of all the new religions that claim a Christian identity, the best known and undoubtedly the most controversial is the Unification Church, whose members are popularly known as the 'Moonies'. They attracted attention in the late 1960s and the 1970s for their methods of fund-raising and their evangelization tactics: the UC was one of the first groups to incur the charge of 'brainwashing'.

It is in some ways ironic that the evangelical Christians should be amongst the most vociferous critics of the Unification Church, since the UC's inception was, arguably, due to the mishandling of Christian missionary activity in Korea. When any religious mission penetrates a new culture, it is not immediately obvious what elements of the host country are cultural and what are religious. If the distinction seems impossible to draw, as it nearly always does, this only goes to demonstrate the problems which the missionary faces in deciding which cultural elements are incompatible with the missionary religion and which are not. In the case of the Unification Church, the problem was particularly exacerbated by the fact that the Christian missionary message was largely passed on by word of mouth, by new converts who were not well acquainted with the Christian faith. As a consequence, various elements of Korean folk shamanism, Confucianism and Mahayana Buddhism became blended with evangelical Protestantism. How precisely these elements intertwine in Unificationist theology is a complex topic, which I have discussed elsewhere (Chryssides, 1991). In what follows, I shall examine the teachings which are given at various stages of acquaintance with the UC.

In *The Advent of Sun Myung Moon* I pointed out a distinction between exoteric and esoteric teachings. This distinction has become somewhat more blurred in recent years. Unificationists will argue that, as members increasingly 'pay indemnity' – that is to say, make personal sacrifices for the movement that will assist the process of restoration – revelations, either those previously known only to the Rev. Moon himself or ones which are known only to members and a few trusted researchers, can be more widely disseminated. Another possible factor in the democratization of the esoteric elements is the fact that academic researchers have progressively revealed what these are. When *The Advent of Sun Myung Moon* first appeared, UC members were not at all happy with my disclosures about the various ceremonies surrounding the 'Blessing' (or the 'mass marriage', as the media insist on calling it). However, the fact that writers have progressively disclosed esoteric elements may well have caused Unificationists to feel that there can no longer be any point in trying to keep such elements hidden from the public. Today, information about all of these ceremonies, including the Indemnity Ceremony (also known as the Chastening Ceremony), can be easily found on the Internet, although new enquirers to the movement would be introduced more or less exclusively to the contents of *Divine Principle*.

According to *Divine Principle*, everything in the universe is subject to three stages of progress: Formation, Growth and Completion. A tree, for example, begins as a seed (Formation), then grows into a sapling (Growth) and finally into a mature tree (Completion); a human being starts as a baby (Formation), becoming a child (Growth) and then a man or woman (Completion).

God intended the first human beings, Adam and Eve, who were created at the Formation Stage, to grow to spiritual Completion. They would do this by obeying God's instruction to 'be fruitful, multiply, and have dominion over the earth' (Genesis 1:28). This is taken to mean becoming perfect individuals ('being fruitful'), marrying and establishing perfect families under God ('multiplying'), and bringing about a perfect world ('having dominion over the earth'). Alas, Adam and Eve did not achieve these goals: at the age of only 16 Eve was seduced by Satan in the Garden of Eden, and went on to have sexual intercourse with Adam, before either of them were of marriageable age. (If it is asked where these non-scriptural additions come from, such as Adam's and Eve's ages, these are

ascribed to revelations given to the Rev. Moon in the spirit world.)
Prior to their 'Fall', Adam and Eve had been at the top of the Growth
stage, but their disobedience put them into the 'unprincipled realm',
which lies beneath the Formation–Growth–Completion spectrum.

Adam and Eve had engaged in a 'give and take' relationship (to
use UC terminology) with Satan, and had thus established a 'false
lineage' for their progeny. The whole of the human race thus became
affected by the original parents' sin. In order to restore humanity
back into the 'principled realm' a messiah is needed. If it is asked
why it has specifically to be a 'messiah' rather than a teacher or a
prophet, the answer is that a messiah is someone who is an ideal,
sinless person. This is held to be important because the Fall resulted
in four kinds of sin: individual sin (Adam and Eve's personal
disobedience), original sin (humanity's inherited fallen nature, as
acknowledged by writers like Augustine and Calvin in mainstream
Christianity), collective sin (sin attributed to a whole group of people
– in this case, the human race), and ancestral sin (sin which is
transmitted through one's 'blood lineage' to one's descendants).
Unlike a teacher or a prophet, the messiah is free of all of these types
of sin, and is therefore in a position to restore humanity, providing
them with a new lineage into which previously sinful men and
women can become engrafted. Only once they are restored to this
new lineage can men and women progress to achieve the stages of
Growth and Completion, which Adam and Eve failed to do.

Although the messiah can redeem the human race, he must
nevertheless be prepared for by human effort. When a wrong is
committed, it is normally incumbent on the perpetrator to make
amends by paying some form of compensation. Unificationists call
this 'indemnity' (*t'ang gam* in Korean). Indemnity need not be
equivalent to the amount of damage incurred by the wronged party;
as in a court of law, the prescribed compensation can be either
greater or less than the damage. In the case of the divine–human
relationship, it is up to God to determine how much 'indemnity' is
appropriate: he has determined that humanity need not make
amends in full for all its sins, which would be an impossible price to
pay, but they must pay something in order to prepare the way for the
messiah. Not only is the human preparation a matter of justice,
entailed by the principle of 'indemnity', but it is important to 'lay the
foundation' for the messiah in the physical world. If the messiah's
mission lacks a proper human foundation to support it, the messiah's

mission will fail.

The history of Israel, as recounted in the Christian Old Testament, is the history of humanity's preparation for this messiah. A number of criteria must be satisfied if the messiah is to come and to be successful in his mission. First, two types of 'foundation' must be laid: a 'vertical' and a 'horizontal'. What this means is that, since there were two types of relationship which the Fall seriously damaged – physical human relationships (the 'horizontal') and divine–human relationships (the 'vertical') – both these relationships must be restored. This requires a 'foundation of substance' and a 'foundation of faith'.

Establishing the foundation of faith requires that a divinely chosen character assumes the role of 'central figure'. He stands in Adam's *position* (this is why it is 'he', not 'she', incidentally), and, by making a sacrifice, restores Adam's failure. The sacrifice is described as a 'symbolic offering': this means that it serves as payment of the indemnity that God asks, but, as previously explained, it is not the full amount that humanity owes. Once the vertical relationship is properly restored, the horizontal (inter-human) relationships can then be re-established in their proper 'principled' manner.

The first central figure is Abel. Abel makes an offering to God (Genesis 4:3), which proves to be acceptable, thus restoring the vertical relationship. Restoring the horizontal relationship fails, however, since Cain murders Abel, thereby preventing Abel from fulfilling his role in ushering in the messiah. The lineage now passes to Seth (Adam and Eve's third, less well-known, son), but owing to the fact that human sin has now been increased, more indemnity needs to be paid, and a greater time-span needs to elapse before the next central figure can arrive. (*Divine Principle* provides some numerical principles which show why particular central figures arrive at their appointed times, and which are too complex to discuss here.)

The next central figure is Noah, whose symbolic offering is the ark, in which human and animal life is saved from the flood. However, although Noah restores the horizontal relationship, he fails to restore the vertical one, because of a rather obscure incident in which he becomes drunk and is seen naked by his three sons (Genesis 9:20–1). Noah's nakedness is not a sin: in fact, Noah is attempting to recapitulate Adam's sin in the Garden of Eden, when he was 'naked and not ashamed' (Genesis 2.:25). However, Ham,

Noah's eldest son, covers his father's body and, in doing so, annuls Noah's attempt to restore humanity.

Divine Principle goes on to recount how Abraham, Moses and Joshua are assigned the roles of central figures, and how in each case they fail to accomplish their mission, thus preventing the messiah's coming. Finally, John the Baptist arrives to herald Jesus as the messiah. At first John proclaims Jesus faithfully: he baptizes Jesus, proclaiming him as 'the lamb of God who takes away the sins of the world', but, as Jesus' mission progresses, Unificationists claim, he loses faith – for example, when he sends his disciples to ask Jesus, 'Are you the one who was to come, or should we expect someone else?' (Matthew 11:3). Being the son of Zacharias the priest, John's testimony would have been highly influential in rallying the people to acknowledge Jesus as the messiah. Faced with John's disloyalty, Jesus had two remaining options: one was simply to flee, perhaps into the desert, having accomplished nothing; the other was to remain in Judaea and face crucifixion.

The latter option afforded Jesus a limited outcome of his mission. According to God's plan, once the foundations had been laid to receive the messiah, the messiah would then marry a bride whom God had been preparing, and who would give birth to sinless children in the new messianic blood lineage. Unificationists insist that Jesus' inability to accomplish this part of his mission was not failure on his part, and they react unfavourably when Christian commentators ascribe to them the teaching that Jesus failed in his mission. It was not Jesus who failed, but other human beings, and in particular John the Baptist. Jesus did in fact accomplish something on the cross: Satan had entered into a transaction with God, in which God agreed that Satan could have Jesus' life in exchange for the opening up of Paradise. In accordance with its principle of Formation, Growth and Completion, the spiritual world consists of three realms, or stages through which departed spirits may progress. Until the time of Jesus, only the Formation Stage was open to those who had died. When Jesus said to the dying thief, 'Today you will be with me in Paradise' (Luke 23:43), he was referring to the opening of the Growth stage in the spirit world, alternatively called 'Paradise'. The third (Completion) stage, which still awaits opening at this point, is the Kingdom of Heaven. The incompleteness of Jesus' mission entails that the process must begin again to lay the foundation for a new messiah.

A long, complicated section of *Divine Principle* now follows, in an attempt to establish the time and place at which this will occur. The precise details are again too complicated to explain here, but in broad outline the argument of *Divine Principle* is as follows. The advent of Jesus heralded the completion of the Old Testament Era; we are now emerging from the New Testament Era, a period of equal length, which will terminate with the coming of the 'Lord of the Second Advent', or 'Lord of the Second Coming', as he is sometimes called. The approximate date of the arrival of the new messiah is determined by noticing a number of 'historical parallels'. Four hundred years of Israelite slavery in Egypt parallels 400 years of Roman persecution of the early Christians; 400 years of rule by judges parallels 400 years of Christian patriarchs; 120 years of a single monarchy in Israel parallels 120 years of the Carolingian Holy Roman Empire; a further 400 years marks the political split between Israel and Judah in the Old Testament Era, and a 400-year division between the East and West Franks in the New Testament Era; the final period from the last prophet (Malachi) until Jesus Christ's advent is 400 years, corresponding to the 400 years which lie between Martin Luther, who is taken to mark the beginning of the Protestant Reformation, and the present day. If one assumes that the Protestant Reformation commenced in 1517, with the pinning of Luther's 95 Theses to the Schlosskirche at Wittenberg, a 400-year advance would take us to 1917.

Sometimes critics have tried to suggest that there are discrepancies in the UC's calculations of dates, and that the correspondences between the Old Testament and New Testament eras are inexact. *Divine Principle*'s scheme, however, allows some leeway, for the appearance of central figures depends on humanity playing its part in the restoration process. Since humans have free will, men and women may make decisions that either speed up or slow down God's plans to some degree. The date of the new messiah's arrival cannot therefore be pinpointed exactly, but it is stated that the earliest possible time for his birth is 1917, and the latest 1930 (Kwak, 1980, p. 306).

Unificationists argue that the notion of a returning messiah is true to scripture, since Jesus himself predicted a second coming. Conservative mainstream Christians of course will insist that Jesus himself will return, on the clouds of heaven, and will take up his followers to reign eternally with him. Unificationists believe that such references are to be understood figuratively rather than literally, and that a second coming will involve a normal physical birth. They point out that the original Jewish notion of a messiah is of a physical human being, rather than supernatural spiritual one. (Today Jews still hold that any messiah would be human, not divine.)

There a sense in which the new messiah will be the returned Jesus Christ: Jesus Christ will 'connect' with this messiah, especially co-operating with him from the spirit world. The idea that spirits can return and provide especial influence on those who are living is known as 'returning resurrection'. Unificationists do not accept that Jesus' body was resurrected, but rather that Jesus went on to live in the spirit world, from which he can co-operate with the Lord of the Second Coming.

Where, then, will the second messiah be born? Israel is rejected on the grounds that it has already had its opportunity to bear the messiah, and has failed to ensure that the messiah's mission was fulfilled. The nation cannot be communist, since communism is satanic; it must be Christian, but not western, since the Book of Revelation speaks of an angel arising from the east (Revelation 7:2). The chosen nation must be on the battleground in which God (who is represented by democracy) and Satan (who is represented by communism) are fighting; it must have paid sufficient indemnity through its sufferings, and there must have been messianic prophecies. Korea, being divided between the communist north and the democratic south, satisfies these conditions and is hence the place from which the messiah will emerge.

Sun Myung Moon, of course, having been born in Korea in 1920, is the obvious candidate to fill this role. UC seminar leaders used to be somewhat unforthcoming if any attendee asked whether Moon was this messiah, sometimes taking the view that this was a matter on which seekers had to decide for themselves. However, as Moon's mission is believed to have been increasingly accomplished, his status has been made much more explicit. In 1992 he announced:

> In early July, I spoke in five cities around Korea at rallies held by the Women's Federation for World Peace. There, I declared that my wife, WFWP President Hak Ja Han Moon, and I are the True Parents of all humanity. I declared that we are the Savior, the Lord of the Second Advent, the Messiah. (Moon, 1992, p. 5)

It should be noted that Moon mentions two messiahs, not just one: since it is incumbent on the messiah to marry, Sun Myung Moon and his wife Hak Ja Han are jointly deemed to be the messiahs of the present age. Their marriage took place in 1960, and they have become the parents of 13 children in all, 12 of whom are still alive.

A seminar would normally end with an account of Sun Myung's life, without which, they say, it is impossible to understand the Principle. Their accounts tells of how Sun Myung Moon from an early age went to the Korean mountains to pray, and on Easter morning, when he was only 16 years old, received a vision in which Jesus appeared to him, commissioning him to complete his unfinished mission. Moon was brought up in North Korea, was arrested for political activities and imprisoned on two occasions, but was liberated in 1950, when UN forces moved into the north. Together with a disciple, Moon fled to Pusan in the far south, where Moon dictated the first version of *Divine Principle*.

Sun Myung Moon's marriage to Hak Ja Han was the messianic wedding which Jesus was unable to have, and the children born of these 'True Parents' are the sinless children who are free of original, collective and ancestral sin, and thus the True Family has been established. The Blessing ceremony, which the movement offers, is a means by which those who are not in the physical lineage of the True Parents can become 'engrafted' into the true family. (Engrafting is a metaphor which Paul uses in the Bible to show how followers of Christ can become part of God's covenant offered to the Jewish people.)

The messianic commission which Moon received included the responsibility of restoring a world of true parents and true families. This is enacted by means of the famous Blessing ceremony – or 'mass wedding' as the media insist on calling it. Although the Blessing, in which up to 3.6 million couples (the figure given for the 1997 Blessing) are simultaneously married, is the phenomenon which the majority of the public associate with the Unification Church, mention of this is not normally made at the introductory public seminars, but divulged after further acquaintance with the movement.

Recent developments in the Unification Church

Within the past decade a number of changes have taken place within the Unification Church that are likely to change its character. In past times the Unification Church was enthusiastic about persuading others of the veracity of Moon's revelations and the need to accept his teachings to unify the world's religions. The principal ventures were therefore proselytizing and organizing large gatherings attended by academics and religious leaders. Today there is much more emphasis on the Blessing itself. Entering the Kingdom of Heaven is something that can be done only by couples, not by individuals. Originally the Blessing ceremony was offered only to UC members. By the late 1980s Unificationists had invited several sympathizers to take part, together with some academics and clergy that they had come to know over the years. (At one point I was approached, but declined.) Today the Blessing is now publicly available. The Unification Church decided to change its name to the Family Federation for World Peace and Unification: ostensibly this was to indicate the emphasis on the importance of families, although abandoning the name 'Unification Church' ensured that old prejudices were not aroused. FFWPU supporters then set up stands in major cities, disseminating information about the importance of stable marriages. Enquirers were asked if they wanted to reaffirm their marriage vows, and then encouraged to sign a brief document which read:

1. As a mature man and woman, we pledge that we will become an eternal husband and wife, consummating the ideal of God's creation with absolute fidelity.
2. We pledge that we will inherit and maintain the tradition of family unity and pass this tradition on to the future generations of our family and humankind.
3. We pledge that as true parents we will raise our children to live up to God's will, and educate them to be sexually abstinent until marriage.
4. We pledge that we will support all families to uplift these ideals, beyond race, religion and nation, by participating in the Blessing of Marriage, helping create the Kingdom of God on Earth and in Heaven.

The signatories were then offered a small glass of wine, reminiscent to Unificationists of the Holy Wine Ceremony, although such connotations were not normally mentioned to the couple. (It is not true, as has been rumoured, that one can receive the Blessing via the Internet: the holy wine is an essential component, which cannot be mediated through modern communications technology.) The number of people who have their marriage blessed is recorded, and at the next large Blessing ceremony such couples are counted as statistics, although they are under no obligation to attend. When it is stated that the Rev. Moon has blessed 3.6 million couples, this figure includes everyone since the previous Blessing who has restored their marriage in whatever way.

Other issues concern the future of the UC leadership. At the time of writing, Sun Myung is advancing in years, and this inevitably raises the question of how the movement will continue after he dies. At one point in time, members thought that the movement would gain renewed impetus through a Zimbabwean member, whose identity was kept anonymous, but whose name is now known to be Cleopus Kundiona. Kundiona claimed to be the mouthpiece of Moon's dead son Heung Jin (1966–84), and attempted to impose renewed discipline on members, a number of whom had become lax in their spirituality. In the end, Kundiona's presence proved to be too strong for the movement, and when he suggested that Moon was not the messiah, but only in the position of John the Baptist – the implication being that he, Kundiona, was the Lord of the Second Coming – this proved too much for all but a small handful of members. Kundiona now heads his own schismatical Unificationist sect.

More disturbing for the UC's future are recent events within Moon's own family. The possibility of Moon's own family serving to ensure the future of the movement seemed a logical one, and at one point Moon actually nominated his eldest son, Hyo Jin, as his successor. (Hyo Jin has an elder sister, incidentally, which indicated that Moon saw the future leadership lineage as patriarchal) (Chryssides, 1991, p. 177). For some time it was rumoured that there were serious problems among the Moon children, particularly relating to Hyo Jin: allegedly he was an alcoholic, addicted to cocaine, slept with prostitutes and was cruel to his wife Nansook Hong. Nansook Hong eventually filed for a divorce, and decided to go public, commissioning a ghost writer to record her experiences, which were published under the title of *In the Shadow of the Moons* (Hong, 1998). What has shocked members is not merely that the rumours about Hyo Jin were confirmed, but that the Rev. and Mrs Moon were unsupportive, and continued to pamper Hyo Jin, providing him with monies to continue with his outrageous lifestyle. Not only were the events inherently shocking, but they raised a number of theological issues. How does one reconcile the existence of True Children with their ability to sin? Are they still placed in a superior spiritual situation by virtue of their birth, or are they in no better a position than those who have joined the UC as ordinary people, with a lineage of ancestral sin? Such questions did not merely relate to Hyo Jin; another daughter had stated that she did not believe that her father was the messiah.

Other concerns relate to the UC's finances. Having substantial investments in Korea, the Unification Church was severely hit by Korea's economic crisis in 1997. Faced with these problems, Moon decided to transfer much of his capital and resources to Central America. Some members are critical of the church's financial management, and one member quite openly expressed anxiety to me about whether he could continue to believe in Moon's messianic status if he could not manage the movement's monies better. Some members are resentful too because they helped to raise a good proportion of the UC assets through their own efforts.

The Korean origins of the UC raise other issues too. The UC has always had shamanic elements within it – a fact which Nansook Hong corroborates in her account of how a Korean shaman was consulted before her marriage with Hyo Jin was arranged. Hak Ja Han's deceased mother has been the focus of a cult within the movement, and is believed to communicate through a medium. Members are currently being sent out to Korea to take part in ceremonies that seem more obviously related to Korean folk shamanism than to Christianity. One ex-member told me that the UC likes to present an outer appearance of being a legitimate form of Christianity, but inwardly is shot through with beliefs in spirits and shamanic practices.

It would be foolish to attempt to say how affairs will develop within the Unification Church. In the meantime the importance of Hak Ja Han is growing. When Moon finally dies, it seems likely that she will preside over the Blessing ceremonies, and will continue to lead the movement as the remaining True Parent. Being considerably younger than Moon, the question of the future leadership may not become a pressing issue in the more immediate future.

The Family (formerly Children of God)

Next to the Unification Church, The Family must surely rate as one of the most controversial NRMs of the New Christian variety.

Formerly known (and perhaps better known) as the 'Children of God', its sexual permissiveness secured it a prominent place in public attention. In its earlier years the movement gained notoriety for its practice of 'flirty fishing' (FFing), allegedly attracting converts by means of offering them sexual favours. More recently, allegations have focused on child abuse, the public suspecting that sexual liberality included having sex with minors, and police raids have taken place in four different countries, with some 600 Family children having been taken into care.

It can be inappropriate to let media controversies, especially scandalmongering ones, dictate the agenda for a Religious Studies approach to a new religious movement. In the case of The Family, however, it is true that attitudes to sex, the body and the physical world are almost as important to their theology as they are in public attention. However, it is necessary to place the movement's liberal attitudes to sex in context, both historically and theologically, as I shall endeavour to do.

The Family originated in California, the birthplace of so many NRMs, as part of the 1960s post-hippie, post-psychedelic 'Jesus Revolution'. The 'Jesus Freaks', as some of them were called, were made up of elements of the youth culture with a background in free sex and drugs; they practised communal living and shared assets, in line with the practice of the early Church, demanding total commitment, with fairly aggressive proselytizing, which resulted from a sense of urgency in the face of Christ's expected imminent return.

David Brandt Berg (1919–94), the founder-leader of The Family, came from a long lineage of Christian evangelists and pastors. Berg's mother's ancestors were Jewish Christians, who had left Germany to become Mennonite farmers. His maternal grandfather became a millionaire and built some 50 churches, and his mother founded the Alliance Tabernacle Church in 1925, apparently in thanksgiving for having received a miraculous cure for paralysis. David Berg's own career began when he became an evangelist in the Christian and Missionary Alliance. Part of his evangelism was done through radio and television, where he jointly presented 'Church in the Home' (1964–7) with Fred Jordan, a Pentecostalist preacher. He also ran the American Soul Clinic, Inc.

In 1944 Berg had married Jane Miller, who became known to the movement as 'Mother Eve'. After David's media ministry, both he and Jane joined his mother at Huntingdon Beach, California, where she was ministering to the hippies. The Bergs' movement was known variously as 'Revolutionaries for Jesus' and 'Teens for Christ'. (The word 'teenager' had only recently gained common currency at that time.) 'Children of God' was originally a press nickname. David Berg grew his hair long, and helped with the distribution of peanut butter sandwiches, in an attempt to provide the counter-culture with meagre subsistence. Live music was an important feature in the worship, and David's general iconoclastic anti-establishment approach proved to be highly effective.

Following his mother's death in 1968, Berg felt no commitment to remain at Huntingdon Beach, and the next year the Children of God began to travel around the USA, eventually settling in Canada. In the latter country, Berg claimed that a new church had come into being, replacing the old. The old was corrupt, and was represented by his wife Jane; accordingly, he took a new wife – Karen Zerby, who had joined the movement in Arizona – and who came to be known as 'Maria'. Maria and David became joint leaders, and, after David's death in 1994, Maria remains at the head of the movement.

It was shortly after leaving California that David Berg came to call himself 'Moses David', one of several names by which he is referred to by his followers. Other appellations are 'Father David', 'Mo' or simply 'Dad'. The assumption of these Old Testament names served to reinforce Berg's claim to have direct revelations from God, and Berg was frequently referred to as a modern-day prophet.

In 1970 Berg led the Texas Soul Clinic Ranch, a religious community which was owned by Jordan, and which grew to a massive 2000 members by the following year. Members were required to renounce the world, and were subjected to spiritual oversight by 'shepherds' (Lewis and Melton, 1994, p. 43). Despite Berg's reputation for sexual permissiveness, the community's sexual morality was straight-laced: dating was prohibited, the virtues of celibacy were taught, and members were even forbidden to hold hands.

It was around 1972 that Berg's movement began to attract unfavourable media publicity. His followers had staged public demonstrations, mainly publicizing their firm belief in the world's imminent end, declaring that a massive earthquake would destroy the entire city of Los Angeles. Other controversial elements took their rise from around this time: Father David (as he was now more commonly known) began to publish *True Comix,* which presented the group's message in down-to-earth comic strip form, and the notorious *MO Letters,* by means of which Berg communicated his thoughts and instructions to his closest full-time following. *The Jesus Book* was the title of their paperback edition of the New Testament. Berg had little direct contact with rank and file members, most of whom never met him at any point during their membership: the MO Letters were his main form of teaching his following. The movement spread to Europe, their international headquarters having been established in London in 1981. By 1973 the Children of God was a truly international movement, with 200 'homes' (originally called 'colonies') in 50 countries, including Latin America, Australia and New Zealand.

It was in 1973 that CoG's sexual liberality commenced. Berg's wife Maria began to have sexual encounters with other men, in order to 'witness' (proclaim the gospel) to them. Father David published a MO Letter entitled 'Revolutionary Sex', in which he proclaimed that the only prohibitions on sex were on fornication, adultery, incest and sodomy; masturbation and nudity were declared acceptable, and even lesbianism, he declared, was not explicitly forbidden in the Bible (Melton, in Lewis and Melton, 1994, p. 73). Maria's experiment marked the beginning of the much discussed practice of FFing, and was sanctioned by a 1974 MO Letter entitled 'Flirty Little Fishy'. The reference to 'fish' harked back to Jesus' call to his earliest disciples, in which he promised that they would become 'fishers of men' (Matthew 4:19); the 'flirting' was Berg's own innovation, of course. The practice was piloted in the Canary Islands during 1974–6, and then more widely. Berg seems to have thought of it as a female ministry, although – at least in theory – men could 'flirtily fish' for women seekers. From 1978 onwards, the practice was worldwide.

Some other evangelization practices are worth noting. Members were concerned that only a limited number of people could be reached by way of direct 'witnessing'. Accordingly, the practice of 'litnessing' was adopted, whereby members engaged in widespread literature distribution. In addition, CoG members produced tapes and videos, and featured on radio and television programmes. Many videos showed CoG members somewhat scantily dressed: no doubt this was designed to arouse viewers' attention, but, as we shall see, part of CoG's theology is that the body is nothing about which to be ashamed. A further tactic was known as 'provisioning': a van load of CoG members would typically stop at a restaurant and persuade the manager to allow their children to perform to the diners. (Family members train their children in the performing arts to a high standard, and encourage them not to have inhibitions about displaying their skills.) Winning the customers' favour by a free polished performance of song and dance, they were then able to talk to them about Christ, and in many cases persuade them to pray, inviting Jesus into their hearts. Performances often resulted in the manager offering the group a free meal, thus enabling them simultaneously to satisfy their own bodily needs and to win others for Christ.

The year 1978, when FFing was at its height, was also the year of the Jonestown massacre, which fuelled public anxiety about NRMs in general, but particularly concerning movements like CoG, which had established such controversial practices. CoG therefore sought to get out of the limelight, and members fled to Spain, then Portugal, Switzerland, Malta, and France (Lewis and Melton, 1994, p. 10). The year 1978 was also significant in another way, heralding a massive reorganization of CoG. Father David believed that some of the leaders had been misusing their authority, and dismissed all of them, including his daughter Linda, who subsequently wrote a scurrilous book denouncing her father and the organization. A number of letters, known as the *RNR Letters* (Reorganizaton and Nationaliza-tion Revolution), were sent out, and Berg invited the remaining members to join him in forming a new organization. The Children of God was dissolved, giving way to the new Family of Love, as the group became known.

Perhaps predictably, some of the female members of FoL began to pay the price for their sexual freedom, and contracted various venereal diseases. The AIDS epidemic had started, and was a cause for concern too. Initially Berg was of the opinion that God would protect members against sexually transmitted diseases; later he accepted that such risks were real, but had to be taken for the sake of the gospel. The risk, he claimed, was analogous to Christ's own sacrifice on the cross, and Berg cited Jesus' words, 'Greater love hath no man than this, that a man lay down his life for his friends' (Lewis and Melton, 1994, p. 242). One much publicized MO Letter bore an illustration of a naked woman lying on a couch, arms outspread and with a large nail penetrating her vagina. Above her was the figure of Jesus Christ, arms outspread on the cross.

In 1983 a famous MO Letter entitled 'Ban the Bomb!' rescinded the FFing policy, and new rules began to be formulated on sexual relationships. Members who already were having sex with their 'fish' were required to use condoms, and FFing gave way to 'ESing', the use of Escort Agencies to establish contacts with seekers. For those who lived in communes, a six-month period had to elapse before sexual intercourse was permitted. By 1987 FFing was a thing of the past. Berg wrote, 'All sex with outsiders is banned! – Which means ESing and FFing with sex is now out!' (Lewis and Melton, 1994, p. 242) The practice that was now 'in' was 'DFing', the provision of 'Daily Food', meaning the spiritual nourishment of new converts; health problems apart, FoL 'fishers' had frequently encountered difficulty in making the transition from a physical sexual relationship to a situation in which the 'fish' could develop spiritually.

Until 1989 a significant proportion of CoG members resided in the Philippines, but they began to attract bad publicity there too, and a number decided to return to Britain. The year 1991 saw another name change: instead of being called the Family of Love, they were now to be known as The Family, which remains their current name at the time of writing. By 1994 there were 10,000 members in 50 countries, and Family members had begun evangelizing in Eastern Europe, a new field that had become ripe for missionizing following the demise of communism.

The theology of The Family

Millikan summarizes The Family's theological position thus: 'In matters of doctrine, The Family's theology is a mix of apocalypticism, evangelical southern American Protestantism, and universalism' (Millikan, in Lewis and Melton, 1994, p. 191). Basically fundamentalist, The Family has a simple faith in the Bible, deploring the 'modernism' of academic scholarly approaches, and espousing creationism in the face of Darwinism. Members affirm all the key doctrines of mainstream Christianity, in its Protestant evangelical form. The Family believes in a triune God who created a perfect universe in six days, culminating in the creation of man and woman, who were tempted by Satan and thus fell from grace. Members firmly believe in the reality of Satan and his demons, who support him in his battle against God. Unable to redeem themselves, they could only gain salvation through God's grace, manifested in the sending of his only begotten Son, born of a virgin and perfectly sinless, who, by offering his life, achieved vicarious atonement for humanity. He rose from the dead and ascended into heaven, after which the Holy Spirit descended on his disciples, enabling them to speak in tongues and to exhibit the various 'gifts of the Spirit' which the apostle Paul describes (1 Corinthians 12). In common with mainstream Christianity, The Family celebrates the Lord's Supper, or Communion, as a memorial of Christ's death, and as an anticipation of the day of his return to earth: as Paul enjoins, the Christian should celebrate the Lord's death 'till he come' (1 Corinthians 11:26).

As far as baptism is concerned, 'Our Statement of Faith' makes no mention of 'water baptism', preferring instead to speak of 'the baptism of the Holy Spirit'. The Family tends not to use words like 'sacrament', which are probably much too 'establishment' for them, and expresses no interest in traditional Protestant–Catholic controversies about whether they are two or seven in number. In common with Christianity's evangelical wing, the crucially important element in gaining salvation is not baptism but personal commitment to Jesus Christ: 'We are saved by believing in and personally receiving Jesus Christ into our hearts and lives, thus becoming spiritually regenerated or "born again"' (Family, 1992a, p. 2). 'Inviting Jesus into your heart' is the key: if this seems simple or all too easy, it should be remembered that salvation comes through divine grace, and not through any human effort. This explains why members of The Family were able to believe that they could actually 'save' several souls in a restaurant while they were 'provisioning': just a simple prayer would suffice. Furthermore, once saved, a believer always remains saved. If the quality of one's life remains unaffected by inviting Christ into one's heart, that does not cancel one's salvation, although it can affect the degree of reward which is meted out at Christ's second coming.

Moses Berg's status and the MO Letters

Despite this apparent congruence with evangelical Protestantism, The Family has been criticized for the status accorded to Moses

David, who has been described as 'the final Prophet' who has come in fulfilment of Hebrew prophecy: 'And I will set up over them one shepherd, my Servant David, and he shall feed them' (Ezekiel 34:23). Some critics have suggested that his MO Letters were accorded equal status with the Bible, or possibly even superseded it (Millikan, in Lewis and Melton, 1994, p. 237). One MO Letter stated, 'We don't even need to read the Book of Acts', implying that the revelations received by Moses David, which were transmitted through the MO Letters, were themselves sufficient to enable followers to know how to live out their faith (quoted in Millikan, in Lewis and Moore, 1994, p. 237).

Berg's revelations were believed to have come to him from contacts with the spirit world. In particular, a spirit called Abrahim [*sic*] was believed frequently to have guided him throughout his life, furnishing him with new insights. However, although Berg was given the status of 'prophet' and Maria that of 'prophetess' after Berg's death, revelations from the spirit world are not exclusive to the leaders, and can be experienced by all. There are three kinds of spirit. There are angels ('angelic ministering spirits') – literally messengers of God – who watch over and protect his people; they are usually invisible, but they can occasionally manifest themselves in physical form, as scripture affirms (Hebrews 13:2; Family, 1992a, p. 3 cites other proof texts). There are 'spirits of departed saints', who deliver messages to those on earth. Finally, there exist Satan's demons, who attempt to thwart God's plans, seeking to tempt and deceive human beings.

The MO Letters, by which Berg's revelations were transmitted, certainly had a limited circulation: they were sent exclusively to 'DOs', that is to say 'Doers Only', the nucleus of totally committed followers who lived in CoG communes. This fact alone, I think, discredits the view that these letters were to be regarded as 'scripture'. CoG clearly held that Christianity's traditional scriptures contained all that was needed for salvation, and thus no extra merit or privileged access to salvation accrued from Father David's revelations. As far as his 'sexual revolution' was concerned, the group's sexual practices were permissions, designed to demonstrate that followers were no longer bound by the constraints of the Jewish law: sexual licentiousness did not itself lead to salvation, which comes from grace, not works. No doubt because of adverse criticism, the role of the MO Letters tends now to be played down. A few still circulate amongst The Family, but they have not been systematically preserved, and in Family homes many – especially the more controversial ones – are not even owned, let alone used.

One cannot discuss the MO Letters without discussing sex, and, more generally, The Family's teachings on the human body. While unreservedly endorsing the doctrine of original sin, The Family points out that this state was the result of the Fall, and that in humanity's prelapsarian state God's creation was completely perfect. This included the first man and woman, who were 'naked and not ashamed' (Genesis 2:25). God's first commandment to Adam and Eve was, 'Be fruitful and multiply' (Genesis 1:28), meaning that they should have sexual intercourse. God's first commandment, Berg once said, was to have lots of sex! The human body is therefore nothing to be ashamed of, and sex is something to be enjoyed.

Much of Berg's writing is explicitly sexual, and deliberately so. He was concerned to extol the pleasures of sex, in contrast to his perception of mainstream Christianity, which tended to downgrade sex, portraying it as evil or disgusting. Thus one MO Letter gives advice on how to maximize the pleasure of masturbation, while another, entitled 'The Love of David! – Your Session with the King!', is a detailed description of David Berg having intercourse with a 'handmaiden', for each detail of which he gives thanks to Jesus.

Marriage in The Family was originally called 'betrothal'. One's true spouse is Jesus, to whom one's primary commitment lies. 'MARRIAGE IN THE FAMILY IS TO JESUS and they are *all* "Jesus babies"! And we are *all* married to each other in His Love' (quoted in Palmer, in Lewis and Melton, 1994, p. 15). As Palmer states, marriages can be arranged as a result of dreams, or by recommendations from the leaders. Although marriage is a lifelong commitment, and divorce discouraged, marriage does not require exclusive sexual fidelity to one's spouse. In its FFing days, marriage did not preclude offering sexual gratification to seekers, and indeed Berg's wife Maria became pregnant as a result of such an encounter in 1975. Her son, Davidito, was accepted by David, who brought him up as his own son.

It would not be accurate to say that the Children of God ever believed in 'free sex'. Flirty fishing was not primarily a means of sexual self-gratification, but served a two-fold function. First, it was intended as an attempt to recognize that people had physical needs, which included sexual ones. Members who recall CoG's FFing days tell me that the activity sometimes entailed having sex with people whom they found singularly unattractive. Second, it afforded an opportunity to 'witness', not only by virtue of the CoG member and seeker being alone together, but because it was reckoned that a seeker was in a better position to listen to the Christian message when his or her physical needs had been satisfied. As one member described it, 'Flirty fishing was a sacrificial, humble ministry of giving one's life to another, so that someone else could find the Lord and have purpose and a life of happiness' ('Bert', n.d., p. 8).

During the FFing period, the dangers of the practice were recognized. Female members could become pregnant, and, if married, their husbands could find themselves fathering children who were not theirs. Male members could find themselves impregnating female non-members – a situation that was particularly problematic if the woman was uninterested in joining. Given that Berg forbade the use of any form of contraception, these situations were very real.

The controversial sexual practice that remains within The Family is 'sharing' – the practice of having a physical relationship with another member (other than one's spouse) of the home in which one resides. 'Sharing' usually involves sex, although it need not do so: it may simply involve, say, a married male member taking out a female member to dinner, and perhaps engaging in some physical contact. Family members claim that this can be a means of satisfying someone's physical and emotional needs when his or her spouse is away for some time on a mission. To interpret the sixth commandment as entailing only having one sex partner is to act in accordance with the law. Berg insisted that the Christian is 'not under law', but under grace. Further, Berg pointed out that scripture condones the practice of having many sexual partners:

> If you look at Bible history you'll make the shocking discovery that most of God's greats had oodles of wives, women, mistresses, harlots & what have you, as well as multitudes of children. (David, quoted in Harrison, 1990, p. 118)

Again, there are rules governing 'sharing': it is certainly not the case that a member can have sex with any other member at will. All spouses must agree; 'sharing' can only be practised within one home, and not between different homes or with outsiders; one cannot 'share' with more than one member in any one month. It also needs the permission of the 'Home Mother' and is only done after 'much discussion and prayer'. Although 'sharing' has aroused much adverse criticism outside the organization, members claim that it is preferable by far to make extra-marital relationships open and explicit, rather than have the clandestine affairs that are common within mainstream society. Divorce rates in The Family are said to be low, and one does not commit adultery by having sex with someone who is not one's spouse; having extra-marital sex without one's partner's permission is what is really harmful. Berg consistently insisted that the 'law of love' was the key to right action: if sex is hurtful and destructive, then it should be avoided; if it is pleasurable and harms no one, then it can be lovingly entered into.

There are restrictions on sexual activities too. Homosexuality is disallowed, being contrary to scripture, and is an excommunicable offence. Lesbianism is also banned, although The Family acknowledges that there is no explicit mention of it in the Bible. Anal intercourse and group sex are prohibited as well. Contraception is banned: The Family holds that life begins at the moment of conception, hence an IUD device or contraceptive pills can destroy a life that has just begun. Natural methods, such as coitus interruptus, are also unacceptable: this was the sin for which Onan was punished (Genesis 38:8–10).

Something briefly needs to be mentioned about sexual practices that are attributed to The Family, but vehemently denied. It has variously been accused of paedophilia, encouraging under-age sex, incest and pornography. Berg certainly aimed to shock, and he was concerned to remove taboos and prohibitions relating to the human body. As he wrote:

> To hell with the proper way! ... The proper way is of man! The unexpected and the improper, the unconventional and untraditional, the unorthodox and unceremonious, contrary to man's natural expectation – This is the way God usually works! 'For My thoughts are not your thoughts, neither are your ways My ways, saith the Lord. For as the heavens are higher than the earth, so are My ways higher than your ways, and My thoughts than your thoughts! Who can know the mind of the Lord, and who can show Him anything?' (MO Letter No. 35, 2 January 1971, para. 13, p. 4)

The Family firmly believes that sex should be perceived as 'beautiful' rather than smutty (Family, 1992a, p. 28).

In 1986 Berg issued a policy statement on 'teen sex': teenagers must avoid sex until at least their fifteenth birthday; in 1989 this was changed to one's sixteenth birthday, and in 1991 to one's eighteenth, except in countries where marriage under the age of 18 was permitted. The issuing of such a policy statement may itself be an indication that sex involving under-15s was previously occurring. Certainly Berg stated that he could see no reason why marriage should not follow puberty, although one researcher believes that his remarks were purely theoretical, and not practised to any extent (Lewis and Melton, 1994, p. 83). Berg as an infant had a Mexican nanny who used to attempt to put him to sleep by manipulating his penis – a fairly widespread Mexican practice. Berg also tells how he experimented with sex as a child, and on one occasion attempted at age seven to have sex with his cousin. No doubt these frank accounts have helped to fuel rumours that similar practices were condoned or even encouraged within CoG, but, to the best of my knowledge, there is no concrete evidence.

Regarding pornography, The Family has been accused of encouraging its children to take part in indecent videos. FoL produced 'dance videos' in the 1980s, the aim of the dances being 'to glorify God and to glorify sex' (Lewis and Melton, 1994, p. 87), and they have been described as 'soft porn'. The practice was discontinued in 1987. In the FFing days in the Philippines, some of the 'fish' asked members to watch pornography as part of the sexual service CoG members provided. Berg made a point of viewing some of the pornographic materials available there, and claims that he was shocked, writing:

IN FACT, UNTIL I SAW SOME PORNO MOVIES, I NEVER REALIZED SEX COULD BE SO UGLY & SO SICKENING & SO PERVERTED AND SO HORRIBLE! (quoted in Melton, in Lewis and Melton, 1994, p. 85)

The Family's current policy statement outlaws pornography:

We oppose debasing human sexuality and presenting the body in a form that has no aesthetic, artistic or socially redeeming value. We do not allow the possession or viewing of sexually offensive pornographic films and materials. We do not approve of any kind of ugly, unloving, or perverse form of sexual behaviour. (Family, 1992a, p. 29)

Previously, classical art was acceptable, but even this is now disallowed (Family, 1992b, p. 3). No doubt this is a conservative move in response to media criticism.

Eschatology

Although Berg and The Family have laid great emphasis on the physical body, there is of course a world and a goal that lie beyond the world which we currently inhabit. This present world is a temporary one, and will soon come to an end. It therefore follows that one should not put down too many roots in the present world. The Family consequently does not believe in amassing wealth, and they prefer to rent property rather than to buy it, since it will be used only for a limited period of time before Christ returns. In the meantime, one can experience communications from this other, better world: angels can materialize physically and come to one's assistance, and spirits of departed saints such as Moses and Elijah can deliver messages to humans.

The Family's declaration, 'Our Statement of Faith', contains quite detailed interpretation of the more obscure apocalyptic passages of scripture, notably the second half of Daniel and the Book of Revelation. Being in the last days, we should not be surprised that ancient prophecies are being fulfilled in present-day events. As Millikan comments, 'Berg believes that the Bible can be read as a virtual textbook of the events leading up to the end of the world' (Millikan, in Lewis and Melton, 1994, p. 203). Although Berg has made a remarkable synthesis of the various end-time events described in disparate sections of Jewish and Christian scripture, it should be noted that The Family does acknowledge that its analysis of such details is less certain than the other main doctrines that I have outlined above. As 'Our Statement of Faith' parenthetically notes:

> (While we hold the following doctrines and teachings to be true and sound, they differ from the aforementioned beliefs in that they are not addressing dogma based on evident and clear-cut statements by our Lord, but are dealing with the rather more mysterious subject of Biblical prophecies, which, for the most part, are yet to be fulfilled. Therefore, as we recognize that these eschatological positions are considerably more open to interpretation than the previous statements, we do not call for the same degree of adherence to these teachings as to the more evident tenets covered earlier.) (Family, 1992a, p. 8)

The 'signs of the times' that we should heed include humanity's increasing wickedness, and specifically the rise of Russia as a world power. It is from Russia that the Antichrist will emerge: The Family makes no exact identification between the Antichrist and any specific individual, but speculates that this 'man of sin' is (or will be) one of the principal antagonists, possibly a Jew, in the Middle East conflict (Lewis and Melton, 1994, p. 203). He will be a signatory to a compromise between Jews, Arabs and Christians, as a result of which the Jews will be permitted to rebuild the Jerusalem Temple on the Temple Mount. The Antichrist will restore the practice of animal sacrifices in the Temple, and then he will set up his own image in the Temple precincts, attempting to coerce the human race to worship him. Some will hail him as the messiah, while others will recognize his true identity, together with that of the False Prophet, the Antichrist's 'right-hand man' (Lewis and Melton, 1994, p. 204).

These events will herald the 'great tribulation' mentioned by Matthew (Matthew 24:21). The Antichrist will attempt to control the entire world, and he will use modern technology to do this. One example involves the 'mark of the beast', described in the Book of Revelation as follows:

> And he causeth all, both small and great, rich and poor, free and bond, to receive a mark in their right hand, or in their foreheads: and that no man might buy or sell, save he that had the mark, or the name of the beast, or the number of his name. (Revelation 13:16–17)

In common with a number of Christian evangelical groups who talk of the new world order, The Family takes this text to refer to the computerization of commercial transactions, currently manifested in money-free transactions, using bar codes and credit cards. It has been speculated that a further development in commercial computer systems would be for consumers to be issued with an implanted silicon chip, either on their wrist or on their forehead, which could then be scanned at supermarket checkouts and other outlets, thus reducing risks of theft and forgery!

The Great Tribulation will last for three and a half years (Daniel 12:7; Revelation 12:14), after which Christ will return on the clouds of heaven, and 'rapture' those of his followers who are alive on earth. The faithful who have died will be resurrected and 'reunited with their new glorified bodies' (Family, 1992a, p. 9). Then follows the 'Marriage Supper of the Lamb', in which the saved will come before Christ's judgement seat and receive their various rewards for their life on earth, while God's wrath and all manner of plagues will be meted out to the unfaithful, who remain on earth. These events lead on to the Battle of Armageddon, in which Christ and his angels decisively

147

defeat the Antichrist and his forces, and Christ is able to begin his millennial rule. (It should be noted that the primal Christian meaning of 'millennium' is not the period commencing in the year 2000 or 2001 CE, but this thousand-year period of Christ's reign.)

The thousand-year period, although long, is not the final eschaton. When this time has elapsed, Satan will be unbound and released for 'a little season' (Revelation 20:3). Satan and his recalcitrant followers will then continue their rebellion in the Battle of Gog and Magog (Revelation 20:8). In this battle, God will send a fire upon them, which will be so great that it will melt the entire earth. Seas will turn to vapour and the earth's atmosphere will be destroyed. 'The heavens shall pass away with a great noise, and the elements shall melt with fervent heat, the Earth also and the works that are therein shall be burned up' (2 Peter 3:10, quoted in Family, 1992a, p. 9).

After this, the New Heaven and the New Earth, described in the Book of Revelation, will be established, and the 'White Throne Judgement' will commence. At this second judgement, the un-redeemed who have died throughout the ages will be made to appear before God: on Berg's interpretation, this affords an opportunity of salvation for those who have been unable to hear and accept the gospel during their lifetime. Berg has sometimes been described as a 'universalist', but this is not strictly accurate: Berg did not hold that all would eventually be saved, but rather implied that a further opportunity for salvation might be afforded to those who failed to secure admission to the 'marriage of the lamb'.

In the afterlife one will continue to experience many of the features of the present one, apart of course from suffering and sin. People will not lose their gender or their sexuality. Indeed God himself is ascribed gender, the Father being male and the Holy Spirit being God's female aspect. Human reproduction will still occur, and one piece of The Family's religious art depicts a baby being born in heaven. One member of The Family recently informed me that, although Jesus said there would be no marriage in heaven, this does not mean that there will be no sex!

The Jesus Army

The Jesus Fellowship Church, also known as the Jesus Army, is noteworthy for several reasons. First, it is one of the few examples of a distinctively British movement: although a few of its members live abroad and affiliate from afar, the Jesus Army currently has no plans to spread itself to Europe more widely or to the USA. Second, the group is thoroughly orthodox, professing allegiance to Christianity's historic creeds; it neither seeks to add to scripture nor claims new present-day prophets, although, in common with many mainstream Christians, it believes in continuing revelation through the Holy Spirit's inspiration.

The Jesus Fellowship Church began as a village Baptist church, in Bugbrooke, Northamptonshire, in England. Founded in 1805, the congregation saw the completion of their chapel in 1808. Within ten years the congregation exceeded 100 members and was able to plant other congregations. However, in common with many Christian congregations, it experienced a post-war decline and was at a low ebb by 1951. The crusades of the American evangelist Billy Graham brought some signs of renewal in 1954, but the Graham-inspired revival was temporary.

In 1957 the congregation was in need of a minister, and Noel Stanton, who continues to lead the Jesus Fellowship Church, was recommended to them. Stanton was born in 1926, of farming parents, and left school to work in a bank. He was conscripted to the Royal Navy during the Second World War, where his travels took him to Sydney in Australia. There he was approached in the street by a man who asked him where he expected to spend eternity; this question made a great impression on him and he subsequently 'gave his life to Christ' (Cooper and Farrant, 1997, p. 25). After leaving the Navy, he received baptism from a Pentecostalist pastor and felt a call to the ministry. Having trained at All Nations Bible College, he became deputy secretary to the West Amazon Mission; then, following a couple of jobs in the world of business, he offered himself to the Ministry Committee of the Baptist Union and was accepted.

The congregation continued along traditional Baptist lines, showing little hope of revival, until 1968. Stanton had been holding a series of Saturday night prayer meetings in his manse, in the course of which the dozen or so attendees studied the Book of Acts to find out the early Church's secret of success. One recurring theme was the presence of the Holy Spirit and the phenomenon of 'speaking in tongues', a matter about which neither Stanton nor the rest of the congregation had been particularly enthusiastic. However, the

149

charismatic movement was well under way, and the members of Bugbrooke Baptist Church had heard reports of friends in other churches not only speaking in tongues but praying that the Bugbrooke congregation would receive this gift of the Spirit also. Stanton had also been reading David Wilkerson's popular book *The Cross and the Switchblade,* a Pentecostalist minister's autobiographical account of how, under the Holy Spirit's influence, he penetrated the gangs of New York City, and enabled many of them to renounce their lives of drugs and violence.

Stanton himself describes how he received the 'baptism of the Spirit' several months later, while praying at his manse:

> it was so intoxicating, so exhilarating, and so intense that I felt I was just not going to live any more! I became filled with the intensity of God. This went on for hours and hours and I moved into speaking in tongues and praising the Lord. It was a tremendous experience of life and fullness from which I didn't come down for a long time – and this was the changing point in my life. (quoted in Cooper and Farrant, 1997, p. 30)

At that time also, some of the young people in the Bugbrooke congregation had received this gift and Stanton preached about the experience in church. This 'gift of the Spirit' incorporates several elements: the feeling that one is taken over by the Holy Spirit (the 'anointing of the Spirit', as the early disciples were at Pentecost (Acts 2)), resultant glossolaliation, and in some instances accompanying miracles, such as healings and – less frequently – experiences of supernatural visitations. (Sometimes they are angels, at other times the visitors are less readily identifiable. One member recounts trying to rescue someone from a gang fight, to find that a man in a suit, carrying a copy of the *Jesus Army Streetpaper*, intervened to fend off his opponents' blows. When no one else acknowledged having seen this man, he concluded that he had been offered supernatural protection.) Other 'fruits of the Spirit' include 'deliverance', the power to cast out demons, who can be found living within people. Not infrequently, members of the Jesus Fellowship Church experience 'laughing in the Spirit' – a feeling of euphoria which accompanies Spirit-possession and which makes members laugh uncontrollably, often lying on their backs.

'Baptism in the Spirit' is alluded to in a few places in the New Testament, and charismatic Christians insist that it was an authentic and highly important phenomenon in the early Church. When describing Jesus' mission, John the Baptist says:

I baptise you with water for repentance. But after me will come one who is more powerful than I, whose sandals I am not fit to carry. He will baptise you with the Holy Spirit and with fire. (Matthew 3:11)

The imagery of 'fire', which is frequently used in the context of Spirit baptism, harks back to John the Baptist's statement, as well as the Pentecost incident in which the Holy Spirit is said to have appeared on the disciples' heads as 'tongues of fire' (Acts 2:3). Fire imagery also connotes the burning passion with which the charismatics desire to proclaim their gospel message.

Although some of the older members also received the gift of the Spirit, the phenomenon deeply divided the congregation, and, in all, 43 of its members resigned in the early 1970s, leaving the Bugbrooke Jesus Fellowship to belong predominantly to the youth culture. When word got around about the anointing of the Spirit that the Bugbrooke Fellowship Church had received, various elements of the youth counter-culture became attracted to it. Seekers included bikers, drug users, glue sniffers, New Agers and others who had emerged from hippie culture. Converts to the new Jesus lifestyle were encouraged to burn the paraphernalia that belonged to their previous life, such as Tarot cards and literature about Krishna consciousness.

When the news of the Toronto Blessing (see above) swept through North America and on into Europe in 1994, the Jesus Fellowship Church welcomed the renewal of spirit baptism which the phenomenon afforded. However, the Toronto Blessing did not offer JFC members anything they did not already possess, and, unlike the most eager of the evangelical Christians, it was not on the agenda of JFC members to visit the Toronto church in which the event first happened. The Jesus Fellowship Church had more pressing things to do at home, and believed that such blessings of the Spirit had to be viewed within a wider perspective.

The desire for Spirit baptism was simply one element of the first-century Christian Church, and 'restorationist' Christian communities often feel a desire to consider the whole range of features that characterized original Christianity. The Book of Acts also speaks of communal living and of common property ownership (Acts 5:32). It is not surprising, then, that the Bugbrooke Jesus Fellowship should move in this direction, and in 1977 the community decided that those who wished to do so could participate in residential membership. There were thus two categories of member, residential and non-residential, and of the (then) 600 members 75 per cent opted for residential living. To mark the transition, the name of the Bugbrooke church was changed to 'The Jesus Fellowship Church', and 'The New Creation Christian Community' became the name of the residential group, together with other members who were closely associated with the residential community.

The Jesus Fellowship Church does not share the view that is sometimes expressed, that the notion of communal ownership was an early Christian experiment which was abandoned as a failure. The life of poverty was an important hallmark of the early Christians, and Jesus himself taught that seekers should sell their possessions and abandon their wealth, giving it away to the poor. Following Jesus therefore entails a recognition that Jesus was poor, and members of the Jesus Fellowship Church have little sympathy with the 'prosperity theology' espoused by evangelists such as John Avanzini and the Word-Faith Movement. Members of the Jesus Fellowship Church are usually proud of the fact that they have no possessions and hence no earthly ties to worry about or to distract them from their mission.

Those who have seen the Jesus Fellowship Church in operation may be more familiar with the name 'The Jesus Army' and the paramilitary style uniforms its members wear. The Jesus Army was established in 1987, not as an independent organization, but rather as the campaigning wing of the Jesus Fellowship Church. It has no independent existence, either in law or in terms of membership. Its inception was designed to give a visible presence to the work of the Jesus Fellowship Church, and, at a pragmatic level, the army-style uniforms provided an inexpensive form of clothing for members.

'Christians at war!' was the slogan on the Jesus Army's first venture, an Easter rally, at which members marched through Northampton with trumpets and drums and wearing their new uniforms, including scarves bearing the name 'Jesus Army', much to the surprise of the local inhabitants. The march ended at the Guildhall, where a 'commissioning' service took place. The Jesus Army's new manifesto was read out at this gathering, part of which runs as follows:

> The Jesus Army is the campaigning arm of the Jesus Fellowship Church. It is created in response to God's call for his church to be an army of his kingdom conquering the spiritual powers of darkness ...
>
> The Jesus Army campaigns aggressively against the social evils so common in our ungodly British society, and also against religious hypocrisy ...

The Jesus Army will go where others will not go. It will take the gospel to the 'forgotten people', the crowds outside the influence of Christian religion. It will bring healing to the sick and deliverance to the oppressed ...

The Jesus Army respects all Christians and churches, and will not deliberately compete. It will not however allow the necessary all-out offensive to be slowed down, nor the prophetic word silenced, because churches are defensive.

Jesus Army soldiers pledge full loyalty. They will receive any training to make victory possible and are committed to sacrifice and hardship ...

The Jesus Army unites believers into holy and loving church-communities, which show the end of all divisions and demonstrate a sharing lifestyle, true brotherhood, and a light to this world ... (Cooper and Farrant, 1997, pp. 243–4)

The concept of a spiritual army proliferated a host of military metaphors. 'Onward Christian Soldiers' was, of course, one of the hymns selected for the commissioning ceremony, and 'The Jesus Army declares War!' was the slogan used in the same year for a large rally at Battersea Park in London. As has become its practice, the Jesus Army erected its 1000-seater 'golden marquee' in the Park, and organized a 'March for Jesus' from Hyde Park to Trafalgar Square.

Other slogans included 'Love, Power and Sacrifice' – the slogan which is emblazoned on the Jesus Army's banners and on its fleet of buses which travel up and down the country – and 'Blood, Fire and Covenant'. Other militaristic allusions included the 'JAWBONE War Fund' ('JAWBONE' is an acronym for 'Jesus Army War Battle Operations Network'), 'Operation MARK – commandos', setting up 'battle stations', 'All out war', and – inevitably – 'blood, sweat and tears' (Cooper and Farrant, 1997, pp. 190, 236, 239).

Particularly at a time when some other churches are becoming embarrassed by militaristic imagery, it is not surprising that the Jesus Army has been accused of projecting a 'macho' image and being 'a Rambo cult'. Other religious organizations might well have been embarrassed by the following piece of publicity, which Cooper and Farrant describe:

We were now enamoured with the Army image. *Join Us!* carried a photo of an Irish lad: 'Sign Up! Mark has joined the Jesus Army!' The next one read: 'Urgent! Join the Jesus Rebellion' and showed a grinning street lad with a cross around his neck, badges, army jumper, and a broken nose! (Cooper and Farrant, 1997, p. 234)

Stanton has defended the use of such imagery, comparing the new Jesus Army to the older, better known, Salvation Army, and one Jesus Army leader has explained, 'The combat jackets are just the Church taking a militant stand against the evils of society. Like the Salvation Army we find that uniforms, flags and banners convey the message of Christ' (quoted in *Fair News*, October 1987). As another leader comments, 'It's spiritual warfare; it's not physical or violent in any way ... We are an army of love, power and sacrifice' (quoted in *Fair News*, Autumn 1988).

The Jesus Fellowship Church's mission is essentially one to the poor, the disadvantaged and the marginalized. Members ministered, both locally and further afield, to glue sniffers, pimps, prostitutes and criminals. Missions variously targeted the homeless (some work was done in 'Cardboard City' in London), the lonely and, on at least one occasion, gypsies. All this was not without its cost to members: two were arrested in Soho in London while trying to create opportunities to preach to those involved in the sex industry. Black people and Asians were also targeted: Cooper and Farrant note that on one occasion a young Sikh woman was converted, but that success with Asian and Afro-Caribbean communities was very limited. They also note that the biker and hippie elements tended to fall away after a short period, an observation which is endorsed by an independent commentator, who suggests that the Jesus Fellowship Church tended not to attract converts directly from the British subculture. He suggests that those who join had often already converted to Christianity and come through some intermediary spiritual home, wanting to deepen their commitment by entering a community whose lifestyle was more demanding.

Once a community was established, expansion was effected by means of the principle, 'grow, divide and plant' (Cooper and Farrant, 1997, p. 202). In 1977 two more community houses were opened, one in Daventry, Northamptonshire and another in a nearby village. As these cellular communities grew, a number of members would move off elsewhere to establish yet another residence, and by 1987 they had established 'battle stations' in over 20 British towns (*Fair News*, October 1987).

Joining a community entails handing over all one's wealth and possessions. However, there is a corollary to this: if someone who joins is in debt, the church may sometimes pay off what is owed, to enable the seeker to participate fully in the community's activities.

Styles of membership

The Jesus Fellowship Church offers the seeker a variety of levels of commitment. The loosest form of membership is that of the 'cultural disciple': these are people who are otherwise unchurched, but who come along occasionally. Some of them may still be on drugs or alcohol, having not yet renounced their old lifestyle. 'Cell group members' are those who attend a weeknight 'cell group' (usually on a Wednesday), but have other commitments on a Sunday, perhaps because of their work. 'Congregational members' attend on Sundays, but do little else for the church.

These forms of commitment fall short of the baptized member: it is the Jesus Fellowship Church's hope that people will be led to express their commitment to Christ by participating in this rite, which not only symbolizes cleansing – the obvious connotation of the water – but, as the apostle Paul asserted, is a recapitulation of the death and resurrection of Christ, in which the new convert proclaims death to his or her old life, and a rising to a new one (Romans 6:4). Over the years the Jesus Army – on its own acknowledgement – has slightly changed its stance on a candidate's eligibility for baptism. In the mid-1970s one had to give up smoking, for example, and prove oneself to be truly stable before one could be accepted for baptism. At the time of writing, some 25 years on, much more emphasis is placed on the power that baptism mediates: baptism is the power that enables a transformation of one's character, rather than a rite requiring purification as a prerequisite. At baptism one can experience being filled with the Holy Spirit, speaking in tongues, even miracles, but – perhaps especially – it brings the healing of hurts. One informant described how a member who had received a leg amputation after being run over by a bus came to terms with this cruel injury at his baptism; more commonly, however, members will testify that human relationships have been healed as a consequence, for example, resentments harboured by divorcees.

Stemming from the Baptist tradition, the Jesus Fellowship Church believes in adult, not child, baptism, since baptism entails a profession of commitment, which cannot be made by infants. Baptism is never administered to anyone less than 14 or 15 years old. It is done by total immersion, not by affusion: in this respect the Jesus Fellowship Church holds that it is being true to scripture and to the earliest New Testament practice, since scripture at no point records any instance of infant baptism or of sprinkling. If someone has been baptized by total immersion in another church, this is acceptable to the Jesus Army, who in any case would see re-baptism as contrary to scripture (Ephesians 4:5). Like The Family, the Jesus Fellowship Church does not claim to possess the sole means of salvation, but sees itself as part of the wider universal Church. Baptized members see the Jesus Fellowship Church as their church, at least for the foreseeable future, and they are attached to one of the Jesus Army households, and share in many of their activities.

The threshold of commitment for which the Jesus Army aims is that of the covenant member. A 'covenant' is a biblical concept, in which an agreement is made between God and his people; in the Jewish ('Old Testament') scriptures God makes covenants with Noah, Abraham, Jacob and Moses, offering promises of deliverance or salvation in return for obedience. In the New Testament Jesus is declared the mediator of the 'new covenant', offering redemption not in exchange for obedience to the law, but through his sacrificial death on the cross. The covenant, then, for the baptized member of the Jesus Fellowship Church is a profession of commitment, in which members are introduced on stage at a public service, and pledge their commitment for the rest of their life. They are offered the 'right hand of covenant' by a leader, and from then onwards are entitled to wear their personal Jesus Army jacket. (On occasions, a non-covenant member may borrow a jacket for a Jesus March, or some other event: covenanting confers the right of personal ownership.)

In all, there are four 'styles' of covenant membership. 'Style 1' is the non-resident, whose membership is similar to that of most members of a mainstream church. 'Style 2' are temporary guests within Jesus Army communities: those who stay for longer than a few days are asked to contribute towards their board and lodging, and have 'voluntary accountability of income over expenditure' (Jesus Fellowship Church, 1992, p. 2). This means that they can allow their finances to be scrutinized by their 'shepherd' and receive financial counselling. (Counselling is also offered on aspects of life such as time management.)

'Style 3' involves full residential community living, in which all income, wealth and possessions are shared. 'Style 4' membership is distance membership. Some members may be working abroad or living in some part of Britain that the Jesus Army has not yet reached. Others may be in prison, perhaps having met the Jesus Army before being sentenced for a past crime (Jesus Fellowship Church, 1992, p. 7).

One distinctive practice of the Jesus Army is the giving of 'virtue names' to its covenant members. Originally a device for distinguishing members who possessed the same forename, Jesus Army members are referred to variously as John 'Gentle', Steve 'Faithful', Mick 'Temperate' and so on, in place of their normal surnames. The practice applies equally to women, who bear names such as Stephanie 'Trusting', Helen 'Pioneering' and Debbie 'Refreshing'. The practice is perhaps more akin to giving someone a nickname, rather than the practice of giving 'spiritual names' which is employed by communities such as the Western Buddhist Order or ISKCON, although it serves to remind the member of an important virtue to maintain. The Bible also refers to a few individuals who underwent name changes (Abram to Abraham, Jacob to Israel, Simon to Peter, Saul to Paul), signifying entry into a new kind of life.

Living in a community entails a simple lifestyle, which enables members to deepen their spiritual commitment and to reduce contact with the outside world, except when campaigning. Alcohol is forbidden, although meat-eating is not, having been permitted by the early Church. (Cooper and Farrant mention one New Age vegetarian, who gave up his vegetarianism after joining in the interests of maintaining an authentic original Christian lifestyle.) Radios and televisions are not found within the community houses, and even reading newspapers is discouraged. The New Creation Christian Community (the JFC's community aspect) decided not to establish its own schools, but to allow children to participate in the state education system. Contact with other pupils is reduced, however: they are expected to come home at lunchtime, and are not permitted to participate in sport and drama. Competitive sports are generally prohibited within the Jesus Fellowship Church.

Within the Jesus Fellowship Church, men and woman have distinctive gender roles: Noel Stanton deplores present-day society's 'unisex' trend, whereby male and female roles become virtually indistinguishable. As Cooper and Farrant write:

> We valued individual character and refused the trend towards unisex, which we saw as unbiblical and psychologically off-beam. Equality between the sexes wasn't the point. Rather, it was being the personality God intended. Women began to enjoy their femininity more and

developed a strong sense of sisterhood. Brothers found that their manly sharing produced manliness and appreciated the friendship and reality of brotherhood. 'As iron sharpens iron,' said the wise man, 'so one man sharpens another.' (Proverbs 27:17; Cooper and Farrant, 1997, pp. 119–20)

Since men should look like men, beards are encouraged (but not obligatory), and short hair is preferable to long hair, which is deemed more becoming of a woman.

It is important that sexual feelings should not be a distraction to the community's mission. Women must therefore dress modestly, wearing dresses and not jeans, and the practice of sharing clothes helps to reduce any tendencies towards personal vanity. Cosmetics and jewellery are not permitted, with the exception of crosses. As the Bible says, 'Your beauty should not come from outward adornment ... Instead, it should be ... the unfading beauty of a gentle and quiet spirit' (1 Peter 3:3-4; quoted in Cooper and Farrant, 1997, p. 120).

Many of the New Creation Christian Community practise celibacy, which is described as 'a precious gem' (Cooper and Farrant, 1997, p. 150). As Paul said, 'Are you unmarried? Do not look for a wife' (1 Corinthians 7:27). This is certainly unusual within a Protestant group, since Protestantism has generally abandoned monasticism, extolling marriage and family life as ideals, and allowing, even encouraging, clergy and laity alike to marry. Celibacy and marriage are regarded as alternative lifestyles, and members are not pressurized to espouse one rather than the other. Some 200 members are committed to celibacy, plus a further 100 or so probationers, a commitment which is undertaken by making a public vow. Because it can be tempting to break or to reconsider a vow of celibacy, it is important that it should not be entered into lightly. There have been instances where committed celibates have subsequently entered into married life: in such situations it is possible to undergo marriage within the Jesus Fellowship Church, but there can be sanctions – for example, having one's leadership responsibilities reduced. It is therefore often recommended that a member undertakes 'committed singleness' without a vow, for a trial period, and normally celibate vows are not made until the member is at least 21. Another scenario is that one can vow to be a committed single up to the age of 25, and then take stock again of the desirability of such a lifestyle; a further alternative possibility is to make a vow for a probationary year. The celibacy vow is made publicly, and some members express this commitment by wearing a silver ring on the fourth finger of one hand. Stanton himself is a celibate, and the senior leadership is made up of roughly 50 per cent celibates and 50 per cent who are involved in family life.

There is a proper procedure for becoming married within a community. It is improper for a man directly to approach a woman and ask for a date: to do this would be to incur a 'flirtatious relationship'. The correct protocol is for marriage partners to be approved by the elders: this may be done either by elders suggesting possible marriage partners or by a 'relating procedure' (Cooper and Farrant, 1997, p. 149). If a brother is contemplating a relationship with a sister, he approaches the latter's pastor, who will then ascertain if any other male is interested in her; the sister can then decide which brother she should get to know first. The couple will then be permitted to spend some time together, after which they can decide whether or not a more permanent relationship between them is desirable.

Any religious community has the problem of how to sustain itself financially. Having been in the world of business, Stanton was able to help establish a number of businesses in the Northampton area for which full-time members work. These include Goodness Foods (a health food company founded in 1976); House of Goodness Ltd; Skaino Service (a building trade firm whose name derives from the Greek word *skenos,* meaning 'tent': Luke tells us the apostle Paul was a tentmaker); Towcester Building Supplies Ltd; Jeans Plus (a clothes shop); as well as some farming interests. Member-workers are paid a basic wage, but are encouraged to plough money back into the movement. Since JFC is a mission to the disadvantaged, collections are not taken at meetings. Although anti-cult critics often harbour the suspicion that a movement's leader benefits financially from any business interests, Noel Stanton, in common with all the other JFC members, has transferred his assets to the community (Cooper and Farrant, 1997, p. 118).

Christian group or NRM?

Is the Jesus Army an expression of mainstream Christianity, or is it a new religious movement? In terms of its message, the Jesus Fellowship Church is a fundamentalist Christian group, accepting, in common with mainstream conservative evangelical Christians, the inerrancy of scripture, and rejecting theories such as evolution on the grounds that they are in conflict with the Bible's authority. Unlike the Mormon Church, the organization does not add to scripture, and Noel Stanton, unlike Unificationist leader Sun Myung Moon, claims no special revelation that is not accessible to any other member. Unlike the Jehovah's Witnesses, the Jesus Army does not regard the traditional Christian creeds as being in conflict with or subsequent accretions that go beyond the Bible: in this respect the Jesus Army is more 'orthodox' even than other Baptist churches, who are not formally committed to any credal affirmation. Although the average Jesus Army member is not a trained theologian, and – like most Christians – is somewhat vague about the relationship between creeds and scripture, the Apostles' Creed is sometimes sung as a favourite song, and its contents are at least known and accepted.

Although Jesus Army members may look distinctive, the organization is not exclusivist, acknowledging that salvation may be obtained in the Christian Church more widely. The baptism of other churches is acknowledged and accepted, with the proviso that it must be of adults and by total immersion – a position which is no different from the Baptist Church as a whole. Indeed its leader Noel Stanton was trained within and was accredited by the Baptist Church.

However, the Jesus' Army's main difficulties stem from its relationship with the Baptist Union and the Evangelical Alliance in Britain. Although local Baptist churches are self-governing and autonomous, most of them belong to the Baptist Union, an organization that oversees and co-ordinates the interests and work of Baptist churches at a national level. Being a local Baptist church in origin, the Bugbrooke Jesus Fellowship had belonged to the Baptist Union. In 1986 they were expelled, for three reasons. The first and main problem related to the Jesus Fellowship Church's institutional structures: church government and authority in the Baptist Church is normally from a single congregation, whereas the enthusiastic – some would say aggressive – evangelizing of the Jesus Army had caused it to become a nationwide organization: it had become the wrong kind of institution to affiliate to the Baptist Union. Second, its membership of the Baptist Union had been nominal for a number of years, since the Jesus Army's evangelical missions and work amidst the counter-culture took precedence over denominational matters.

Third, the Baptist Union had found the amount of adverse publicity embarrassing. The rise of the Jesus Fellowship Church began shortly before the Jonestown massacre, which caused the vast majority of people in the USA and Europe to be suspicious of new 'cults'. It was also unfortunate for them that their rise coincided with the inception of Family Action Information and Rescue (FAIR) in 1976. FAIR carefully and consistently monitored the Jesus Fellowship Church's development, even from its early Bugbrooke days, giving it adverse publicity in its quarterly magazine *FAIR News*. Not only did FAIR give prominence to the fact that many members handed over all their possessions to the Church, and to its disputes with the Baptist Union and Evangelical Alliance, unjustly portraying Stanton as an authoritarian leader who claimed an exclusive 'hotline to God', the untimely deaths of three young members – two in rather strange, although not suspicious, circumstances – helped to fuel fears about this new charismatic group (Cooper and Farrant, 1997, pp. 130–1, 142).

Similar considerations affected the Jesus Army's relationship with the Evangelical Alliance, where a number of member churches threatened that they would pull out if the Jesus Fellowship Church was allowed to remain in. After discussions with the Evangelical Alliance's leaders, the Jesus Fellowship Church thought it best to resign in 1985. The JFC was therefore left on the margins of the Baptist denomination, although ironically one Baptist minister was at the time living within the JFC on sabbatical.

The militaristic imagery in itself should not make the Jesus Army sectarian or 'cultic', since war metaphors are not uncommon in Christianity, going right back to the New Testament itself. The writer to the Ephesians talks about putting on 'the full armour of God ... the belt of truth buckled around your waist, with the breastplate of righteousness ... the shield of faith ... the helmet of salvation and the sword of the Spirit, which is the word of God', explaining that 'our struggle is not against flesh and blood, but against the rulers, against the authorities, against the powers of this dark world and against the spiritual forces of evil in the heavenly realms' (Ephesians 6:13–17). However, although some Christians may maintain that 'Onward Christian Soldiers' encapsulates the Christian's conflict better than the image of the Christian peacemaker, the combat uniforms certainly single out the Jesus Army member from other British denominations. A century earlier, the Salvation Army found similar problems about winning confidence in certain circles on account of their military-style organization and uniforms, and has only recently gained acceptance within mainstream Councils of Churches.

Equally important in contributing to the Jesus Army's distinctive identity is their community living, their common sharing of possessions, their commitment to a life of poverty and, in many cases, celibacy. Although some forms of Christianity such as Roman Catholicism have their monastic orders, monasticism is only one wing of this branch of the Church. Christianity, especially in most of its Protestant varieties, has been world-affirming, and, apart from the clergy, its members have combined their Christian faith with secular employment and living within the 'fallen' world. In a world where 'serial monogamy' is the norm and in churches where marriage and family life are the most highly favoured forms of human relationship, a religious community with different ideals seems an oddity. Having said this, members of the Jesus Army will often point to the fact that the mainstream Christian denominations' emphasis on the family, such as advertising 'family services', serves to exclude those for whom family life is not the norm: the single, the homeless, the divorced and so on. By insisting on practising a radical expression of Christianity, and energetically promoting it, the Jesus Army certainly presents a form of the Christian faith which mainstream Christians are bound to find disconcerting.

Conclusion

It is remarkable that one should find so many different attempts to express Christianity in the New Christian movements. Of the three organizations considered in this chapter, the Unification Church is clearly the most radical, teaching the incomplete mission of Jesus, a new messiah and a new definitive religious text. The Judaeo-Christian scriptures, being complex and multifaceted, raise considerable problems of interpretation and generate (real or apparent) contradictions. The Unification Church cuts through all problems of interpretation by making Moon's revelations the final arbiter of religious truth, and by suggesting that parts of the Bible are symbolic rather than literal. The Family and the Jesus Army, by contrast, are expressions of Christian fundamentalism, and hence are committed to a literal belief in the entire Bible – with the obvious exceptions of clearly intended metaphors and parables. This generates obvious problems: for example, should a believer in the Bible practise celibacy or enjoy multiple sex partners? On this question, The Family appeals to the Old Testament, while the theologically more conservative Jesus Army appeals to the practice of Jesus and the early Church.

Allied to belief in the Bible is belief in prophecy. The three groups I have considered show gradations in their attitudes to prophecy. The Unification Church does not talk about having prophets, and simply uses the term historically to describe key figures in the Old Testament. By virtue of the claim that its founder-leader is no mere prophet but the messiah, the Lord of the Second Advent, there can be no higher human authority. A prophet is someone who speaks on God's behalf: as we have seen, the UC teaches that it is not simply God who communicates with humanity, but spirits. With such possibilities of access to the spirit world, present-day prophecy becomes unnecessary. By contrast, The Family, which acknowledges no new messiah, but accepts the prophethood of Moses David, tends to regard his role as a definitive interpreter of God's word. Although his pronouncements on sex may seem startling to those outside the organization, they are nonetheless offered as interpretations of scripture, and draw attention to Old Testament ideas – for example, about polygamy – which Christians tend simply to ignore. The Jesus Army seldom speaks of prophecy, but more typically views the Church as the bearer of the prophetic role, pointing out social ills and caring for the under-privileged. The Jesus Army, therefore, tends not to kindle interest in eclipsed passages in scripture, but – although committed to the inerrancy of scripture – focuses on its less problematic components, in common with the majority of Christian fundamentalists.

Innovation tends to lead to exclusivity. The Unification Church, by virtue of its new revelations, can claim that its Blessing ceremony is the sole vehicle for entry into the Kingdom of Heaven. At the other extreme, the theologically conservative Jesus Army claims to offer teachings that do not differ substantially from those of Protestant Christianity more widely. The Family stands between these two extremes: it is innovative, but claims not to deny Christianity's fundamental teachings, and hence does not offer the sole path to salvation. Of the three movements, it is the Jesus Army, being the most orthodox, that is currently the most likely to gain recognition by mainstream Christians in the foreseeable future.

5. New religions in the Hindu tradition

Western converts and the Hindu tradition

To claim that any religion in the Hindu tradition is a new religion is highly problematic. Several Hindu NRMs claim an ancient lineage: for example, the International Society for Krishna Consciousness (ISKCON) can certainly trace its origins to the Gaudiya Math movement of the nineteenth century, and plausibly to Chaitanya (*c.* 1485–1533). If ISKCON devotees are correct, the movement goes back even further, to Krishna himself, who is deemed to have lived some five thousand years ago.

In a previous chapter I identified a defining characteristic of NRMs as being outside the mainstream. This immediately raises the question of how we are to identify any 'mainstream Hinduism' among a miscellany of diverse and loosely structured forms of Indian spirituality. Although theoretically Hinduism originates in the Vedas and the Upanishads, the four ancient Vedas (the Rig Veda, the Sama Veda, the Atharva Veda and the Yajur Veda) are not used as part of living Hinduism. The later texts, the Upanishads, admit of a wide variety of interpretations, giving rise to the *dvaita* (personalist) and *advaita* (impersonalist) understandings of God, emanating from the respective schools of Shankara (trad. 788-820 CE) and Ramanuja (*c.* 11/12 CE) respectively. Whether or not one regards God as personal has repercussions regarding one's spiritual path (yoga), and Hindus may variously pursue *jnana yoga* (the path of wisdom or insight), *bhakti yoga* (the path of devotion), or *karma yoga* (the path of action). As far as devotion is concerned, the various forms of Hindu deity are many. One can identify some main strands of devotionalism such as Vaishnavism (devotion to Vishnu), Saivism (devotion to Shiva), the shakti cults which worship the deity in male and female aspects, and the cult of Kali, but there is no uniform path of devotion, and in any case the Hindu-related NRMs can usually be classified within these broad categories. Even a concept like caste does not flow uniformly through Indian culture: although it offers a means of organizing Indian society, there are forms of Indian spirituality which have either claimed that true caste is related to one's level of spirituality or denied the reality of caste altogether.

If the Hindu religions had remained confined to India or to ethnically Indian communities in the west, questions of orthodoxy and unorthodoxy might not have arisen. For expatriate Hindus the problems of practising Hinduism in Europe and the USA are almost entirely pragmatic. In the early days of immigration, problems of maintaining one's religious identity consisted of finding a suitable meeting place for worship, purchasing premises for a temple, securing its acceptance as a legitimate place to conduct marriages, perhaps raising money and making arrangements to have a qualified priest preside over the temple's congregation, maintaining one's traditional rites of passage, and so on.

For a westerner wishing to convert to Hinduism, however, it is a very different story. A white westerner does not already belong to a Hindu religious community, but has probably read books on religion, and possibly Hindu scriptures such as the Upanishads or the Bhagavad Gita. He or she may well have come across key concepts such as reincarnation, and been attracted to them in preference to the views of the dominant religion – Christianity – concerning life after death. The starting point probably lies in the ideas rather than the practice, and therefore the version of Hinduism that the westerner has is probably an intellectualized one. Propitiating devas to fend off smallpox, exorcising evil spirits or using astrological charts to fix the date of a family wedding are not live concerns. Many educated Hindus today regard such practices as superstitions, and some have even given up their religion as a consequence.

Even if the western seeker decides to pursue his or her studies of Hinduism by finding a place of worship, a traditional Hindu temple poses several difficulties. Most obviously, a white westerner will stand out, not only as someone who is different from the rest of the worshippers, but as someone who plainly has lived most of his or her life outside the Hindu tradition. There is evidence, too, that Hindus,

Muslims and Sikhs in the west tend to group into communities on the grounds of their ethnicity, perhaps even to a greater degree than the religious tradition to which they belong. However welcoming a Hindu congregation may be, the western enquirer will always remain visibly an outsider.

Allied to ethnicity is language, which again proves a formidable barrier to western seekers. Worship in a Hindu temple will tend to be conducted in Indian languages such as Gujarati or Bengali, and when scriptures are used the language will be Sanskrit. Western seekers are likely to gain little by attaching themselves to a community where the liturgical language almost totally precludes any understanding.

Finally, there is the phenomenon of caste. Although differences of belief can be found amongst Indian religious communities, most Indians have a caste, which is determined exclusively by one's birth. For most westerners the whole notion of caste is problematic, and even writers such as John Hick, who are normally empathetic to faiths other than Christianity, describe caste as an evil. Even if westerners can surmount intellectual and moral objections to caste, the insurmountable problem is finding a caste niche in which to fit, for unless one is born into a caste one has no caste at all.

For westerners who are interested in forms of Hinduism, but are likely to find these factors problematical, Hindu-related NRMs offer an attractive alternative. By virtue of the fact that many who join are white, there need be no fear of standing out from any expatriate Hindu community. Because Hindu NRMs accept westerners there is no need to belong to an Indian ethnic group or any caste. The language which is spoken is generally the vernacular. Although organizations like ISKCON will often quote the Bhagavad Gita and the Srimad Bhagavatam in their original Sanskrit, this is done more for the effect of assuring the largely western congregation that they are going back to the original meaning of these texts, and the Sanskrit is always translated for the audience.

However one assesses their 'orthodoxy', the three movements discussed in this chapter (ISKCON, Sai Baba and Brahma Kumaris) are certainly new in terms of the age of the organization, and, unlike most expressions of Hinduism in India and overseas, they stand out in terms of their large western following.

ISKCON

Although the International Society for Krishna Consciousness – better known to the public as the 'Hare Krishna' movement – regards itself an ancient religion going back several thousands of years, its historically traceable ancestry is inevitably much later. Certainly, Krishna Consciousness as a religious movement goes back as far as the Indian saint Chaitanya (*c.* 1485–1533), and of course the myths of Krishna themselves are to be found in the Bhagavad Gita and the Srimad Bhagavatam. The dating of these texts is a matter for debate, and western estimates of the date of the Bhagavad Gita vary from 600 BCE to around 250 CE. (ISKCON devotees, however, place the writing of the Bhagavad Gita at around 3000 BCE.)

Chaitanya

Chaitanya was certainly a historical figure, his original name being Vishvambhara Misra. He was born in Bengal, but came to be known as the 'golden avatar', the avatar of the kali yuga, who is popularly worshipped in Navadwip in Bengal. The name 'golden avatar' alludes to the way in which he is depicted in Hindu iconography: he is fair rather than dark, and typically painted in yellow or gold, in contrast to Krishna who is traditionally dark, and portrayed in a blue colour. Chaitanya, however, is not a separate deity from Krishna, but is said to be jointly the avatar of Krishna and Radha.

Chaitanya was originally a scholar and a teacher. However, his direction in life changed radically after visiting Gaya when he was 22 years old to perform funeral rites on behalf of his father. There he met Ishvara Puri, a devotee of Krishna, who initiated him with a Krishna mantra. After this he became a 'Krishna-intoxicated ecstatic' (Brooks, 1992, p. 45), leading kirtans and chanting, dancing and even inducing trance states in devotion to Krishna. Chaitanya thus became the focus of a new Krishna cult, and is accredited with having taught the 'maha mantra', made famous by ISKCON devotees:

Hare Krishna; Hare Krishna
Krishna Krishna; Hare Hare
Hare Rama; Hare Rama
Rama Rama; Hare Hare.

In 1510 he became initiated as a sannyasin, and, at the young age of 24, left his family behind in pursuit of devotion to Krishna and in spreading Krishna Consciousness. From this point onwards he became known as 'Sri Krishna Chaitanya', meaning 'one who awakens the spirit of Krishna in his heart' (Brooks, 1992, p. 46). Chaitanya's followers taught the supremacy of Krishna. Six of them were particularly close disciples of Chaitanya: they became known as the 'six goswamis', and all but one wrote commentaries on the Vedas and Puranas; they are often depicted in Hindu art as dancing ecstatically with Chaitanya.

The Chaitanya movement extolled the virtues of honouring Krishna by bhakti, renouncing one's secular life in order to follow the path of devotion, and the visiting of shrines. Special attention was given to those scriptures that told of Krishna: Chaitanya was principally influenced by the Srimad Bhagavatam, which recounts the exploits of Krishna and the gopis (the milkmaids) in the region of Govardhan. Chaitanya and his followers renounced caste, as was taught in the Srimad Bhagavatam: true religion, they taught, stems from one's inner nature and devotion. They declined to wear the sacred thread, which is characteristic of the higher castes in India, and accepted full commensality with everyone, regardless of their status. Chaitanya and his followers were vegetarian, avoiding all meat and fish, and renouncing worship of deities who demanded animal sacrifice. Contact was to be avoided with those who sacrificed animals.

From an early age, Chaitanya had expressed a desire to visit the city of Vrindaban. He finally achieved this in 1515. His chief disciple Lokanath prepared the ground for this visit, 'reclaiming' several sacred sites and establishing the Gokulananda Temple there. On his arrival, Chaitanya designated the locations of the principal events in Krishna's life, where they remain places of pilgrimage. Although ISKCON devotees firmly believe in the authenticity of these sites, it is debatable whether such sacred places ever existed before Chaitanya designated them as such. Chaitanya's presence in Vrindaban also served, in the course of time, to establish sacred sites that commemorated incidents in his own life, for example, the tamarind tree under which he is said to have chanted daily.

Vrindaban now is the home of ISKCON's international head-quarters, where its impressive Krishna-Balaram temple was opened by Prabhupada in 1975. The city is compact and intimate, with a total population of around 30,000. Six miles south of Vrindaban lies the town of Mathura, which is said to be the site of Krishna's birth, and a journey of a further 12 miles brings the pilgrim to Govardhan, where Krishna is said to have lifted Govardhan Hill with his little finger, in order to protect humanity from the god Indra's storms.

Little is known about Vrindaban before the time of Chaitanya, although probably it was principally a forest in his time. 'Vrindaban' is the name of Krishna's paradise, thus imposing on the community the very name of the spiritual goal to which human beings should aspire. The earthly Vrindaban thus represents Krishna's plan for the world, which is often characterized in Hindu theology as *lila* – literally, 'sport' or 'play' – thus indicating that God created the world initially for his own pleasure. Consequently it is important, as ISKCON devotees concur, to live one's life and perform one's devotion in such a way as to please God. The Puranas relate the tales of Krishna, Radha and the gopis in and around this holy city, and thus this particular part of the physical world has become in a very literal sense the setting for God's lila. Krishna enjoys life; he flirts and dances with the gopis, and some of the stories have erotic connotations – for example, the incident in which he stole their clothes while they were bathing in the River Jamuna, and refused to return them until they performed due obeisance to him. This story combines the themes of love, play (lila) and devotion (bhakti). It is worth noting that the emphasis on the Puranas, which is found in the Chaitanya movement and preserved within ISKCON, is because these texts demonstrate the way in which bhakti should be conducted. The Bhagavad Gita, which is the text more generally studied by scholars and students outside this movement, was regarded as highly important by Prabhupada, but tends to illustrate Krishna's divine nature itself, rather than the means that one should use to venerate him.

Gaudiya Math

Religious ecstasy can be difficult to maintain, and during the seventeenth century the Chaitanya movement lost much of its original ecstatic zeal. A later Hindu movement, the Gaudiya Sampradaya, subsequently arose as an attempt to revive Chaitanyite ecstasy, and proved to be an important influence on ISKCON's inception.

The Gaudiya Math organization was founded in 1918 by Bhaktisiddhanta Saraswati, and has been described as 'the first organised monastic institution within Vaishnavism' (Brooks, 1992, p. 87). It sought to revive and renew Chaitanyaism, encouraging devotion, abolition of caste distinctions and a veneration of the sacred sites associated with Krishna, Radha and Chaitanya. One of its practices was to encourage an annual circumambulation of Vrindaban.

Prabhupada's relationship with the Gaudiya Math movement is difficult to untangle. After Bhaktisiddhanta's death, there were disputes over the mission's ownership, although apparently Prabhupada staked no claim on it. What is more important to ISKCON is Prabhupada's disciplic succession (parampara) which he traces back to this mission. It is particularly important in the Hindu tradition that a guru should be able to trace an accredited lineage of teachers in order to establish his own credentials as an authentic teacher and as one who passes on the body of teaching entrusted to him, without addition or alteration. ISKCON temples will typically contain pictures of Prabhupada beside three other gurus who make up the lineage: Bhaktisiddhanta (1873–1936), Srila Srila Bhaktivinoda Thakura (1838–1914), and Gaurkishor Das Babaji. As has been mentioned, Bhaktisiddhanta was the founder of the Gaudiya Math mission, Bhaktivinoda was his father, and Gaurkishor was an illiterate ascetic who initiated Bhaktisiddhanta in 1900.

Prabhupada's translation of the *Bhagavad-Gita As It Is* sets out the disciplic succession, claiming an unbroken lineage extending back through Chaitanya himself to Krishna. However, there are problems regarding the *parampara* immediately preceding Prabhupada. It is alleged that Bhaktisiddhanta did not receive direct initiation from Bhaktivinoda Thakura, but through a dream or perhaps through a self-initiation in front of an image of the guru. Prabhupada himself did not accept his sannyasa vows until some two years after Bhaktisiddhanta's death, when the latter appeared to him in a dream. If this is the case, then this calls into question the legitimacy of the *parampara* both for the Gaudiya Math and for ISKCON. When controversies about the succession first emerged, a few ISKCON devotees left the movement to find a guru who had a greater claim to a direct lineage. Others, however, regard such 'mystical' initiations as superior to the more usual ones: Brooks records one of his informants as saying, 'The proof is in the pudding.

What if the initiation was in a dream? In my mind a mystical initiation is cent per cent better' (Brooks, 1992, p. 87n; Satsvarupa, 1983, p. xxxi).

Prabhupada

Prabhupada certainly took over Bhaktisiddhanta's mission to bring Krishna Consciousness to the west. Born in Calcutta, his original secular name was Abhay Charan De (1896–1977), the son of a cloth merchant. An astrologer predicted that, at the age of 70, Abhay would cross the ocean. The family worshipped in the Radha-Govinda Temple, which was 'pure Vaishnava'.

In 1922 Abhay met for the first time Bhaktisiddhanta, who invited him to become a preacher. Three years later, he visited Vrindaban on a pilgrimage, and eventually in 1932 Abhay received *diksha* (first initiation) from Bhaktisiddhanta. Bhaktisiddhanta told Abhay, 'If you ever get money, print books.' Thus book distribution assumes a high degree of importance in ISKCON: Prabhupada's ambition was to replace 'mundane' literature with 'transcendental' material; in each home there should be at least one piece of literature on Krishna Consciousness.

The outbreak of the Second World War had an inevitable impact upon the mission. Abhay had started to produce *Back to Godhead,* which continues to be ISKCON's principal journal, but paper was rationed and Abhay had insufficient funds to produce regular issues. Copies appeared on an occasional basis, duplicated from stencils. In the period immediately after the war, Abhay's business began to fail. He had problems with his home life too: his wife was unsupportive, and he continually reprimanded her for drinking tea. (Tea, containing caffeine, is unacceptable to ISKCON devotees.) Abhay, it is said, returned home one day and discovered that his wife had sold his only copy of the Srimad Bhagavatam in order to buy some tea biscuits. He left her, and took his poor material fortunes as a signal to move on to the spiritual life.

In 1956 Abhay took up residence in Vrindaban, to make arrangements for the continued existence of the magazine. It was at this stage that Abhay had his dream: his guru Bhaktisiddhanta appeared to him, inviting him to take the sannyasin vows. Abhay agreed, and his decision was followed by a ceremony in Vrindaban,

after which he became known as Abhay Caranaravinda Bhaktivedanta Swami (Satsvarupa, 1983, p. xxxii). His name, as it appears in
his translations and commentaries, is more usually given as A.C.
Bhaktivedanta Swami Prabhupada. 'Prabhupada' means 'one at
whose feet (pada) there are many Prabhus', and 'one who is always
found at the lotus feet of Krishna' (Satsvarupa, 1983, p. 158).
Devotees normally refer to him affectionately as 'Srila Prabhupad'.

Prabhupada came to believe that a more permanent record of
teachings about Krishna was needed, beyond oral teachings, leaflets
and magazines. He resolved to translate the Srimad Bhagavatam and
add his commentary to it. This was an ambitious project: the Srimad
Bhagavatam comprises 12 cantos, and contains some 18,000 verses:
this would require at least 60 volumes, and between five and seven
years' constant work. Would-be authors know only too well the
sheer difficulty of persuading publishers to commission even a single
seemingly promising volume: a publisher needs to be persuaded that
there is a likely readership to make the book sell, and that the author
can inspire confidence that he or she will produce a competent piece
of writing. Measured against such criteria, Prabhupada's project
looked decidedly unpromising. However, Prabhupada had one
important advantage: he could claim *parampara;* no other aspiring
writer could claim to transmit ancient knowledge in an unbroken
lineage.

Prabhupada commenced work in Vrindaban. By 1965 Prabhupada
had brought out three volumes, through a little-known publisher.
Then a sponsor, who was the head of Scindia Steamship Lines,
provided him with a free journey from Calcutta to New York on a
freight steamer. Prabhupada was thus in a position to commence his
mission to the west, which brought him to fame (Brooks, 1992, p.
75).

Prabhupada arrived at New York harbour in 1965, with only 40
rupees in cash and 20 dollars from book sales to the captain
(Satsvarupa, 1983, p. 5). After residing for a short period with a
sponsor in Pennsylvania, Prabhupada moved to New York City,
taking up residence in an area that was frequented by the younger
'hippie' generation. He shortly found a disused shop called
Matchless Gifts. ('Matchless Gifts' remains the name under which
some of ISKCON's products are marketed.) It was there that
Prabhupada founded the International Society for Krishna Consciousness, and advertised lectures on the Bhagavad Gita. In the

course of these classes, his audience, many of whom had been on LSD, peyote and 'magic mushrooms' were introduced to the 'Hare Krishna' chant. Two important events served to bring Prabhupada to wider public attention. A 'Mantra-Rock Dance', organized in San Francisco in 1967, attended by the poet Allen Ginsberg and Timothy Leary, the celebrated psychedelic author of the 1960s, and at which a number of leading rock groups performed, included dancing to the Hare Krishna Maha Mantra. Prabhupada was there, and, despite his position as a Hindu swami, joined in. Ginsberg addressed the audience, and extolled the advantages of Krishna Consciousness as a means of stabilizing re-entry for those who wanted to come off drugs. Prabhupada had taught his psychedelic enquirers that Krishna Consciousness could enable the devotee to acquire an 'all-time' high that was not dependent on constant drug taking. One ISKCON handbill read: 'Stay high forever! No more coming down. Practice Krishna Consciousness. Expand your consciousness by practicing the Transcendental Sound Vibration' (Satsvarupa, 1983, p. 72). Not only did the Maha Mantra Rock Dance enable Krishna Consciousness to gain wider public attention, but the event raised some 2000 dollars for the new San Francisco ISKCON temple.

A further important impetus for ISKCON was provided by the Beatles. They had gained publicity by going to India in 1968 to meet the Maharishi Mahesh Yogi, the guru of Transcendental Meditation. In the same year Beatle George Harrison met a devotee at Apple Records (ISKCON was deliberately trying to making contact with the group), and this led to Harrison's recording of 'My Sweet Lord'. In 1969 the Beatles hosted Prabhupada in England. When Prabhupada's first volume of the trilogy *Krsna* was published in 1973, it contained a foreword by George Harrison, and sold well amongst the young concert-goers. Also, in 1973, Harrison purchased Bhaktivedanta Manor on ISKCON's behalf: previously devotees had met in a modest flat near London's British Museum. This imposing building was converted into a shrine and a training college for sannyasins, and remains ISKCON's British headquarters.

During the period 1970–3 ISKCON succeeded in opening no less than 21 temples. ISKCON's temples now include the Mayapur Chandrodaya Mandir (also known as the Temple of Human Understanding), which is ISKCON's world headquarters. Since it is Chaitanya's birthplace, it is planned to make Mayapur 'the spiritual capital of the world' and 'a model for all other cities'

(Satsvarupa, 1983, pp. 223, 266). In Vrindaban, Prabhupada opened the Krishna Balaram Madir, the city's largest temple, in 1975. Another ISKCON temple, recently opened in Bombay, is said to be the largest Hindu temple in the world.

ISKCON teachings

When Prabhupada founded ISKCON, he initially considered the phrase 'God consciousness' as part of the title, the word 'God' of course being more familiar to westerners than to Krishna devotees. He swiftly rejected this idea, believing that the word 'God' had insufficiently personal connotations. What is important for the ISKCON devotee is to realize that God has personality, and that the form Krishna is the supreme representation of this form. This is not to declare totally wrong the impersonalist tradition that is represented by Shankara and his followers, but rather to understand that any impersonal characteristics emanate from the person of God, rather than vice versa.

The belief that Krishna is primordial entails that all other forms of deity are really forms of Krishna. Western textbooks – as well as many Vaishnavites – typically teach that there are ten principal avatars of Vishnu, and that he has appeared at various times in human history (variously in the form of a fish, a turtle, a boar, a lion-man, a dwarf, a brahmin, Rama, Krishna and the Buddha, with Kalki as the coming avatar). The teaching of Gaudiya Math and of ISKCON is that it is not Vishnu who is primordial, but Krishna, and that all the principal avatars are actually forms of Krishna, with Vishnu as an emanation. (Vishnu emanating from Krishna is described in the great theophany passage in chapter 11 of the Bhagavad Gita.)

Thus the most important aspect of Krishna Consciousness is devotion (bhakti) to Krishna. A mantra typically has power rather than literal meaning, and devotees believe that, even if one chants the mantra in ignorance of its significance, it is still enormously efficacious. Prabhupada's explanation of the mantra's meaning was that 'Hare' meant 'O energy of the Lord', the word 'Lord' referring to Krishna. 'Rama', he explained, is also a name of the Supreme Lord, meaning 'the highest pleasure'. Great claims are made concerning the power of bhakti and of the Maha Mantra.

Prabhupada insisted that bhakti was the only way to change karma, and that chanting 'Hare Krishna' is 'the only panacea for all material diseases', the antidote to societal ills such as poverty and crime (Satsvarupa, 1983, pp. 81, 273, 316–17).

The mantra is recited using 'japa beads', usually made from the sacred tulsi plant, with 108 beads on a string. (108 is a sacred number in Hinduism and Buddhism.) The required number of 'rounds' is 16: in other words, one is required to chant the mantra once on every bead, 108 beads constituting a 'round'; the devotee thus recites the mantra 1728 times each day, an activity which takes around two hours. This chanting need not be done at one continuous stretch, but can be carried out as one walks around, as well as in a temple. At first Prabhupada prescribed 64 rounds a day, claiming that his spiritual master Bhaktisiddhanta had declared that anyone who did less was 'fallen'. However, when Prabhupada's western followers protested, he finally agreed that 16 rounds would suffice (Satsvarupa, 1983, p. 60).

The practice of chanting 16 rounds a day is a firm obligation only to initiates, however. Like many religious movements one can belong at various levels: ordinary membership simply involves payment of a subscription and entitlement to the receipt of information and discounts on ISKCON merchandise. Those who are initiated, however, take on four additional vows: (1) avoidance of meat, fish and eggs; (2) no intoxicants or stimulants; (3) no illicit sex; and (4) no gambling.

The fourth vow is self-explanatory, but some comment is needed about the others. Being committed to non-violence, ISKCON holds that respect should be shown to all living beings, and hence a vegetarian diet is required. Although this includes the avoidance of fish and eggs (an egg being a potential form of life), the ISKCON diet is not vegan, and the consumption of dairy products is actually encouraged. To those who suggest that the production of milk and butter exploits animals, devotees would reply that, although dairy farming can be exploitative, ISKCON communities often keep their own cows, thus demonstrating that this is possible. Many devotees support cow protection programmes: since the cow is a sacred animal in India many Hindus regard it as quite unacceptable to kill a cow when her productive life is ended, and cow protection programmes ensure that a 'retired' cow continues to enjoy a good life, even when she is no longer economically beneficial to humans.

Meat-eating does not only involve direct violence to the animal whose life is forfeited. ISKCON also teaches that meat-eating encourages human aggression, and contributes to human conflict and war. It is worth recalling that ISKCON's inception in the west coincided with the American involvement in the Vietnam conflict, and that Prabhupada saw Krishna Consciousness as a practical means of ending military confrontation.

Food is also associated with the Hindu doctrine of the three *gunas* (literally, 'strands' – aspects which are found throughout the entire physical and mental world). The Bhagavad Gita teaches that everything in the universe is a mixture (in varying degrees) of *sattva* (the light or perfect element), *rajas* (the fiery or aggressive) and *tamas* (the dull or ignorant). It is therefore important to eat 'sattvic' food – vegetarian, of the highest quality – and to avoid foods that contain the two lower elements. Highly spiced foods or meat products can thus give rise to aggression, while other foods can dull the mind and impair one's spiritual practice. Not only does Krishna Consciousness prohibit meat, but devotees will not eat mushrooms, onions and garlic, since these are believed to cloud the mind.

The second principle – the avoidance of intoxicants and stimulants – prescribes the avoidance of drugs that alter one's state of consciousness, either by dulling it (as with alcohol and some recreational drugs) or over-stimulating it (as happens with caffeine). Devotees will not drink tea or coffee, or introduce drugs like nicotine into their system by smoking tobacco. Drugs that are prescribed by a medical doctor are acceptable, although ISKCON prefers Ayurvedic medicine – the traditional remedies that have been used in India.

The third principle (the avoidance of illicit sex) goes further than simply forbidding fornication and adultery: even within marriage sex may only be used for the deliberate purpose of procreation. This goes considerably further than the traditional Roman Catholic position, where 'unnatural' contraception is forbidden. ISKCON devotees by contrast must only have intercourse at those times when procreation is likely. This rule applies to those who have taken the first initiation (*diksha*). Those who have undertaken the second initiation, as a sannyasin, are committed to complete celibacy. Sex can therefore be part of one's spiritual journey (ISKCON even allows the concept of the 'householder priest'), but it is something that should ultimately be transcended. Until the devotee is ready for such a decision, sex is something that is 'spiritualized' (although not something inherently spiritual). As one devotee explained, the sex act is inviting children into the world: they already exist, since all living beings are subject to the process of reincarnation.

Marriage is therefore permissible within ISKCON. In contrast with the practice of Indians and expatriate Hindus, marriages are not arranged, but permission must first be obtained from the Temple president. The president can arrange introductions, if these are sought. Since the purpose of sex is procreation, homosexuality is disapproved of, and may not be actively practised. I am told that there are many homosexuals who are connected with ISKCON: pop star Boy George is one well-known example, but his support of the movement by no means implies that ISKCON supports homosexuality.

Clearly the observation of these four principles is demanding, and in ISKCON's early days required a complete reversal of the lifestyle of the former hippies. Prabhupada refused to compromise his message for American youth culture, since this was the 'parampara message of Krishna Consciousness' (Satsvarupa, 1983, pp. 85, 102).

Equally demanding is the members' lifestyle. For the full-time devotee in an ISKCON temple the day begins at 4 a.m., when the deity is awakened. An *arati* (worship ceremony using incense, flowers and fire) will take place, after which devotees will shower before having breakfast. Members will undertake their particular tasks: some will distribute Krishna Consciousness literature in town centres, while others are engaged in visiting schools. (ISKCON organizes education programmes for teachers and educators.) Others will be involved with the general running of the temple, ensuring that it is suitably maintained. Some devotees will be designated the task of attending to the deities: ISKCON is strict in ensuring that, once murtis (images of deities) are installed in a Krishna temple, they are dressed meticulously and regularly (twice daily in the case of their larger temples). Devotees must also ensure that regular puja (worship) and kirtan (congregational singing) are carried out at the appropriate times: in the early and late morning, at noon, in the afternoon, at dusk and at night. The number of ceremonies and the elaborateness of the murtis' dress make this a considerable undertaking, with several devotees working around the clock to make garlands, and to look after the wardrobe, ensuring that the murtis' clothes are clean. Some smaller ISKCON communities lack sufficient members to do all this: these smaller centres are designated as 'missions' rather than 'temples', and use two-dimensional framed images of the deities rather than full murtis.

Although ISKCON has all the hallmarks of a world-renouncing religion, it has no objection to its members enjoying food, and indeed from its early days it made a feature out of its 'love feasts'. It has even described itself as the 'kitchen religion', providing worshippers with prasadam – often in the form of a complete vegetarian meal – after worship. 'Prasadam' literally means 'mercy': it is a token of divine grace, and Prabhupada regarded it as a reward for subduing the senses.

Some issues

I mentioned earlier that NRMs like ISKCON provide an acceptable way for westerners to embrace a form of Hinduism. This is not without its problems, however. Hinduism is very much bound up with caste, which is typically viewed as a matter of birth. Although some scholars have questioned whether caste is a religious rather than a social phenomenon, nonetheless the phenomenon of the white brahmin, which ISKCON appears to have created, is somewhat of an anomaly. Prabhupada was also iconoclastic by giving initiation to westerners, particularly since they were often young: sannyasin vows are generally for those who have passed beyond the householder (*grihastha*) stage and who are in the final years of their earthly existence.

In his discussion of the white brahmin, Brooks identifies three different positions which are held in India. The conservative position relates caste to what is prescribed in the ancient laws of Manu, which entails that one's caste status is given at birth and is unchangeable. A second position is that Vaishnavism transcends caste, and that those who are devoted to Vishnu (and this of course includes Krishna) are regarded as equal in status, and can engage in endogamy and commensality. A third position, held by the Gaudiya Math, is that caste is irrelevant: whatever one's position at birth, one can become a brahmin through knowledge, ability and the appropriate initiations. According to some, Vrindaban itself entails the absence of caste. However, the advent of the westerner is a new phenomenon even for the liberal Gaudiya Math devotee, and indeed Brooks reports that commensality and endogamy lack consistent practice, which varies according to time and to the particular devotees involved. There have been occasions where a brahmin has offered a daughter in marriage to an ISKCON devotee, and when he has agreed to share a table at a meal.

Another controversial issue surrounds ceremonies, temples and deities. Anyone who has visited India will know that there exist temples that are clearly designated for 'Hindus only', denying access to the western tourist. In the case of the Orissa Temple at Puri in Bengal, the resident deities – the Jaggernatha – were not to be seen by any non-Hindu, except annually in procession. Until ISKCON's inception it was unacceptable for westerners to handle the Jaggernatha. (The 'Jaggernatha' are said to be forms of Krishna, Balaram and Subhadra, and are distinctive in their singular lack of features: they are not normally worshipped directly, but give 'darshan' – literally, 'view' – by being publicly processed.) Within ISKCON the Jaggernatha can be freely seen in their temples, by Hindu and westerner alike.

When the Jaggernatha were first installed in the ISKCON temple in San Francisco, it was impossible to follow the standard Indian brahmanical procedure, as Prabhupada himself acknowledged. When the Krishna Balaram ISKCON temple in Vrindaban was opened, however, Prabhupada was much more concerned to ensure that the installation of the murtis was uncontroversially authentic: it would have been a serious blow for ISKCON to own a temple which Hindus would not use. Accordingly, ritual specialists from Mathura and Vrindaban were invited and participated in the installation of the murtis. This was not done at a later stage in Mayapur, but the absence of such specialists apparently did not prevent indigenous Hindus from coming to the temple.

Although ISKCON remains controversial among Hindus, their temples are used by western convert and Hindu expatriate alike. Although the practices of Gaudiya Math may be unfamiliar to many Hindus, ISKCON nevertheless offers them a temple in which daily worship is offered and festivals celebrated.

Sai Baba

In contrast with ISKCON, the Sai Baba movement emanates from the Saivite tradition. Of all the Indian gurus Sai Baba is undoubtedly the most famous of all the Hindu miracle workers, and anyone who has heard of Sai Baba will know of him as the 'man of miracles', materializing rings, pendants and lockets for his followers and enabling the mysterious ash, known as *vibhuti,* to appear inexplicably and multiply. One writer describes him as 'the most sought out, worshipped and famous yogi in modern times' (Agehananda Bharati, 1982, p. 54).

It is perhaps surprising that Sai Baba attracts so little attention from anti-cult organizations, since the movement possesses a considerable number of characteristics that are associated with the notion of 'cult' in its sociological senses. Although the movement has its institutional structures, the wider following is loosely organized, and there is no one mandatory set of practices. It centres on a single guru who claims to be divine, and who is believed to have omniscience, offering definitive teachings and demanding obedience: by his clairvoyant powers he is believed to keep a watchful eye on all his followers, offering help, and meting out sanctions when he perceives lack of obedience.

Sai Baba's relative immunity from criticism has no doubt been due in part to the fact that the movement was brought to the west by Gujaratis from East Africa, to whom it belonged as part of their own indigenous faith. Another important factor is that Sai Baba has never been involved in any sexual or financial scandal, but has lived true to his teachings. The only major controversy generated by the movement relates to the miracles themselves. Sai Baba has been criticized by the Indian Rationalist Association as one of India's many spurious miracle workers, preying on the superstition of an inadequately educated Indian population. Yet, although many view with suspicion his claims to miraculous and paranormal powers, his miracles have never been conclusively discredited. Sai Baba himself says he is opposed to superstition, and offers a spiritual path based on firm evidence rather than blind faith.

Shirdi Sai Baba

Sai Baba is reckoned to be an incarnation of a previous holy man, now deceased, also known as Sai Baba. In order to distinguish the two babas, the first is generally called Shirdi Sai Baba (1838–1918), and the second Satya Sai Baba. (In what follows it should be clear which is being referred to; when I straightforwardly use the name 'Sai Baba' without indication, I am referring to the one who is currently alive.)

Shirdi Sai Baba was born into a Hindu brahmin family who lived in Patri in Hyderabad. Shiridi is near the River Godavari, the 'Ganges of the South'; it is a sacred river. He was cared for by a Muslim fakir, and associated alike with Hindus and Muslims, equally belonging to both religious communities. He is regarded as having been an incarnation of the Hindu-Sufi mystic poet Kabir (trad. 1398–1518). Shirdi Sai Baba came to the Shri Khandoba temple in Shirdi, where the caretaker welcomed him with the greeting, 'Aao Sai Baba, Aao' ('Welcome Sai Baba, welcome'), as a consequence of which he adopted the name Sai Baba. He settled in Shirdi in 1872.

Like Satya Sai Baba, Shirdi Sai Baba is also acclaimed as a miracle worker, effecting healings and protecting his followers against evil. He is said to have possessed the full range of siddhis, being able to control the weather, and engage in astral travel and materialize in the guise of a beggar, a hermit, a dog or a cat. One of his miracles is particularly significant. The local shopkeeper once refused to sell him oil for the temple lamps, possibly at the instigation of some of the local youths, who followed him back to the temple to see what he would do. Unperturbed, Shirdi Sai Baba filled the lamps with water, which miraculously fuelled them, enabling them to continue to burn. A fire continually burned in the temple, where it burns to this day with logs placed on it by devotees: it is a place of pilgrimage for Hindus, Muslims, Parsees, Buddhists and Christians alike. The word for ash is 'udhi', and it has been speculated that the prominent place afforded to vibhuti in the Sai Baba tradition can be traced back to the ash from Shirdi Sai Baba's fire, which was believed to have miraculous powers (Murphet, 1971/1997, pp. 20–1).

Shirdi Sai Baba died on 15 October 1918, in the afternoon of Vijayadashmi day. He still continues to visit devotees, guiding them in dreams, offering them protection, and blessing them 'for fulfilment of their deserving desires'. As a holy man, his body was buried rather than cremated, and lies in the Shri Sai Samadhi Mandir. In 1952 devotees installed a statue of him at his samadhi (resting place). Some say that they feel, when looking at the statue, that Shirdi Sai Baba continues to gaze at them, and others claim that the statue miraculously generates vibhuti.

History of Satya Sai Baba

Satya Sai Baba was born as Satyanarayana Rajuin in 1926. Satyanarayana means 'true all-pervading God'. Shortly after his birth, under his bed was found under a cobra, who proclaimed Sai Baba's role as Sheshiasa, Lord of the Serpents. (The cobra is the symbol of Shiva.)

As a child, Sai Baba disliked seeing suffering: he became vegetarian, and tried to spare animals from being eaten. He avoided cock-fighting, bear-baiting and bullock cart races. He was kind to beggars, even from the age of four. At school he is said to have worked miracles on behalf of his class mates. If a fellow pupil lost a pencil, he could materialize another; if a fellow pupil was sick he could conjure up healing herbs. He became leader of the school prayer group, performing pujas for the pupils. As a boy, Sai Baba was asked for a sign of his spiritual status. He asked for jasmine flowers to be placed in his hand and threw them to the floor, where they clearly formed the name 'Sai Baba' in Telegu.

In 1940 Sai Baba was apparently bitten by a scorpion in the town of Shirdi. He became unconscious for two entire months, and was subjected to treatment by a local healer, who cut his head in three places and applied herbs. When Sai Baba regained consciousness, he appeared to have undergone a radical personality change, and proclaimed himself to be the returned Sai Baba of Shirdi. Sai Baba was taken to someone who had personally known Shirdi Sai Baba, and this person authenticated Satya Sai Baba's claim.

After some time, Sai Baba was able to return to school, where he continued to materialize objects, but now tended to effect materializations that associated him with Shirdi Sai Baba, in particular vibhuti. Devotees sometimes regard Sai Baba's life as falling into three stages: the first 16 years consist of the 'bal lilas' – the childish pranks that are attributed to him, such as making clocks run backwards instead of forwards, or rendering people unable to rise from their seats; the second 16 years, which are characterized by the 'mahimas' ('glorious activities'); and, thirdly, the period from 1958 onwards, in which Sai Baba engages in 'upadesh', the serious teaching of erring humanity.

One particular childhood miracle is noteworthy – the miracle of the kalpataru, or 'wish-fulfilling tree'. According to accounts, there existed a tree on top of a hill, where Sai Baba would often challenge his fellow pupils to race him to the top. Sai Baba invariably used his miraculous powers to get there first, sometimes levitating up to the tree. The kalpataru tree was a tamarind tree, but Sai Baba would invite his friends to name whatever fruit they wanted to appear on it, miraculously producing apples, oranges and mangoes on its branches, or whatever fruit they named (Murphet, 1971/1977, p. 71).

His fame spread rapidly, and within a very short time a complex was established at Prasanthi Nilayam (the name means 'abode of peace'); in 1967 it became an independent town. During the 1950s Sai Baba's following grew. He went on tours, and by 1980 there were 3600 main centres and over 10,000 sub-centres. Sai Baba's attraction grew as westerners became increasingly interested in meditation, vegetarianism and paranormal phenomena. The movement began in Britain in 1966, considerably before the widespread establishment of Hindu temples in the country. The groups therefore helped to provide support for those who had recently immigrated, and this in turn helped the Satya Sai Baba movement to gain further momentum. This form of bhakti did not require brahmin priests, so it was relatively easy to get going.

Sai Baba's status

At the very least Sai Baba is regarded as an authoritative guru and a holy man. This is the minimal import of the title 'baba' which he has assumed. 'Baba' is simply an affectionate Indian term that can be suffixed to the names of babies and old men, as a term of endearment and familiarity. Thus the term 'baba', when applied to a holy man, connotes the child's innocence and the old man's wisdom. Devotees, however, will add a further piece of explanation to this. 'Sai', they claim, means 'Universal Mother' and 'Baba' means 'father'; thus Sai Baba is the father and the mother of the universe, embodying both male and female aspects of deity. Shirdi Sai Baba was not only regarded as a reincarnation of the Hindu-Muslim mystic-saint Kabir, but also the incarnation of Lord Shiva. Satya Sai Baba is held, additionally, to embody the nature of Shakti, Shiva's female consort. Thus Satya Sai Baba embodies both the male and the female aspects of divinity, being simultaneously the avatar of Shiva and Shakti.

Textbooks on Hinduism tend to mention Vishnu's avatars and not

Shiva's. However, both sets of avatars are mentioned in the Puranas: the Srimad Bhagavatam mentions ten of Vishnu, and the Skanda Purana outlines 28 pertaining to Shiva. Sai Baba teaches that the first eight of the former are indeed avatars of Vishnu, but that the Buddha and Kalki emanate from Shiva. Sai Baba is regarded as the promised Kalki, and, although claiming to emanate from Shiva, he is sometimes also stated to be an avatar of Vishnu. (Since ultimately all the great gods are one in any case, there is no particular theological difficulty in claiming to be an avatar of two major forms of deity.) Although Kalki comes at the end of the tenfold list of principal avatars, it is not expected that Sai Baba will be the last. His next incarnation will be as Sri Prema Sai Baba (meaning the Sai Baba of love), who will be the avatar of Shakti alone (Ruhela, 1994, p. 13). Sai Baba has specified the exact year in which he will relinquish his present physical body, and make way for the new avatar: this will occur in 2022, when Sai Baba will have reached the human age of 96 years.

Although Sai Baba is variously referred to as 'bhagwan' ('supreme Lord') and 'avatar', he has also instructed: 'Do not try to understand who I am! You will never succeed! Come – experience for yourself and then accept' (Gadhia, 1989, p. 4). This invitation indicates that it is not necessary to affirm that Sai Baba has any particular status in order to belong to the movement; indeed, a scepticism about the miracles need not be a barrier to the seeker. However, although according divine status to Sai Baba may not be a formal requirement, it is clear that devotees regard him as God incarnate. He is said to possess 'samku chakram' on the soles of his feet, a mark which is indicative of avatarship.

Sai Baba's status is believed to be attested by his powerful miracles. If he is the creator of the universe, as devotees believe, then materializing rings, pendants and necklaces is no problem whatsoever for him. Such miracles are often described as 'lila', drawing on the Hindu notion that the universe as a whole is a lila, an object created solely for God's pleasure. Sai Baba's miracles are not confined to materializations of trinkets or vibhuti; Sai Baba has been known to produce murtis out of sand, sometimes accompanied by bowls of amrit (a sacred sweet liquid), which of course would be difficult to secrete in sand. At times, Sai Baba can materialize the sacred lingam from his mouth, the lingam being the symbol of Shiva, thus offering tangible proof of his relationship with the high God. These lingams are said to be quite large; Murphet recalls being told that Sai had materialized one that was three inches high, fixed on a five-inch broad pedestal (Murphet, 1971/1997, p. 47). Since these objects were often apparently produced after Sai had been speaking for an hour or more, they could not have been secreted in his mouth. The lingams are said to dematerialize again in many cases; Shiva's symbol requires proper regular performance of puja (worship), which few are in a position to carry out. However, some are given away to devotees.

Sai Baba's teachings

Sai Baba now gives little by way of teaching. He no longer gives discourses, his pronouncements being limited to occasional remarks he might make to devotees. When Sai Baba appears, he does so to give darshan – that is to say, blessing by appearance. The fact that Sai Baba's appearances are described as 'darshan' underlines his followers' belief that he is God incarnate. However, Sai Baba has already taught four important principles that continue to be known amongst his devotees: Satya (truth), Dharma (duty), Shanti (peace) and Prema (divine love). He has stated, 'Within them they contain the answer to all the problems of human existence and illuminate man's path to his rightful destiny.'

SATYA (TRUTH)

Satya is not merely an ethical principle entailing the need for true speech. Truth is wider and more fundamental, and it is important that a devotee – indeed the whole of humankind – understands the truth about the world, God, and the place of the individual within the created order. Much of Sai Baba's teaching on these basic and important matters derives from ancient Hindu tradition, drawing on the Vedas, the Upanishads and other classical Hindu writings.

The principal teaching of the Upanishads is the identity between the individual soul and God, between atman and brahman. If this is so, this raises the question of whether Sai Baba's divinity really differentiates him from his followers. Murphet suggests that there are degrees of avatarship, while Ruhela claims that there are two distinct types of avatar: the amsa-avatar and the purna-avatar. All human beings are the former – a partial incarnation of the divine –

and are caught up in maya (illusion, which characterizes the whole of the physical world), developing a sense of individual ego and an attachment to the world. The purna-avatar transcends maya, seeing things as they really are (Murphet, 1971/1977, p. 202; Ruhela, 1994, p. 11).

One might put it this way. The ordinary mortal is one who is born in accordance with his or her karma – that is to say, the effects of one's deeds in past lives – and who is faced with the task of giving selfless service and achieving liberation, the twin goals of the Sai Baba movement. The second of these goals entails seeing the true self behind several 'sheaths' that veil the atman, and recognizing one's oneness with brahman. The avatar, by contrast, is a being who is already aware of his (not so often her) divine identity, and who chooses to descend ('avatar' literally means 'descent') into a physical form because of a particular need on earth.

Sai Baba literature contains various lists of qualities that distinguish an avatar from ordinary human beings: one eightfold list itemizes splendour, righteousness, wisdom, fame, prosperity, non-attachment, powers of creation and destruction, and omniscience (Gadhia, 1989, p. 25). The miracles, of course, are intended to bear witness to Sai Baba's avatarship, although the fact that Sai Baba has a human body imposes limitations on his powers: he must work in accordance with the laws of nature to effect any change, 'otherwise life would become incomprehensible and chaotic' (Gadhia, 1989, p. 25). Although Sai Baba can dispense grace, he can do so only in accordance with the law of karma: Sai Baba is not simply a magician, and, if one receives a boon from him, this may well be due to 'forgotten' good karma.

The powers of creation and destruction are particularly relevant to the God Shiva, of whom Sai Baba is believed to be an embodiment. Shiva's destroying powers should not be seen in a negative way: Sai Baba has taught that it is not his role to destroy the wicked, but rather that destruction is necessary within the universe for the regenerative process to take place. Although Sai Baba's miracles are commonly perceived as conferring benefits on their recipients, Sai Baba can also 'lay dooms', causing some people to incur suffering in order to burn out some of the bad karma they have accumulated. Sai Baba's avatarship confers on him clairvoyant powers, enabling him to see into the workings of the law of karma in ways in which ordinary mortals cannot.

DHARMA (DUTY)

Dharma is Sai Baba's second principle. In its typical usage within Hinduism more widely, the term refers to one's religious, social and moral obligations. Since the Sai Baba movement rejects caste, however, it follows that there can be no specifically caste dharma ('jati dharma'), but only general dharma ('sadharan dharma') that applies to all. Sai Baba teaches the equality of all, regardless of caste, creed, colour and race. Men and women are said to be equal – although sexual equality is perhaps not what a western feminist would understand by the notion. Sai Baba has said, for example, that 'motherhood is God's great gift', which suggests that rearing children is preferable to pursuing a career.

Traditionally, Hinduism has defined four stages in life: the brahmacarin (the youth), the grihastha (householder), the vanaprastha (hermit), and finally the sannyasin – the ascetic who renounces worldly living to pursue the spiritual life. Although Sai Baba himself leads a celibate and fairly austere life, his followers are not encouraged to renounce the world. Unlike ISKCON, there are no sannyasins within the movement and no separate communities in which celibacy or monasticism is pursued. If any member chooses to be celibate, that is his or her own choice. The grihastha state is regarded as totally acceptable, indeed the norm, and one's dharma includes having the right attitudes to one's work, the implication being that earning one's living in a conventional everyday way is to be expected. Having the right attitude, however, implies doing one's work as if one were working directly for God. To gain liberation, a combination of the three traditional spiritual paths (yogas) is needed: karma (deeds), jnana (wisdom) and bhakti (devotion). As Sai Baba puts it, the relationship between the self and the world is like a boat and the water in which it sails: the boat must enter the water, but the water must not enter the boat.

Also included in one's dharma is right eating. Sais are vegetarian, viewing this as an entailment of non-violence. Peace (shanti) – the third principle – includes the non-harming of any living being, hence the avoidance of meat. Sais also avoid alcohol. Devotees sometimes report that at an early stage of their acquaintance with the Sai Baba movement they acquire feelings of guilt about meat-eating, and some have even felt that Sai Baba himself was reprimanding them for their action. One informant described how he had begun to take an interest in Sai Baba and had started to read Howard Murphet's *Sai*

Baba, Man of Miracles during his lunch break. He had dropped off to sleep, when he felt as if someone was slapping him on the face and saying, 'Meat! Meat!' Waking up, he found what appeared to be the imprint of a hand on his face, and took this as a reprimand from Sai Baba for having eaten meat sandwiches.

The concept of dharma serves to explain Sai Baba's attitude to other religions. Just as Shirdi Sai Baba sought to reconcile Hindus and Muslims without obscuring their distinctive identities, so Satya Sai Baba teaches that seekers should continue to follow their own religion in a conscientious way. As he has said, 'I have not come to set afoot a new cult' (Ruhela, 1994, p. 125).

The connection with dharma here is that the root meaning of the Sanskrit word *dharma* is 'essential nature' or 'essence'. Thus it is the essential nature of humanity to refrain from killing and stealing; it is the essence of the brahmin to study and of the camar to make leather goods. (Neither Hindu nor Buddhist thought acknowledges the distinction between 'prescriptive' and 'descriptive' laws, which has often been championed in the west.) By this same logic, if one is a Hindu, that is one's essential nature, but equally if one is a Buddhist, a Christian or a Muslim, these too are aspects of one's essence. Sai Baba's own essence as the living deity is no different from the essential nature of the God of Judaism, Christianity, Islam and Sikhism, or from the other forms of deity pertaining to the Hindu religions. To quote Sai Baba:

> I affirm that this Sai form is the form of all the various names that man uses for the adoration of the Divine. So I am teaching that no distinction should be made between the names – Ram, Krishna, Ishwara, Sai – for they are all My names ... Continue your worship of your chosen God along the lines already familiar to you. Then you will find that you are coming nearer and nearer to Me; for all names are Mine and all forms are Mine. There is no need to change your chosen God and adopt a new one when you have seen Me and heard Me. (Ruhela, 1994, p. 125)

Sai Baba regards himself as having been predicted by faiths outside the Hindu tradition. For example, he sees references to himself in Christian scripture. Commenting on the Book of Revelation, Sai Baba provides the following by way of exegesis:

> He who sent me among you will come again; and he pointed to a lamb.
>   The Lamb is merely a symbol, a sign. It stands for the voice (the sound of bleating) ba ba; the announcement was of the advent of Baba. His name will be truth, Christ declared. Sathya means Truth. 'He wears a

robe of red, a blood red robe' Christ said. (Here, Sai Baba pointed to the robe he was wearing). Christ said 'He will be short, with a crown (of hair). The Lamb is the sign and symbol of love. Christ did not declare that he would come again.' That ba ba is this Baba. (Gadhia, 1989, p. 42)

As Sai Baba has pointed out, Jesus proclaimed that 'I and the Father are one,' and hence Jesus was also an avatar. Devotees point out that Jesus, too, was a miracle worker. Some devotees view Jesus as the avatar of the astrological Age of Pisces, and Sai Baba as the new avatar of the Age of Aquarius (Bowen, 1988, p. 226). In Sai Baba temples one characteristically finds icons pertaining to a variety of faiths, including images of Rama, Krishna, Vishnu and Jesus, as well as Shiva.

Having said this, Sai Baba teaches that only in India can an avatar be born 'because only in India are the Shastras understood. And only in India do the sages constantly experiment and practise. It is like a gold mine' (Ruhela, 1994, p. 12). This statement may appear to rest uneasily with the claim that Jesus was an avatar, although Sai Baba – to whom is attributed knowledge of facts that are not generally accessible to the rest of humankind – claims that Jesus lived in India, not after the resurrection (as writers like Kersten (1986/1994) have speculated) but between the age of 12 and the beginning of his ministry.

SHANTI (PEACE)

The great avatars do not arrive on earth in an arbitrary way. The Bhagavad Gita teaches that, when the Dharma is lost, the avatar descends and rescues humanity from its predicament. Devotees therefore believe that Sai Baba, as one of the great avatars, has come to earth to rescue humankind from destruction.

The great disasters which threaten humanity in the twentieth and twenty-first centuries are not hard to find. The most serious of all the threats is the threat of nuclear annihilation, but rising population, global warming, deforestation, the possibility of economic collapse, and a general decline in moral values (evidenced by the rise in pornography, amongst other social ills) all attest to the fact that humanity is at a time of great crisis. Sai Baba can help humankind to attain peace, both in the sense of absence of war and in the sense of attaining peace with one's fellow humans and our environment.

Sai Baba will use his avataric powers to fend off nuclear war, but his success depends on humanity's efforts; as he points out, the Bhagavad Gita begins with a battle scene, in which Arjuna (Krishna's charioteer) attempts to make peace with his opponents, but eventually has no option but to fight them. Likewise, humanity can either dismantle its nuclear arsenal or bring about Armageddon. Sai Baba rejects fatalistic assumptions: a global holocaust is not inevitable, but humanity has the choice regarding its future. The world is like the wish-fulfilling tree of Sai Baba's miracle: we have the choice regarding the fruit we want from our thoughts and actions (Murphet, 1971/1997, p. 235).

Although humanity has choice, Sai Baba is optimistic about humanity's future, predicting that the new golden age, the Sat Yuga, will dawn in 1999, leading into the era of the next avatar in 2030. He describes it thus:

> When the Golden Age dawns there will be harmony throughout the world and love will flow everywhere. All thoughts of hatred will disappear. Today you cannot visualise such a state because there is chaos everywhere, fighting, scheming, hatred, evil; all the negative emotions are in the ascendant. But eventually the change will come.
>
> The arrival of the Golden Age will be heralded by a New Coming as well as some upheavals, sufficient to uproot the evil that is so prevalent today. (Ruhela, 1994, p. 213)

PREMA (DIVINE LOVE)

Finally, it is love that will determine the future of humankind: love for one's fellow human beings, but most especially love for Sai Baba, which of course is the same as love for God. Sai Baba is himself venerated as an object of devotion.

There is no set form to congregational worship (Ruhela, 1994, p. 80). The satsang (religious fellowship) meets once a week for Bhajan Manda, its most important event. As the name implies, this largely consists of singing bhajans (spiritual songs), most of which have been composed by Sai Baba himself. Shat-Laksharchan is another form of worship which includes the recitation of the mantra, 'Aum Sri Sathya Sai Krishnaya Namah', and Namasmarna Sadhna (chanting the divine name).

Devotees also celebrate a number of festivals throughout the year. These include those that are widely recognized by Hindus generally, such as Diwali (in October/November) and Janmasthami (in the early autumn). Mahashivaratri (around February/March) is particularly important, being the birthday of Lord Shiva. This festival is the one at which Sai Baba will often materialize Shiva lingams.

Sai Baba's birthday is on 23 November, and on the nearest weekend a number of satsangs will often combine to have a large celebration which includes a meal followed by devotions, entertainments and talks by devotees. On leaving, one receives a piece of Sai Baba's birthday cake and often a small packet of vibhuti. In the English Midlands, this is attended by members of various faiths, including Jains, Sikhs and a few Christians. The Christian Christmas is also acknowledged in Baba's liturgical calendar, and is a major day of celebration, with a Christmas tree, nativity plays and a large torchlight procession, which culminates with 1000 candles being waved by devotees.

If it is at all possible, devotees will endeavour to see Sai Baba give darshan, which usually takes places at one of the ashrams, such as Prasanthi Nilayam in Andhra State, or Whitefield (Brindavanam) near Bangalore. For those who cannot see Sai Baba in person, having a photograph of him is sufficient: the image can provide one's own darshan, and Sai Baba, being omnipresent, is just as near to the devotee who cannot visit one of the ashrams, at his or her own home.

Some devotees keep a special room in their homes, prepared as Sai Baba's own room, as one would prepare a room for an important guest to visit. A bed is made up, with fine coverings, a chair is set out, and food and drink are placed each night for him to eat. Two of my informants have declared that occasionally the bed is disturbed, that food has been eaten, or that traces of his footprints have been seen. One even claims to have seen him in the building, even though he is in some far distant part of the world: Sai Baba's siddhic powers enable him to be in more than one place at a time.

Conclusion

Sai Baba's critics claim that he is little more than a showman, a charlatan who makes extravagant claims to divinity while materializing his trinkets through sleight of hand, like a stage magician. Even if he can, they ask, what purpose do such tricks serve? Sai Baba has described them as 'bait', attracting attention so that seekers will learn his true message of truth, duty, peace and love. Unlike Jesus, who chastized those who only 'sought the loaves and fishes', Sai Baba does not discourage people from seeking material benefits, but teaches that, if this is all one wants, then it is all one will get. The real miracle, he claims, is not the remarkable materializations, but the way in which the Sai Baba organization changes the lives of those who are affected by it. As Ruhela writes:

> People sometimes are puzzled by the miracles of Sai Baba; some critics and fanatics have, out of their helplessness and ignorance, even ridiculed and challenged Sai Baba for producing holy ash, icons, lockets, diamonds, etc. But the greatest of all his miracles, visible to anyone in any country, is how the daily lives of Sai devotees and activities of Sri Sathya Sai Service Organization units throughout the world today are being regulated in a set, dignified, moral, honest and efficient manner, all working in perfect unison ...
>
> The self-control exercised through the inner promptings of every heart, propelled by Baba's divine will, ultimately lends the real strength to the movement. There are very few, almost rare, cases of disobedience, delinquency or exploitation in this global movement of millions of people. (Ruhela, 1994, p. 171)

Brahma Kumaris

Brahma Kumaris is seldom discussed in literature on NRMs. It is not mentioned by Walter Martin (1965/1985), Bob Larson (1989), Josh McDowell and Don Stuart (1992), or indeed most anti-cult writers, and receives little mention in academic literature. There are no doubt several reasons for this. There have been no major scandals involving BKs, who not only have stressed the virtues of purity, chastity and peace, but have very consistently put their ideals into practice. They have worked extensively within the inter-faith movement, having had a major part in some highly significant events, such as the World's Parliament of Religions in Chicago in 1993, and have enjoyed close links with the World Congress of Faiths and the International Association for Religious Freedom. In 1980 Brahma Kumaris became affiliated to the Department of Public Information of the United Nations; three years later it gained consultative status with the UN Economic and Social Council, and also with UNICEF in 1988.

The BKs have consistently avoided most of the tactics that have aroused public criticism of NRMs. They have avoided name changes and variant names, consistently using their original name of 'Brahma Kumaris', or 'Brahma Kumaris World Spiritual University', and in pursuit of their ideals they have not set up their own rival organizations for similar purposes. They have avoided aggressive proselytizing, stating clearly that they have no wish for seekers to leave their own religion (if they have one) in order to become a BK. They allow members and sympathizers to donate as they are willing: they are thus self-supporting, and have never engaged in street peddling or other methods of eliciting donations from the public.

Two other factors have no doubt caused those who know the BKs to be rather more sympathetic to them than to many other NRMs. First, to some degree they can be perceived as Indian: their headquarters is in India, and their founder-leader Dada Lekhraj spent his entire life working in the Indian subcontinent. Unlike Prabhupada, for example, he made no pilgrimage to the west in order to spread his message to Americans and Europeans, and hence BKs are much less likely to be labelled as a cult that emanates from the USA. Second, Brahma Kumaris accords a high status to women, who are largely responsible for the teaching and for the adminis-trative organization of the movement – a feature which undoubtedly endears them to western feminists.

All this may raise the question of the extent to which one should categorize Brahma Kumaris as a new religious movement, rather than straightforwardly as a form of Saivite Hinduism. However, they are recent, having been established by Dada Lekhraj in 1938, and having reached the west in 1971. Although Saivite, there are distinctive doctrines and practices that distinguish the movement from other forms of Hinduism: it has been pointed out, for example, that Brahma Kumaris is unusual in aiming at the creation of a physical utopia rather than the state of *moksha* (liberation), and BKs state clearly that Rajayoga is not a Hindu sect (Bowker, 1997, p. 163; Hassija, n.d. a, Part 1, p. 7). The movement, too, has attracted westerners, having a worldwide rather than simply an indigenous Indian following.

Origins of Brahma Kumaris

Dada Lekhraj (1876–1969), the organization's founder-leader, was a wealthy jeweller, who lived in Hyderabad. He specialized in diamonds and became a multi-millionaire. In 1936, at the relatively late age of 60, Dada Lekhraj had a series of visions which were to cause him to abandon his business in favour of the spiritual life. He described these as being surrounded by a flow of warm energy, which filled him with light, and which unravelled the mysteries of God's nature, the inherent nature of the human soul, and the process by which the physical world would become transformed.

Dada Lekhraj attracted a small group of followers – about 300 men, women and children – in Hyderabad, and the group was known as 'Om Mandali'. A year later, in 1937, the group moved to Karachi. Although now part of Pakistan, both Hyderabad and Karachi belonged at that time to colonial India, prior to the 1948 India–Pakistan partition. Dada Lekhraj established a small management committee, consisting of eight young women, and the following year, 1938, he handed over all his material wealth into a trust, the sole management of which was entrusted to these women.

The Om Mandali group lived self-sufficiently in Karachi, engaging in study, meditation ('Raja Yoga') and 'self-transformation', until 1950, when they moved to Mount Abu, an extremely tranquil location in Rajasthan's Aravali mountains, then comprised of a number of small caves in which a few recluses attempted to pursue the spiritual life. Mount Abu now comprises a place of pilgrimage, with a large meditation retreat centre, far removed from the bustle of Indian city life. The headquarters of Brahma Kumaris is now in Madhuban.

In 1952 Dada Lekhraj – also known as Brahma Baba by that time – felt that the time was right to expand his movement beyond Rajasthan, and accordingly some 'sisters' were sent to Delhi and Bombay to establish centres for the study of Raja Yoga. Expansion outside India, however, did not take place until after Dada Lekhraj's death. After he died in 1969, the administrative leadership passed to Dadi Prakashmai and Didi Manmohini, who saw a new wave of expansion of the movement. In 1971 two centres were established in London and Hong Kong, and by 1980 there were centres in over 40 countries. By 1996 approximately 3200 centres had taken root in 70 countries, with over 450,000 students.

Teachings

The BK organization claims that enrolment for courses in the Brahma Kumaris World Spiritual University is open to all, independent of religious or political affiliation, and I know several BK members who simultaneously belong to some other religious community. Nevertheless, Brahma Kumaris has a distinctive set of teachings that relate to God, humanity and the universe.

BK teachings substantially derive from Dada Lekhraj's revelations. BKs state that he is not a guru, possibly meaning that he claims no lineage (or *parampara*), and he is certainly not regarded as an avatar. However, since his visions are believed to come directly from Shiva, they are imbued with authority. Lekhraj is described as the 'corporeal medium' of Shiva.

Lekhraj first became Shiva's medium at a satsang (congregational gathering) in 1936. His wife and daughter saw his eyes turn red, like red light bulbs, and heard a voice from Dada's mouth saying:

> I am the Blissful self, I am Shiva, I am Shiva.
> I am the Knowledgeful self, I am Shiva, I am Shiva.
> I am the Luminous self, I am Shiva, I am Shiva.

Lekhraj is said to have a further decisive vision, this time from Vishnu, who appeared to him in his four-armed form, saying, 'Thou art that' – an allusion to the famous statement of the Chandogya Upanishad.

Other visions of Lekhraj included an apparition of Shiva in the form of a self-luminous ball of light. Shiva bestowed the name of 'Prajapati Brahma' upon him, 'Prajapati' and 'Brahma' being different names for the creator God in Hinduism. (The name 'Brahma Kumaris' is related to this.) Lekhraj was also afforded visions of the world's destruction by large-scale bombing, apparently before the invention of the atomic and hydrogen bombs: there would be traumatic upheaval and change in the world, before a golden age would dawn on humankind. Lekhraj's visions also identified the underlying cause of sorrow and suffering, namely 'body consciousness', its main vices being sexual lust, anger, greed, conceit, attachment and lethargy, all of which had to be removed. Lekhraj was at first persecuted for declaring these visions. He received verbal abuse, and on one occasion his house was set on fire. However, the visions serve to define the underlying theology and ideology of the BK movement.

Dada Lekhraj taught that everyone should see themselves as a 'tiny star, a minute point of invisible luminous energy that is the soul' (Brahma Kumaris, 1997). Those stars centred round Shiva, who was the brightest luminary. Nearest to Shiva was Krishna, followed by Lakshmi. The various beings of light wanted to 'explore', and visited the physical world: Krishna and Lakshmi went first, followed by others. In order to survive in this physical world the souls needed to assume physical bodies, just as an astronaut needs a space suit.

The world into which they entered was originally a paradise. However, as the voyagers settled in the physical world, they began to become attached to it, desiring sensual pleasures, such as the desire to acquire material things and to accumulate wealth, possessions and power. Such desire was often satiated at the expense of the well-being of others, leading to injustice and exploitation, which in turn gave rise to anger, hatred and resentment. Human conflict was an inevitable outcome.

There was another consequence of the souls having assumed physical bodies: there were two kinds of body, male and female, and each gender found itself attracted to the other. To Brahma Kumaris, sex is something destructive, having an effect on the soul for many subsequent rebirths. Dada Lekhraj emphatically stated: 'Hence you should treat it as the great enemy, the greatest source of violence that an individual can commit on another. It is indeed the greatest vice which needs to be totally renounced' (quoted in Puttick, 1997, p. 109). As Dada Lekhraj once said:

> Sex-Lust is the dreaded enemy of the man of knowledge. It is the gateway to hell. Any connection, based on sex-lust, amounts to making people drink poison. It is what is called 'criminal assault'. The lustful one is a *Shudra,* a low man, no better than a dustbin. In one sense, sexual intercourse is like plunging into a gutter or like carrying a basket of muck and dirt on one's head. (Brahma Kumaris, n.d. a, p. 30)

It is perhaps not surprising therefore that Elizabeth Puttick, in her research on women in new religions, found that, by and large, Brahma Kumaris tended to attract women who were uninterested in sex!

The BKs' objections to sex occur on a variety of levels. Philosophically speaking, obsession with sex, or even allowing it to assume any degree of importance, is to identify the self with the physical body. If we think of ourselves in terms of gender ('I am a woman' or 'I am a man'), we forget that the true self is a spiritual being, that 'I am a soul, my body is a garment' (Puttick, 1997, p. 109). Since people are souls, they should endeavour to lose awareness of physical relationships. The soul, by contrast, gains awareness of its spiritual relationship with God.

Pragmatically speaking, sex leads to societal problems, over-population being the most obvious and urgent, particularly in a country such as India. Most educated Indians cite overpopulation as their country's most serious problem. Other alleged consequences of sex include rape, promiscuity, illegitimate children and pornography (Brahma Kumaris, n.d. b, p. 30). Sex also lies at the root of inequalities in human relationships: the woman is typically expected to be subservient to her husband (Puttick, 1997, p. 110). Most of the active BK members are celibate women, and, as Puttick notes, celibacy is in fact required of full-time BKs. For those who are already married prior to joining, chastity should be observed within marriage.

Following Dada Lekhraj's death, the leadership of the movement was entrusted to two senior women within the organization. Dadi Prakashmani, who was one of Lekhraj's original trustees, was appointed as Chief Administrator in 1969. Dadi Janki (b. 1915), who joined the movement at its inception in 1936, became 'Additional Administrative Head'; she travelled to cities in 70 countries, after visiting London in 1974 to establish one of the first meditation centres there. It should not be thought that women's roles are confined to administration; on the contrary, women are teachers, and, more often than not, are entrusted with the responsibility of leading meditations and seminars.

Dada Lekhraj's decision to entrust the movement's affairs largely to women stems from a desire to see traditionally feminine virtues displayed amongst BKs. As they state:

> The soundness of that decision to choose women and young girls as administrators and spiritual teachers can be seen in the increasing recognition of the need for the more traditionally feminine qualities of patience, tolerance, sacrifice, kindness and love as core values necessary for personal growth, human relations, and caring communities. (Brahma Kumaris, 1997)

BKs are typically called 'Sister', but, as Puttick notes, it is motherliness that is more commonly regarded as the key virtue, being associated with teaching, patience, nurturing and compassion, in contrast with the more 'typically' male characteristics of strength and competitiveness (Puttick, 1997, p. 194). However, Brahma Kumaris is not an exclusively women's movement: both men and women can belong and 'participate in a process of self-growth and personal development' (Brahma Kumaris, 1997).

> To a soul born in a male costume, as a man, the characteristics are probably going to be bossiness and ego; for a woman it will probably be timidity, dependence and fear. But when the awakening of the spirit takes place ... then the man who is a yogi will have the strength of being a man but it will be tinged with gentleness, humility, so that ego and bossiness disappear. And for a woman, having the experience of detachment from the body and being in yoga brings a lot of strength, a lot of courage so that she is fearless now. (Bancroft, 1976/1989, pp. 126–7; quoted in Puttick, 1997, pp. 179–80)

Although Dada Lekhraj's teachings seem to suggest that perfected men and women will share each other's traditional characteristics, BKs seem to assume that the traditional feminine traits are inherently desirable. Women, he taught, are fully 'surrendered': women, being used to renunciation and hardship, are accustomed to humility and service, the very characteristics of the devotee (Puttick, 1997, p. 180). Bhakti, by its very nature, entails submission, and both men and women should be surrendered and submissive to Shiva.

Sexuality, then, belongs to the body, an aspect that pertains to one's nature at a mere conventional level, but which is in no way a genuine aspect of the soul. Similarly, one can confuse bodily and spiritual characteristics by equating one's identity either with other aspects of one's physical body or with attributes that relate to the physical world, such as one's nationality or profession. At a conventional level we may need to identify ourselves in such ways, for example, when we are searching for a job, or applying for a passport. However, it is crucially important not to confuse these features of 'secondary-level reality' with the true reality that pertains to the soul. What we need is 'identity transference', so that, in striving to become perfected individuals, we do not confuse such ephemeral characteristics with eternal spiritual qualities.

The true self, then, is the soul and not the body. This soul contains three separate faculties: mind, intellect and impressions. Although they are separate and have a different function, BKs explain that they are really the same energy operating 'on three different but closely connected levels' (Brahma Kumaris, 1997). The mind forms thoughts, formulates ideas and imagines; thoughts form the basis of emotions, desires and sensations. The intellect interprets and processes the thoughts, engaging in reasoning, memorizing, discrimination and decision-making; the intellect, being an aspect of the soul, is not to be confused with the brain, which is the physical focus of the nervous system. Impressions are the result of actions, which leave their mark on the soul in the form of habits, tendencies, temperaments and personality traits. These 'stimulate the mind and influence the quality of thought' (Brahma Kumaris, 1997).

Because the soul becomes attached to the physical world, reincarnation takes place. BKs believe in the law of karma, and that one will be reborn according to one's state of consciousness. However, BKs also believe that the present 'iron age' is coming to an end, and that a new golden age – the sat yuga – is dawning. Instead of being attached to the physical world by means of greed, desire, hatred, sexual lust and so on, the new age will entail self-control, giving and sharing, compassion, humility and the spirit of service, heralding a new culture, in which the lifestyle of human beings recognizes the inherent dignity of each human individual. This golden age will be an age of peace, tranquillity and prosperity, and the BKs' description of it shares much in common with the utopia envisaged by other major world faiths:

> There is no animosity even between a lion and a lamb, for love has eliminated hatred and fear so much so that a lamb can lie in perfect peace in the lap or under the neck of a lion who, as a species, hase [sic] no trace of ferocity. Birds play with human beings, the former unafraid of the latter and in a spirit of friendly sports. The animals are not pegged nor are they killed for man's food, for they are considered as members of the wider family. In this culture, everyone is thankful to everyone and no one has a grudge or grumble against anyone because they really love each other heartily. (Brahma Kumaris, n.d. b, p. 15)

Achieving this utopia will involve a radical transformation on the part of human beings, a 'spiritual alchemy', as one BK has put it. Attachment, acquisitiveness and grasping will be superseded by the virtues of love and compassion, sharing, and respect for each individual and for the environment.

The characteristics of this perfect society are set out in a 27-point list in a short work entitled *Vision of a Better World* (Brahma Kumaris, n.d. b). In sum, this vision includes the following:

1. *A personal vision.* All human beings will have self respect, and enjoy good health (especially freedom from psycho-somatic disorders), adequate clothing and shelter, good inter-personal relationships with friends and family, opportunities for creative expression, and adequate leisure-time sports and

entertainments. Everyone will be engaged in music making, dancing, drama, painting and sport: 'life itself is a dance, song or drama of joy and merry-making. For them, life has a rhythm, a meaning and a method' (Brahma Kumaris, n.d. b, p. 15).

2. *An environmental vision.* The earth will be clean, free from pollution of land, air and water. There will be generous amounts of vegetation to provide adequate fruit and vegetables to feed everyone. Since BKs are vegetarian, there is of course no expectation that land should be used for rearing cattle. Energy will be clean, sustainable and adequate for human needs.

3. *A social vision.* The final goal will be an age of peace, which will be led by a responsible and caring world government. It will be an open government, with freedom of information. There will be justice for all, with law and order perfectly maintained. There will be sustainable population, with good communications amongst all its citizens. Education will be holistic and universal.

In this ideal world, there will no longer exist armies or armaments manufacturers, since it would be an age of uninterrupted peace. No people would be needed to enforce law and order, and the legal profession would disappear, since there would be no further need for litigation. There would be no courts or judges, since every citizen would behave impeccably; indeed BKs believe that there would be no need even for laws, since each person in this golden age would be able to listen to his or her own voice of conscience and to implement its dictates, without any need for external sanctions. There will be no tobacco, alcohol or 'intoxicating drugs'. (BKs do not smoke or consume alcohol.)

What is more, as this golden age dawns, the need for religion too will be superseded:

> Further, since all will be pure in thought, word and deed and will be peaceful and stabilised in the self, there will be no need for any formal religions or places of worship or scriptures. (Brahma Kumaris, n.d. b, p. 16)

The key virtues that will herald this new golden age are: (1) self-control; (2) giving and sharing; (3) compassion; and (4) humility and the spirit of service.

As with all utopias, the obvious question is how such an ambitious goal can ever be attained. First, it is claimed that evil is inherently self-destructive. Violence, war, crime, destruction of the environment, overpopulation and so on are self-limiting: they can endure for a while, but they will soon reach a stage where their effects are felt with such a force that these vices will be brought to an end. Violence will cause its perpetrators to die out, and environmental pollution will give rise to resultant natural disasters. The last decade of the second millennium, BKs believe, will see the demise of evil and its replacement by an age of virtue (Brahma Kumaris, n.d. b, p. 21).

Might the utopia be achieved by political means? BKs have had an interest in politics, particularly in human rights issues. Many nations have drawn up constitutions that affirm the intrinsic worth of human individuals (for example, the USA, France, Germany, Japan and the former USSR), and various international bodies have drawn up declarations affirming the dignity and worth of human beings (for example, the United Nations Charter and the Universal Declaration of Human Rights). However, BKs believe that such declarations are not based on clear universal principles that express the true nature of human identity on the basis of which such rights exist. What is important is to recognize human beings' 'transcendental identity', which accords them the status of souls – a status that transcends race, nationality, religion or any other category that pertains to the physical world.

Rather than pursue their aims through political channels, the method of bringing about the golden age is spiritual. To this end the practice of Raja Yoga is crucial. The practice, BKs claim, is related to the Yoga Sutras of Patanjali (300 CE), but immensely simplified. One does not have to assume any specific physical postures, for example, or even to close one's eyes: the follower simply sits tranquilly in front of the image of Dada Lekhraj, which is projected on to a screen. 'Yoga' means 'union', and 'raja' means 'highest' or – by extension – 'ruler'. Thus the aim of Raja Yoga is for the mind to rule one's physical body, and to attain union between the atman (individual soul) and the paramatman (supreme soul), so that God, the paramatman, becomes the ruler of one's mind.

The practice of Raja Yoga involves five 'affirmations'. First, the meditator affirms the soul as an eternal, infinitesimal point of light. Second, one affirms one's original nature as purity, love and peace.

Third, one acknowledges that one has come from the world of souls, the centre of which is Shiva's golden red light, and that one will return there. Fourth, the meditator affirms that his or her soul is the eternal child of God, and expresses love for God, who is both father and mother, friend, teacher ('philosopher') and guide. Finally, one resolves to do good, to act out of universal love, and to live peacefully.

Raja Yoga is believed to benefit the meditator at a number of levels. It is calming, and capable of alleviating stress; however, unlike certain forms of Buddhist meditation, its aim is not to calm the mind with a view to eliminating all thought. This form of yoga helps to instil a belief in the world's original goodness, to provide a philosophy for living, and to imbue the mind with enthusiasm for the attainment of one's goals. Many of these goals are pragmatic, and BKs unashamedly promote Raja Yoga on the grounds that it can promote successful business and management skills. Indeed one of their publications outlines 22 characteristics of the successful manager, and explains the role of Raja Yoga in acquiring these. Brahma Kumaris is therefore pragmatic, and, despite having certain world-renouncing features (notably chastity and community living for full-time BKs), BKs find no problem about entering into the world of trade and commerce, provided of course that this is done honestly and for the right motives. As mentioned above, the golden age will consist of men and women engaging in gainful employment.

As increasing numbers of individuals take up the practice of Raja Yoga, a certain 'critical mass' will be reached, which will secure the arrival of the sat yuga. This claim relates to the BKs' firm belief in the law of karma: if one's sows the seeds of love, justice, peace and prosperity, one will inevitably reap them in the age that is dawning. Once the sat yuga appears, then the souls will be ready for their return to the light source in Shiva's soul realm. Although this returning to the source entails a recognition of one's true identity as a soul rather than a physical body, BKs do not believe that the return to existence in Shiva's soul world will be a permanent state. The souls will want to 'explore' again at some future time, and will return to the physical world to assume new physical bodies. There will therefore be a new kalpa, in which the events of the previous one are repeated.

Conclusion

As these three case studies have indicated, there are wide varieties of Hindu-related NRMs, reflecting the variety of expressions of Hindu devotion and practice. At the beginning of this chapter I argued that the Hindu-related NRMs provide a possible way for westerners to align themselves with a form of Hinduism to which they feel drawn. The three movements which I have discussed no doubt appeal for different reasons. As Puttick has argued, the Brahma Kumaris provide an obvious spiritual home for Hindu sympathizers who have sympathies with the feminist cause, particularly, although not exclusively, women. Its emphasis on Raja Yoga sells itself to those who are more drawn to jnana yoga than to forms of bhakti. By contrast, Sai Baba enlists devotion, providing the opportunity for present-day devotees to receive darshan of a living avatar. No doubt too, there are followers who are intrigued by the possibility of miracles, and who thus bite on Sai Baba's 'bait'. Of the three movements, ISKCON is the most intellectual form of Hindu-related NRM: although it is a bhakti movement, members are offered considerable verbal teachings, in the form of exposition of the Puranas and the Bhagavad Gita by its sannyasins, and the quantity and availability of ISKCON literature afford considerable opportunities for devotees to study as well as chant the Maha Mantra.

One feature that is typically missing from these NRMs is the distinctively Indian village practices. There are no exorcisms, no prayers to local devas to fend off disasters or secure good fortune, no concept of caste and its associated concepts of purity and pollution; there is little mention of ghosts and demons. Since these movements find a substantial following amongst educated westerners, the version of Hinduism one finds is a somewhat intellectualized one. These movements emphasize teachings ('transcendental philosophy' in the case of ISKCON), and have shed the village elements that are less palatable to westerners. This is not necessarily deliberate, of course, but it illustrates yet another way in which religions adapt to new cultural environments.

6. New forms of Buddhism

During the post-war period, Europe and the USA have seen escalating interest in various forms of Buddhism. Many westerners have perceived Buddhism to be the 'religion of reason'. Buddhists often do not welcome the term 'faith' as a description of their religion, since the Buddha is said to have taught that no one should accept his teachings simply on his authority, but should test them out by means of his or her own experience. Only then should Buddhist doctrines be believed.

The notion of Buddhism as the religion of reason was originally propagated by Christian missionaries, some of whom upheld Buddhism as the best example of what could be achieved by the human intellect, unaided by the eyes of faith and divine grace. It was second best only to Christianity. For many today who find belief in God an article of faith which stretches reason beyond its limits, Buddhism has first place, offering a non-theistic form of religion, a world-view without a deity, but yet a way of life, with a code of conduct and rituals – often colourful – which they find conducive to spiritual progress. The code of ethics itself often holds an appeal, teaching non-attachment in a materialistic world, and non-violence, which is congruent with the peace movement, campaigns for nuclear disarmament, opposition to blood sports and the increasing uptake of vegetarianism.

The spread of Buddhism to the west came in several stages. T.W. Rhys Davids' translations of the Pali canon in the late nineteenth century made Buddhist scriptures accessible to western readers. The Theosophical Society stimulated a further interest, particularly since Henry Steel Olcott had taken a keen interest in the Buddhist religion, and done much to help Sinhalese Buddhists to re-assert their Buddhism in the wake of Christian missionizing. Christmas Humphreys, a leading British lawyer who became the first president of the Buddhist Society of Britain and Ireland, introduced Buddhism through the Theosophical Lodge in London. Allan Bennett, an Englishman, travelled to Burma where he became ordained as a Buddhist monk, assuming the monastic name of Ananda Metteyya, by which he is better known. Metteyya returned to England in 1908 to start the first Buddhist mission. Christmas Humphreys did much to popularize Buddhism. The brand of Buddhism that he espoused was Zen, but his Penguin paperback, simply entitled *Buddhism*, (Humphreys, 1951), helped to arouse widespread interest in Buddhism in all its varieties.

Meanwhile, in the USA, Zen had made its appearance in a different way. When the World's Parliament of Religions met in Chicago in 1893, one of the participants was Soen Shaku, a Zen master in the Rinzai tradition. Paul Carus (1852–1919), a highly influential publisher, was much impressed by Soen Shaku's teachings, and wanted to publish material on Zen. Soen Shaku recommended and introduced his pupil Daisetz Teitaro Suzuki (1870–1966) to Carus. Suzuki wrote prolifically on Zen, and his writings were read widely in the USA and in Britain.

The version of Zen that developed in the USA in the 1960s differed from that of Suzuki. Taken up by the beatniks and hippies of that time, the notions of spontaneity and of finding one's own buddha-nature within were interpreted as a do-as-you-please philosophy, in which 'anything goes'. This form of Zen became known as 'Beat Zen'; encouraged by the writings of Alan Watts, who helped to define the philosophy of the movements, and also writers such as Jack Kerouac, Gary Snyder and Allen Ginsberg. Kerouac's novels *The Dharma Bums* and *On the Road* depict a community of drop-outs who have studied Buddhism after their own fashion, and who seek to combine a kind of oneness with nature with alcohol, sex, and generally doing outrageous things. Alan Watts (1915–73) deserves particular mention as an exponent of Zen: trained as an Anglican priest, he gave up Anglicanism in favour of Zen. His first book, *The Spirit of Zen,* was published when he was only 20, and was the first of several writings that helped to popularize Zen, particularly from the 1960s onwards, on both sides of the Atlantic.

The Tibetan Buddhist tradition reached its zenith about a decade after Zen. It is sometimes said that Zen was the counter-cultural religion of the 1960s, whereas Tibetan Buddhism was the religious alternative of the 1970s. The Chinese invasion of Tibet in 1959 caused a large number of Tibetan monks, as well as the Dalai Lama, to flee the country. Several sought refuge in the USA and in Europe, including Geshe Kelsang Gyatso, the founder-leader of the New Kadampa Tradition, which will be discussed below. At a popular level, the writings of T. Lobsang Rampa (1911–81), who purported to have been a Tibetan lama, were voraciously read by a largely unsuspecting public who did not realize that Rampa's real identity was Cyril Hoskins, a plumber's son from Devon in England. His most famous book, *The Third Eye*, describes a somewhat bizarre surgical operation performed on his head to open a 'third eye' and bestow amazing psychic powers. Although the book is consistently scorned by Buddhist scholars, it is certainly a good read, and played at least some part in arousing interest in Tibet's distinctive brand of Buddhism.

Rajneesh/Osho

Of all the Buddhist-related new religious movements Rajneesh – or Osho, as it is now known – is certainly the most outrageous and the most controversial. I have classified it as a Buddhist-related NRM, although Osho's ideas were decidedly eclectic. Born into a Jain family, Osho drew not only on Buddhist sources, but on Taoist, Christian, Hindu and Sufi ideas, as well as the ideas of Gurdjieff and elements of secular western philosophy. The various traditions can intertwine: for example, Rajneesh believed that Jesus did not die on the cross, but was taken to Kashmir to learn meditation; the individual is inherently divine, but this key Hindu teaching does not need to be accompanied by respecting Hindu customs, even in a Hindu society. After his death, Osho's followers have continued his tendency to syncretize, adding New Age in the form of an Osho Zen Tarot – launched in 1994 – and the Osho Zen Runes two years later.

However, despite Osho's eclecticism, one's immediate impression of the 'Multiversity' at Poona in India creates the impression that its principal focus is Buddhist: the main meditation hall is clearly designated 'The Gautama Buddha Auditorium'; Osho has published commentaries on Buddhist scripture, and frequently emphasized Zen and concepts of enlightenment. It is essentially a form of 'Beat Zen', although apparently developed in isolation from the principal American 'Beat Zen' exponents mentioned earlier.

Rajneesh Chandra Mohan (1931–90) – Osho's given name – was a sick child. He suffered from asthma – a condition that dogged him throughout his life – as well as migraines and at times anorexia – unusual for a boy. At times he was very close to death, which no doubt gave impetus to his search for meaning in life. Rajneesh acquainted himself with eastern scriptures and western philosophers, but tended to rebel and mock rather than align himself with any particular school of thought. He found it difficult, even impossible, to accept authority, and was aggressive and arrogant. Because of his personality he tended, even as a youth, to acquire disciples rather than friends: his interpersonal relationships were certainly not reciprocal ones.

At the age of 14, Rajneesh experienced what he regarded as his first enlightenment (or 'satori'). He was later to tell his followers that in a previous birth he had only just fallen short of enlightenment: 700 years earlier, he was killed only three days before satori would have occurred. Rajneesh left high school in 1951, going on to Hitkarini College in Jabalpur. It was during this period as a student that his poor health was exacerbated, and in 1953 he induced an experience that was designed to be reminiscent of Gautama the Buddha's enlightenment: Rajneesh is said to have sat down under a tree, and remained there for seven days until enlightenment dawned. Unlike the historical Buddha, however, this 'enlightenment' was ecstatic, rather than peaceful and contemplative. This 'greater enlightenment' put an end to Rajneesh's illnesses, at least for a while.

It is unfortunate that commentators describe Osho's teachings variously as 'a pot-pourri of all the great religious leaders of the past' (Storr, 1996, p. 51) and 'a mixture of homespun philosophy and deep spiritual insights' (Barrett, 1996, p. 145). Rajneesh was no amateur philosopher. Not only did he obtain a BA degree in philosophy in 1955 and an MA from Sangar University in 1957, but he went on to become Assistant Professor of Philosophy at the University of Jabalpur, a post which he held from 1960 to 1966. Whether or not one accepts his teachings, he was no charlatan when it came to expounding the ideas of others. If Rajneesh's ideas seem less than systematic in his teaching, this is no doubt because of two factors. First, the propagation of spiritual teachings is an importantly different activity from delivering philosophy lectures, being designed to effect changes in one's audience, which go beyond making a difference to levels of understanding; however, an early lecturing tour proved sufficiently controversial for his audiences. Second, his pronounced leanings towards a philosophy of Zen led Rajneesh to make pronouncements that appear outrageous, lacking in systematization, and even at times contradictory. That is the nature of Zen.

In 1964 Rajneesh organized his first 'meditation camp', which lasted for ten days, and in which participants were taught 'dynamic meditation'. In 1966 he resigned his academic post, calling himself Acharya Rajneesh. 'Acharya' is a term used in Hinduism, Jainism and Buddhism, signifying a spiritual teacher who has the right to transmit the teachings of his or her lineage and to initiate disciples. In 1971 Rajneesh changed his title to 'Bhagwan': although the term is predominantly used in Hinduism to designate the supreme personal God, it should be remembered that the Upanishads teach the identity between the soul and the divine, and hence Rajneesh's use of the title serves to underline his notion that God is to be found within oneself and not in some eternal metaphysical realm. Critical as he was of theism, Rajneesh could hardly have claimed identity with a God whose existence he denied, or to be one of his avatars, as is sometimes suggested. As Osho wrote, 'God does not exist and has never been in existence. Life exists. Celebrate life' (Osho, 1989, dust jacket).

Rajneesh initiated his first sannyasins in 1970 into the 'Neo-Sannyasin International Movement'. At first, the movement was unsuccessful in Bombay, but it gained momentum from 1974 onwards when Rajneesh and his followers purchased farm land at Kailash, where they lived as a community. It was at this point that its 419 members assumed the four 'agreements': (1) they were required to wear clothes 'of the colours of the rising or setting sun' – normally orange, which earned Rajneeshees the nickname of 'the orange people'; (2) a string of 108 mala beads were worn around the neck; (3) sannyasins assumed a new spiritual name, which began with 'Ma' in the case of women, and 'Swami' for men; the new name signified that the initiated member was discarding the past; and (4) there was the daily meditation. In the same year Rajneesh purchased a six-acre site – the Shree Rajneesh Ashram – at Poona (Pune), with 6000 followers. (There are now 30,000 visitors each year, and one sannyasin has described it as 'a six-acre Buddhafield'.) The Rajneeshees were unpopular with the local community, since they violated Indian religious traditions, permitting smoking, drinking, meat-eating, dressing indecently and publicly expressing intimacy between men and women. (There were also rumours that sannyasins used drugs, but Rajneesh never knowingly permitted this.) The Indian government revoked the community's tax-exempt status.

Health proved a problem at Kailash, and Rajneesh's health problems began to recur. In 1979 Rajneesh took a vow of silence and declined to give any further teachings, only darshan. It has been suggested that Bhagwan was suffering from depression, and that the period of silence, which lasted two and half years, was a consequence of his medical condition. Whatever the explanation of the silence, it became obvious that Rajneesh needed treatment that was not available in India, and which, he believed, could be found only in the USA. Accordingly, in 1981 Rajneesh was admitted to the Chidvilas Rajneesh Meditation Center, Montclair, New Jersey. Although ostensibly the journey was for medical purposes, for which Rajneesh was only granted a visitor's visa, it was clear from an early stage after his arrival that he intended to use his presence in the USA to propagate his teachings. As he declared, 'I am the Messiah America has been waiting for.'

Rajneesh and his sannyasins bought 126 square miles of land in Oregon, 20 miles from Antelope, the nearest town. The area was known as 'Big Muddy Ranch', and was barely inhabitable on their arrival. Rajneesh's aim was to build an ideal community, which would be self-sufficient, growing its own crops and rearing its own cattle. Supporters also bought property from the residents of Antelope, a number of whom moved away. Only two weeks' residence was needed to secure voting rights, so sannyasins could be brought in before local elections. In 1982 a sannyasin mayor gained office, and Big Muddy Ranch was incorporated as a city, having been renamed Rajneeshpuram ('expression of Rajneesh'). Sannyasins described Rajneeshpuram as 'America's first enlightened city', although its distinctively religious nature was a violation of the US constitution, which demands a clear separation of civil and religious affairs.

The incorporation of Rajneeshpuram as a city meant that the community had its own city council and could run its own affairs. For obvious reasons this did not please the original residents of the area. A local park was set aside for nude sunbathing, for example, and the non-Rajneeshees felt not only that the original character of their area had radically changed, but that they no longer had an effective say in local government. Even the council proceedings, it had been decided, had to begin and end with one of Bhagwan's jokes! (Mullan, 1983, p. 133). It has since been established beyond doubt that the Rajneeshees' gaining of office was not achieved by fair means. Not only did they stack the odds in their own favour by ensuring an influx of their own supporters into the area (there were 2000 by 1983), but Ma Anand Sheela, Rajneesh's personal adviser, had apparently gone round local restaurants infecting salad bars with salmonella bacteria shortly before the election, with the result that many of the local residents had to stay at home through illness, and were effectively disenfranchised.

Affairs went downhill after 1982. One decisive event was an explosion in a hotel in Portland owned by Rajneeshees. Only the bomber was injured, but the incident led to Rajneesh's followers deciding that they needed to arm themselves for protection. A special Rajneeshpuram police force was established, and there is evidence of telephone tapping by sannyasins. A further problem was the AIDS epidemic that was advancing alarmingly by 1984. For Rajneesh's followers this was more than a scare because sexually transmitted diseases had come to be a problem: at first gonorrhoea and herpes were the most common infections amongst Rajneeshees, but subsequently 11 sannyasins were diagnosed as HIV positive. They were segregated, and Rajneesh gave his orders that sex should only be engaged in if the partners used a condom and rubber gloves.

Following the election-rigging scandal, federal police moved in on the community in 1985. Sheela had absconded and fled to Germany, where she was arrested: she pleaded guilty. Osho's followers firmly believe that Sheela had taken it upon herself to act as she did, and that Rajneesh had not known about the salmonella incident. Rajneesh was arrested also, but released.

In 1987 Rajneesh returned to Poona. At the end of his Oregon period, Bhagwan had declared that 'Rajneeshism is dead.' In 1988 he assumed the title 'Osho', the name by which his organization is now known. The name 'Osho' has been variously explained as meaning 'friend' or 'oceanic' (referring to the drop dissolving in the ocean of being); it is also taken to mean 'The Blessed One on Whom the Sky Showers Flowers' (Appleton, n.d., inside front cover). In 1990 Osho died. Many of his followers believe that he was poisoned by the federal authorities, although others suggest that he was poisoned by Sheela, or that he died of AIDS. The Osho organization lives on, however, disseminating literature and video lectures by Osho, as well as subsequent innovations such as the Osho Tarot and runes.

Teachings

Rajneesh has been variously referred to as the 'sex guru' and the 'rich man's guru'. Normally the world that the Indian sannyasin renounces includes wealth and sex. The Rajneesh/Osho sannyasin renounces neither: all one needs to renounce is attachment to these things.

Rajneesh is popularly dubbed the 'sex guru' because of his seemingly outrageous ideas about sex as a means to enlightenment, and was famed for his acquisition of a total of 93 Rolls-Royces at his ashram in Oregon. Osho liked to shock: his lectures are peppered with quite insulting comments on Christianity in particular, and it was his normal practice to include at least one dirty joke in each speech. Like the traditional Zen master, Osho's technique was to attempt to give his hearers a jolt, so that they might call into question their conventional ways of thinking, and assume the highly unconventional path of the Osho 'sannyasin'. Osho's first ashram is said to have borne at the entrance a notice that read, 'Leave your shoes and your minds behind.' Osho's point was not that one should allow oneself to be brainwashed, but rather that enlightenment cannot be gained through rational activity, only by intuitive insight.

According to Rajneesh, we are all buddhas, identical with God ('brahma'). All that exists is divine, and hence the world should be affirmed, not renounced. However, there is a gulf between one's common experience and the divine: this gulf is the mind. The mind is the mechanism that is needed for physical and societal survival: thus it is not without its uses. The mind interposes taboos and prohibitions that run counter to our inner nature, and the mind projects a God 'out there', with the result that it pays undue credence to supposed intermediaries such as gurus and prophets. As Osho taught:

> [God's] death means man has come of age. He is no longer a child and he does not need a father figure. He can stand on his own feet. He is not a sheep, as all the religions have been telling him, and he does not need any shepherds. Jesus, Krishna, Mahavira, Mohammed, Moses ... no prophets are needed, no saviors are needed, no messengers of God are needed. They were all megalomaniacs, and in the name of God they have been pushing human consciousness to the lowest levels of existence. (Osho, 1989, p. 4)

211

The mind needs to let go, to surrender. Much of our thinking tends to be conditioned by various institutions to which we belong, shaped by societal conventions or an established religious organization. The depths to which humans could sink is illustrated by their conformity to the ideals of Nazi regime: if only one could be true to oneself rather than conform to the dictates of a powerful collective organization! The same holds true of the Roman Catholic Church, which seeks to impose strict rules governing one's sexual behaviour. Yet, by and large, such rules are felt to be oppressive, and do not reflect what we truly want to do, inside ourselves. Most people enjoy sexual intercourse, and seek a stable relationship with a partner, but do not necessarily want to impose upon themselves a permanent liaison, as is dictated by the institution of marriage. It is better to enjoy life and to enjoy sex, being true to one's inner nature.

Regarding wealth, the Rajneesh/Osho movement is certainly upmarket: Heelas and Thompson report that over 60 per cent of supporters in 1986 had university degrees, 80 per cent were professional white-collar workers, and 90 per cent considered themselves 'successful'. Members were most commonly in their thirties, and thus Osho can hardly be considered as a youth movement or an organization that stemmed from the 1960s counter-culture. His acquisition of the 93 Rolls-Royces in Oregon supremely emphasized the high regard in which he held material wealth. Some sannyasins' cars bore a sticker which read, 'Jesus saves; Moses invests; Bhagwan spends' (Heelas and Thompson, 1986, p. 91). Rajneesh never appears to have seen himself as having a mission to the underprivileged, and at the Poona ashram beggars are consistently turned away. Material wealth is to be welcomed, with the proviso that one simply should not be attached to it.

To suppose that religion demands poverty or world renunciation is to think and act collectively. Such thinking assumes that one should follow a religion, and that enlightenment comes from such renunciation. Such suppositions run contrary to the buddha-nature within, which seeks to satisfy material desire as well as to seek spiritual truth. Accordingly, Osho has emphasized the concept of 'Zorba the Buddha': although the Buddha is the epitome of the enlightened being who has attained the supreme spiritual goal, Zorba is the Greek who remains passionate and hedonistic, even amidst disaster (Osho, 1989). True enlightenment involves reconciling one's hedonism with one's buddha-nature. If this seems a new way of looking at spirituality, a 'religionless religiousness' as Mullan has described it, Rajneesh agreed. As he said, 'This is a revolution... I am burning scriptures here, uprooting traditions' (quoted in Martin, 1965/1985, p. 355). (Osho is of course alluding to Zen monks' supposed practice of tearing up scriptures, since they inhibit the spontaneous emergence of the buddha-nature.) As Ma Anand Sheela explained, 'What he is teaching is to be individual, to become free, free of all limitations, free of all conditioning, and just become an integrated individual, a free being ...' (quoted in Drury, 1989, p. 109).

Osho meditation

Although Rajneesh taught the need for individuality, spontaneity, and discovering one's own inner buddha-nature, he nevertheless provided a number of spiritual techniques to facilitate this. The Rajneesh/Osho movement is particularly known for its somewhat controversial 'dynamic meditation'.

The Rajneesh/Osho meditation involved a number of stages – either four or five. In the course of time the practice underwent certain changes; hence one finds different descriptions of Rajneesh's 'dynamic meditation' in different accounts. The five-stage meditation, each part of ten minutes' duration, ran as follows. In the first stage sannyasins breathed fast and chaotically, through their noses. The second stage was 'cathartic'; participants would shout, jump, dance, scream, or whatever they felt like doing, to rid themselves of painful emotions by releasing pent-up energies. Third came the 'energetic' stage in which sannyasins chanted the Sufi-derived mantra 'hoo'; it was taught that this hit the 'sex centre', stimulating sexual energy and releasing spiritual power. At the fourth stage, on a signal from Bhagwan – or the leader – the whole gathering became quiet, slumping on the floor and remaining motionless: one was instructed to 'just be'. Finally came the 'celebration stage', in which sannyasins expressed their thanks and celebrated their buddhahood, moving, dancing and relaxing to music.

As well as dynamic meditation, other spiritual practices included sessions in which participants engaged with the question, 'Who am I?', somewhat in the style of a Zen koan. There could also be guided fantasy, 'bio-energetic' breathing exercises, and role-playing. The purpose of such activities was to enable the participant to see how 'unnatural' one normally is, and to unblock one's inhibitions, clearing the self of the 'garbage' that one allows to accumulate. In one of these sessions, one could behave freely and find acceptance in doing so by the rest of the group.

A number of festivals are also typically celebrated: the Bhagwan's Enlightenment (21 March), Guru Purnima Day (full moon in July, in which enlightened Rajneeshees are celebrated), Bhagwan's Birthday (11 December) and Mahaparinirvana Day (8 September, the anniversary of Bhagawan's death and final liberation). Various conventional festivals are also celebrated in the west (Heelas and Thompson, 1986, p. 102).

An appraisal

As Heelas and Thompson point out, there are many strange contradictions associated with Rajneesh/Osho. For example, Osho stressed freedom and spontaneity, urging his followers to find the Buddha within themselves, while simultaneously urging them to 'surrender to me'. Although one was recommended to enjoy inner freedom, communal life required order to the extent that Rajneeshpuram was described as a 'concentration camp': a strict programme for the day, a highly structured meditation system, and dietary rules such as vegetarianism. There was to be free love, yet there were strict rules governing sex. Although Osho and his followers claimed to be 'religionless', Osho offered a religion, and drew on the teachings of a variety of religious systems. As Mullan too points out, the movement was at once experiential and intellectual, recommending 'no thought' but lots of words. (The Heart Sutra, which can be printed on a single page, elicits 12 volumes of commentary by Osho!) No doubt these are some of the paradoxes entailed by a form of Zen, and they certainly did not prove to be so contradictory as to be impossible to follow in practice. As Mullan writes, Osho was 'consistently inconsistent'! (Mullan, 1983, p. 32).

Soka Gakkai International

Soka Gakkai International is quite a different brand of Buddhism from that of Osho. A form of Nichiren Buddhism, it traces its origins back to its historical founder Nichiren (1222–82). Nichiren, the son of a poor fisherman in Kominato Village in Japan, was sent to study in a Tendai Buddhist temple at Seichoji. From there he travelled extensively, in a quest to find the 'true' form of Buddhism. After studying all the major Buddhist schools, and acquainting himself with their scriptures, Nichiren concluded that the Lotus Sutra was the one true form of Buddhism for the age in which he lived, and that this classical Mahayana text encapsulated all of Buddhism's authentic teachings. Its essence, he taught, was encapsulated in the mantra *nam myoho renge kyo* – translated as 'Homage to the Lotus Sutra' – and chanted assiduously by present-day Soka Gakkai members.

According to the Lotus Sutra, the teachings of the historical Buddha, Gautama, were 'provisional': that is to say, they did not contain the whole truth about Buddhism, but merely what humankind was ready to hear in the sixth century BCE. A buddha must use 'skilful means' to enable his hearers to make what spiritual progress they can, within the constraints of their time and place. When followers are ready, then new truths can be delivered, and this is what the Lotus Sutra purports to do.

Although the Lotus Sutra's teachings appear to be innovatory, the sutra purports to be a sermon preached by Gautama (also known as Shakyamuni). Although SGI members ascribe the sutra to Shakyamuni, most western scholars would regard it as originating considerably later, possibly around 250 CE. The sutra teaches that – perhaps surprisingly – the Buddha did not gain enlightenment under the pipal tree at Bodh Gaya. He was already enlightened, but merely pretended that he was not, as part of the skilful means of imparting provisional teachings: by assuming the role of the unenlightened, he was apparently providing them with a demonstration of how nirvana could be reached. Gautama the Buddha was in fact an emanation of a primal buddha, or *adi-buddha*, assuming a conjured-up physical body as a means to accomplishing his task of teaching and showing the way to enlightenment. SGI members regard this *adi-buddha* as none other than Nichiren himself, and thus Nichiren assumes a greater significance than Gautama. To underline their veneration of Nichiren, members will always refer to him as 'Nichiren Daishonin' (*daishonin* meaning 'great sage'), and consider it disrespectful baldly to call him Nichiren without this title.

The interest in Nichiren Buddhism tended to wane somewhat until the middle of the nineteenth century, when the Nichiren schools experienced a revival. Amongst other Nichiren groups, the best known are the Reiyukai, the Rissho-Kosei-kai and the Nipponzan Myohoji. According to legend, when Nichiren died, six principal disciples remained to continue the movement. According to the SGI, five of them contaminated Nichiren's teachings with elements of Tendai Buddhism, while the sixth, Nikko, preserved Nichiren's teachings in their pure unadulterated form. Nikko left them, departed to Taiseki-ji with the Dai-Gohonzon, his teacher's writings and the ashes of his cremated body. There he and his followers built the Dai-bo, their main temple. Like many myths which are devised to explain the parting of the ways between rival schools, it is capable of being interpreted in more than one way: those Nichiren Buddhists who do not belong to the SGI might agree that Nikko departed with a gohonzon, but that this was only one of several which were inscribed by Nichiren. The story, they will say, only serves to demonstrate the sectarian nature of the SGI, indicating Nikko's inability to co-exist with his fellow disciples.

The modern Soka Gakkai movement can be traced back to the 1930s, when Tsunesaburo Makiguchi (1871–1944), who converted to Nichiren Shoshu Buddhism in the 1920s, together with Josei Toda (1900-58), established the Soka Kyoiku Gakkai – literally the 'Value Creating Education Society' – which was primarily aimed at achieving educational reforms. During the Second World War, the Japanese government demanded that all its citizens should install Shinto shrines in their homes for the purpose of emperor worship, seeking to impose a national religious unity. Nichiren Shoshu Buddhists felt unable to introduce Shinto elements into their practice, and a number of their leaders (including Makiguchi and Toda) refused, and received prison sentences. Makiguchi died in gaol, leaving Toda to assume sole leadership. Toda believed that education reform was too narrow a goal, and widened the organization's scope, renaming it the Soka Gakkai ('Value Creation Society'). Under Toda's leadership a massive drive for new members was begun, and it is from this period that the controversial proselytizing practice of *shakubuku* ('break and subdue') commenced. Believing, as they did, that all other forms of Buddhism were false, impure and corrupt, it seemed important to demonstrate this vigorously, although Soka Gakkai Buddhists deny rumours that such tactics involved physical violence. *Shakubuku* entails a refusal to compromise with opposing views, or other forms of Buddhism, and an attempt to win converts by demonstrating the falsity of their views. After Toda's death in 1958, Daisaku Ikeda (b. 1928) became the organization's president, and, at the time of writing, remains in office. Under his leadership, the movement has gained international renown, spreading to the west, with some 5000 active followers in Britain alone by 1988.

Anyone who is unfamiliar with the Soka Gakkai might be forgiven for wondering what connection its teachings and practices have with traditional Buddhism. One finds no viharas or monasteries, no monks in saffron robes, no disciples engaged in silent breathing meditation, no images of the Buddha, and little, if any, reference to the essential teachings attributed to the Buddha, such as the Four Noble Truths, the Eightfold Path or the Precepts. Indeed the whole ethos of the movement might seem to be quite the reverse of the Buddha's teachings. Instead of renouncing the world and seeking to eliminate selfish desire, the Soka Gakkai seems world-affirming, seeking to improve their own professional and material lot in society: Barrett encapsulates their outlook on life in the expression 'materialistic Buddhism' (Barrett, 1996, p. 157).

Because of the supreme importance of the mantra *nam myoho renge kyo,* the basic practice of Soka Gakkai members is to chant the mantra twice daily, in the morning and the evening, for 20 minutes each time. A small rosary of plastic beads is held in both hands and rubbed during the chant. Since mantras are held to have power, and since this mantra, having been taught by Nichiren, has tremendous power to achieve practical results, members seldom undertake the chant without some specific purpose in mind.

The power of the chant is said to enable the follower to attain all manner of benefits, both spiritual and – perhaps more commonly – material. Thus, if someone needs a car, a fur coat or a girlfriend (their examples, not mine!), the power of the chant can help to provide them. It is perhaps worth mentioning that SGI members are generally not naive enough to assume that a successful outcome is automatically guaranteed. There can also be inappropriate objects to seek through chanting: to take an extreme example (although one which I have heard an SGI member discuss), if an intending rapist chanted to find appropriate victims, the power of the chant would be unlikely to assist; if the chant were sincerely used, that person might more appropriately come to see the error of his ways and mend his life accordingly. Perhaps more realistically, the SGI student who chants that he or she might pass an exam is not offered a cast-iron guarantee of success; failure is still a possibility, but the power of the chant should enable this student to come to terms with failure and learn from it.

In addition to private chanting, the Soka Gakkai have regular collective gatherings. A *gongyo* ceremony is the most common form of ritual. ('Gongyo' literally means 'assiduous practice'.) It normally takes place unpretentiously in the home of a member who possesses a *gohonzon* – a scroll which is inscribed in ink, in Japanese characters, with the mantra *nam myoho renge kyo* – contained within a *butsudan*, which is a little black cupboard which contains the scroll and keeps it out of view when the ceremony is over. The meeting consists of about a dozen members, who constitute a 'chapter', and who recite in Japanese the words of a small red book entitled *The Liturgy of the Nichiren Shoshu*. The book is an abridged form of the Lotus Sutra, containing part of chapter 2 (called the 'Hoben' chapter) and chapter 16 (the 'Juryo' chapter). Most members have not read the Lotus Sutra in its entirety, even though it is considerably shorter than the Christian New Testament. These two chapters are regarded as a distillation of the Lotus Sutra, and the Liturgy consists of a parallel text, in transliterated Japanese with an English translation. The Japanese text is recited by members several times in succession.

After the chanting, the meeting admits of a variety of forms, and, in contrast with the chanting, is fairly informal. Members may give testimony about their practice, telling the others what they have sought to achieve through their chanting and what degree of success they have achieved. Someone might have been commissioned to prepare a brief talk – normally about Nichiren or the Lotus Sutra – to introduce discussion. The meeting ends with refreshments, or even adjourning to a local pub. (There is no prohibtion on alcohol.)

Although the Hoben and Juryo chapters are short, the mantra *nam myoho renge kyo* in itself contains the essence of the Lotus Sutra. As Nichiren himself is reputed to have said:

> included within the title, Nam-myoho-renge-kyo, is the entire sutra consisting of all eight volumes, twenty-eight chapters and 69,384 characters without exception. (Cowan, 1982, p. 54)

And since the Lotus Sutra encapsulates the whole of Buddhism, *nam myoho renge kyo* sums up everything else. Consequently, when questioned about the place of Buddhist precepts, or the Four Noble Truths and the Eightfold Path, SGI members will insist that, like everything else in Buddhism, it is all encapsulated in 'nam myoho renge kyo'.

The notion that one can use Buddhist practice to satisfy desire rather than eliminate it might seem a far cry from the Buddha's Four Noble Truths, where it is taught that unsatisfactoriness (*dukkha*, or 'suffering') is caused by desire and that selfish desire is to be eliminated. SGI appears to teach that enlightenment is achieved *through* desire, rather than by removing it.

SGI members explain the paradox by claiming that human nature has two sides: there is *bonno* (evil desires) and there is enlightenment. The two are inseparable, and it would be a mistake to believe that desire was unequivocally evil; after all, one cannot be human without having desires for food and drink, sleep and sex. SGI rejects the idea of Pure Land Buddhist teaching, that there is a perfect buddha-world which transcends the unsatisfactory earthly world that we currently inhabit. The state of enlightenment cannot be separated from the state of *bonno*.

As Jim Cowan, an exponent of Soka Gakkai Buddhism, explains:

> if the minds of the people are impure, their land is also impure, but if their minds are pure, so is their land. There are not two lands, pure and impure in themselves. The difference lies solely in the good or evil of our minds. (Cowan, 1982, p. 60)

In this context, SGI sometimes draws an analogy with the lotus, one of the traditional Buddhist symbols. Although the lotus is a very beautiful flower, it typically grows in a muddy swamp, and indeed cannot grow without it. The relationship between the flower and the swamp is analogous to the relationship between enlightenment and *bonno*. A muddy swamp without lotuses would be extremely ugly, hence the swamp needs the lotus flower; but equally the lotus flower needs the swamp, otherwise it could not grow at all. Similarly, one's buddha-nature must emanate from the swamp of desire; if there were no desire, there would no humanity to gain enlightenment. Equally, however, one should not be content simply with desire, for each individual is capable of flowering into buddhahood.

Because of the interconnection between desire and enlightenment, the SGI sees justification in using the power inherent in 'nam myoho renge kyo' as a means for satisfying earthly desires, such as health, wealth or other forms of material prosperity. However, one's practice should not cease there, and one should come to realize that the whole earth can be a paradise for which one should strive. SGI members are therefore concerned about issues such as conserving the environment, and, in particular, the ideal of world peace, which is a very strong concern on the part of SGI, and the object of much chanting.

The 1991 schism

Until very recently, the Soka Gakkai was a lay society, associated with the Nichiren Shoshu and its priesthood. The Nichiren Shoshu high priest presides over the main temple at Taiseki-ji, at the foot of Mount Fuji, where he is responsible for the safe keeping of the Dai-Gohonzon (the original gohonzon said to have been inscribed by Nichiren), and where he inscribes the gohonzons for members to use in their homes. Since the distribution of the gohonzon could not take place without the priesthood, the Nichiren Shoshu priests have regarded themselves as the linchpin of the organization, the supreme authority without whom the laity could not practise Nichiren Shoshu Buddhism. The priests also had the duty of officiating at funerals and installing memorial tablets at Nichiren Shoshu temples. In return for such services, the laity provided funds and premises for the practice of their religion.

As Wilson and Dobbelaere (1998) point out, the priesthood, having its seat of authority within the Taiseki-ji Temple, had never ventured beyond Japan's borders, and tended to be insular and traditional, as well as more supportive of Japanese culture, in contrast to the Soka Gakkai, which had become an international movement with a large worldwide following. The Nichiren Shoshu priesthood and the Soka Gakkai laity therefore found themselves pulling their brand of Buddhism in different directions, and, almost since the Soka Gakkai's inception, experienced mutual friction.

One early source of resentment related to the use of Shinto symbols. Shortly after the Second World War, the Nichiren priesthood agreed to wear Shinto amulets, and even to install a Shinto shrine at the Taiseki-ji Temple. Mindful of the fact that Makiguchi and Toda had been prepared to serve prison sentences for refusing to make such concessions towards Shinto, the Soka Gakkai movement was outraged, and throughout the 1950s relationships

NEW FORMS OF BUDDHISM

were strained, to say the least. At one point the priesthood even threatened to deprive Toda of his office and bar him from entering the Taiseki-ji Temple.

As an international movement, the Soka Gakkai felt a need to adapt and grow, in contrast with the Nichiren Shoshu priesthood, who wanted to maintain their traditions. The head temple at Taiseki-ji was remote from European and American supporters, and attempts at laicization were inevitable. Western Soka Gakkai members could still receive gohonzons inscribed by the Japanese priesthood, but, gohonzons apart, the western lay members functioned largely in the absence of the Nichiren Shoshu priests. What Ikeda taught was rather like Protestant Christianity's notion of 'the priesthood of all believers': one's heart was the true priest, one could 'fuse with the gohonzon', and the lay movement itself could claim a direct connection with Nichiren, without the priesthood serving as intermediaries. Ikeda claimed that this understanding of the laity's role found support in statements by Nittatsu Hotoi, who was High Priest until his death in 1979. Nittatsu had stated,

> Regardless of whether their heads are shaven or not, all those who chant *Nam-myoho-renge-kyo* before the *Dai-Gohonzon* in the High Sanctuary constitute a single religious community in which lay members are absolutely equal in rank with those of us who are members of the clergy. (quoted in Wilson and Dobbelaere, 1998, p. 234)

Whatever Nittatsu meant by asserting the equality of the priesthood and laity, he clearly did not mean to imply an identity of function. Ikeda published *A History of Buddhism* – a collection of speeches made in 1976 and 1977 – in which he asserted that 'the Soka Gakkai is an organization that carries out the function of both the priests and the lay believers' (quoted in Wilson and Dobbelaere, 1998, p. 234). Allegedly the Soka Gakkai conducted their own weddings and memorials without the presence of a Nichiren priest, Ikeda having claimed that the Soka Gakkai centres were equivalent to Nichiren temples. Soka Gakkai leaders were also accused of having distributed gohonzons without the proper documentation. In 1978 the Soka Gakkai conceded that they had made errors of judgement: they affirmed that there was no priesthood apart from that which had the High Priest as its head; they also agreed to take better care in the issuing of gohonzons. Despite this attempt at reconciliation, friction still persisted during the 1980s, and this even led to a split in the priesthood, when over 200 anti-Gakkai priests demonstrated against the Soka Gakkai, calling for Ikeda to be dismissed from his position as head of SGI, and even challenging the authority of the High Priest Nikken, who had succeeded Nittatsu. For these acts of defiance the rebel priests were removed from office and expelled.

Things came to a head again in 1990, when Ikeda had addressed the Headquarters Leaders' Meeting in Britain. Although there was dispute between the two parties about what Ikeda had actually said, the essence of the accusations against him was that he had diluted Nichiren's teachings, denying the necessity of *shakubuku* declining, to convert others by refuting the teachings of rival Buddhist and other spiritual groups. By way of response, the Taiseki-ji Temple sent out a number of their priests to inaugurate a new movement called *Danto* ('believer'), to which a number of European members transferred their allegiance. Taiseki-ji officials barred SGI members from visiting the Taiseki-ji Temple as pilgrims – a move that had serious economic repercussions at Fujinomya. Deprived of the services of the Nichiren Shoshu priests, the SGI had little alternative but to conduct weddings and funerals independently.

Other allegations and counter-allegations followed. The controversy spanned issues as diverse as the cost of memorial tablets (*toba*), which the Taiseki-ji Temple authorities had increased, to allegations about Nikken's personal life: he was accused of having used the services of a prostitute. The priesthood itself became divided, and about 500 priests defected, in some cases causing their temples to disaffiliate with the Nichiren Shoshu. In December 1991 over 16 million Soka Gakkai members demanded Nikken's resignation.

In 1992 the Nichiren Shoshu of the United Kingdom officially changed its name to Soka Gakkai International. Its essential practices remain intact, namely the chanting of *nam myoho renge kyo* and the *gongyo* ceremony. In practical terms, the only real problem relates to *gohonzon* and the *gojukai* ceremony – the official ceremony for installing it, which must be performed by a Nichiren Shoshu priest. SGI members are concerned that a high priest whom they regard as corrupt has the responsibility for looking after the dai gohonzon, although there is currently little that can be done to change this state of affairs. Because of the rift between lay members and the priesthood, no more gohonzons are being inscribed and issued to SGI members. Conversely, disused gohonzons (from those who have died or left the movement) are no longer returned to the

High Priest. In Britain they are currently stored at the SGI headquarters in Taplow in Berkshire. The lack of availability of new gohonzons has caused some British members to reappraise them: one informant explained to me that this was not an insuperable problem, since the true gohonzon was in one's heart.

At the time of writing, the rift remains and outstanding controversies are unresolved, with no sign of a solution. What is to happen to the stored gohonzons has not been determined. The unavailability of new gohonzons of course presents problems, but causes members to reflect on their purpose rather than their material nature: 'the real gohonzon is within yourself', a physical receptacle being no more than a dispensable symbol which is much inferior to the state of mind which would previously have been expected to accompany its possession.

Western Buddhist Order

As religions migrate, they tend to take on many of the characteristics of the culture into which they come. Sometimes this can be an unconscious process, in which converts to the immigrant religion are unaware of sets of assumptions that they retain from their own culture. At other times – and this is the case with the Western Buddhist Order – practitioners of a religion may quite deliberately wish to make changes and adaptations in order to make it seem more appropriate to the indigenous culture. It is in the nature of Buddhism to adapt itself as it has travelled through time and place: as we have seen, the Mahayana tradition regards the Buddha's teachings as 'provisional'. Christmas Humphreys suggested that there might emerge a new form of Buddhism particularly appropriate to the west.

> Why should there not be in time a Western Buddhism, a Nava-yana or 'new vehicle' ... ? There is no reason why it should not grow happily alongside, and even blend with the best of Western science, psychology and social science, and thus affect the ever-changing field of Western thought. It will not be Theravada or Zen, Prajnaparamita intuitive philosophy or Tibetan ritual. Just what it will be we do not know, nor does it matter at the present time. The Dharma as such is immortal, but its forms must ever change to serve the ever-changing human need. (Humphreys, 1968, p. 80)

Humphreys was no doubt barely aware that as he wrote these words a new and distinctive form of Buddhism was taking its rise, specifically aimed at attracting westerners: the Western Buddhist Order.

Sangharakshita – the Order's founder-leader – and his followers have been highly critical of the type of Buddhism that was practised in the west in the first half of the twentieth century. By and large, he claims, it consisted of westerners who were interested in Buddhism as an intellectual pursuit or exotic hobby – reading books and attending lectures – but whose lifestyle remained largely unchanged. They still ate meat and drank alcohol, they supported the war effort, women wore fur coats, and so on. Some were prepared to support a traditional Sangha through donations, but the lifestyle of the Sangha was strictly for monks, whose world-renunciation was made possible through the laity's support. 'Buddhism and beefsteaks do not go together,' Sangharakshita once declared. 'A difference must make a difference.'

As well as being a radical development of Buddhism, the Western Buddhist Order can be seen as deliberately, even provocatively, presenting an alternative to Christianity. Although those who characterize Buddhism as a 'godless religion' normally fail to appreciate that the gods are simply of little importance to Buddhist thought and practice, members of the Western Buddhist Order, consisting predominantly of westerners, have consciously and deliberately turned their backs on the God of Christianity. This rejection of God is often important to them, and such a rejection can be accommodated within Buddhism. Indeed, the WBO founder-leader Sangharakshita has encouraged the rejection of the God of Judaeo-Christianity: in the wake of a well-publicized blasphemy trial in England, where blasphemy laws are still on the statute books, he wrote:

> One who was brought up under the influence of Christianity, – under the oppressive and coercive influence of theological monarchism, – and who as a result of that influence is tormented by irrational feelings of fear and guilt, has the right to rid himself of those feelings by openly expressing his resentment against the Power that bears the ultimate responsibility for their being instilled into him, i.e. by committing blasphemy. (Sangharakshita, 1978, p. 23)

The Western Buddhist Order was founded by the Venerable Maha Sthavira Sangharakshita. 'Sangharakshita' (which literally means 'guardian of the Sangha') is the founder's spiritual or monastic name.

Born in London as Dennis Lingwood in 1925, and baptized in the Church of England, he read widely in his childhood and adolescence. His explorations of occultist ideas led him to read Madame Blavatsky's *Isis Unveiled,* which, he said, made him realize that he was not a Christian. At the age of 16 he discovered two Buddhist texts, the Diamond Sutra and the Sutra of Hui Neng (sometimes called the 'Platform Sutra') – both principal Zen texts – and these made him realize that he was really a Buddhist. Lingwood consequently joined the Buddhist Society of Great Britain, which at that time was under the leadership of Christmas Humphreys. With the advent of the Second World War, Lingwood joined the army in 1943, serving variously in India, Ceylon (now Sri Lanka) and Singapore as a radio engineer. In 1946 he deserted his post, then tore up his identification papers, and wandered through India as a world-renouncer. He entered the Buddhist Sangha in 1949, receiving *shramanera* (novice) ordination at Kusinara, the birthplace of the Buddha. (A *shramanera* is, literally, one who hears: during the probationary months of ordination, the novice is not permitted to give teachings to others, but must listen to those of other fully ordained monks.) Eighteen months later this was followed by full ordination as a bhikkhu, this time at Sarnath, the place at which the Buddha preached his first sermon, outlining the Four Noble Truths and the Eightfold Path.

Sangharakshita settled in Kalimpong from 1950 until 1964, during which period he did considerable work with the untouchables. He founded a Young Men's Buddhist Association, which aimed to provide young men with general education as well as instruction in Buddhism. In 1957 Sangharakshita established the 'Triyana Vardhana Vihara'; the name literally means 'the dwelling-place where the three vehicles flourish', the three 'vehicles' being Buddhism's three *yanas* or spiritual paths: the 'Hinayana', the Mahayana and the Vajrayana. During this period Sangharakshita received instruction and initiations from a number of teachers, and the vihara's name indicates the equal recognition that Sangharakshita wanted to give to all the major Buddhist traditions – a feature that was later to become central to the Western Buddhist Order.

During this period Sangharakshita came into contact with Dr Bhimrao Ramji Ambedkar (1891–1956). Ambedkar was particularly renowned for his work as a Hindu reformer, who sought to improve the lot of the untouchables, to whom he belonged. One way in which untouchables could shed their low caste status was by converting away from Hinduism, and Buddhism afforded an important refuge for them. Ambedkar converted to Buddhism in 1956 – the last year of his life. Sangharakshita was not present at the ceremony in Nagpur at which between 300,000 and 400,000 untouchables 'took refuge' – the initiation rite which formally marks one's entry into Buddhism. When Sangharakshita came to Nagpur some six weeks later, he was informed that Ambedkar had died only a few hours previously. Sangharakshita was able to offer consolation and guidance to the large numbers of new Buddhist converts, and he later presided over a ceremony at which a further 200,000 untouchables took refuge.

In 1964 Sangharakshita was invited back to England by the Sangha Trust at the Buddhist Vihara at Hampstead in London. This vihara, founded in 1956 and in the Theravada tradition, was the first English vihara to be established in Britain, and was the precursor of the Amaravati Forest Hermitage, with which Ajahn Chah was associated. Having accepted the invitation, disagreements emerged between Sangharakshita and other Sangha members. When he returned briefly to India in 1966, he received a letter from the Trust informing him that he would not be allowed to resume his former post as incumbent of the vihara. Different explanations have been offered for Sangharakshita's dismissal. In his biography of Sangharakshita, Subhuti (1994) – one of the most senior WBO members – suggests that this was owing to the fact that Sangharakshita gave Mahayana as well as Theravada teachings, in his attempt to give equal recognition to all traditions. However, one senior WBO member offered an alternative explanation: Sangharakshita, he stated, was falsely accused of homosexuality.

When Sangharakshita returned to Britain, he decided to form his own Buddhist organization, and in 1967 the Friends of the Western Sangha was formed. Since the name 'Sangha' was not self-explanatory in British culture, the name was swiftly changed to 'Friends of the Western Buddhist Order'. The following year, 13 men and women were ordained as *upasakas* or (in the case of the women) *upasikas*. This was the beginning of the Western Buddhist Order (as distinct from the Friends of the Western Buddhist Order). Upasakas and upasikas are given a spiritual name, which they can prefix with 'Dharmachari' if male, and 'Dharmacharini' if female:

these terms, which are of Sangharakshita's creation, mean 'followers of the Dharma'.

The Unity of Buddhism

The Western Buddhist Order has two linchpins. First, it aims to express an authentic form of Buddhism, but yet a version which is accessible to westerners. Second, as we have seen, Sangharakshita has taught that all the major traditions of Buddhism have an equal contribution to an understanding of Buddhist doctrine and to one's spiritual development. The varieties of Buddhism, although different, form a unity.

In what sense is Buddhism a unity? Firstly, Sangharakshita regards Buddhism as having a *methodological unity*. It should be noted, he says, that the three main strands of Buddhism – 'Hinayana', Mahayana and Vajrayana – are *yanas,* or 'vehicles', and the purpose of a vehicle is to enable the traveller to arrive at his or her destination. The particular vehicle (or yana) that one chooses is therefore a means to an end, and the true Dharma is what is conducive to gaining enlightenment, to eliminating *tanha* (craving) and to quenching the three fires of hatred, greed and delusion (the three fundamental Buddhist vices). Each Buddhist school provides different means of enlightenment, appropriate to the time and place at which it arose, and therefore meets the different spiritual needs of different people; however, each contains the basics of Buddhism. The White Lotus Sutra tells a parable of a rain cloud: the cloud delivers the same rain, but enables different kinds of plant to grow. Thus the same basic Buddhism is delivered throughout the three distinctive yanas, enabling different types of spiritual seeker to make spiritual progress.

What, then, is this basic Buddhism that can be found in all three traditions? The answer lies in what can be traced back to the earliest traditions that stem from the Buddha himself. All three traditions are historical developments of Buddhism's early traditions, and thus have *historical unity*. Sangharakshita believes in the legitimacy of modern western critical scholarship, which suggests that it is not possible to ascertain with certainty what the Buddha himself taught. However, it is possible to determine Buddhism's earliest strands, and, he believes, it is reasonable to assume that these were inspired by the Buddha. Among such aspects of basic Buddhism are the Four Noble Truths, the Eightfold Path, the three 'marks of existence' (insubstantiality, impermanence and unsatisfactoriness), the doctrine of the 'middle way', and the earliest monastic precepts. Sangharakshita believes that therefore Nichiren Buddhism does not preserve these aspects of basic Buddhism, since it ignores all of them, propagating sectarian teaching.

Sangharakshita points out too that Buddhism's three yanas do not set out to be mutually contradictory. Mahayana does not reject what is in the Hinayana, nor does the Vajrayana negate the Mahayana. They are successive layers of spirituality, and hence represent a *unity of spiritual development*. The Hinayana tradition's contribution to Buddhism was its ethics, its stress on the monastic life and its metaphysics. The Mahayana rejected none of these, but opened Buddhism up to the layperson, bringing in the devotional elements. The Vajrayana contributed the imaginative and mythical insights by means of its complex and colourful symbolic ritual elements. As a religion develops, Sangharakshita has argued, the initial experiential and spontaneous elements tend to crystallize into doctrines, and it is tempting for followers of the religion to assume that these crystallizations are the final form. To make such an assumption is to close the door to further experience and spontaneity. Thus, when the Hinayana tradition has been accused of being narrow-minded, such a criticism has force, not against its basic teachings, but against those followers who insist that it contains the final truths.

By the same logic, it should not be assumed that the final truth rests with the Vajrayana. Such an assumption would involve ossifying Buddhism by letting it crystallize in its Vajrayana form. Sangharakshita has therefore made a point of ensuring that other aspects of religious thought are allowed to enhance Buddhist belief and practice. Sangharakshita has given a series of talks on Al-Ghazali's *The Duties of Brotherhood in Islam,* he has encouraged members to take up martial arts such as t'ai chi, karate and aikido, and western poetry and music have been allowed to colour the lifestyle of WBO members.

If a Western Buddhist Order is be truly western and to make an impact on western minds, it must pay due regard to the findings of modern science. One example of this is in Sangharakshita's treatment of the concept of enlightenment, where he has allowed evolutionary theory to shed light on the path to its attainment. Traditionally, the cycle of samsara has been explained in terms of 'dependent origination' – the 12 nidanas, in which a chain of 12 links is postulated, each of which is said to give rise to the other: ignorance, karma formations, consciousness, name and form, the six senses (the western five senses plus thought), contact, feeling, craving, grasping, becoming, birth, old age and death. Each link is the 'condition' of the next, and, unless one of the links is removed (for example, by eliminating craving), then death will act as the condition of ignorance and the whole cycle will begin again. Nirvana, by contrast, is the 'unconditioned', and is gained when this chain of conditioning is made to cease.

Sangharakshita suggests that this is a somewhat negative way of viewing enlightenment. It portrays nirvana in negative terms, signifying the 'blowing out' of hatred, greed and delusion. Instead, Sangharakshita proposes the following 'evolutionary' model of understanding the path to enlightenment. The mind, he says, has a reactive and a creative element. The former belongs to the realm of samsara, and is lower, being concerned with the survival of one's social group, one's nation, one's caste or – especially – one's family. The latter is the 'nirvanic', and is concerned with spiritual evolution, rather than cyclical 'becoming'; it is concerned with the spiritual community rather than secular social groupings. Sangharakshita refers to a chain of conditioned arising, which – like the nidanas – has 12 elements: dependence on suffering, faith, joy, rapture, serenity, bliss, concentration, knowledge and vision of things as they really are, withdrawal, passionlessness, liberation, and finally knowledge and destruction of the poisons, which is enlightenment. (This is a somewhat curious list, relying more on Hinduism than on Buddhism: it seems to carry the implication that nirvana is 'conditioned' – that is, dependent on other factors for its being.)

From the 'Hinayana' tradition comes the practice of meditation. Indeed the WBO sees as one of the weaknesses of the earlier generation of British Buddhists that their commitment to Buddhism was largely confined to studying writings about it. WBO meditations are traditional rather than innovative: visitors to its meditation sessions might typically find themselves introduced to 'The Mindfulness of Breathing' – a breathing meditation in which the meditator is guided in following one's breath – or the 'Metta Bhavana' (literally, 'awareness of compassion') – a meditation designed to cultivate equanimity of affection, so that one regards oneself, one's close friends, people to whom one is indifferent, and one's enemies with an equalness of warmth. Upasakas and upasikas, who are inevitably more experienced in meditation than members of the public who attend the WBO meditation classes, undertake 'visualization' – a traditional meditative practice which is particularly carried out within the Pure Land and the Tibetan schools of Mahayana Buddhism. In visualization, the meditator uses a pictorial representation of a buddha or bodhisattva and attempts to reconstruct each detail of the picture within one's own mind: ultimately one should be able to do this without the assistance of pictorial data. The object of such practice is to cultivate the attributes of the buddha or bodhisattva figure within one's own nature: for example, the bodhisattva Manjushri is particularly associated with wisdom, whereas Avalokiteshvara represents compassion.

The three main Buddhist traditions – Theravada, Mahayana and Vajrayana – have often been viewed as complementary rather than contradictory, and the WBO combines their various elements in this spirit. In common with the Theravada schools, the WBO acknowledges the story of Gautama the Buddha and how he came to gain enlightenment, his basic teachings of the 'middle way' (avoiding extremes of wealth and poverty), the Four Noble Truths and the Eightfold Path. It also acknowledges his analysis of existence, that it essentially bears three 'marks' (or 'signs of being'), namely anatta ('no soul'), anicca (constant change) and dukkha (unsatisfactoriness, or 'suffering'). There being no permanent enduring soul, the self is merely a construct, but nevertheless one's deeds generate karma, which of necessity must burn out itself out. Accordingly, any 'karmic energy' which is outstanding at death will result in the rebirth of another being in the chain of samsara (the wheel of birth and rebirth). One may be reborn in one of six successive states – gods, asuras (anti-gods), humans, animals, hungry ghosts or hell-beings – until one finally attains release in nirvana.

From the Mahayana tradition comes the ideal of the bodhisattva: a being who has become enlightened, but renounces entry into full nirvana, continuing to incarnate in order to help one's fellow living beings. Nirvana thus encapsulates not just wisdom, which was a distinctive characteristic of enlightenment in the Theravada schools, but compassion combined with wisdom. Mahayana Buddhism also taught that there exists a multiplicity of buddhas, not just one single buddha (such as Gautama) in any one age. The multiplicity of buddhas and bodhisattvas encouraged the rise of a rich set of devotional practices: indeed it is arguably the case that the various bodhisattva devotional cults originally derived from the indigenous worship of gods and goddesses in their various countries of origin. The WBO incorporates devotional practices, directed towards the most popular buddhas and bodhisattvas, such as the buddhas Amitabha, Akshobya and Vairochana and the bodhisattvas Manjushri, Avalokiteshvara and Tara.

As far as the Tibetan tradition is concerned, members of the Western Buddhist Order typically study the history of the Tibetan tradition, and, more especially, its symbolic-ritual elements. Some of its devotional practices, for instance, make use of mantras derived from the Vajrayana tradition, and inspiration is drawn from figures in Tibetan Buddhist history such as Padmasambhava (the philosopher-magician), Milarepa (the austere yogi), Atisha (the scholar) and Tsongkhapa (the scholar-saint).

Redefining the Sangha

The WBO offers a radical and practical critique of the Sangha. Instead of being led by monks, and instead of portraying the monastic life as the ideal that is most conducive to making spiritual progress towards nirvana, the WBO is essentially a lay movement. Apart from Sangharakshita himself, none of the leaders have undergone monastic ordination, and even Sangharakshita does not dress in traditional monk's robes, but in conventional western attire. The basic level of support is that of the *mitra* ('friend'), but the deeper level of commitment is by receiving ordination as a *dharmachari* (male) or *dharmacharini* (female).

Some of the dharmacharis and dharmacharinis live in WBO communities, dedicating their lives to the WBO. More commonly, however, they will continue to pursue their own secular employment, provided of course that it is compatible with observing the Buddhist precepts. The only feature that visibly distinguishes them from laypeople is a cloth band which is worn around the neck, with a small medallion on it. This is normally worn at official meetings, not in one's everyday role outside the organization. It should therefore be obvious that this ordination does not involve anything like as radical a change in lifestyle as traditional monastic ordination, where the monk renounces the world and, as far as possible, avoids any contacts which might lead to worldly desires.

Also, WBO ordination can be given more swiftly than traditional monastic ordination. As someone once suggested to me, becoming ordained as a dharmachari or dharmacharini is parallel to confirmation in the Church of England, rather than full ordination as a deacon or priest. It is an expression of commitment, rather than a decision to follow the religion full-time as a career.

There are ten precepts to be observed by Order members:

I undertake to abstain from taking life.
I undertake to abstain from taking the not-given.
I undertake to abstain from sexual misconduct.
I undertake to abstain from false speech.
I undertake to abstain from harsh speech.
I undertake to abstain from useless speech.
I undertake to abstain from slanderous speech.
I undertake to abstain from covetousness.
I undertake to abstain from animosity.
I undertake to abstain from false views.

(Western Buddhist Order, 1975, p. 7)

This set of ten precepts differs from the *Digha-Nikaya*'s ten monastic precepts which are quoted in most standard textbooks. The WBO's list comes from an untitled sutra in which the Buddha instructs Cunda, a silversmith, concerning the Dharma. Cunda, being a layperson, is of course not required to assume the precepts that relate to a monastic lifestyle, such as the requirement that one does not eat at inappropriate times (normally after noon), that one's resting place is not over-luxurious, or that one does not handle money. The Western Buddhist Order is a lay order. Notwithstanding its continued contacts with traditional Buddhist groups, Sangharakshita and his followers tend to disapprove of a monastic lifestyle which relies exclusively on lay support. Sangharakshita has compared this with begging, and has encouraged his distinctive brand of Buddhism to make a transition 'from beggars to business'. Instead of asking less fully committed lay supporters to support the WBO financially, WBO communities have been set up to run in a self-sufficient manner. Mitrata run various WBO small businesses, which have spanned vegetarian restaurants, DIY shops, second-hand book shops, a printing press and so on. WBO also markets its own religious artefacts, stationery and publications. These enterprises are organized as 'Pure Land Co-operatives' and are run on a joint ownership basis: each member owns a share which is non-transferable, and which is surrendered when he or she leaves.

Such policies enable the WBO effectively to redefine the concept of the Sangha. The Sangha is thus not a distinct, specially 'spiritual' set of people who detach themselves from the laity but yet depend on them for survival. The WBO emphasizes the precept of 'right livelihood', claiming that followers of the Buddhist path have a duty to ensure that they are earning their living honestly, rather than 'begging' it from charitable laypeople.

Some members participate in community living: such communities tend to be single-sex, and members commit themselves to strict chastity. This entails an avoidance of heterosexual relationships, which Sangharakshita has viewed as distracting from the spiritual life, encouraging 'neurotic dependence'. He views heterosexual relationships that develop into western-style nuclear families as undesirable, since a family lifestyle is not conducive to the spiritual life. Sangharakshita has not taken the same view of homosexuality, however, and indeed members have even been encouraged to develop homosexual relationships, which he says are 'hardly sexual at all' (Rawlinson, 1997, p. 506).

In some respects the WBO's advent served to ensure a greater authenticity of Buddhist teachings. The previous brand of Buddhism propounded by writers such as Christmas Humphreys originally stemmed from Theosophy. In common with the Theosophists, Humphreys taught in the name of Buddhism that one could not be demoted in the wheel of samsara: once a human, always a human, until nirvana was attained. Notwithstanding Humphreys's status within British Buddhism, this doctrine is certainly not accepted as standard Buddhist teaching, and the WBO have done Buddhism a service in pointing out the more idiosyncratic doctrines that the previous generation passed off as Buddhist teachings. At the same time, it is true to say that the WBO has its own distinctive features too, since it especially aims to propound a form of Buddhism which will be more amenable to westerners.

The New Kadampa Tradition

While organizations like the Western Buddhist Order aim to develop new forms of Buddhism that they believe are more relevant to the

233

present-day world, for other western converts to Buddhism it is authenticity and maintenance of ancient practice that are important. This is witnessed by the tendency of many westerners to seek out traditional Theravada Buddhist groups, and in some case to establish branches of the Sangha that consist almost exclusively of westerners. One such example in Britain is the English Sangha Trust, founded under the leadership of the Thai teacher Ajahn Chah (1918–92) and now headed by an American Buddhist monk, the Ven Sumedho.

Western seekers who came into contact with exiled Tibetan teachers no doubt found much in Tibetan Buddhism to appeal to them. Its rich variety of imagery evidences a high degree of what one might call 'religious imagination'. Anyone visiting a Tibetan shrine room will undoubtedly be struck by the profusion and variety of images, and the elaborate ritual and symbolism characteristic of Tibetan ceremonies. To those who feel drawn to the Tibetan tradition, it is plain that there is a depth of spirituality that does not stand and deliver its meaning instantly to the impatient: its profundity can be learned only through long and intense periods of instruction, study and meditation, under the guidance of an accredited spiritual teacher.

Tibetan traditions

Tibetan Buddhism is usually classified into four main schools. There is the Nyingmapa school, which is the most ancient, and which draws widely on ancient pre-Buddhist myths and practices, which are largely shamanic. Of the four schools, the Nyingmapa is most renowned for its emphasis on magic and the paranormal, and lamas in this tradition are accredited with remarkable psychic and psycho-kinetic powers. Because of the scale on which the Nyingmapa draw on ancient pre-Buddhist practice they are sometimes referred to as the 'unreformed' school of Buddhism. Two further schools are the Kargyupa and the Sakyapa: these are known as the 'semi-reformed' schools, still retaining some of the pre-Buddhist elements. The fourth – the 'reformed' school – is of particular interest: the Gelugpa tradition, of which the Dalai Lama is the spiritual head. This is the school to which the vast majority of Tibetans have given their allegiance.

The New Kadampa Tradition is Gelugpa in character. Like other NRMs that I have discussed, NKT might well question its inclusion in this volume, particularly since followers claim to adopt an ancient form of Buddhism that goes back at least to the time of the Tibetan saint-scholar Tsongkhapa (1357–1419) and to be purifying his form of Buddhism of non-Buddhist elements that have no place in pure practice. Indeed some see the NKT as practising a form of Buddhism that is purer than that of the Dalai Lama himself. The organization came prominently into public attention in 1996 on account of the Dorje Shugden controversy: after veneration of this deity had been banned by the Dalai Lama, not only did NKT members pay no regard to his ruling, but publicly demonstrated outside a public meeting that the Dalai Lama was addressing. While Buddhists have occasionally engaged in active protests about actions and policies which they regarded as serious contraventions of Buddhist teaching (such as the Vietnam war in the 1960s), a demonstration against fellow Buddhists, and particularly against such a respected leader as the Dalai Lama was surprising, to say the least.

If the Dalai Lama is to be regarded as the spiritual leader and the focal point of Tibetan Buddhism, then any group that attempts to challenge his teachings, arguably, places itself outside the mainstream. As Thubten Jigme Nobu, the Dalai Lama's brother, has emphatically stated, 'The worship of Dorje Shugden is not a religion at all. It is a cult' (quoted in Lopez, 1998a, p. 67). Part of the controversy, as will become apparent, relates to another salient feature of NRMs, namely the fact that it is typically followed by westerners. Although a Tibetan lama presides over the movement, the vast majority of its followers are white British converts, and a number of its teachers are British. Organizationally, the movement is new: Geshe Kelsang Gyatso, its founder-leader, arrived in England in 1977, and the organization established itself under the name of 'New Kadampa Tradition' in 1991. Kelsang Gyatso was born in Tibet in 1932, having studied under several Tibetan lamas including Trijang Rinpoche (1901–81), who also taught the present Dalai Lama. Gyatso is a prolific writer, having completed 16 books over the past decade.

NKT aims 'to preserve and promote the essence of Buddha's teachings in a form that is suited to the Western mind and way of life. It is a new organization making an ancient tradition accessible to all' (New Kadampa Tradition, 1998a). Simultaneously with endeavouring to preserve the purity of the ancient Gelugpa tradition, NKT is concerned with westernization, and has grown rapidly since its inception.

Gyatso's work in Britain began with the Manjushri Institute (now the Manjushri Centre), a former Christian nunnery set in extensive grounds in the village of Ulverston in England's Lake District. In its early days Geshe Kelsang Gyatso presided over a small group of students of both genders who had taken up the Gelugpa monastic life, the majority of whom had embarked on the Institute's *geshe* programme. (A geshe is a teacher who has undergone extensive training, usually over a period of around nine years.) In addition to the geshe programme, the Manjushri Institute offered short residential courses, mainly on Buddhism, which members of the public could attend. Much work had to be done in repairing and renovating the premises, and this was largely carried out by the Manjushri students.

A typical daily programme would begin around 7 a.m. with meditation. This would normally involve Manjushri puja – the chanting in veneration of Manjushri, the bodhisattva who is said to represent wisdom. Within this ceremony there would normally be an opportunity to meditate on one's yidam. A yidam is a pictorial image that is used for visualization. Practitioners sit with their image in front of them, aiming to familiarize themselves with all its details, so that they are ultimately able to conjure up the picture of Manjushri (or some other buddha or bodhisattva who has been prescribed by one's teacher) in their own mind without the aid of the image. The purpose of such practice is to 'attain oneness' with the buddha or bodhisattva, realizing the virtues of this celestial being within oneself. Buddhism teaches that there is no individual self or soul; hence at an 'ultimate' level there is no distinction between what I regard as 'myself' and the essence of any buddha or bodhisattva. What I need is to realize this.

Daytime activities at the centre depend, obviously, on the programme on which one has embarked. Those on the geshe programme will receive teachings, while visitors will attend the seminars for which they have come, meditate in the shrine room, or simply go for walks in the area: it is perfectly acceptable to stay at the Centre for purely recreational purposes. In the early evening a further puja takes place. Most often this will be Chenrezig puja, Chenrezig being more familiarly known as Avalokiteshvara or Kwan Yin outside the Tibetan tradition. (The lineage of Dalai Lamas are believed to be incarnations, or emanations, of Chenrezig.) On special days other ceremonies take place: Lama Chöpa Tsog Day is celebrated twice in the lunar month, as is Tara Day. Other Buddhist festivals are marked too, such as the Buddha's Enlightenment, his Turning the Wheel of Dharma, and Je Tsongkhapa Day. Veneration is also given to 'protector deities', a practice to which I shall return shortly.

When I first visited the Manjushri Institute in 1981, all the ceremonies were in Tibetan, although it was possible to understand them by means of a service book which had an English and Tibetan parallel text. In order to enable English speakers to understand the practices better, NKT decided during the early 1990s to use English, rather than Tibetan, as the principal language for these rituals. A further adaptation, which can be found in NKT centres, is the availability of chairs rather than meditation cushions. In most Buddhist groups the meditation cushion is the hallmark of authentic practice, and westerners often take a pride in being able to sit unsupported for long periods. NKT thus combines Tibetan tradition with western adaptation.

The Dorje Shugden controversy

The historical origins of New Kadampa go back the scholar-saint Tsongkhapa (1357–1419). Tsongkhapa introduced various reforms into Tibetan Buddhism, laying particular emphasis on renewing the monastic life, and endeavouring to rid Tibetan of its pre-Buddhist shamanic elements. Tsongkhapa drew from all the existing Tibetan traditions, devising a new synthesis in doctrine, ethics and practice. He called his group Kadam Sarpa (New Kadam) at first. Kadampa means 'those who put all of Buddha's teachings into practice through practising the instructions on Lamrim (Stages of the Path)'.

The first Dalai Lama was a leading disciple of Tsongkhapa. A Dalai Lama, however, is not merely initiated within the Gelugpa school from which he emanates, but receives initiation into various Buddhist lineages. This not only explains their characteristically liberal outlook – Dalai Lamas have seldom proclaimed that their particular brand of Buddhism is superior to the others – but why they are revered not merely within their own tradition but by all Tibetan Buddhists (with the current exception of NKT).

The fifth Dalai Lama (1617–82) began his rule in 1642. He belonged to Gelugpa, but also used Nyingmapa teachings, enjoying a mystical rapport with Padmasambhava (Batchelor, 1998, p. 62).

237

This Dalai Lama had a rival, a tulku by the name of Drakpa Gyaltsen. (A tulku is an incarnate lama, identified specifically as a previous lama who has died. As is widely known, when a high lama dies, including the Dalai Lama, searches are conducted to ascertain who is his new incarnation.) According to legend, Tulku Drakpa Gyaltsen once defeated the Dalai Lama in debate, and was mysteriously found dead shortly afterwards, a ceremonial scarf having been forced down his throat. Whether this was murder, or whether he committed suicide, is uncertain. Dorje Shugden is held to be the spirit of this dead lama.

Drakpa Gyaltsen enjoyed the support of the King of Tsang, a region of Tibet, but this king was defeated by the Mongol ruler Gushri Khan, who gave the Dalai Lama supreme authority over the entire country of Tibet, thus endowing him with unprecedented authority. However, there were resentments as the Gelugpas attempted to weaken the other three main schools, not simply by debate and legislation, but by pillaging their monasteries and forcibly turning them into Gelugpa establishments.

Several calamities subsequently befell the fifth Dalai Lama. On one occasion dishes were apparently overturned by a mysterious invisible force as the Dalai Lama began his midday meal. This incident was attributed to Drakpa Gyaltsen's spirit, and several magicians and lamas were summoned to perform exorcisms. When they were unsuccessful, the Dalai Lama and other high lamas began to make offerings to placate the spirit, and thus Dorje Shugden came to be regarded as a Gelugpa protector. He was believed to protect the Gelugpa from Nyingmapa influence, punishing those who sought to introduce Nyingmapa elements into their practice. ('Dorje Shugden' literally means 'powerful thunderbolt'.)

Dorje Shugden practice tended to fall into neglect until the early twentieth century, when Pabongka (1878–1943) led a Dorje Shugden revival. Pabongka was the teacher of Trijang Rinpoche (1901–81), who taught both Kelsang Gyatso and the present Dalai Lama (Thapa, 1998). However, the thirteenth Dalai Lama (1876–1933), who came to office in 1895 when he was 19, had several Nyingmapa teachers, and incorporated Nyingmapa teachings into his practices. Pabongka was thus a rival, since he used Dorje Shugden practice to maintain the purity of the Gelugpa tradition. The thirteenth Dalai Lama therefore ordered Pabongka to cease to venerate Dorje Shugden. Pabongka complied, but subsequently became ill and attributed his illness to the cessation of Shugden practice. After condemning Dorje Shugden, the thirteenth Dalai Lama is said to have changed his mind on the issue and taken up the practice himself.

In 1973 the fourteenth (present) Dalai Lama condemned Zemey Rinpoche (1927–96), who had written down oral teachings relating to Dorje Shugden which he had received from his teacher. The text recounts the calamities of those who practise Nyingmapa teachings (the previous three Panchen Lamas, senior government officials of the thirteenth Dalai Lama, and even Pabongka), thus displeasing Dorje Shugden. The Dalai Lama condemned this material, despite the fact that Trijang Rinpoche had been his own tutor. (Ling Rinpoche was another tutor of the Dalai Lama who practised Dorje Shugden (Deus, 1997).) The Dalai Lama had himself been engaged in Nyingmapa practices under the guidance of Dilgo Khyentse Rinpoche, thus proving himself not to be in favour of 'purifying' the Gelugpa tradition by ridding it of these supposedly extraneous elements. The Dalai Lama subsequently refused to give tantric initiation to those who practised Dorje Shugden.

Following the Chinese invasion, the Dalai Lama fled from Tibet in 1959, in a remarkable escape in which he disguised himself as an ordinary monk. The escape was planned in fine detail by his tutor Trijang Rinpoche, possibly after consultation with one of Dorje Shugden's oracles. The Dalai Lama, apparently, relies on several oracles, including Tenma and Nechung, which enable him to make many of his political decisions. The state oracle, however, was said to have become jealous and began to defame Dorje Shugden.

Having fled from Tibet, the Dalai Lama appointed two Dorje Shugden worshippers in 1961 as his assistants: Geshe Rabten and Lati Rinpoche, and NKT members relate as evidence that Dalai Lama changed his mind about Shugden over the years. Affairs came to a head in March 1996, when the Dalai Lama formally pronounced his opposition to Dorje Shugden, saying: 'It has become fairly clear that Dolgyal (i.e., Shugden) is a spirit of the dark forces' (Batchelor, 1998, p. 64). The Tibetan government in exile is said to have conducted house searches, demanding that people sign a declaration stating that they have abandoned Dorje Shugden practice (Batchelor, 1998, p. 64).

It was the Dalai Lama's 1996 declaration that caused NKT's wave of protest. NKT members formed the Shugden Supporters Community, and, when the Dalai Lama visited Britain later that year, the group organized a picket outside the Buddhist Society headquarters in London where he was speaking. One placard bore the slogan, 'Your smiles charm, your actions harm' (*Guardian*, 6 July 1996). In the same year the Dorje Shugden Devotees Charitable and Religious Society was formed. A petition was drawn up, and NKT members were asked to sign. A further petition was circulated in 1998. After seeking legal advice, they were recommended to take the case to the supreme court in India, since it was reckoned that the Tibetan government in exile was violating Indian religious freedom laws. This has not been done, allegedly as a mark of respect for the Dalai Lama. The media portrayed NKT as a fanatical, 'fundamentalist' organization of demon worshippers, and, if Shugden supporters believed that the media would be encouraged to champion their case, they were very much mistaken. The Dalai Lama is held in too high regard in the west, and continues to serve as a symbol of Chinese communist oppression.

Events took a sinister turn when in February 1997 Geshe Lobsang Gyatso, Principal of the Institute of Buddhist Dialectics, and two of his disciples were murdered in Dharamsala. Lobsang Gyatso had supported the Dalai Lama on the issue of Shugden practice, and hence Shugden monks were blamed for the deaths – an accusation which, of course, Kelsang Gyatso denies. Equally, there are rumours of a secret society – the Secret Organization of External and Internal Enemy Eliminators (of Tibet) – who seek to kill anyone who practises Dorje Shugden. The Dalai Lama's brother is even alleged to be involved in such killings. Whatever the veracity of such rumours it is certainly true that, in July 1997, 200 of the Dalai Lama's followers physically attacked Shugden supporters (Deus, 1997).

The Dorje Shugden controversy hinges on his status within Buddhist cosmology. It is common for Mahayana Buddhist temples to have a *dharmapala,* or 'protector deity', who presides over the sacred space of the temple or shrine area. Officially the dharmapala protects the Dharma (the Buddha's teachings), although at a more popular level the protector deity can be construed as providing pragmatic benefits, such as good fortune or protection against illness. Herein lies part of the controversy: a buddha or bodhisattva only presides over a temple to protect the Dharma, not to offer worldly benefits, and a protector deity who merely offers earthly boons cannot be more than a god, who is subject to birth and rebirth in the same way as human beings.

What, then, is the status of Dorje Shugden? Dorje Shugden

opponents describe him as a 'dabla' – an enemy-defeating god. Dabla can bestow material benefits and provide protection to their supporters. Tibet is a dangerous country, on account of its climate, its high mountains, and its poor arability, and many Tibetans believe it to be populated with terrifying demons and spirits. Dorje Shugden personifies these fears, but is more: Dorje Shugden's anger can cause calamity, so many Tibetans 'entrust their lives' to him. The Dalai Lama has claimed that Dorje Shugden is a worldly god; although he previously offered puja to Shugden, he now claims that this is not beneficial, and even that the continued practice is a threat to his health and even to his life. He is supported by Ganden Lama, head of the Gelugpa school, and the College of the Sera monastery – one of Tibet's three most prestigious institutions – has expelled Kelsang Gyatso. His brother even questioned his status as a god, claiming that as the spirit of Drakpa Gyaltsen he can be no more than a ghost. Such characterizations of Dorje Shugden are of course repudiated by Kelsang Gyatso and followers of NKT. For them, Shugden is, like Tsongkhapa, an emanation of Manjushri, and equal in status.

The status of the Dalai Lama

The dispute between Kelsang Gyatso and the Dalai Lama admits of no obvious resolution. The Dalai Lama stands accused of restricting the religious freedom of followers of Tibetan Buddhism, and of causing widespread suffering to Shugden supporters, who are not denied access to their protector deity, but who are the victims of persecution, being unable to get jobs that relate to the Tibetan government-in-exile (for example, in schools), and are denied humanitarian assistance.

What is more, NKT members accuse the Dalai Lama of being superstitious, worshipping worldly spirits, and making decisions based on oracles, interpretation of dreams and divination. The Dalai Lama has increasingly relied on the Tibetan state oracle since 1970s (Deus, 1997). One practice which is repeatedly mentioned in this connection is a form of divination that involves throwing a pair of small dough-balls in the air, and deciding one's course of action on the basis of the way in which they land. He appears to believe too that his well-being might be adversely affected by Dorje Shugden practice. NKT members see all this as running counter to the picture of the Dalai Lama which the media portray and which westerners absorb. He is typically perceived as rational, presenting a form of religion that appeals to western intellectuals, who claim that it is thoroughly compatible with western science. Yet he does not call on his fellow Tibetans to abandon belief in dablas, oracles, divination, and other elements that are deeply embedded in an outmoded world-view and which would normally be regarded as superstitions in the west.

While the west has come to perceive the Dalai Lama as the good-hearted, good-humoured religious leader who embodies all that is good in the Buddhist religion, NKT claim that westerners have uncritically imbibed a highly sanitized version of Tibet and its religion, a version that has been fuelled by books like *Seven Years in Tibet* (and its recent film version). The pre-invasion Tibetan government, they claim, was ruthless: people were regularly beaten by police, living conditions were rough, and Buddhism far from 'pure'; the Dalai Lama was even prepared to include the old Bön religion, originally highly hostile to the Buddhists, as a form of Buddhism (Thapa, 1998).

Traditionally, the Dalai Lama has been regarded as an incarnation of Chenrezig, who embodies the Mahayana ideals of wisdom and compassion, but, if NKT is right, how can a bodhisattva be in such serious error and cause so much suffering? Kelsang Gyatso therefore questions the traditional status attributed to the Dalai Lama. As he recently stated:

> It is not possible for the Dalai Lama to be a Buddha and then to degenerate; therefore, the only possibility is that he is an ordinary being and his actions are showing it. A real Buddhist does not need to be afraid of spirits, so why should he be? (Dwang, interviewed by Deus, 1997)

Supporters of the Dalai Lama are resentful of NKT, regarding its members largely as westerners who have no first-hand familiarity with Tibet, but who are trying to reform a tradition that they do not understand fully. They accuse them of sectarianism, alleging that NKT members must offer unquestioning loyalty to Kelsang Gyatso, whose writings form the sole focus of their study.

The dispute shows no signs of any resolution, and the most likely outcome is that NKT and the Dalai Lama's followers will simply go their separate ways. Both parties continue to campaign. On the one side, the Shugden Supporters Community and the Dorje Shugden

Devotees Charitable and Religious Society continue to petition the
Dalai Lama. On the other, the Dalai Lama's supporters continue to
campaign for Buddhists' allegiance; the Tibetan Youth Congress has
travelled to various monasteries in India campaigning for monks to
affirm their continued loyalty to the Dalai Lama.

Conclusion

This chapter has examined four quite diverse expressions of
Buddhism in the west. At the time of writing, there is no single
form of the Buddhist religion for which westerners have a clear
preference. The different varieties offer different benefits: Osho and
Soka Gakkai offer pragmatic help with everyday living and are
markedly world-affirming; the Western Buddhist Order and the New
Kadampa Tradition give more emphasis to making spiritual
progress, while making their respective versions of Buddhism
available to the laity. Although there are some westerners who have
managed to take up a full-time monastic existence, such a lifestyle is
generally not possible for the average westerner whose interest in
Buddhism has been aroused. In the case of Soka Gakkai and NKT,
their aim has been to offer Buddhism to a lay following, but yet to
maintain its authenticity. For Osho and the WBO, by contrast,
adaptation is desirable, indeed necessary for the west.

Eastern tradition and western uptake cause tensions, as can be
seen from the confrontational stances assumed by the Nichiren
Shoshu priesthood and the Soka Gakkai laity, by western NKT
supporters and the Dalai Lama. Osho, of course, has deliberately
confronted all the mainstream religions by his outrageous criticisms
of them. The WBO stands in an uneasy relationship with other
mainstream Buddhist groups, often supporting their activities, but at
the same time presenting a form of Buddhism which arouses
suspicion, particularly in the wake of the recent homosexuality
controversy. Seeking to resolve such tensions, or at least learning to
live with them, will certainly be an important part of western
Buddhism's agenda over the next few decades. In the meantime, its
varieties continue to provide an attractive alternative to seekers who
are unable to accept the God of Christian theism.

7. Independent new religions

Jewish and Islamic new religious movements are perhaps not so well known or documented as the New Christian movements or the Hindu- and Buddhist-related NRMs discussed in other chapters. Apart from certain Sufi groups that have a western following, and which may or may not be considered 'authentic' forms of Sufism, NRMs that are derived from Judaism and Islam tend to be restricted in their evangelistic scope. Although it is possible for gentiles to convert to Judaism, a Jew is technically someone who is born of a Jewish mother, and hence there is a clear distinction between someone who is a Jew by birth and someone who is a proselyte. In some new Jewish groups one's affiliation presupposes that one is already a Jew: for example, the 'messianic Jews' seek to combine their Jewish identity with a recognition of Jesus of Nazareth as the messiah; similarly the Lubavich Jews are already Jews, but claim that the messiah has now come in the form of their leader Rabbi Menachem M. Schneerson.

In the case of Islamic groups, such as the Black Power movements led by George Jackson, Malcolm X (the Nation of Islam), and Michael X, allegiance presupposes a black Muslim identity which serves to exclude any white westerners who may have sympathy with their cause. The same holds true of Black Power Jewish groups. Although the vast majority of Rastafarians are black, it is worth noting that there are a few Afro-Chinese and Afro-East Indian Rastafarians as well as a small handful of white Rastas.

None of the groups selected for discussion in this chapter (the Rastafarians, the Baha'i and Subud) would claim a Jewish or Muslim identity. However, there can be little doubt regarding the influence of Islam on the Baha'i and Subud, both of whose founder-leaders

244

were Muslims. The Rastafarians are more problematic in terms of the taxonomy I have adopted in this volume. In Turner's scheme they are 'Hebraist': although the majority of converts to Rastafarianism either were practising Christians or came from Christian homes, the movement emphatically rejects Christianity. Rastafarians do not accept that the Christian New Testament refers to Jesus Christ, but reinterprets certain parts as prophecies heralding their present-day saviour, Haile Selassie. Arguably they are closer to Judaism than Christianity, although they make no pretence of claiming an identity in either faith.

The Baha'i faith

Of all the new and emergent religions of the world, the Baha'i faith has probably elicited the greatest degree of public sympathy, for two main reasons. First, its ideals are commendable: who indeed could fail to admire a faith that pursues the virtues of justice, love, trustworthiness and truth, purity and chastity, and service for others? (Momen, 1997, pp. 12–20).

Second, far from being the perpetrators of the kinds of atrocity attributed to NRMs, the Baha'i have been the victims of severe persecution, and thus have elicited much public sympathy. In its early years, some 9000 of Baha'u'llah's followers are estimated to have been murdered by the Persian authorities, and in more recent times over 200 have lost their lives in Iran, following the 1979 Islamic revolution (Martin, 1965/1985, p. 272; Baha'i, 1992, p. 59).

The origins of the Baha'i

Examining the origins and development of the Baha'i faith is somewhat problematical. The vast majority of writings on the Baha'i faith tend to be written by practising Baha'is, and the few textbooks which give separate coverage to the faith appear to have appropriated the Baha'i version of events, without subjecting it to critical scrutiny. Moreover, as MacEoin (1998) points out, the writings of the Baha'i founder-leaders – the Bab, Baha'u'llah and Abdu'l-baha – although vast, are not available in full, and tend to be largely unknown, even to Baha'is, who merely possess short selections of the writings of Baha'u'llah, which they use for devotional purposes. The Baha'i scriptures tend to have eluded scholarly attention, partly because of this lack of available sources, and partly through a relative lack of interest on the part of western scholars.

The account of Baha'i history that Baha'i sympathizers normally give is as follows. Siyyid Ali Muhammad (1819-50) was a descendant of Muhammad, and an Iranian merchant. He claimed to be 'the herald of one greater than himself', the witness to 'him whom God shall manifest'. He introduced a number of innovatory religious practices, relating principally to prayers and to rules for living. These innovations heralded the dawning of a new age, and Siyyid Ali Muhammad became known as 'the Bab', which means 'the gate' – signifying the opening of this new era. The Bab gathered followers around himself, from which he drew 18 principal disciples, whom he called 'Letters of the Living'. All except one was an immediate male follower living in Shiraz; the one woman lived some distance away, but had written a letter to the Bab expressing her commitment to him. She became known as 'Tahirih', meaning 'the pure one'. The Bab's disciples travelled through various parts of Iran, spreading his message. In 1844 the Bab went on pilgrimage to Makkah: on the night of 22 May in that year he declared that God's 'manifestation' was present on earth. Baha'is regard this date as marking the beginning of the Baha'i faith, and this is signified by the distinctive Baha'i calendar, which defines all other dates from this point.

The Bab was charged with heresy against Islam. Some of his followers were involved in a plot to assassinate the Shah, but Baha'is insist that they were not involved in this. He was arrested in 1844, and again in 1846. His followers were persecuted, and many lost their lives. The Bab himself was executed in 1850. His tomb can be visited at Haifa in modern Israel.

After the Bab's death, Mirza Husayn Ali (1817–92), now better known to his followers as Baha'u'llah, claimed to be the fulfilment of the Bab's prophecy. Baha'u'llah was born in Tehran, of a wealthy family. Although his father was a minister of state, Ali was not interested in politics, but in spiritual matters (Sheppherd, 1992, p. 29). His mission is said to have commenced in August 1852. At that time he had begun to serve a prison sentence for alleged conspiracy against the Shah. While in prison he experienced a revelation, which Baha'is compare with those of Moses, Jesus and

Muhammad – a kind of inaugural vision. (Momen, 1997, p. 119.) Given the option between exile in Russia or in Iraq, Baha'u'llah chose the latter. During the following ten years, Baha'u'llah attempted to establish a small community around him in Baghdad, but did not disclose his revelation. When the Baghdad authorities forced him to leave in 1863, he decided to declare his mission to his followers: this occurred during a 12-day period in a garden called 'Ridvan' (meaning 'paradise'). The Declaration of Baha'u'llah marks the transition of the movement from Babism to Baha'ism. The Baha'i continue to celebrate the Declaration of Baha'u'llah in the Feast of Ridvan, a 12-day festival spanning late April and early May. Faced with the spread of Baha'u'llah's message, the authorities moved Baha'u'llah on, first to Istanbul, then Edirne, and finally Akka (Acre), near Haifa, where he was imprisoned for two years.

In Edirne, Baha'u'llah composed letters to various world political leaders, including Napoleon III, Kaiser William I, Tsar Alexander II, Queen Victoria and Pope Pius IX. In these letters, Baha'u'llah discussed their policies and responsibilities, declaring his aim of world peace (the 'Most Great Peace'), and proclaiming himself as the Messenger of God. He informed the Pope that the return of Christ had occurred in his advent. Queen Victoria, apparently, was the only state authority to take Baha'u'llah's letters seriously, commenting, 'If this is of God, it will endure; if it is not, it can do no harm' (Sheppherd, 1992, pp. 44–5).

Baha'u'llah died in Bahji, near Akka, in 1892. On his death, Muslims (Sunni and Shi'ite), Christians, Jews and Druzes all came to pay their respects, which indicates the high regard in which he had come to be held by the various major faiths.

After Baha'u'llah's death, the Baha'i leadership passed to Abdu'l-Baha (1844–1921), who had accompanied his father on his mission since the age of eight, and whom Baha'is recognize as Baha'u'llah's authorized interpreter. (The name Abdu'l-Baha means 'the servant of splendour'.) Abdu'l-Baha travelled widely: to Egypt, Europe and North America. The first western converts were gained in 1894, and by 1900 there were several thousand Baha'is in North America, and a few small groups in Europe.

One final figure must be mentioned in this outline of Baha'i history. He is Shoghi Effendi (1897–1957), Abdu'l-Baha's grandson, whom Abdu'l-Baha appointed as 'Guardian of the Faith' and 'Interpreter of Scripture'. Shoghi Effendi had an important role to play in the institutionalization of the Baha'i faith, paving the way for the establishment of the Universal House of Justice, the supreme ruling body of the Baha'i, which came into existence in 1963, shortly after his death. Shoghi Effendi was responsible for a second wave of worldwide proclamation of the Baha'i message, initiating a Ten-Year World Crusade (1953-63), which in fact outlived him. It was during this period of outreach that the Baha'i faith attracted a substantial following from Third World countries, particularly Uganda, Bolivia, Indonesia and India, where the faith did much to address the problems of poverty and illiteracy.

Shoghi Effendi died in London in 1957, without children. This raised a problem of succession, which hitherto had been through progeny. His authority passed to the 'Hands of the Cause of God' – some 27 people whom Effendi had appointed as 'Chief Stewards of the Faith'. Today the Baha'i seat of authority is in the Universal House of Justice, in Haifa in Israel, which was established in 1963, and which consists of nine elected men whose decisions are binding on the rest of the Baha'i community. Below this body are the National Spiritual Assemblies in each country, and Local Spiritual Assemblies. LSAs are democratically elected by local members, and NSAs by democratic vote within the LSAs. Similarly, the nine men in the House of Justice are appointed from the NSAs. Individual Baha'is are not allowed to campaign for election, since their suitability for the task should be more important than any personal magnetism or persuasiveness that they might bring to bear. Decisions of Baha'i bodies are binding on each lower echelon of authority, down to the individual member; however, any individual has the right of appeal against any decision, which he or she can take as far as the Universal House of Justice.

Baha'i beliefs and practices

One of the key principles of the Baha'i faith is unity. Baha'ism acknowledges the insights of all religions, all of which have had their own messengers, who have passed on their insights into the true nature of God and God's message to humanity at their particular time and place. Baha'is typically refer to these messengers as 'Manifestations of God' and believe that they appear at roughly 1000-year intervals with teachings appropriate for that age. Thus

Abraham, Krishna, Moses, Zoroaster, Buddha, Jesus, Muhammad, the Bab and Baha'u'llah are all divine manifestations, with Baha'u'llah being the last of this line of messengers, and the Manifestation for the present era. Baha'is view divine revelation as progressive: although Baha'u'llah is the culmination point of all these other past messengers, he will not be the last: another messenger can be expected, although not for another 900 years or so.

Since the various world religions have given rise to their respective divine messengers, it follows that the God of each religion is one and the same. The Baha'i affirm the unity of God, although all attempts to define him are inevitably limited. As Baha'u'llah taught:

> All that the sages and mystics have said or written have never exceeded, nor can they ever hope to exceed, the limitations to which man's finite mind hath been strictly subjected. (Momen, 1997, p. 92)

God can be referred to in terms of his attributes: he is All-Wise, Ever-Forgiving, the Most Generous, the Almighty, the All-Glorious, the Most-Bountiful, to cite but a few terms that Baha'is typically attribute to God. However, these are only partial indicators of God's nature. While the Abrahamic traditions are inclined to use personalistic metaphors to describe God's nature, certain forms of eastern spirituality, such as Advaita Vedanta, conceive of ultimate reality in a more impersonalistic way: thus brahman is not a person, but an impersonal cosmic ground of all there is. Although Baha'is may appear to favour using personalistic descriptors for God, Baha'is claim that eastern and western religions do not assume different concepts of ultimate reality, but are really looking at it from a different standpoint. Abdu'l-Baha claimed, 'The differences among the religions of the world are due to the varying types of minds' (Abdu'l-Baha, quoted in Momen, 1997, p. 92), and each type of mind can only claim limited relative truth. A similar point applies to gender-specific characterizations of God. Baha'i literature explains:

> Like previous Messengers of God, Baha'u'llah used the masculine pronoun when referring to the Creator. To have done anything else would have violated all conventions of Arabic – the principal language in which Baha'u'llah wrote.
>
> Baha'u'llah stated explicitly, however, that God is beyond any comparison to human form or gender. Accordingly, the issue of whether to refer to God as 'He,' 'She,' or 'It' does not arise in Baha'i discussions. (Baha'i, 1992, p. 34)

One's soul is similar to the divine essence. Attributes like gender, colour and race are attributes of our physical bodies. They do not belong to the soul, which is separate from the body, the seat of one's true self, and the substance that survives death to attain eternal existence. In particular, the prophets and the Manifestations of God 'perfectly reflect all of the names and attributes of God' (Momen, 1997, p. 94): they stand in place of God in the physical world, and if we want to conceptualize God's attributes, this can be best accomplished by considering his Manifestations. Although identical to God in its attributes, the soul is not identical to God in terms of its substance: in western philosophical jargon, it is not 'numerically identical' with God. Similarly, the universe is not identical with God: God is separate from creation, whose purpose is that men and women should cultivate God's love.

Baha'is espouse a number of principles, attributed to Baha'u'llah. These are:

- the oneness of humanity
- the equality of women and men
- the elimination of prejudice
- the elimination of extremes of wealth and poverty
- the independent investigation of truth
- universal education
- religious tolerance
- the harmony of science and religion
- a world commonwealth of nations
- a universal auxiliary language. (quoted from Bah'ai, 1992, p. 28)

Elimination of prejudice entails non-discrimination against individuals on the grounds of religion, race, class or gender. (Baha'is do not mention sexual orientation in this context: homosexuality is disapproved of.) The reference to religion presupposes that other religions will not simply vanish, with Baha'ism solely remaining: as we have noted, all other religions are worthy of respect, and many will continue to follow them. The Baha'i were opposed to the racism and Nazism of the two world wars; however, they have not at all been reassured by the alternative emergent ideologies of western capitalism and religious fundamentalism. Under capitalism, the strong exploit the weak, and fundamentalism brings with it fanaticism and persecution.

The equality of the sexes entails that education should be available for boys and girls, for men and women. Indeed, if resources are insufficient to provide education for all, women should be given priority, on the grounds that they will be the ones who will educate the next generation. Baha'is believe that traditionally female tasks such as child-rearing should be given due recognition as equally important activities to paid employment. They also claim that differences in the roles of men and women are culture-specific, and not endemic.

In terms of the institutional structures of the Baha'i faith, women have equal eligibility to hold office in any of the Local and National Assemblies; there is but one area in which women are excluded from office: unlike men, they may not be members of the Universal House of Justice (Momen, 1997, p. 40). Abdu'l-Baha said that the reasons for this would one day become clear. (Roger Cooper (1982) identifies other areas in which men and women receive differential treatment: women receive less inheritance, and their possessions are deemed to belong to their husbands, unless they can demonstrate that the husband has specifically assigned belongings to them. Additionally, only men may undertake Baha'i pilgrimages.)

Justice is a prevalent theme in the above list. Baha'u'llah taught, 'The best beloved of all things in My sight is Justice' (Sheppherd, 1992, p. 72). While Baha'is extol the virtues of economic justice, they seek to eliminate extremes of wealth and poverty, rather than promote a strict egalitarianism. They also believe that sharing should be voluntary, rather than imposed by some egalitarian political system. Baha'is currently collect from members a voluntary wealth tax (huququ'llah), which amounts to 19 per cent of a member's surplus of income over expenditure. This money goes to the World Centre of the Baha'i Faith.

In championing the independent investigation of truth and the harmony of science and religion, Baha'is believe that a religion should not lay down in advance what is scientifically true, or issue defined lists of books that may not safely be read. A well-educated community will be able independently to undertake intellectual enquiry and distinguish truth from error. On the creationist–evolutionist controversy, Baha'ism agrees with Darwinism that species evolve, but denies that human beings evolved from a lower species: humanity is a separate creation of God.

Education underpins economic justice and intellectual enquiry; hence Baha'is have been actively involved in education projects, particularly in the Third World, teaching villagers literacy, rural technology, health and hygiene, and a number of women's crafts. Education, they hold, should not merely include teaching the traditional pragmatic skills, but also spiritual education – an essential component if the Baha'i goals are to become a reality.

The Baha'i vision of an ideal world goes beyond economic justice and scientific enquiry: it aims to achieve an entirely new world order, involving a global civilization, a world under a single government, which will rule through international courts of justice and enforce its law through an international military force. It will be a world in which poverty, injustice and discrimination are eliminated, a world in which there will be universal lasting peace. Unity will be the key theme, and men and women will share a system of universal weights and measures, a universal single currency, and a universal common 'auxiliary' language, in order to communicate and promote mutual understanding. Note that the language is typically described as 'auxiliary': it is not envisaged that the new world order's common language will supersede the variety of languages and dialects that already exist on earth. The universal language may be English, being one of the most commonly spoken, or it may be a new artificially created language (perhaps like Esperanto). Whatever transpires, retention of one's cultural identity will remain important.

If this all sounds unattainable, Baha'is ask whether it is not even more unrealistic to suppose that humankind's current ideologies will achieve an ideal world order. Nationalism, racism and communism have all failed, and capitalism and religious fundamentalism show no signs of bringing about a world in which all men and women live together in total harmony.

In view of the fact that a large proportion of Baha'i teachings are about political and ideological systems, it may seem surprising that, until recently, Baha'is taught that their members should abstain from involvement with politics. Many Baha'is have viewed politics as essentially adversarial, concerned with winning and losing, with party interests promoting at best the interests of majorities rather than the well-being of all, and emphasizing the material rather than the spiritual. They have therefore avoided any attempts to attain their goals either through creating a specifically Baha'i political party or by championing the cause of one particular party-political organization. To create this new world order, people need to be educated spiritually, in order to see the futility of materialistic attempts to solve the world's problems.

In the 1980s Baha'i policy began to change. The Baha'i International Community gained consultative status as a non-governmental organization with several of the United Nations' subsidiary organizations, such as ECOSOC and UNICEF. It has a similar role in the European Community and supports organizations such as the Worldwide Fund for Nature (Sheppherd, 1992, p. 104). Individual Baha'is are permitted to vote in elections, although they may not themselves seek political office, and party political matters are considered inappropriate for discussion amongst Baha'i members. Until such time as the new world order is achieved, Baha'is undertake to obey the laws of the country in which they reside.

The new world will not truly be achieved, however, until everyone is persuaded of the truth of the Baha'i message. However, Baha'u'llah himself forbade aggressive proselytizing: in particular, threatening non-believers with hell was declared particularly unacceptable. One highly popular Baha'i meeting is known as the 'fireside' – gatherings at Baha'i homes for disseminating information and stimulating discussion. Baha'is have sometimes deliberately moved into areas where there is a low or non-existent Baha'i population, to maintain a presence there. (This is called 'pioneering'.) In these ways the Baha'is share their vision, confidently envisaging that the Baha'i faith will become the religion of the world within this 'cycle' (1000 years).

Spiritual practice

Baha'is affirm and endeavour to abide by the Ten Commandments, and Baha'u'llah stressed the value of 'honesty, trustworthiness, chastity, service to others, purity of motive, generosity, deeds over words, unity' and 'work as a form of worship' (Baha'i, 1992, p. 28). There are no specific dietary laws that Baha'is observe, although they abstain from alcohol (including foods that contain alcohol as an ingredient). Baha'is are meat-eaters (unlike Muslims, they will even eat pork), although Baha'u'llah once said that, in the new world order, men and women would live on fruit, nuts and grains.

The taking of recreational drugs is unacceptable, and so is gambling, which fuels materialism. Although smoking is permitted, it is discouraged. Sex should only be practised within marriage: premarital and extramarital sexual relationships are prohibited: 'The

Baha'is do not believe in the suppression of the sex impulse but in its regulation and control' (Shoghi Effendi, quoted in Momen, 1997, p. 17). Marriage is encouraged, although it is not compulsory. 'Backbiting' is said to have been the offence against which Baha'u'llah spoke most strongly (Sheppherd, 1992, p. 70): speaking ill of others and criticizing them behind their backs was something which, he taught, was particularly destructive and reprehensible. Baha'u'llah's version of the 'golden rule' was specifically targeted to one's speech:

> O Son of Being! Ascribe not to any soul that which thou wouldst not have ascribed to thee, and say not that which thou doest not. This is My command unto thee, do thou observe it. (quoted in Sheppherd, 1992, p. 68)

The spiritual life

Baha'is should pray and read from their sacred writings every day. There are three 'obligatory prayers' to be recited daily: one is long, one is of medium length and one is short. The long prayer, which takes 15 minutes to recite, may be said at any time of the day; the second is to be recited three times a day, in the morning, at noon and in the evening, and the third – the shortest – is also for noon time. Prayers are to be said out loud, not merely rehearsed internally, although in private, and they should be said facing Bahji, where Baha'u'llah is buried. Prayer is undertaken exclusively for one's own edification: it is not for the purpose of giving God some list of instructions to carry out on behalf of human beings. Baha'is are also encouraged to 'meditate', although there is no prescribed form that the meditation must take. One might chant 'Allahu Abha' ('God is most glorious'), which Baha'u'llah recommended should be chanted 95 times a day. Scriptures should be read twice daily, in the morning and at night: there is no set lectionary, the choice being left to the individual follower. Prayer and meditation should form the initial stages of a five-point progression: prayer, meditation, inspiration, volition and faith, and finally action (Sheppherd, 1992, p. 90).

Baha'ism has a variety of festivals which are celebrated throughout the year. Baha'ism has defined its own calendar, dating from the Declaration of the Bab (23 May 1844). Thus, for the Baha'i, the year 2000 CE is 156 BE, 'BE' signifying 'Baha'i Era'. There are 19 months, each of 19 days, making a total of 361. To make it a solar calendar, four intercalary days are added between 26 February and 1 March, with a further additional day every leap year. These intercalary days are for preparation for the month of fasting, and are days of hospitality, giving and parties.

Each month bears the name of one of God's attributes (for example, Azamat, meaning 'grandeur', and Nur, meaning 'light'), and begins with a 'feast'. The year begins on 21 March with the festival ('feast') of Naw-Ruz (New Year). The 'feast', which heralds each new month, is not a large banquet, but rather a day in which a Baha'i family will offer food and hospitality to other members. The celebration normally has three parts: devotional, consultative and social. Close non-Baha'i friends and sympathizers may sometimes be invited to the social aspect. There is no fixed formula for such events: it is the host who normally selects readings from Baha'i scriptures and devises entertainments.

Other Baha'i Holy Days include the Ascension of Baha'u'llah (29 May), the Martyrdom of the Bab (9 July), the Birth of the Bab (20 October), and the Birth of Baha'u'llah (12 November). Ridvan is the 'Lord of Feasts', and commemorates the Declaration of Baha'u'llah. Hence it is the most important day in the Baha'i calendar, marking the 12 days spent by Baha'u'llah in the Ridvan garden before he left Baghdad, in the course of which he made his Declaration.

The month of Ala is the month of fasting. No food or drink may be consumed between sunrise and sunset, and no smoking is permitted during this period. There are certain exemptions, however. Baha'is who are under 15 or over 70 need not undertake the fast, and the sick, travellers, pregnant women, menstruating women and mothers who are breast-feeding are also exempt. The fasting is symbolic, indicating the need to abstain from fleshly desires, and to renew oneself. The fast ends with Naw-Ruz.

In addition to the festival year, pilgrimage is encouraged, although restricted to men only. Previously the two main pilgrimage shrines (the 'Greater Pilgrimage') were the House of the Bab in Shiraz and the House of Baha'u'llah in Baghdad, at which fairly elaborate ceremonies were performed. The former, however, was destroyed in 1979 following the Iranian revolution, and there are obvious difficulties about making a pilgrimage to any Baha'i sacred place inside Iran. Hence, if one cannot make the 'Greater Pilgrimage', a 'Lesser Pilgrimage' will suffice, and many Baha'is visit the tombs of the Bab and Baha'u'llah.

Life-cycle rites

Various life-cycle events are placed within the context of the Baha'i faith. These consist of the naming of a newly born child, marriage and death. The naming ceremony is a simple and fairly informal act of dedication and thanksgiving; unlike Judaism or Islam, there is no ritual obligation such as circumcision. The marriage ceremony again is informal, and has no fixed pattern. In order to become joined in marriage, however, it is necessary for all the living parents of the bride and groom to give their consent.

When a Baha'i member dies, he or she should be buried no more than an hour's journey from the place of death. Cremation is discouraged. The feet of the deceased should face the 'qiblah' at Akka. Prayers for the dead are recited: it is believed that one can assist them in the afterlife by means of prayer and good works. Saying prayers on behalf of the dead is in fact the only time that Baha'i prayers are recited communally.

Baha'u'llah also taught the importance of preparing for death. It is the duty of a Baha'i to make a will, and, if a Baha'i dies intestate, there is a specific method of distributing his or her estate, in accordance with Baha'u'llah's teachings.

Life after death

Baha'is believe that there is something beyond our mortal existence on earth, but that the afterdeath state is beyond human ability to encapsulate in language. Metaphors, however, are helpful, and the analogy of coming from the womb into the world is an image that Baha'is frequently draw upon. As Sheppherd writes, 'This world is the womb of the next' (Sheppherd, 1992, p. 60). The 'womb' metaphor conveys both the inadequacy of our present concepts to encapsulate the world to come and the firm belief that one's earthly life is a period of preparation for this future state.

Just as there is nothing that 'enters' the newborn child on birth into the physical world, so the soul does not literally 'enter' the body, either at the moment of conception or at birth. Abdu'l-Baha explained that words like 'descent' and 'entrance' apply to bodily entities that can be spatially related to each other, and of course no such relationship holds between soul and body. After the death of the body, the soul simply continues its eternal existence, independent of a physical body.

Preparing the soul for this world to come is more important than theological speculation. Ideally this preparation will have already started, with prayer, meditation, obedience to God's laws and service: with these eternal life has already commenced. According to the quality of one's life one may expect to experience 'heaven' or 'hell', not in the sense of places of paradise and torment respectively, but rather in the sense of proximity or remoteness to God. The soul that has gained salvation is the one in which the divine light has manifested itself in the human self. By contrast, those who have not paid due attention to the spiritual life will find themselves far removed from God's presence, although this state is not unalterable. Most souls in fact can expect to pass through many worlds in order finally to reach God. One can assist the progress of those who have died by means of prayer, and for this reason Baha'is will often intercede on behalf of the dead.

Newest world religion or NRM?

The historian Arnold Toynbee wrote:

> Bahaism is an independent religion on a par with Islam, Christianity, and the other recognized world religions. Bahaism is not a sect of some other religion; it is a separate religion, and it has the same status as the other recognized religions. (quoted in Baha'i, 1992, p. 10)

The majority of scholars of world religions are more cautious, with some justification. The grounds for the Baha'is' claim are: (1) they are numerically strong, with membership running into millions of followers; (2) they do not regard themselves as either an Islamic sect or a syncretistic group; (3) they are a worldwide movement like Christianity, Buddhism and Islam; and (4) a number of Baha'is are uncomfortable at being classed as a new religion, pointing out that their origin can be traced back to the mid-nineteenth century.

As far as numbers are concerned, the Baha'is' total membership is currently around 5.6 million. Baha'is therefore constitute only 0.09 per cent of the world's population, and there are less than half as many Baha'is as there are Jews or Sikhs. This places them, arguably, at about level pegging with the Church of Scientology (also an international organization), and there are only half as many Baha'is as attendees at the Jehovah's Witnesses' annual Memorial.

Despite the Baha'is' insistence that they are not an Islamic sect, several features of the Baha'i faith are fairly distinctively Islamic. MacEoin (1998) points to the strong influence of Shaykhism within Shi'ite Islam in the 1820s and 1830s. Emphasis was given to the need for continuing inspiration in Islam and the 'age of inner truth' (1840s). When the leader of the Shaykhi sect of Islam died in Iraq in 1844, the question arose as to who should succeed him, and it was in this context that many turned to 'the Bab' as a possible successor. The Bab claimed to be Mahdi, the hidden imam, consistently with the expectations of certain Shi'ite groups that their leader had not died, but merely gone into hiding, from whence he would one day return.

As MacEoin points out, the notion of religious truth as directly revealed through God is Islamic, and the term 'manifestations of God' comes from Shi'ism and 'theosophical Sufism'. The idea that history contains a series of prophets, from Adam to Jesus Christ and eventually Muhammad is thoroughly Islamic. The Baha'i innovation, of course, is to incorporate figures from other world faiths (such as Krishna, Zoroaster and the Buddha), and to contend that Muhammad was not the 'seal of the prophets', to be superseded by the Bab and Baha'u'llah. The fact that Baha'u'llah delivers an ethical-social-legal system with a view to establishing a universal world government in which there is no separation of religion and politics is again very reminiscent of the Islamic system of shar'ia, where religious law is binding on individual, society and government alike.

Additionally, the religious obligations of the Baha'i bear striking similarities to the Five Pillars of Islam. There is the Baha'i Confession of Faith: 'There is one God. All knowledge comes to man from God through His Messengers ... The Messenger of God for this age is Baha'u'llah.' Compare this with the Muslim *shahadah:* 'There is no God but God (Allah), and Muhammad is his prophet.' There is prayer at prescribed hours, although it is true that Baha'u'llah simplified the practice and reduced the number of prayer times from five to three. There is the obligation to give to the poor and thus level out inequalities of wealth. The month of fasting corresponds to Ramadan, and the list of those who are exempt is almost identical in both faiths. Finally, the importance of pilgrimage is held in common by Muslims and Baha'is alike, and, as MacEoin points out, the idea of visiting saints' shrines is very much in the Sufi tradition.

The Baha'is' emphasis on the continuity between Babism and Baha'ism helps to support the argument that the Baha'i faith has a tradition that spans a century and a half, and hence that it is a world faith rather than a new religion. However, there are several significant differences between the earlier Babism and the later Baha'ism which subsequently developed. The Bab was very much part of the Islamic Shaykhi sect; hence his movement was not a worldwide movement, but a distinctively Islamic one, with laws against unbelievers. The Bab was militant, advocating 'the striking of necks, the burning of books and papers, the destruction of shrines, and the universal slaughter of all save those who believed and were faithful' (quoted in McEoin, 1998, p. 632). The later Baha'i ideal of the unity of religions and world peace is far removed from such teaching.

When the Bab died, the question of succession was controversial. There were several claimants to be the predicted 'Manifestation', of whom the Baha'u'llah was one. Indeed, despite claims sometimes made by Baha'is that the movement is unified and unbroken by schisms, a number of splinter groups have formed over the years, some of which have been the result of disputes about succession of leadership: Barrett (1996) mentions the New History Society (founded in 1929 in New York), the Baha'i World Union (also known as the World Union of Universal Religion and Universal Peace, founded by Amin Effendi in 1930), Baha'is Under the Hereditary Guardianship (also known as the Orthodox Baha'is, founded in 1960), and Baha'is Under the Provisions of the Covenant (a breakaway group from the previous one, founded in 1971).

The Baha'is' claim to be an emergent world religion provides an interesting example of how an original small group within a major world religion gradually moves from being a sect to an independent movement. However, the Baha'i movement needs further growth and spread before it gains wider recognition as a new world religion.

Subud

Although the Baha'i enjoy a fairly high profile in religious circles, Subud is relatively unknown. In common with several other NRMs discussed in this volume, Subud denies being a religion. Subud claims to have no creeds or teachings: followers are encouraged to find their own spiritual truth, mediated through their main spiritual practice, the latihan. Subud does not seek to attract its followers away from the religion into which they were born, but rather aims to awaken the soul (*jiwa*), opening the door of the inner self to a direct recognition of the Great Source of Life.

Since Subud does not exist as an additional religion that competes for allegiance against other traditions, Subud's founder-leader, Subuh, suggested that it should be regarded more as an association or a fraternity.

From the scholar's standpoint, Subud is clearly religious. It has a firm belief in the supernatural, offering its members a means to contact the Great Source of Life and to maintain a relationship with God. Subud operates functionally as a religion, since the latihan mediates guidance for life to its followers, offering explanations of birth, marriage and death, and a distinctive way of regarding the world. It defines the ultimate concerns of purifying the soul and rising beyond the lower levels of human existence. Finally, Subud exhibits the characteristic features of a religion, principally an experiential dimension, coupled with ritual, ethical and (to a more limited degree) mythological components; and it has a clearly defined institutional structure. Subud's claim to have no teachings is somewhat of an exaggeration; even in religions that profess to have no dogma, there are usually elements of a world-view that underpin their other salient features. This is no less true of Subud, which offers distinctive beliefs which are not normally shared by mainstream Buddhists, Christians, Hindus and Muslims.

Subud's founder-leader is Muhammad Sukarno Sumohadiwidjojo (1901-87), who was born in the village of Kedungjati in Java and raised as a Muslim. He is better known to his followers as Subuh, or as 'Bapak' (which means 'Father'); sometimes members combine these two names and refer to him as Pak Subuh. 'Sukarno' was Subud's given name at birth, but – so it is said – he became ill in his early childhood, whereupon a wandering mendicant informed his parents that he had been inappropriately named, and that they should change his name to 'Muhammad' (Needleman, 1970, p. 110).

Subuh's inaugural experience occurred in 1924 when he was a young man. He worked during the day in the town of Semarang as a civil servant, and studied book-keeping when he got home, often until midnight. After finishing studying, he would put his books away and go out for a walk. On one such walk he became suddenly aware of an extremely bright light in the sky which appeared to descend upon him. His body began to shake violently and his chest pulsated. Thinking that he was experiencing the onset of a heart attack, he hurried home, went directly to bed and committed himself to God in anticipation of a possible imminent death. To Subuh's surprise, he survived, but continued to feel as if this radiant light filled his entire body, an experience which, he later said, continued for a thousand nights. This was Subuh's 'opening', the first *'latihan kejiwaan* of Subud'* (Lyle, 1983, pp. 11–13).

After 1928 Subuh stopped having these spontaneous experiences. He married and had children. A number of acquaintances, however, came to regard him as someone with special insight, and in 1933 he received a revelation about his mission: anyone who wished to share Subuh's experience could receive the same divine contact as Subuh. The first latihan took place in 1932. The term *latihan kejiwaan* literally means 'spiritual exercise' or 'training of the spirit' and became Subud's core religious practice. The following year Subuh felt that he was receiving guidance through the latihan to give up his paid employment. This involved financial hardship, but he was able to manage, he believed, through God's grace. In 1945, at the end of the Second World War, he went to Jogjakarta to join the Army Medical Corps. During his service there he conducted 'openings' on Tuesdays and Saturdays. In 1948, however, he felt that he was receiving guidance that he should not be working with the armed forces, and he resigned, returning to civilian life as a builder.

Subuh did not want the latihan to be accessible only in Java, but to be available throughout the world. The opportunity for disseminating the latihan internationally arose in 1954 when Husein Rofé, an English Muslim, visited Subuh in Jakarta and received the 'opening'. Rofé travelled to Turkey and Cyprus, spreading the message, finally returning to England, where he invited Subuh to come at his expense. Subuh was hosted at Coombe Springs, where John Bennett – then a follower of Gurdjieff – received the 'opening'. Bennett later wrote *Concerning Subud* (1958), one of the first detailed introductions to the movement.

The group adopted the name 'Subud', an acronym for 'SUsila, BUdhi, Dharma', which Subud followers translate respectively as 'good morals', 'inner force' and 'submission' or 'surrender'. The

Hindu-Buddhist terminology that features in this explanation is significant. Subud literature uses ideas and vocabulary from a variety of traditional religions, seeking to enhance them rather than compete with them. The only forms of religion to which Subud is opposed are 'cults' (Rieu, 1983, p. 124). By this is meant eastern forms of paranormal practice, some of which have recently gained in popularity in the west, particularly in New Age thought. Rieu mentions especially the practices of magic, fire walking, and the techniques of fakirs and other holy men who seek to amaze their audiences rather than to improve the state of their souls. Followers of Subud do not deny that such powers exist, but insist that they are confusing, inefficacious and even dangerous. Those who possess such powers are likely to find that they disappear as a result of the latihan.

The name 'Subud' only coincidentally resembles 'Subuh', and is in no way intended to signify some special status that is accorded to the organization's founder-leader. Subuh made no pretentious claims either about his own person or about his message, which is simple and clear. He did not regard himself, nor is he regarded by his followers, as a prophet, a saint or even as a teacher. He described himself as a *mogol,* that is to say a Muslim who is not well versed in Islamic sacred texts. He never claimed to have achieved perfection, and his followers regard him as having had faults and failings like everyone else. Asked about his spiritual status, Subuh once remarked, 'Bapak is just Bapak.'

Being unversed in scripture and claiming no special status, Subuh said he had no teachings to impart to members. During his lifetime, however, he gave numerous talks to followers: these were always spontaneous and unprepared, and spanned a variety of topics, ranging from the latihan to marriage, education, business and politics. These addresses were delivered entirely in Indonesian, and when his audience was non-Indonesian his talks were simultaneously translated, and later transcribed for future reference.

The latihan

The latihan is central to Subud. An enquirer who wanted to participate would first be assigned to a 'helper' of the same gender, for a three-month period. (The three-month waiting period is waived in the case of those over 63, and no one under the age of 18 is accepted for the latihan.) The helper will answer any questions that the enquirer wishes to ask, and the three-month period serves to ensure that the seeker is serious and is sure of his or her wish to join. Subud members use the term 'contact' to describe the initial transmission of the experience, and at his or her first latihan the new member is said to receive 'opening', with the aid of the helper.

Followers typically emphasize a number of respects in which the latihan differs from other eastern forms of meditation. It differs from yoga and other forms of breathing meditation in that there are no prescribed breathing exercises or special instructions that are given to the follower. Unlike certain forms of tantric practice, one is not required to have attained any special status as an adept before one is admitted: the latihan is open to all, without payment, and is not surrounded by secrecy; in fact Subud has been described as the 'Path of the Ordinary Man'. The latihan does not result in some altered state of consciousness, loss of freedom, or hallucinatory visions.

Members normally meet for the latihan two or three times during the week: early in the week (Sunday, Monday or Tuesday) and on a Friday. The event takes place in a room or a hall with open space, uncluttered by furniture. The sexes are segregated, and meet in different rooms. The meeting begins with participants sitting quietly, until a helper stands, and announces the latihan's start. Members then stand and simply wait to 'receive'. There are no special instructions or theories about what should be done: God himself is the trainer, and God does the 'opening'. One needs to empty one's mind, banishing all problems and questions in it, and simply 'surrendering' to God. Unlike certain forms of Buddhist meditation, practitioners are given no instructions about how to clear the mind from distracting thoughts, or how to focus on some 'no-thought'. One waits to hear the 'voice of silence', which can manifest itself in a number of ways.

During the latihan members may find that they move, make noises (sometimes animal noises), walk around, dance, jump or skip. What happens is in accordance with one's inner state. Such activities are said to be purificatory, bringing out the spiritual and physical poisons that exist in the soul, and changing the soul from within. As a consequence, one gains responsibility, and becomes an 'actor' or agent, rather than an instrument. Latihan also strengthens and reinforces one's religious observance (*shariat*), the study of one's

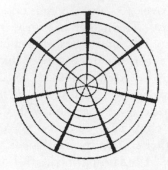

Figure 7.1

religion (*karekat*) and the awareness of the 'reality of religion' (*hakekat*) (Rieu, 1983, p. 112). Such awareness does not normally contradict the teachings of the religion to which one belongs, but serves to grant great conviction. Bennett cites the example of a follower who found himself reciting the Apostles' Creed during the latihan and became convinced of its absolute truth; until then he had regarded himself as a 'rational Christian' and had been sceptical of the Church's traditional creeds (Bennett, 1958, p. 182).

The latihan in fact offers unlimited spiritual development. The Subud symbol consists of seven concentric circles, cut into seven equal segments by spokes that emanate from the centre (see Figure 7.1).

The circles illustrate seven powers, or 'the seven great spheres of universal life' (Bennett, 1958, p. 113), which are:

(1) Material Power
(2) Vegetative Power
(3) Animal Power
(4) Human Power
(5) The Power of the Complete Man
(6) The Power of Compassion
(7) The Power of the Supreme Lord

The seven radial lines in the emblem signify that each of the seven powers permeates each of the seven levels of spiritual development, although in different degrees. Apart from the first, each of these powers grows out of the previous one on the list, and the level that each individual has attained depends on which of the seven powers is dominant.

264

This can be illustrated by the first power. Whatever our state of spirituality, we are all of necessity in contact with the material world; indeed our senses – the very source of the mind's knowledge – could not operate if there were not things to see, hear, taste, smell and touch. The very sensory images that the mind forms are those of material objects: if someone uses a word like 'table', we instantly conjure up the mental image of a material table. However, if we let Material Power dominate our existence, we become attached to our material possessions, feeling secure only when we have them, and fearing that we might lose them. In its worst form, those who are dominated by Material Power will resort to violence, stealing or even killing in order to acquire the material possessions that they desire. Thus Material Power is also said to be satanic power.

Plant Power transcends Material Power, since plants are alive and since plant life supports other forms of life in the world. It is also held to be 'the source of all the diverse impulses that form the "nature" of men and animals' (Bennett, 1958, p. 117). Vegetative Power, it is taught, is the 'force of desire', and men and women who are dominated by Plant Power have strong, clear impulses. Animal Power is the source of character: although one is human in physical shape, it is possible that, in terms of one's character, one is more like a dog or a pig. Animal Power gives beings their personality.

Human Power is available to those whose souls have been awakened. As with the other Powers, Human Power is both a set of qualities that permeate the universe and a level of spiritual attainment. Depending on one's level of spiritual attainment, one's external human qualities can manifest themselves in different ways. One example that Subuh frequently discussed is sex. Sex is essential to human existence, firstly because it is through procreation that humans come into being, and secondly because human beings are gendered, usually with accompanying sexual impulses. Most men and women's sexual activities, Subuh taught, emanate from their animal impulses, but, when they are carried out at the level of Human Power, they fulfil God's purpose and further the soul's perfection.

The first four Powers are called 'the four lower powers' (Bennett, 1958, p. 115), and only these four are accessible to men and women. The Power of the Complete Man and the Power of Compassion 'are entirely beyond the apprehension of the human mind' (Bennett, 1958, p. 114), and cannot be encapsulated in words or mental images. The seventh, the Power of the Supreme Lord, 'is beyond the highest possible human consciousness' (Bennett, 1958, p. 114). Because of their ineffability, there is therefore little that can be said about these higher Powers.

One further point about the Subud emblem needs to be made. The circles and spokes constitute the visible content of the symbol, depicting the seven qualities and levels. What the symbol does not illustrate is how it is possible to make the transition from one level to another, or how they are united with each other. The emblem is therefore said to have an invisible content containing 'two further essences': the Primal Essence (or the Great Life Force) and the Holy Essence (Sacred Essence, or Holy Spirit). The Great Life Force is not a personal God, but an impersonal force which permeates everything in the universe; it is responsible for the exchange of substances which is vital to the maintenance of the universe's life. The Holy Essence proceeds from God's will, and this Essence makes it possible for essences to 'return to their source'; Bennett equates this Holy Essence with 'The Lord and Giver of Life' mentioned in Christianity's Nicene Creed.

According to Subuh, human beings have already existed as *jiwas* (souls) before birth. As a result of their entry into the material world, however, they have become caught up with material objects and desires. The latihan awakens them and enables them to be adept at living in the world. Subud does not advocate asceticism, which Subuh described as *diledek* – meaning 'being tantalized'; the ascetic, in other words, never finally attains the desired state of complete attainment, but, like Tantalus in the ancient Greek myth, has to perform the same onerous tasks time and time again. The normal expectation, although by no means a requirement, is that members live ordinary lives in the normal world of work, engaging in business and economic transactions, marrying and bringing up families, but with honesty and integrity, aiming to eliminate *nafsu* (the Indonesian term for 'passions'), and attempting to eliminate the typically human failings of impatience, complaining, criticizing and harbouring hostile feelings towards others. Bettering human life in this world is one of Subud's principal aims. Rieu, writing on behalf of the Subud organization, describes Subud's 'main worldly objective' as 'the founding and funding of various kinds of welfare project' (Rieu, 1983, p. 190).

Although Subuh did not extol austerity, a number of Muslim

followers observe the month's fast at Ramadan, and were encouraged to do so. Some Christian members have believed that they were guided to observe Lent. A few Subud members have on occasion decided to observe both periods of fasting. Subuh taught that fasting was not obligatory; if it was done at all, it should be done with honesty, and for the purpose of subduing *nafsu*. It should not be a perfunctory act which one was glad to have finished with at the end of the fasting period, but an opportunity to subdue one's desires, so that one reached a position of not wanting cigarettes, alcohol or whatever one relinquished for that period. Subuh did not extol the practice of one religion above another: Ramadan and Lent, he taught, were of equal value.

Spiritual benefits of latihan

The latihan provides the means for the soul to return to its Source. At one level, this implies awareness of God's presence and the receiving of the Power of the Spirit to enable followers to live their lives to the full. However, the practice of latihan affects the way in which one meets death. Subuh regarded both spiritualism and reincarnation as offering somewhat unsatisfactory accounts of life after death, although he was influenced by both. Since humans consist of souls and bodies and can expect bodily resurrection (a belief common to Christianity, Islam and Zoroastrianism), the likelihood of being transformed at death from one's earthly abode to the 'second Abode' with a 'second body' depends on the degree of presence of the soul in the body. The soul is not present in the 'ordinary man's' body (that is, the person who has not experienced the 'opening' in the latihan), and a soul-less body can only return to earth to experience physical life once again. Those whose bodies are imbued with their soul can progress to the spiritual realm. They can also be helped by the actions of those on earth, and the latihan can be performed by the bereaved to assist loved ones who have died. One's deeds are significant in determining one's passage in the afterlife; for example, Subud stresses sexual purity, and the effects of a promiscuous sex-life would be likely to result in a significant period in purgatory to cleanse the effects of such misconduct.

It is believed that God has created man and woman to attain union in the afterlife. This is one principal reason for marital fidelity

267

and appropriate sexual behaviour. It also explains why Subud does not encourage the monastic life or other lifestyles that involve celibacy, but encourages 'this-worldly' activities, including marriage and marital sex. Male and female partners can expect to be reunited after death. In the case of those who firmly believe that the latihan has guided them into a celibate lifestyle, they can have the opportunity to meet their true spouse after death (Bennett, 1958, p. 165). Of course, there have been religious leaders, such as Jesus of Nazareth, who have lived an unmarried life. In the case of Jesus, Subuh taught that he was a complete soul, containing male and female attributes in undivided union. Jesus' virginity was therefore not like human virginity, and hence there will be no celestial wedding banquet in which Jesus will be united with a chosen, separate bride.

If the latihan is so important, it may be asked why humanity has had to wait for so many centuries before it became available. Subuh's answer was that the time was now right for it to come, since the development of science and technology had caused men and women to become cut off from their inner being. The latihan provides the opportunity to regain contact with one's inner self or soul.

The Subud latihan is regarded as being too powerful to do more frequently than twice a week. However, it was said that Subuh was in latihan all the time, and in 1977 the idea of all Subud members being in continuous latihan gained momentum. During a tour of Britain, a follower had mentioned to Subuh the problem that, owing to life's pressures, it took up to half an hour in the latihan before he could commence the practice untrammelled. Subuh's reply was that followers should not think of the latihan as a brief twice-weekly occurrence, but something that permeated one's life, work and leisure. The following extract from one of Subuh's addresses illustrates this:

> This is our latihan. The latihan is life. It is a life that is within our life and encompasses our whole life. It is something that goes on forever. It has no boundary, and this is why Bapak said that once we have received the latihan, once we are open, the latihan is our possession, it is part of us, it goes with us wherever we are and whatever we do. So that this latihan, this vibration or this movement of life that is within our life, is the grace of God which is called in Islam the *qadar ilham* or the essence or nature of God, the essence of God's power which is given to us in our normal life as we normally are. (Rieu, 1983, p. 28)

According to Subuh the latihan was more powerful than the Muslim *salat* (prayer). A pious Muslim who observes the set times of prayer prays to Allah for a total of 75 minutes per day; a continuous latihan lasts 24 hours a day! (Rieu, 1983, p. 30).

Islamic, syncretistic or non-religious?

Indigenous Pacific religion centres around nature, with myths involving a marriage between the earth and the sky, the former being female (as in 'mother nature') and the latter male. The forces of mother earth and father sky combine to ensure the production of rice, the divine plant. To maintain the cosmic order that is required for the growth of adequate crops, correct behaviour (*adat*) is required, not only of humans but of spirits and animals. Belief in an impersonal supernatural force that pervades the world is prevalent. Javanese mystical thinking posits a higher form of knowledge that can be gained through the acquisition of inner intuitive feelings by the soul. This soul is regarded as a kind of substance that can be expanded within the self, and is held to exist alongside a personal spirit. Through various techniques the spirit world can be helped by the activities of humans on earth.

There are some affinities here with the ideas of Subud: the interaction between higher and lower powers and forms of knowledge; the notion of a soul that exists in varying degrees within the self, and which can be expanded; and a belief in personal and impersonal spiritual forces alongside one another. The idea that animals and humans must be true to their own nature to ensure spiritual progress, together with the essentially pragmatic nature of Javanese religion, may well have had a bearing on Subud and, in particular, on its founder-leader. Religions are seldom, if ever, 'pure' or completely innovative, and this is no less true of Subud. Being little known, despite having been in existence for over 50 years, it offers scope for further scholarly research into its origins and sources.

Rastafarianism

Rastafarianism is more of a movement than a single homogeneous religion. Rastafarians have no agreed creed; practices vary, and there

269

are many groups with different leaders and different messages. There are of course recurring themes. Most groups draw on the Black Power movement that swept through Jamaica from the 1940s onwards, seeing the black population's future in a return to Africa, specifically to the country of Ethiopia, whose former leader Haile Selassie is hailed as God, the messiah and the saviour of the black people. Rastafarianism can therefore be considered as a 'cult' in Troeltsch's sense of the term, being loosely organized, and outside the dominant culture.

Origins

The black Jamaicans were descendants of the Caribbean slave population, four million of whom had been brought by the whites in the four centuries of the slave trade (*c*. 1460–*c*. 1860). Obedient and submissive to the white population, the slaves had been conditioned by Christian missionaries to believe that slavery was part of God's ordering of society, and they found little condemnation of it by the Christian churches. Despite the emancipation of slaves in 1835, Jamaica continued to be governed by the British until 1962.

The 1930s in Jamaica has been described as the 'decade of despair'. The Great Depression brought unemployment, and most of the black population who found work could expect very low wages. In addition, a series of hurricanes wreaked havoc in the Caribbean, destroying crops and living quarters. Some of the black Jamaicans began to organize themselves politically, and there were labour disturbances in 1938, first in Westmorland and then in Kingston. Others, however, saw no future in Jamaica, and a number of 'Back to Africa' movements began to rise. The time was right for the rise of charismatic leaders who would show the black population the way to liberation.

One of the earliest black Jamaican leaders was Marcus Mosiah Garvey (1887–1940). Garvey was not explicitly the founder of the Rastafarians, but his ideas heralded their rise. Known as 'Black Moses', he taught that the black Caribbeans were the lost tribes of Israel, and that their future lay, not in Jamaica, but in the 'promised land' of Africa, where they would emigrate and resettle. Garvey's study of the Bible suggested to him that an African king would be crowned as the messiah-redeemer, and specifically mentioned

Ethiopia as the country. In 1918 Garvey founded the United Negro Improvement Association, and departed for America to propagate his ideas. He was arrested and imprisoned, and in 1927 deported to Jamaica, where he continued his activism. Garveyism tended to lose its momentum in the late 1920s, and Garvey departed for London in 1930. Garvey's ideas influenced the inception of Father Divine's Peace Mission, as well as subsequent Black Muslim and Black Jewish groups.

The Black Power movements gained renewed impetus when Haile Selassie was crowned Emperor of Ethiopia in 1930. At that time, Leonard Howell (d. 1981) had gained prominence as a black leader, and it was Howell who heralded the rise of Rastafarianism as we now know it. According to newspaper reports, Howell taught hatred against the white people, advocating the supremacy of the blacks, and revenge on the whites for their past oppression. However, whereas Garvey had taught political activism and self-reliance, the emergent Rastafarian movement, heralded by Howell, laid much more emphasis on divine help and intervention to remedy the black people's plight. The black population could expect a return to Africa, for which they should prepare, acclaiming Haile Selassie as their supreme ruler. Howell became leader of a community of 500 people at Pinnacle, Jamaica, an isolated village, high in the mountains of St Catherine, and which was only accessible by foot. It was there that Howell instigated the practices that are most typically associated with Rastafarianism, including the smoking of ganja ('the herb' – marijuana). The police raided Pinnacle in 1941, after which the community dispersed, returners taking up residence at Back-O-Wall, a shanty town at Kingston. Howell was charged with sedition: he had sold photographs of Haile Selassie to his supporters for a shilling each, telling them that these would be the passports that would secure them entry to Ethiopia. Howell also distributed a 'Black Man's Bible' – selected portions of scripture which had been 'restored' to their original meaning from the Amharic texts. (Rastafarians typically claim that the original language of the Bible was Amharic and that the white races have distorted its true meaning, to their own advantage.)

Other precursors of Rastafarianism include H. Archibald Dunkley, a Christian, who opened a mission in Kingston in 1933. After studying the Bible for two and a half years, he concluded that Haile Selassie was the messiah, to be identified with Rastafari (God),

271

the 'Root of David' and the 'King of Kings'. Dunkley attracted a number of Garvey's followers.

The interest in Ethiopia and the rise of the Rastafarian movement took great strides in the 1950s, and Rastafarianism spread to other Caribbean Islands, and also to the USA and Britain. Haile Selassie raised Rastafarians' hopes in 1955 when it was announced that he was building a navy, and intended to send ships to America and possibly Jamaica. In the same year he aided the 'Back to Africa' movement by setting aside some 500 acres of Ethiopian land for black resettlement. Haile Selassie's state visit to Jamaica in 1956 was a high point in Rastafarian expectations. In 1958 the first Rastafarian Universal Conventional was held, a major attempt at institutionalizing the movement. However, hopes of reaching Ethiopia were consistently dashed: the rumours of ships to transport the Rastafarians to their promised land never materialized; and, apart from the very small area of Ethiopian land, which was never augmented, the Ethiopian government gave little encouragement for black resettlement, and indicated that mass immigration was simply not feasible.

Rastafarian thought

Rastafarians are generally opposed to Christianity, since it is the 'white man's' religion with its 'white man's Bible'. Christianity has legitimized slavery, and the Bible has been tampered with to suit the white races' own ends. In particular, the Roman Catholic Church is identified with the beast and the harlot, to which the Book of Revelation refers, although Rastafarians seem equally opposed to Protestantism. Some Rastafarians reject the Bible altogether. However, Haile Selassie's coronation as Emperor of Ethiopia in 1930 gave many supporters of the Black Power movement the impetus to study the Bible again and to find new meaning in it. The Bible, they contend, is a primordial source of wisdom, and demonstrates that God's chosen people were black, not white:

> But now they are blacker than soot. (Lamentations 4:8)

> Though I am like a wineskin in the smoke,
> I do not forget your decrees. (Psalm 119:8)

Much of the Bible is symbolic, and needs a key to unlock its true meaning. It highlights God's supremacy over creation, his providence over his people, and the sending of his prophets. Particular emphasis is given to the major prophets of the Hebrew scriptures, notably Isaiah, Jeremiah, Ezekiel and Daniel. The apocalyptic parts of Matthew and Mark's gospels are accepted, as are the prophetic parts of the Psalms, and the Book of Revelation. Revelation is supremely important for Rastafarians, since it contains the titles accorded to the coming King of Kings.

The Bible provides a history of God's oppressed peoples from ancient times to the present day. The story it tells is of a God who once appeared in human form, and was incarnated in a series of avatars: first Moses, then Elijah, and then Jesus Christ. Jesus himself makes statements like, 'Before Abraham was, I am' (John 8:58), thus indicating previous existence many centuries earlier. The fourth and final incarnation is in the form of Ras Tafari, otherwise known as Haile Selassie, the Emperor of Ethiopia, to whom Rastafarians accord the title, 'King of Kings and Lord of Lords' (Revelation 19:16). Haile Selassie is thus the returned Christ, the saviour and redeemer of his people. According to Rastafarian teaching, the four avatars have an important point in common: they did not experience death. Moses is left on Mount Nebo surveying the promised land; Elijah escapes death by being taken up into heaven in his fiery chariot; Jesus, apparently, did not experience death through crucifixion, but simply disappeared to continue life in India.

This belief in the succession of divine avatars is accompanied by a general belief in reincarnation. The black people are held to be the reincarnations of the ancient Israelites, the lost tribes of Israel; like the Israelites of old, they have been exiled from their home country and punished by subjection to slavery. However, their time of slavery is now near its end, as can be seen from the Bible, which is believed to refer to present-day events. For example, 'Ethiopia shall soon stretch out her hands unto God' (Psalm 68:31).

The Book of Daniel tells of 'four great beasts' with wings – one like a lion, a second like a bear, and a third like a four-headed leopard. The fourth is not compared with any animal, but is exceptionally strong, with ten horns and iron teeth, with which it devours and breaks things in pieces, treading down what remains with its feet. The writer continues with the following description:

I beheld till the thrones were cast down, and the Ancient of days did sit, whose garment was white as snow, and the hair of his head like pure wool: his throne was like the fiery flame, and his wheels as burning fire.

273

A fiery stream issued and came forth from before him: thousand thousands ministered unto him, and ten thousand times ten thousand stood before him: the judgment was set, and the books were opened. I beheld then because of the voice of the great words which the horn spake: I beheld even till the beast was slain, and his body destroyed, and given to the burning flame. As concerning the rest of the beasts, they had their dominion taken away: yet their lives were prolonged for a season and time. (Daniel 7:9–12)

The Psalmist's explicit mention of Ethiopia is regarded as highly significant, of course, and Daniel's reference to the hair being like wool is construed as a reference to the 'dreadlocks' that are typically worn by Rastafarians. The mention of the four beasts is held to be a reference to the four incarnations: Moses, Elijah, Jesus and Ras Tafari. The 'King of Kings and Lord of Lords' is not to be regarded as a reference to Jesus, but to Haile Selassie. In fact, Rastafarians have typically used some of the hymns that their forebears were taught by Christian missionaries, substituting the word 'Negus' for 'Jesus'. ('Negus' is a synonym for Haile Selassie.) For example:

Negus shall reign where-e'r the sun
Doth his successive journeys run.

Rastafarians have no agreed concept of God, apart from the belief that the white people have portrayed him as a 'white god' or a 'white man's god', and that such a portrayal needs to be challenged. Some have stated that 'God is black', describing him as a 'thick darkness' that exists in motionless space (Barrett, 1974, p. 174). Some Rastafarians regard the black God as a physical being, who once walked the earth, and who is literally one and the same as Haile Selassie. One informant reasoned that, since Haile Selassie did not die, but remains alive somewhere in Ethiopia, God is a physical being who literally resides somewhere in that country.

Haile Selassie himself never acknowledged either being God or being the redeemer of the black people. He was himself an Ethiopian Orthodox Christian, who worshipped at the local cathedral, and was never in any regular conversations with the Rastafarians. The Rastafarians attribute his failure to assert his messiahship as an act of humility, and claimed to be in 'spiritual communication' with him during his lifetime. The hope of resettlement in Ethiopia received a further setback when Haile Selassie was deposed by a military coup in 1974, and died under house arrest the following year. Firm in their belief that the righteous do not die, some Rastafarians at first denied such reports, dismissing them as part of a 'Babylonian conspiracy'. More prevalent, however, are eschatological expectations associated with the King of Kings: some hold that he will be resurrected, while others expect him to return on the clouds of heaven. Other Rastafarians have 'spiritualized' the concept of Ethiopia, believing that it signals some better age for the black people, but not necessarily a literal return to Africa.

It is sometimes said that Rastafarians do not believe in death. This does not appear to be wholly consistent with the belief that each of the divine incarnations is a reincarnation of the previous one, or that the black people are a reincarnation of Israel's lost tribes. According to Clarke (1986), such apparent inconsistencies are simply attributable to a lack of systematization in Rastafarian thought. However, one can detect harmonizing tendencies, despite considerable diversity of thought. Some have viewed death as a result of a lack of self-preservation or unfaithfulness to the King of Kings. One analogy that has sometimes been used is a game of cricket: if the batsman can be bowled out, it is because of (relative) lack of skill. In theory a batsman could stay in indefinitely, but in practice no cricketer has been sufficiently skilful to escape being caught or bowled. Thus humans are potentially, although not actually, immortal. Other Rastafarians have denied the reality of death by pointing out that no piece of matter ever dies: atoms are only redistributed, not annihilated, and the physical components of someone who dies simply become constituents of other life forms within the universe (Barrett, 1974, p. 179). Whichever view is taken, Rastafarians make a point of having modest funerals, which are only attended by closest family, and they justify these 'low key' rites by reference to biblical injunctions like 'Leave the dead to bury their dead, but go thou and publish abroad the Kingdom of God' (quoted in Barrett, 1974, p. 179).

Lifestyle

Some further aspects of Rastafarian lifestyle are worthy of mention at this juncture. Just as Rastafarians have 'low key' funerals, the same is true of marriage. There is no formal marriage ceremony, only what is called 'changing of hands'. In the early days in Jamaica polygamy was practised (Leonard Howell had 13 wives at Pinnacle), but this is no longer the case. Rastafarians do not believe in birth control, since they regard such measures as the white people's means of oppression, and view birth control as a way of hindering the reincarnation of the lost tribes.

Other aspects of Rastafarian lifestyle are attempts to fulfil the laws which God gave to the Israelites. They observe the basic Jewish dietary laws, avoiding pork, and have very strong leanings towards vegetarianism. While some are staunchly vegetarian, most Rastafarians eat fish. Until recent times, Rastafarians have not owned land: originally this was due to poverty, but more recently this has been through choice, in recognition of the psalmist's statement that 'The earth is Lord's and the fullness thereof' (Psalm 24:1). When Rastafarians have wanted land, they have simply captured it, as indeed was the practice in Old Testament times.

Two practices that are commonly associated with the Rastafarians are the wearing of dreadlocks, and smoking of ganja ('the herb'). The 'locksmen', as they are sometimes called, are to be regarded as Ethiopian warriors, and emulate the description given in the Book of Daniel of the head looking like wool. More generally, there is a taboo on mutilating one's body: Rastafarians will not cut their arms or faces, as some African tribes-people do, as a means of asserting their tribal identity, and they will not allow their bodies to be tattooed.

The practice of ganja smoking has often brought Rastafarians into contact with the law. Ganja is known as 'the herb' or the 'wisdom seed', and it is frequently used in the 'reasoning sessions' in which Rastafarians engage. They claim that it is not harmful, and that more harm is done to the body by tobacco smoking or by over-consumption of Jamaican rum. Again, scriptural warrant is found for the practice. God said to Adam:

> I have given you every herb bearing seed, which is upon the face of all the earth ... to you it shall be for meat. (Genesis 1:29)

> Better a dinner of herbs where love is,
> Than a stalled ox and hatred therewith. (Proverbs 15:17)

Rastafarian meetings, called 'groundations' (etymologically a compound of 'ground' and 'foundations'), almost invariably entail the use of ganja, which is held to be calming and conducive to cool reasoning. Such meetings are democratic: free debate is encouraged, and one may agree or disagree with the outcome. A 'leading brother' – sometimes known as a 'brother priest' – presides over them, and he is assisted by a chaplain. Below the priest and chaplain are the 'recording secretary' and the treasurer. A sergeant-at-arms guards the meeting – a feature which originated under Howell at Pinnacle. The meetings tend to be male dominated, with little – if any – place for women, who may at most be assigned the role of 'leader of songs'.

Rastafarianism in Britain

The substantial immigration into Britain which took place in the late 1950s and 1960s included Afro-Caribbeans, some of whom brought Black Power ideologies, including Rastafarianism, with them. Since the new settlers were economic migrants, attempting to carve out a future in a western-style economy, notions such as returning to Africa, rejecting property ownership, and appropriating land when one's need arose simply were not feasible. As the Rastafarian community experienced economic development, they began to own cars, to run co-operatives, own small businesses and experience an artistic revival. One well-known example of Rastafarian artistic performance is, of course, its reggae music, successfully performed and marketed by singers such as Bob Marley (1945–81). ('Reggae' means 'for the king' – a reference to Haile Selassie.)

Some Afro-Caribbean (as well as African) settlers' allegiances were to Pentecostalism. It was common, however, for them to find indigenous forms of Pentecostalism unwelcoming in Britain, hence the formation of various black-led churches. Faced with this cool reception by British Christians, several Afro-Caribbean Pentecostalists turned away from Christianity altogether and converted to Rastafarianism. The first Rastafarian group took its rise in Britain in the mid-1950s, and there are now a number of strands. One is the Twelve Tribes of Israel, to which Bob Marley belonged, and which upholds the main ideals of Rastafarianism which have been outlined above. The Universal Black Improvement Organisation serves to promote Rastafarian interests, while other Rastafarians, by contrast, have acknowledged more traditional elements of Christianity by way of the Ethiopian Orthodox Church. This British strand of Rastafarianism is much more conservative than the Twelve Tribes of Israel. Its members wear no 'dreads'; they do not expect an imminent return to Africa; and they do not acknowledge Haile Selassie as God.

8. The Human Potential Movement

Anti-cultists have commonly criticized certain new religious movements for being essentially business organizations that masquerade as religions, and there exists a cluster of organizations whose claim to a religious identity may seem tenuous. What they offer the enquirer seems to be primarily pragmatic, the main benefits apparently being increased personal efficiency, improved communication and material success. They appear to be free-standing, bearing no immediately obvious relationship to traditional world religions (with the exception of Transcendental Meditation), and the seeker's involvement consists of pursuing numerous courses or seminars, which are not made freely available to all, but which have to be bought, often for fairly substantial fees. Examples include the Church of Scientology, Erhard Seminar Training (or *est,* subsequently known as The Forum and Landmark), Programmes Ltd (formerly Exegesis), the School of Economic Science, and Transcendental Meditation.

Paul Heelas has suggested the term 'self religions' as an umbrella label for such organizations (Heelas, 1982). Certainly they focus on self-improvement, and appear to place humanity at the centre of their endeavours, encouraging feelings of self-worth and almost unlimited potential, in contrast with mainstream Christian notions of original sin and Calvinist ideas of humanity's 'total depravity'. These ideas have understandably attracted criticism from Protestant evangelical circles; thus Blewett has accused such groups of 'three persistent and recurring ancient heresies, synchretism [*sic*], gnosticism and pelagianism' (Blewett, n.d., p. 20).

The term 'self religions' is not without its problems, however. First, a number of Scientologists are critical of the word 'self' in this context, pointing out that the Self is only the first of the Eight Dynamics, and that Scientology additionally addresses 'creativity', 'group survival', 'species', 'life forms', the 'physical universe', the 'spiritual dynamic' and finally 'infinity'. Its scope therefore purports to be much broader and more ambitious than simple self-improvement. Bearing this in mind, Tipton's term 'human potential' movement seems more apt in characterizing such groups, since they largely address human problems and concerns, but go beyond the Self (Tipton, 1981).

Second, Transcendental Meditation and the Erhard groups have consistently denied being religions, regarding themselves as 'techniques' or 'tools' to enable participants to deal better with life, society or work. Scientologists, by contrast, insist that their organization is indeed religious, since it treats humans as spiritual beings and deals with the 'infinite'. In recent times, Scientologists have compiled a dossier of endorsements by some academics and clergy which corroborated its claim to a religious identity, and in 1993 the Church of Scientology won an important court case in the USA, which granted it tax-exempt status as a religion.

Cynics will argue that the self-identity of such groups is determined by the perceived benefits. TM was able to have the Maharishi Mahesh Yogi's techniques taught for a while in American schools, on the grounds that it was not religious. (Religious education is illegal in the USA's education system.) When some Christian evangelicals challenged this claim successfully by taking it to law, the teaching of TM in US schools had to be dropped (although TM still insists that it is not religious and deplores the court's decision).

As well as setting out the principal ideas and practices of the selected human potential groups, this chapter provides a good opportunity for exploring the edges of religion. When is a religion not a religion? Whatever the religious identity of the human potential groups, there is a degree of perverseness on the part of their critics: Scientology, which claims to be a religion, is accused of not being a genuine religion at all, whereas TM and *est*, which take strong exception to being classified as religious, are told that they are really religions in disguise. One wonders what the anti-cult movement's response would have been if TM and *est* had claimed a religious identity but Scientologists had not!

Because of the uncertainty as to whether such groups should be classified as religions or not, some writers have adopted the term 'para-religions' as a general descriptor, thus indicating that they only partly fulfil the criteria that religions must satisfy. At the conclusion of this chapter I shall give an appraisal of the claims and counterclaims that the three selected organizations – Scientology, *est* and TM – are religions. In the meantime, for the reasons mentioned above, I propose to use Tipton's label 'Human Potential Movement' in preference to Heelas's 'self religions' in the ensuing discussion.

The movement's origins can be traced back to the 1940s, in which one finds the beginnings of 'sensitivity training' and the study of group dynamics. According to Finkelstein *et al.* (1982), the movement began to get under way in the 1950s, and the name itself began to be employed two decades later. One writer has characterized the goal of HPM as the 'self-transcendence of merging with the infinite cosmic energy or ground of all being' (Stone, 1975; quoted in Blewett, n.d., p. 6). Those who follow HPM seek considerably more than a few practical tips on how to become more efficient or how to make more money. HPM typically leads seekers to understand that their potential is much greater: they have within themselves a divine quality, which endows them with unlimited potential, and encourages them to allow this godlike or enlightened quality to control their lives.

Scientology

Despite its high profile, Scientology has received sparse treatment from academics. This is no doubt due to several factors. L. Ron Hubbard's writings are vast: according to Scientology sources he wrote 40 million words on Dianetics and Scientology, spoke 25 million words in 3000 lectures, not to mention his 500 novels and short stories. Not all of this is accessible: the Operating Thetan material can be divulged only to those who possess the necessary prerequisites, which include becoming 'clear'. Once disclosed, the OT material is confidential and may not be passed on to unauthorized people. Thorough investigation of Scientology would therefore be long and expensive, and, even if successfully accomplished, would present researchers with serious problems of research ethics if they attempted to disseminate their findings.

The life of L. Ron Hubbard

Even with modern founder-leaders it is difficult to disentangle hagiographic myth from historical fact, and Lafayette Ronald Hubbard (1911–86) is no exception. That he was born on 13 March 1911 in Tilden, Nebraska is undisputed. According to the Church of Scientology, Ron was a precocious child, reading widely and familiarizing himself with life in a variety of societies. At the age of four, he was able to ride, lasso and break broncos, and at age six he was reading Shakespeare and the writings of ancient Greek philosophers. He was particularly interested in 'primitive tribes', becoming a blood brother of the Blackfeet, also at the age of six. At age twelve he made his first acquaintance with Freudian psychology. Because his father was a naval officer, the young Ron was able to travel widely, meeting magicians in Beijing, learning from Buddhists in West China, and hunting with Pygmies in the Philippines.

> By the age of nineteen, long before the advent of commercial airplane or jet transportation, he had travelled more than a quarter of a million miles, including voyages not only to China but also Japan, Guam, the Philippines and other points in the Orient. In a very real sense, the world itself was his classroom, and he studied in it voraciously. (Church of Scientology, 1998a, p. 32)

However, instead of anthropology Hubbard is said to have studied mathematics and engineering at George Washington University. He also enrolled for a class on nuclear physics, apparently hoping that the subject might enable him to discover 'the Life essence' – a quest which his experience in Asia had suggested to him. Additionally, Hubbard is said to have pursued a wide variety of other subject areas in which he gained expertise. Present-day Scientologists affirm that Hubbard was an expert in no less than 29 subjects.

In 1932 Hubbard set out to participate in two international ethnographical expeditions, first to the Caribbean and then to Puerto Rico. He returned to the USA in 1933, and that year marked the beginning of his writing career. From then until 1950 Hubbard published in a variety of genres, the best known being his science fiction, which continues to sell today. During this period, Hubbard was still questing for the 'common denominator of life': in 1938 he wrote a work entitled *Excalibur,* which developed this thesis, and which became the forerunner of Scientology. In *Excalibur* Hubbard averred that mankind possessed the basic common denominator of *survival* – survival not only of one's self, but of one's social group and one's species.

During the Second World War Hubbard served in the Navy. He was wounded in action, being judged partially blind, and with injuries to his hip and back. He was treated with the drug testosterone, in common with other victims. He noticed the obvious: the drug worked well on some people, but not on others, and he was concerned to find the answer to the question, 'Why?' LRH concluded that it was because of the power of the mind that some people experienced improvements and others did not.

Hubbard's philosophy

Hubbard's followers, of course, believe implicitly in these details of Hubbard's life and his many areas of expertise. Needless to say, Scientology's detractors insist that most of this account of his life is absurd, pointing out that there is no corroborative evidence that Hubbard was a student at George Washington University, and suggesting that, if he ever studied there, he failed in his first year. What is more significant than these claims and counter-claims are the teachings of Dianetics and Scientology. If Scientologists' claims about Hubbard seem to be exaggerated beyond outsiders' credibility, they function as religious myths, serving to underline the high regard with which Hubbard is held, and emphasizing the organization's key tenets.

Hubbard's notion of the unlimited powers of the mind is the key to understanding the ideas of Dianetics and Scientology. In fact, Bartley compares Scientology's ideas to the idealist philosophies of George Berkeley (1685–1752) and G. W. F. Hegel (1770–1831), both of whom viewed the mind as the true reality, and matter as essentially mind-dependent. Bartley, however, suggests that Hubbard's idealism is more eastern than western, noting that Hubbard himself drew from writings such as the Vedas and the *Dhammapada*, and described his ideas as the 'Western world's first workable organization of Eastern philosophy' (Bartley, 1978, p. 152).

In contrast to most forms of philosophical dualism, which claim that the mind or the soul is the essence of the self, Scientology contends that both the mind and the body are things that the self possesses, and that neither are to be identified with the real self. The real self is the 'thetan' or spirit, and is the godlike, creative force, which is immortal. Hubbard wanted to avoid using terms like 'spirit' or 'soul' to describe the true self, since he believed that they were encumbered with the philosophical baggage of many centuries; the word 'thetan' was derived from the Greek letter 'theta', which Hubbard had previously used as an abbreviation to denote the 'life force' for which he had been seeking.

As the creative force, the thetan has been responsible for the creation of matter, energy, space and time ('MEST' in Scientology jargon), the four principal elements which are taken to comprise the physical world. MEST, however, being a product of the thetan, has no independent reality, but only continues to seem real because the vast majority of thetans agree that it exists. The belief that MEST is real is an illusion: humanity has forgotten that it is the creation of thetans, and thus men and women have become entrapped in MEST, forgetting their original, essential, immortal state. Hubbard quotes the Dhammapada in this regard:

> All that we are is the result of what we have thought. It is founded upon our thoughts. It is made up of our thoughts. (quoted by Bartley, 1978, p. 153)

The thetan, being the true reality, is not MEST: it does not consist of matter or energy, and does not exist in space and time.

Not only are humans entrapped in MEST, but some have even come to regard themselves as consisting essentially of MEST. This is particularly true of philosophical materialism and behaviouristic psychology. Scientologists are therefore adamant that 'man is a spiritual being', and does not simply consist of a material body. They are also fiercely opposed to forms of medicine and psychiatry that treat human beings as if they were nothing more than lumps of matter, for example, by treating psychiatric illness by means of chemicals. Men and women need freedom from this entrapment in MEST, in order to regain the freedom and creativity with which MEST interferes. The thetan possesses a mind and a body, but is identical with neither.

The mind is further divided into two types: the analytical mind and the reactive mind. The analytical mind is that part of the mind that thinks and calculates in a rational way, recognizing differences between different objects. The reactive mind, by contrast, is the part of the mind that is in agreement with MEST; it stores memories of unpleasant events, which can reappear to cause pain, fears and blocks. As we all know, an accident such as a fall from a ladder can cause us to fear climbing ladders, or someone who has been stung by bees may develop a phobia about bees, even in a situation that is relatively safe. Dianetics takes this obvious fact a stage or two further. Even if the victim is rendered unconscious, what is going on around him or her goes into the reactive mind: the ambulance's siren, comments that other people are making about the incident, and so on. (For this reason Scientologists are particularly careful about undergoing general anaesthetics in a hospital. They will usually request that any surgery should be carried out silently, lest unwanted data slip into the reactive mind.)

The reactive mind blurs over differences. To use one of Scientology's own examples: if I find a worm in an apple while I am eating it, my reactive mind may associate apples with worms from then on, giving me a revulsion towards apples, whether or not they contain worms. The incident in which I encountered the worm in the apple may became buried in my reactive mind, and thus I may be unaware why I dislike the thought of eating an apple. My reactive mind contains what Scientologists call 'engrams' – traces of past incidents that cause anxieties and fears that can lead to irrational or unsociable behaviour.

As long as engrams remain, the thetan is not yet 'clear'. Attaining the state of 'clear' is achieved through a process called 'auditing', a form of counselling, the root meaning of which is 'listening'. In the auditing session the pre-clear is assigned a trained Dianetics auditor, or else a pair of Dianetics students can simply use Hubbard's book *Dianetics* and audit each other by using the procedures that it prescribes.

Auditing differs from the kind of counselling that is carried out by professional counsellors outside the Church of Scientology. In conventional counselling the counsellor has discretion about how to present the client with alternatives and how to enable him or her to explore problems. Dianetics procedures are quite rigid by comparison, and the auditor must follow an exact sequence of procedures. The auditing session involves asking the pre-clear to confront an incident which he or she can handle comfortably and to describe it to the auditor. Once this has been done, the auditor then instructs the pre-clear to go over the incident again in order to elicit any new data that were not adduced in the initial description. This retracing of the incident is continually repeated until no new data are emerging. Once this has been accomplished, the pre-clear is then invited to confront a similar, earlier incident, which is likely to have given rise to engrams that are affecting the first recounted incident. This procedure can be quite lengthy, and it may take numerous auditing sessions to go through such incidents and rid the reactive mind of the engrams.

A device that often features in auditing sessions is an instrument known as the E-meter (electropsychometer). This consists of two metal cylinders that are held by the pre-clear, with a control panel and dial that the auditor observes. The dial measures the amount of electrical current that passes through the body: this changes when an engram is stimulated, and is picked up by the meter.

Those who have a cursory acquaintance with Dianetics will sometimes remark that auditing appears similar to psychoanalysis, psychiatry or hypnosis. Hubbard himself made it clear that he rejected all three comparisons. While it is certainly true that psychoanalysis aims to bring out ideas that are buried in the subconscious and unknown to the patient, Hubbard emphasized that Freudian psychoanalysis was interpretative, offering the psycho-analyst's own interpretation of what was happening in the patient's mind. Thus certain forms of behaviour could be attributed to an Oedipus complex, sibling rivalry or whatever. In Dianetics auditing, the auditor provides no interpretation whatsoever, simply allowing the pre-clear to run and rerun incidents, until all the details emerge and the engrams vanish.

Scientologists see the forms of psychiatry that emerged after Freud as behaviouristic. The behaviourist school, they claim, treats human beings simply as bodies, either engaging in behaviour modification in forms of treatment such as behaviour therapy, or else they treat conditions either chemically or with electric shock treatment. Over the years Scientologists have campaigned vigorously against psychiatric drugs, electric shock treatment and lobotomy. These ways of treating patients, they believe, are degrading, ineffectual, and treat the human self as nothing more than a physical body, rather than – as Scientologists insist – a 'spiritual being'.

As far as hypnosis is concerned, hypnotic techniques aim to reduce the patient's level of awareness, leading to sleep. Although the pre-clear's eyes remain closed during the auditing, he or she is far from asleep: on the contrary, the auditing session aims to increase the amount of awareness, so that all the details of recounted incidents can be brought out from the reactive mind.

The aim of auditing is not merely to free the reactive mind of

285

engrams, but to eliminate the reactive mind altogether. Once the engrams are disposed of, then the reactive mind ceases to exist and no longer serves as a receptacle for those pieces of information that escape the analytical mind. This is the state of 'clear' and the Operating Thetan can then progress along the various levels of its spiritual path.

Achieving the status of 'clear' is no mean attainment. One recent Scientology source has described it in this way:

> While the Clear is analogous to the state of awareness in Buddhism called the Bodhi, or enlightened one, the Clear is a permanent level of spiritual awareness never attainable prior to Dianetics and Scientology. (Church of Scientology, 1998b, p. 16)

One factor that inhibits the pre-clear is the existence of toxins in one's body. Pre-clears are often directed towards the Purification Rundown course, which aims to eliminate toxins with substantial prescriptions of vitamins and regular saunas, which enable the body to expel toxins by prolonged sweating. Scientologists generally try to avoid ingesting drugs of any kind. Recreational drugs are avoided, and medication is viewed very much as a last resort. Alcohol is not totally forbidden, but it is believed that it can interfere with the auditing process. A pre-clear who undergoes auditing must not have consumed alcohol, even in moderation, within the previous 24 hours, and the use of paracetamol or similar painkillers makes one ineligible for auditing for seven days.

Although the Church of Scientology opposes the use of recreational drugs, caffeine and nicotine are permitted (Lamont, 1986, p. 34). At first sight, Scientology's position on tea, coffee and tobacco may seem inconsistent with the hard stance the Church takes on drugs. However, Scientologists point out that alcohol and recreational drugs such as cannabis lower one's state of consciousness, making the reactive mind unable to recall some of its mental image pictures. By contrast, caffeine and nicotine are stimulants, and hence do not have this effect.

The Eight Dynamics

Thus far it may seem as if Dianetics addresses problems pertaining to individual selves. However, as I have pointed out, the Self is but the first of eight 'dynamics', which are:

Self
Creativity
Group survival
Species
Life forms
Physical universe
Spiritual dynamic
Infinity

The 'self' dynamic concerns not merely the physical survival of one's self, but maintaining a good state of health, and a range of human interests, such as one's hobbies, appreciation of music, theatre and the like. The 'creativity' dynamic is sometimes rendered 'sex/ children', and refers to the maintenance of one's family unit. The third dynamic of 'group survival' underlines the fact that humans are social creatures and organize themselves into groups. Some of these groups may have serious human concerns, such as political organizations, while others may exist for recreational purposes, like sports clubs. The fourth dynamic is 'species', sometimes defined as 'mankind'. Humanity seeks survival and development as an entire species, not merely at the level of its own social groupings. When human beings engage in armed combat, this is a breakdown of the fourth dynamic.

Beyond the human species there are other life forms (animals, birds, insects – the fifth dynamic), which form an important part of life on this planet (the sixth dynamic). Beyond the physical realm lie spiritual beings, some of whom are men and women who have 'dropped the body' and now experience a spiritual existence beyond physical death. The dynamic of 'infinity' is sometimes referred to as the 'God dynamic', since it relates to the supreme divine being who sustains the physical universe. There is little in Dianetics that addresses the eighth dynamic: Dianetics, rather, prepares the individual to reach a state where he or she can apprehend the God dynamic, an exploration of which awaits the OT levels which properly belong to Scientology.

Mention should be made here of Scientology ethics. The ethically correct course of action is that which produces the best possible solution for all eight dynamics. Thus a course of action that benefited one's self, but which was detrimental, say, to one's family and one's social group, would not be a satisfactory policy to pursue. A policy which sacrificed one human being (a loss on the first dynamic) for the good of humankind (a gain on the fourth dynamic) would be likely to be ethically justifiable. Thus Scientology entails an ethic that is rather similar to the utilitarianism of philosophers like Jeremy Bentham and John Stuart Mill.

The Operating Thetan levels

It is difficult to comment on what happens after the state of clear. As I have mentioned, relatively few Scientologists progress beyond this state to the various OT levels. Those who do are introduced to material that is only to be divulged to those who are ready for it – that is to say, those who have the prerequisite of successfully attaining the previous level. There are 15 levels of OT, although no existing Scientologist has advanced beyond OT 8. For those who gain access without being in an appropriate state of readiness, such teachings are believed to be dangerous. 'They would blow your mind out!' one Scientologist told me, and suggested that they could even be damaging to one's physical health.

Inevitably there are a few ex-Scientologists who have attained some of the OT levels and have attempted to divulge the material that they contain, and others have attempted to use Scientology material for their own use. The Church of Scientology has consistently taken the view that they alone are responsible for preserving and administering LRH's teachings and practices, and the Religious Technology Center, which was founded in 1982 as a department of the Church, is entrusted with the preservation of Hubbard's writings and lectures in their authentic form. Scientologists have characteristically taken to litigation when they have believed that their materials were being used in the wrong hands.

On a few occasions Scientology's opponents have attempted to make public some of the OT material. Lamont (1986), for example, describes a creation myth involving a being called Xenu, and which has more than a shade of science fiction about it. Scientologists deny the authenticity of such material, claiming that such accounts are garbled versions of material that was stolen from their British headquarters and quoted out of context in an attempt to discredit the organization. The truth of the matter appears to be that in 1967 Hubbard announced his discovery of the root of human suffering: this is due, apparently, to an event that occurred 75 million years ago on earth, and which had a great impact on the human spirit. Hubbard believed he had found a way of undoing the effects of this disaster, and herein lie the secrets and benefits of OT 3, as well as other OT levels. I am told that Scientologists do not readily discuss these matters, because they believe that a firm grounding in previous levels is needed first. Official Scientology literature describes the states of OT in extremely broad terms:

> The state of Operating Thetan – a being able to operate free of the encumbrances of the material universe – is a central part of the ultimate salvation sought in the Scientology religion. (Church of Scientology, 1998a, p. 55)

Is Scientology a religion?

Is Scientology a religion? The arguments adduced by critics to disqualify Scientology from having a religious status are these. First, the large financial sums that are required to pursue courses in Dianetics and Scientology make it more of a business company than a spiritual community. Second, critics will sometimes allege that Dianetics and Scientology look more like pop psychology or amateur advice for educators and students than anything more spiritual. Third, the fact that it teaches that one need not abandon one's previous religion is often thought to indicate that it cannot be a religion in its own right. These criticisms must now be addressed.

Scientology's charges may be high, although those who remain in the organization affirm that they receive value for money. As one Scientologist recently remarked to me, 'If Scientology cost a million pounds and that was all I had, I would still pay it!' I do not wish to adjudicate on the question of whether Scientology offers good value: this is not relevant to the question of whether or not it is inherently religious in character. An organization does not need to be judged to be good or worthwhile in order to qualify as a religion.

The fact that one has to pay for Scientology and Dianetics does not mean disqualification from being a religion. The Graeco-Roman mystery religions demanded very substantial fees for initiation, but I have not known anyone argue that the mystery religions were not religions. Few religious communities elicit sufficient numbers of benefactors to enable them to exist without their followers handling money, and the Church of Scientology, like any other religious organization, has to devise ways of keeping itself financially solvent. Scientologists will point out that, unlike many other religious groups, they do not organize street collections where the public are asked to support them: all their income comes from their members' payments and occasional donations.

It is important to remember the distinction between Dianetics and Scientology, and the fact that their proponents claim that it is merely the latter that constitutes a religion, whereas the former does not. Dianetics is the set of techniques to prepare the thetan for the spiritual journey through the various levels after attaining clear. As Bryan Wilson suggests, Scientology enables the thetan to be brought into contact with the Infinite – the last of the eight dynamics – which many, although not all, Scientologists would identify with God (Church of Scientology, 1998b, p. 139).

The fact that the Church of Scientology does not call upon its members to abandon their own religion needs some comment. One can be simultaneously a Scientologist and a Christian, Buddhist, Hindu or whatever. This is no mere theory: I have personally known Scientologists who remain members of the Church of England. (I shall leave it to the Church of England to determine whether or not it finds this position acceptable: it certainly is all right with the Church of Scientology! If other religious organizations wish to claim that their followers cannot simultaneously pursue Scientology, then that is their prerogative.) It may be thought that, if one can find one's religion elsewhere, this indicates that Scientology is not religious. However, the notion that one follows only one religion at any one time is a notion that is really confined to the semitic traditions: the God of Judaism, Christianity and Islam brooks no rivals. By contrast, followers of eastern religions are renowned for using a variety of faiths for whatever purpose each can deliver best: it is therefore quite common to be simultaneously a Buddhist, a Confucianist and a shamanist (Chryssides, 1991, p. 46). If Scientologists can use their religion in conjunction with others, this does not disqualify it from being a religion.

When asked about their religious credentials, the most common answer given by Scientologists is that they treat 'man as a spiritual being'. They typically view 'man' as more than a body – a thetan, or spirit, who is capable of being taken through various levels of spiritual attainment in order to make contact with the Infinite. Belief in a Supreme Being, then, is characteristic of many Scientologists.

Furthermore, Scientology possesses features that are characteristically associated with religion: LRH's writings are now coming to be referred to as 'scriptures'. The use of the term 'scripture' began to be introduced sporadically into Scientology literature from around 1997 onwards, but now receives systematic treatment in the definitive 1998 volume, *Scientology: Theology and Practice of a Contemporary Religion*. This work goes so far as to formulate a definitive canon of scripture:

> The Scripture of the Scientology religion consists of the writings and recorded spoken words of L. Ron Hubbard on the subjects of Dianetics and Scientology. (Church of Scientology, 1998a, p. 45)

This definition, for obvious reasons, excludes Hubbard's fictional writings, and the text goes on to mention explicitly fundamental Scientology texts such as *Scientology, the Fundamentals of Thought; Scientology 8-80; Scientology 8-8008; The Creation of Human Ability;* and *Scientology, a New Slant on Life.*

In addition to scripture, there is a Scientologists' creed, and there is an ordained ministry which makes provision for the spiritual life of its people. Many Scientology 'orgs' (churches, or centres) have Sunday services, with readings and a sermon. Functionally, Scientology operates as a religion. Its ordained ministry enables followers to observe rites of passage within the Church: the naming of a baby, marriages and funerals.

Critics have sometimes claimed that Hubbard first set up Dianetics as a business and at a somewhat later stage endowed it with religious status for various state benefits. However, as early as 1955 (the year in which the Church of Scientology was established), Hubbard emphatically proclaimed Scientology's religious status:

> We are on a much higher level in Scientology than the Western religions have been, but we are not on a higher level in Scientology except in our technologies ... If we call Scientology a religion we are calling it a religion out of a much deeper well than the last two thousand years. (Hubbard, 1955, p. 110)

Hubbard regarded the technological aspects as the important innovation in this new religion. Yet it is probably these very aspects that cause non-Scientologists to view it differently. Part of Scientology's problem in being viewed as a religion perhaps lies in its lack of use of overtly, conventional religious vocabulary. It avoids blatantly pious talk, using terms such as 'the tech', 'the org', 'boil off' and 'rundown', speaking in very secular-sounding or quasi-technological vocabulary. Instead of priests and monks wearing dignified robes, Scientologists wear casual secular clothes, with the exception of the Flagship staff, whose attire resembles naval uniforms. Instead of endowing their founder-leader with pious titles, he is simply referred to as 'Ron' or 'LRH'. Some may find such features surprising, but I do not think they are defining characteristics of a religion.

Transcendental Meditation

Transcendental Meditation was founded by the Maharishi Mahesh Yogi. The Maharishi originated within the Hindu tradition, being born at Jabalpur in Central India, and some might expect TM to be treated as a form of Hinduism. There are several reasons for not doing so. First, as we have noted, TM makes no claim to be a form of religion, preferring to be regarded as a 'technique' or a 'tool'; like Scientology, it is said to be compatible with any religion, and able to be followed by anyone, regardless of creed or religious affiliation. Second, Hindus would not affiliate to TM as their preferred form of spirituality, but would practise the technique while attending their own Hindu temple; there are no specially dedicated TM temples, although obviously the movement has its own premises and special locations for pursuing, in particular, the 'siddhi' programme. Third, the whole thrust of TM is about personal, societal and global benefits: TM makes no claims to offer 'enlightenment' or *moksha* to its followers. This is not to imply that its proclaimed benefits are less worthwhile: on the contrary, very bold and startling claims are made about the consequences that TM offers.

Relatively little is known about the early life of the Maharishi Mahesh Yogi: indeed even his date of birth is uncertain – either 1911 or 1918. This lack of firm information is partly due to a tendency of Indian gurus to want to hide their early past, and, perhaps more especially, to the fact that it is the practice of TM that is important to his followers, rather than factual details about the founder-leader's life.

The Maharishi's original name was either Mahesh Prasad Varma or J.N. Srivastava (again there is some uncertainty). 'Maharishi' is an assumed title, meaning 'great seer'. Although little is known about the Maharishi's early years, we can be certain that he went to Allahabad University, where he studied physics and graduated in

1940. For 13 years thereafter he studied Hindu mystical techniques under Swami Brahmananda Saraswati, (Maharaj) Jagadguru, Bhagwan Shankaracharya of Jyotir Math (1869–1953). This swami is more commonly referred to as 'Guru Dev', and is regarded as a 'fully realized man'. TM literature seems more concerned with Guru Dev than with the Maharishi's own life.

Guru Dev accepted the Maharishi for study while he was still a university student, but insisted that he must complete his degree. At first the latter performed menial chores for his guru, but gained increasing responsibility, becoming a Shankaracharya in Jyotir Math monastery and finally Guru Dev's private secretary. The term 'Shankaracharya' implies that Guru Dev and hence the Maharishi were in the Shankara tradition of *advaita Vedanta:* that is to say, they were monists, believing atman and brahman to be identical in an unqualified way. Knowing brahman is thus a matter of looking inside the self (atman), and is achieved through jnana (insight), not bhakti (devotion) or karma (deeds).

After Guru Dev's death in 1953, the Maharishi spent two years in total seclusion in Uttar Kashi, emerging in 1956, when he published his first book on Transcendental Meditation, entitled *The Beacon Light of the Himalayas.* On the last day of 1957, the Maharishi introduced TM to the west, founding the Spiritual Regeneration Movement in Madras. In 1959 SRM had acquired an office in Los Angeles, the only place in the USA where TM could be taught until 1965, when the Students International Meditation Society was established. In 1960 the movement came to Britain, when the Maharishi lectured in the Caxton Hall in London. This aroused some considerable interest from the Study Society, a Gurdjieff/Ouspensky group with which Leon MacLaren (Leonardo da Vinci MacLaren), who went on to found the School of Economic Science, was associated. These groups jointly formed the School of Meditation, which is said to have employed some of the Maharishi's techniques (Bloomfield *et al.*, 1985, p. 248).

In the following year the Maharishi began to train other TM teachers, thus enabling the practice to spread more widely and rapidly. The year 1963 saw the appearance of the Maharishi's *Science of Being and Art of Living,* a key work on the expected benefits that TM offers, and a work which remains a key text of the TM movement. When the Maharishi visited Britain in 1967, the movement caught the imagination of George Harrison, who persuaded the other Beatles to visit him in India in 1968. Although (as we have seen) the Beatles went on to sample other forms of spirituality, their visit was enormously beneficial in attracting the world's attention to TM. TM appealed to students who were disillusioned with the drug experience and who failed to find 'alternative consciousness'.

Philosophy and practice

The Maharishi taught that there are various laws that govern our nature. Not only are there physical laws: the material side of life is insufficient for gaining fulfilment. This can only be gained from *within*, and this inner nature is called 'being' or 'bliss-consciousness'. 'Only Being, an unbounded ocean of energy, creative intelligence and happiness, a field of eternal fullness, nonchanging and absolute, can satisfy the mind' (Forem, 1974, p. 37). Once this inner nature is discovered, it can then emerge to enjoy the multiplicity of pleasures of the physical (relative) creation. Thus there needs to be a union of the two sides of life: the values of the inner Absolute, and the physical world in which one exists. Although technically the physical world is *maya* (illusion), TM is world-affirming, offering physical and mental benefits for the student, society and the world. The Maharishi himself tended to emphasize the positive aspects of humanity, focusing on the good that exists in everyone, and making little mention of one's evil tendencies.

In her important discussion of TM, Una Kroll identifies two strands that are important in understanding TM. First, there are ten states of consciousness which the Maharishi has defined: as one practises TM one's human consciousness expands until it finally attains 'divine consciousness', in which one recognizes one's oneness with the eternal. As one's state of consciousness progresses, one distances oneself from suffering (the second strand), which merely exists on the plane of relative existence (Kroll, 1974/1976, p. 48). As the Maharishi explains:

> All suffering in life would be alleviated if Being were to be established on the conscious level of life where discord and disunity prevail. Since there is a way to establish Being on the level of mind (TM), body and surroundings, perfect health is possible at all levels. (Maharishi, 1963/ 1995, p. 113)

The knowledge of how to enable the Self to transcend the physical world has been lost with the passage of time. Various revivals of this way of understanding life have been brought to humanity by Krishna, the Buddha and Shankara. The TM technique also draws on the *Yoga Sutras* of Patanjali, written some 2000 years ago, although the Maharishi has modified the techniques that are described there, claiming to make them less confusing and more consistent.

Whatever TM's pedigree, all this is not so important to its students as the practice itself, and teachers of TM would be unlikely to delve into the Maharishi's personal history or to the sources that he has brought to bear. It is not even necessary to understand the philosophical ideas of the relationship between the Self, the Absolute and the physical world. As Forem writes, 'TM is a spontaneous process of direct perception ... faith or belief is irrelevant ...' (Forem, 1974, p. 39).

The TM technique is very easy and can be mastered within a few days. The TM organization regards it as a virtue that TM can be learned easily and quickly, and can yield almost immediate benefits. TM teachers see little virtue in pursuing a path that takes years or even decades to complete.

The most usual way of approaching TM is to attend an introductory lecture: these are publicly advertised and open to all. There a lecturer will explain the fundamentals of TM and the benefits it offers. Those who are interested in hearing more are then invited to a second talk, usually on private premises. At this point enquirers are informed of the fees, and those who are interested in committing themselves further are invited to undergo an interview. The interview explores the enquirer's reasons for wanting to learn TM, and he or she is asked to put these reasons in writing.

The next step is a formal initiation ceremony. At this meeting the student appears before the teacher with a clean white handkerchief, flowers and payment. It used to be stated that payment was roughly equivalent to a week's wages, with reduced rates for students. At the time of writing, it is somewhat higher than this, the cost per person being £490 (US $735). TM is therefore not cheap, but its teachers will contend that such amounts are necessary for the running of the organization, and that students are more likely to persist and to obtain the benefits if they have paid a fairly significant sum for their instruction.

The teacher then gives the student a mantra, on which he or she should meditate twice daily for 15 to 20 minutes at each session. Some TM practitioners, particularly Christian ones, have suffered qualms about undergoing an initiation ceremony which is in the Hindu tradition. However, initiation is compulsory, and one cannot proceed without it. If one is tempted to find one's own mantra, perhaps out of a book (of which there are some), TM teachers will insist that the kind of results that TM promises cannot occur.

There are several reasons for this. First, the Maharishi has taught that there are two kinds of mantra: mantras for recluses, and mantras for householders. It is important to use the correct kind, and not to confuse the two. Most mantras that are found in books are for recluses, and are inappropriate for those who are following the 'householder' path. One of TM's claimed benefits is that it can be practised by people from all walks of life, and does not require anyone to abandon the world of work, friends and family in favour of the sannyasin's way of life. Second, the power of the mantra lies in the sound. As soon as the Vedic mantras were committed to writing, the Maharishi claims, an important part of their power was lost; and when the Vedas underwent translation from their original Sanskrit into other languages, even more of their efficacy was forfeited. For this reason the Maharishi claims to have restored a lost tradition, and one of the TM teacher's most important tasks is to convey the mantra's proper sound to the student.

The teacher has a further task in selecting a student's mantra. The mantra is chosen in accordance with the student's 'vibrations': it is therefore personal, and cannot be used by someone else who may wish to attempt TM without payment or initiation. The mantra should be kept secret, known only to the teacher and pupil. This is to ensure that it does not acquire inappropriate connotations or modifications in the practice. Unlike the Hare Krishna mantra, which is verbalized, one's TM mantra is not spoken during the practice, but merely thought inwardly. There is no need for any special postures or rituals when using one's mantra: again, a professed advantage of TM is that it can be done anywhere, without special equipment or ceremony.

Criticism is often made about the allocation of mantras. John Allan (1980), for example, in common with many evangelical Christians, claims that mantras are not individually tailored to students' needs, but are fairly crudely related to one's age. Some students who have given up the practice have divulged their mantras to each other, and found, to their surprise, that they were identical. However, the fact that a mantra is personal does not imply that no two students ever have identical ones. Given that there are now some four million TM practitioners worldwide, it would seem unreasonable to expect that there should exist four million different mantras!

After one's first session with one's teacher, which lasts between one and one and a half hours, three further sessions are held on consecutive days. These are for 'verification' and 'validation' of the student's experiences. It is possible that the meditator may have introduced minor modifications or unauthorized additions, which must be corrected. After this one-to-one tuition a further three sessions are held in groups, where students can share experiences and ask their teacher for any additional advice.

The Maharishi has given very clear and detailed statements about how the TM technique works scientifically. According to the third law of thermodynamics, when physical temperature or activity decreases, a system becomes more orderly. The same is true, he teaches, of the mental world: if one's 'mental temperature' decreases, then the Self becomes calmer and better ordered. During TM, one's breathing rate is said to slow down, 'often almost to the point of suspension' (Griggs, 1993, p. 1). Metabolic activity is reduced, falling up to 20 per cent, allowing space for bodily restoration. There is a drop in the levels of certain chemicals in the blood, such as cortisol and lactates, which contribute to stress. The brain is said to function in a more organized way, with a marked increase in alpha waves: these are the slowest brain waves, inducing calmness and relaxation. As one penetrates beneath the level of conscious awareness, one discovers subtler levels of thought, until finally one is able to penetrate the source of all thought, which is Being itself, pure consciousness, which is totally calm and still.

TM serves to enhance one's state of consciousness rather than to dull it down, as happens in sleep, hypnotic trance or unconsciousness. The benefits from these changed states of consciousness are said to accrue on a number of levels – physical, personal, psychological, societal and global. At a physical level, it is claimed that TM enables practitioners to enjoy better health: they are more relaxed, have greater stamina, are less prone to heart disease, have a lower cholesterol level, and acquire a better immune system, as well as numerous other physical benefits. The TM organization boasts that TM practitioners enjoy 87 per cent fewer hospitalizations, 87 per cent fewer nervous disorders, and 55 per cent fewer tumours (Griggs, 1993, p. 2). TM is also said to arrest the effects of ageing: those who have meditated for more than five years can expect on average to look and feel 12 years younger than their chronological age. Amongst medical disorders which TM claims to improve are asthma, migraine, insomnia, depression, infertility and irritable bowel syndrome. One's vision can also, apparently, undergo improvements. Certain more serious disorders are supposedly assisted: the organization cites angina pectoris, (non-insulin-dependent) diabetes, rheumatoid arthritis, eczema, psoriasis and chronic sinusitis (Transcendental Meditation, 1995, p. 4–5). However, TM is not normally taught to anyone who is seriously ill or who has a psychiatric condition such as schizophrenia. Those who experience problems with smoking and alcoholism can also find TM beneficial. It is not claimed that TM is a panacea, however: it is not a substitute for sleep, for example, and some of these conditions can be addressed by the Maharishi Ayur-Veda Panchakarma Programme, a therapeutic programme, sometimes accompanied by Maharishi herbal preparations, which are used in combination with TM. TM does not merely remove the symptoms of illness, but claims to get to the roots of humans' problems; as the Maharishi has said, 'Water the root to enjoy the fruit' (Russell, 1976/1978, p. 88).

In 1993 in Britain a number of medical doctors attracted media attention by expressing support for TM. Having formed the British Association for the Medical Application of Transcendental Meditation, 136 doctors requested that TM should be made available free of charge on the National Health Service. As well as pointing to its apparently remarkable effectiveness, they pointed out that, as a form of therapy, it was a safe alternative to drugs, not involving any chemically induced changes in the patient's state of consciousness and having no harmful side-effects. Moreover, they claimed, TM was likely to be less expensive for the NHS than the alternative of continued medication for patients. British surgeries are allowed to employ complementary therapists, and, if they are responsible for their own budgets, have discretion about what alternative therapies are available. In theory, therefore, TM can be made available to patients, although I am not aware of any medical practice in which it is a live option (Transcendental Meditation, 1995, p. 3).

At a personal level, it is claimed that TM practitioners are calmer, more confident, less accident-prone, and can cope better with stress, meeting deadlines, heavy workloads and personal problems. TM enables one to contact the 'inner self', increasing creativity, enhancing one's mental abilities, enabling the practitioner to think more clearly, acquire better problem-solving skills, more reliable decision-making, faster reactions, improved self-confidence, greater sense of well-being, better learning capacity, greater alertness, and a greater and broader ability to comprehend and to focus. In short, TM offers 'self-realization', a state in which reality is experienced more clearly and objectively, and in which one experiences a sense of identity, uniqueness and autonomy; there is a greater ability to love others, and hence one experiences better interpersonal relationships, at home and at work.

The benefits that TM purports to offer are those that relate principally to the 'right-hand side of the brain'. The Maharishi believes that the world's educational systems have laid too much emphasis on the left-hand side, stressing logic, reasoning, mathematics, and all the traditional academic subjects, most of which involve rational thinking rather than intuition and creativity. The Maharishi's phrase 'the science of creative intelligence' is therefore important and deliberate. As a practical means of enabling students to attain their full potential, the Maharishi established in 1982 the Maharishi University of Natural Law, at Mentmore Towers in Buckinghamshire, which until recently was the British headquarters.

Although TM denies being a religion, it claims that spiritual benefits can accrue from the practice. One might attain 'cosmic consciousness', which enables 'God consciousness'. The observable physical and psychological benefits derive from the Self's spiritual state, and in self-realization one recognizes the Self's oneness with brahman. To love oneself is to experience the love of God, and the Maharishi has said that religion should not be based on fear of God, but love: it is God's love that percolates into one's human activities.

The benefits of TM extend further than the practitioner, however, and can be experienced on a societal and even a global level. Where sufficient numbers of people practise TM in an area, one can expect fewer accidents, reduced crime rates, an increase in life expectancy, more positive trends in politics and economics, and even improved weather and 'agricultural productivity' (Institute of Natural Law, 1977, p. 10). World peace can be brought nearer, since war and violence can be reduced by a concentration of TM practice. This expected tendency of TM to affect one's environment is known as the 'field effect' or the 'Maharishi effect', having been apparently predicted by the Maharishi in 1960.

The phrase 'field effect' reflects TM's belief that consciousness is like a 'field': just as a field of light radiates from a light bulb or a magnetic field is created by a magnet, so one's consciousness radiates a field of energy to its environment. When there is a sufficient concentration of TM practice within a population, the Maharishi effect is felt. To achieve this, 100 regular practitioners are needed for a population of one million. For larger populations, proportionally fewer TM practitioners are needed: 316 would be sufficient for a 10 million population, and 748 for 56 million (until recently, the population of Britain).

Given the numbers of TM practitioners (4 million worldwide, 160,000 in Britain alone in 1995), it is not surprising that the TM organization has claimed that the Maharishi effect can already be seen. Four million is exactly the number needed to make a difference at a global level. TM claimed to have achieved a measurable reduction in the crime rate in Merseyside, England, between 1987 and 1992, as a result of the concentration of TM practice there. In the USA the national crime rate was said to have decreased when the practice reached 0.34 per cent of the population.

If these claims seem surprising, TM claims that they can be verified by scientific findings, and its literature refers to some 500 studies, some by well-accredited American universities which apparently substantiate such claims. Needless to say, however, such claims have not gone unchallenged, and critics have questioned both the statistical evidence and, where statistics appear supportive, the explanation that societal improvements are due to the so-called 'Maharishi effect'.

The belief that TM can have such a profound effect on the world enabled the Maharishi to formulate a 'world plan' in 1972. There would be one teaching centre for each million of the world's population, with the eventual goal of one meditation teacher per thousand. This would enable the attainment of the following points which constituted the plan:

1. To develop the full potential of the individual.
2. To realize the highest ideal of education.
3. To maximize the intelligent use of the environment.
4. To improve government achievements.

5. To solve the problems of crime, drug abuse and all behaviour that brings unhappiness to the family of man.
6. To bring fulfilment to the economic aspirations of individuals and society.
7. To achieve the spiritual goals of mankind in this generation. (Quoted in Kroll, 1974/1976, p. 23)

Some further projects of the Maharishi are worth noting. In 1976 the TM-Siddhi programme was introduced. 'Siddhi' literally means 'perfection' and the siddhi is a disciple who possesses advanced supernatural spiritual powers. The programme is based on Patanjali's *Yoga Sutras*, according to which there are 52 'siddhas' or special powers which accompany enlightenment. These include the knowledge of one's previous births, the development of compassion, subjugation of hunger and thirst, intuition, ability to leave the body at will, ability to radiate light, knowledge of the positions and motions of the stars, strength equal to that of an elephant, and understanding the sounds of all living beings. The key to attaining these powers is said to be *samyana*, which synthesizes three methods that Patanjali taught: *dharana* (holding one's attention still), *dhyana* (where mind flows along a specific theme), and *samadhi* (transcendental consciousness). The Maharishi believes that these practices, as enumerated by Patanjali, appear to take the practitioner in different directions: thus *dharana* appears to involve a state of calm, while *dhyana* involves mental motion.

The Maharishi's synthesis (*samyama*) incorporates the programme of 'yogic flying', to which the media have drawn considerable attention. At a purely visual level, yogic flying involves practitioners sitting cross-legged on cushions, from whence they propel themselves in the air in a series of short hops: although it is described as 'flying', it is not levitation as it is commonly understood, and siddhis do not remain in the air for any sustained length of time. TM siddhis claim other remarkable psychic powers. Some claim to be able to see objects that are hidden inside closed boxes. Others 'see' friends who are currently resident in other countries. The siddhi might see into the future and the past: some siddhis who are involved in financial affairs claim to have gained paranormal knowledge of movements in the stock market. Others apparently have acquired the ability to know the layout of their internal bodily organs, gaining aptitude in locating sources of illness.

What is reckoned to be more important than these paranormal powers is the general ability to develop and control the mind. Russell (1976/1978) compares siddhic practice to a gymnasium: there is no inherent merit in being able to lift a heavy dumb-bell or to climb ropes and wallbars, but for the gymnast these are all transferable skills, which develop one's body and imbue it with greater physical powers. Similarly, the siddhi programme develops the mind, enabling it to develop maximum human potential or 'enlightenment'. Barrett writes, 'Yogic Flying demonstrates perfect mind–body coordination and is correlated with maximum coherence, indicating maximum orderliness and integration of brain function, as has been measured by EEG research' (Barrett, 1996, p. 251). In Britain a new centre was established in Skelmersdale, where an 'ideal village' was created, and which served as the centre for siddhi practice. Its renowned Golden Dome was completed in 1988.

In 1990 TM assumed a distinctive political identity with the formation of the Natural Law Party. The NLP contested every parliamentary seat in the 1992 British general election, showing demonstrations of yogic flying on television in its party political broadcasts. The NLP was singularly unsuccessful, with no candidates even managing to retain their deposits. The party has fared no better in local or in European elections, and in the 1997 general election only a few NLP candidates stood for office. Notwithstanding such discouragements, the NLP still seeks to become the government of Britain, and has established various 'Ministries' within its organization.

Is TM a religion?

We now come to the question of whether TM is a religion. The Maharishi and his followers insist that it is not. Those who insist that it is a religion may well point to the fact that the Maharishi emanates from a Hindu background, is in a lineage of Hindu teachers, and uses a system of mantras that are characteristic of Indian religious traditions. His writings include a commentary on the Bhagavad Gita, in which he attempts to accommodate the text's ideas to his philosophical monism. In addition, TM has clear ritual elements in the form of the initiation ceremony and the twice-daily mantra practice. The power attributed to the mantra not only offers increased personal benefits, but serves as a radical solution to the world's problems.

Although TM may resemble a religion in these respects, it also lacks a number of key elements. Although one can identify the Maharishi's philosophical tradition, its teachings are in no way binding on TM practitioners. There is no public worship, no code of ethics, no scriptures that are studied, and no rites of passage that are observed within the context of TM. The practitioner has no special obligations, such as dietary laws, giving to the poor, or pilgrimages. In particular, there is no real TM community: practitioners do not characteristically meet together for public worship, but simply recite the mantra, as they have been taught it, not as a religious obligation, but simply as a technique to benefit themselves, their surroundings and the wider world.

est (Erhard Seminars Training) and its successors

Probably even more controversial than TM is *est* and its associated companies and programmes. *est* (an acronym for Erhard Seminars Training, and always spelt in lower casing) came into being in 1971, and aroused much unfavourable media comment, partly on account of allegations about the personal life of its founder Werner Hans Erhard, and also because of the extremely harsh conditions to which participants in *est* seminars were subjected.

Werner Erhard (Jack Rosenberg)

est was founded by Werner Hans Erhard, who was born as John Paul (Jack) Rosenberg in 1935. Rosenberg did not enter higher education, and has no formal training in philosophy, psychology or counselling; as a young man he started his career selling used cars and encyclopedias. He deserted his first wife, Ellen Bryde, and their four children in 1960, with the intention of starting a new life. On the day of his departure he read a magazine article about Werner Braun (a missile scientist) and Ludwig Erhard (a West German politician), and decided to appropriate the name Werner Erhard.

One morning, driving across San Francisco's Golden Gate Bridge, Erhard had an experience that was to prove decisive in shaping his life. He says that he became 'transformed', 'knowing everything and knowing nothing', an experience which he compared with Buddhist enlightenment. As a result of this experience, he founded *est*, with the aim of enabling others to undergo similar transformations.

Erhard's philosophy, on which the *est* seminars and their later successors were based, drew on a variety of sources. The idea of experiencing a radical 'transformation', 'a new and unexpected paradigm', draws primarily on the work of Thomas Kuhn, the celebrated author of the highly influential book *The Structure of Scientific Revolutions* (1962/1970). Another important influence on Erhard was Zen, much in vogue in California in the 1960s. The idea of a sudden recognition of an indefinable 'it' is an important theme that occurs both in Zen and in Erhard's seminars. Other ideas of Erhard are related to the German existentialist philosopher Martin Heidegger (1889–1976), and possibly Jean-Paul Sartre (1905–80). Erhard's ideas are also related to those of the transpersonal psychologists, particularly Abraham Maslow and Carl Rogers, as well as Gestalt Therapy. For Maslow, self-actualization was at the top of the 'hierarchy of needs' and was the individual's ultimate goal. However, despite the influence of transpersonal psychology, *est* never claimed to offer therapy, being aimed at the healthy and the successful.

Erhard also appears to have had contact with a number of extant Human Potential groups. Charlene Afremow, a close aide of Erhard's (who was later dismissed for criticizing the long hours that Erhard's employees worked), is said to have taught Mind Dynamics to Erhard. Some commentators have suggested that there are affinities between *est* and Scientology, and Erhard has even been accused of using Scientology material. There are certainly affinities between Erhard's notion of the two types of mental record (those that threaten survival and those that do not) with Hubbard's distinction between the analytical and reactive mind, but whether there is borrowing or mere similarity is difficult to determine.

Whatever its ingredients or originality, *est*'s professed aim was to offer 'a new and unexpected paradigm', 'a new model for humanity', 'to redefine what it means to be a human being', using a 'technology of transformation'. This emerging new paradigm was not confined to any single field of study, hence *est*'s work was not confined exclusively to its Human Potential seminars, but supported programmes and conferences relating to a wide variety of subject areas, ranging from physics to Tibetan Buddhism.

The seminars themselves offered a 'whole new way of thinking', a method of enlightenment whereby one could view one's Self in an entirely new way. It enabled participants to 'realize their potential to transform the quality of their lives'. To demonstrate the difference between conventional thinking and the kind of enlightened thinking that *est* affords, Erhard offers a parable. A man who has lost a key one night is looking for it beneath a lamp post. His friend asks where he lost it, and is told that it was further along the road. 'Why are you looking for it here, then?' the friend asks. 'Because the light is better!' he replies. The point of the parable is that we often search for life's meaning in places where it seems easiest, but what *est* can offer is the key itself!

According to *est* training, one's life has two elements: content and context. The content includes the facts and circumstances relating to our existence: our genetic make-up, our upbringing, our education, our knowledge and opinions, our occupation, our family and so on. It is very difficult, even impossible, to alter much of this. However, what can be altered is the *context* – the way in which we regard our lives and their environment. Consider one of Erhard's own examples: an employee asks her boss for a day off to visit her sick mother, but finds that her request is denied. One way of interpreting the situation is for her to say, 'My boss doesn't like me: he refused to give me the day off!' Another possible way of looking at it is to think, 'My boss can't do without me: he won't give me the day off!' Thus the same situation is capable of eliciting two radically different responses, each evidencing an importantly different view of one's Self.

What one is meant to recognize is not that one reaction to the situation is superior to another, but that believing in one's self-worth is preferable to believing that one is disliked and persecuted. According to Erhard, the important point to recognize is that we all have the ability to choose how we interpret and react to our life situations. If the woman whose boss will not give her the day off sticks with the opinion that her boss dislikes her, she will then be affected by this belief, letting it control her. In short, her reaction is the *effect* of the situation and her belief that has arisen from it.

What she can do, however, is to 'recontextualize' her opinion, bringing it 'to a context where you are the source'. In the above example the subordinate can assume control and decide for herself whether she is disliked or whether she is indispensable. Either way, she becomes the 'author', 'creator', the one who is responsible for her position; she has recognized that there was a genuine choice to be made and she has chosen, not simply drifted into the most immediately obvious interpretation, or one that her friends have placed on the situation for her.

est training is to be distinguished from 'positive thinking', whereby expressions of self-worth are judged to be superior to expressions of self-depreciation. The boss may really dislike the employee, who might be wise to act accordingly. Positive thinking, Erhard believes, focuses too much on life's 'ups', ignoring the 'downs': 'The training is about life being the way it is – down when it's down and up when it's up – and acknowledging the truth about it' (*est* brochure, n.d., p. 4).

est training should not be thought of as a form of therapy, either. The employee in the illustration is not meant to be paranoid, with a persecution complex to be addressed in some form of treatment. *est* is not primarily for people with problems, and the company executives who have undergone *est* training have not typically been marginal performers, or members of companies experiencing difficulties. (Indeed *est* has given training to companies as successful as British Airways, IBM, HarperCollins, British Telecom, and Saatchi and Saatchi.) *est* aims to provide important benefits to those who are already successful. The already successful can gain 'a new freedom and spontaneity'; the already healthy can acquire 'enhanced sense of vitality and spirit'; the already committed can appreciate other people better and understand more clearly what makes human relationships work; the already accomplished gain increased productivity and better satisfaction, accomplishing what might previously have seemed impossible; and the already knowledgeable achieve greater clarity, superior insight, increased originality and creativity, and more confidence, enabling better choices.

The est seminar

The original *est* seminars were conducted by Erhard himself. As *est* grew, however, it was necessary to delegate the seminar work to other trainers – men and women who had dedicated themselves to *est*, and who are said to have undergone intensive specialist training for periods ranging from three to seven years.

Finkelstein *et al.* (1982) give a detailed description of the sequence of events and conditions that were characteristic of the original *est* seminars, which ran from 1971 to 1984. One's first acquaintance with *est* was normally a 'guest seminar' – an event for which former *est* graduates were invited to bring along a friend who might be interested in participation. As a matter of policy, *est* did not advertise, but relied almost exclusively on word of mouth to gain new participants. At the guest seminar, graduates would typically give their testimony of their experience and how it benefited them, then the structure and purpose of *est* training would be explained. This was accompanied by a structured exercise (called a 'process'), in which participants were guided through various mental images.

For those who expressed an interest, the next stage was a pre-training session, usually held on the Monday before the first seminar weekend. (The main programme ran on two consecutive Saturdays and Sundays.) This session involved reading out the 'ground rules' which governed participation. Trainees should wear comfortable clothes; they must not consume alcohol or take any recreational drugs before the training session; no clock or watch should be brought into the training room; eating, smoking, and going to the toilet would not be allowed except during breaks; one must remain seated and silent unless instructed to speak by the trainer; name badges must be worn; one must not sit near anyone one knows. Trainees were obliged to sign an agreement to these conditions, and to submit this contract with their deposit.

The weekend seminars took place in a hotel conference room, or similar venue, beginning at 8.30 a.m. on Saturday. Some 250 people were seated in rows, with the trainer, smartly dressed and with the appearance of authority, at the front. The trainer interacted with some of the trainees, often subjecting them to abuse, calling them 'assholes' and devaluing their achievements; members of the audience were repeatedly told that their lives simply 'did not work'. The abusive treatment, apparently, was justified on the ground that other trainers who treated their students with greater superficial respect were merely engaging in 'acts'. The trainees were under the control of the trainer, and were allowed to speak only after raising a hand and being acknowledged; they were on the floor until the trainer terminated their contribution by saying 'Thank you' or 'I got it.' These dialogues were interspersed with two or three 'processes', which might consist of a relaxation exercise, or an exercise in guided imagery.

The following day, individual participants were asked to describe their persistent problems: these became the subject matter for the 'Truth Process' which took place later. Members of the audience were then instructed to close their eyes and meditate on a problem they experienced as individuals. They must locate a situation in which this problem occurs, and focus on the detailed physical sensations and images that accompany it. Audience reactions ranged from copious tears, retching and hilarious laughter. Then attendees were given the opportunity to share their experience with others, which they often regard as cathartic. This second day also included what is called the 'Danger Process': participants came up on the dais in groups of 25. They were instructed to 'be themselves': anyone who was deemed to be smiling insincerely or assuming an affected posture was reprimanded.

After a mid-training seminar, the trainer demonstrated on the second Saturday that the participants had failed to keep their agreements. (For example, some may still have had alcohol in their systems.) Some of the philosophy of *est* was then explained, particularly the idea that each one is the 'source' and has responsibility for one's life. This was followed by 'processes' to reinforce what has been said: for example, students could be asked to act out a role that they found embarrassing, thus eliciting the conclusion that the source of the embarrassment was one's Self and how it chose to view the situation.

Sunday was the final culmination of the training. Trainees reported on what they had experienced the previous evening. Then a presentation entitled 'The Anatomy of the Mind' was delivered. Its gist was that the human mind consists of 'multisensory records of successive moments of the individual's life' (Finkelstein *et al.*, 1982, p. 521). There are two types of record: (1) imprints of experiences that threaten survival (ones that resulted in pain, unconsciousness-ness or some other clear threat); and (2) those that are not thus threatening. The mind tends to assign all experiences into the 'threatening' category; thus the presumed 'correctness' of one's beliefs tends to be equated with what is conducive to survival, hence one finds a need to feel vindicated, rather than actually to possess the truth. One is enlightened on recognizing that the (conventional) mind is like a machine that makes illogical associations. (There is more than a shade of Dianetics here.)

At this point, the audience was asked if they had 'got it', and those who had 'got it' were asked to stand – which participants did with various degrees of swiftness. (Had some 'got it' more quickly than others, or did some not like to admit that they had not 'got it'?) Finally, this was followed by a review of the four-day seminar and a 'graduation ceremony', which formed its climax.

What was it that the trainees believed they had 'got'? If 'it' is anything like the experience of *satori* (enlightenment) in Zen, then it cannot be explained verbally, but only experienced. Erhard himself has designed the seminars so that they do not consist simply of downloading information: *est*'s goal is 'empowerment', not factual knowledge. 'Getting it' means finding one's true Self, which is the 'core self', or 'The Self' (with a capital 'S'), which is to be contrasted with the 'Mind State' (our ordinary consciousness). Those who operate from the 'Mind State' are 'uncorrected cybernetic machinery'. Those who 'get it' recognize the assumptions from which the Mind operates, and assume responsibility for their lives by letting this true Self shape their existence without the encumbrances of the conventional mind. We tend to identify ourselves with a particular role in life, which in truth is only a partial descriptor of ourselves: one might describe oneself as a parent, a business executive, a wage earner, a football player or whatever, and we come to identify the Self with these descriptions. We bury the Self in these partial identificators, and hence we need to recover it. 'Getting it' enables one to discover that one has held on to a position and that one can choose to hold or give up. Thus I might do certain things because I think they are expected of me as a university lecturer: but then 'lecturer' is only a partial descriptor of the whole 'me', and I have the responsibility of deciding whether to act as I think a lecturer should, or to act in accordance with some other aspect of my being.

Finkelstein *et al.* (1982) note affinities here between Erhard, Husserl's phenomenology and Heidegger's philosophy of existence. Husserl placed great emphasis on laying bare the presuppositions which underlie one's thinking (the 'Natural Attitude', as he called it, meaning one's ordinary consciousness), and paring them off in order to get 'to the things themselves'. Heidegger too wrote of Being (*Dasein*), which is typically 'fallen', 'inauthentic', and drifts along with the 'They' (the crowd). To be authentic one's must recognize one's true possibilities for Being, and decide one's existence accordingly, taking responsibility for it.

'Getting it' then is enlightenment, finding one's true Self, and assuming responsibility for decision-making, realizing what one's assumptions have been, and that one has been limited in the past by narrow thinking, a restricted view of one's self and the options that lie open. 'Getting it' is therefore not a 'peak experience', a 'high' on which *est* graduates leave the seminar, but something that is meant to last throughout one's life. 'Getting it' entails 'an expanded experience of happiness, love, health, and full self-expression' (*est* brochure, n.d., p. 5).

Self and others?

est's goals are more ambitious than mere Self-enlightenment. *est* literature speaks of 'global transformation', and expresses its aim as being 'to encourage individuals to participate in bringing about a transformation in the quality of life on our planet' (*est* brochure, n.d., p. 2). Accordingly, *est* did more than organize seminars, and generated a range of projects and subsidiary organizations.

It would be tedious to describe them all; some examples will suffice. The Werner Erhard Foundation awarded grants for research, aid for those affected by natural disasters, and Third World development projects. It also sponsored an education exchange scheme with the (then) Soviet Union. The Breakthrough Foundation (founded in 1980) ran a 'Youth at Risk Program', and claimed to have achieved decreases in arrests, violence and substance abuse, as well as increased success at school and work. The 'Holiday Project' encouraged 15,000 volunteers to visit people in hospitals and nursing homes during the Christmas and Chanukah period. 'Prison Possibilities Inc.' instigated a programme aimed at rehabilitating prisoners.

Such projects aroused their share of controversy, most of all Erhard's 'Hunger Project', established in 1977 with headquarters in San Francisco. The Hunger Project aimed to eliminate hunger by the end of the twentieth century, claiming that the measure of success would be a reduction of infant morality in every country to 50 children per year. The project attracted criticism because, although millions of dollars were elicited by way of donations, not a cent found its way to people in famine areas. According to the *Cult Observer* (November 1984), 22.5 per cent was used to produce literature; 77 per cent was for 'general expenses'. Whatever the

Hunger Project did or did not achieve, Erhard did make it clear that its aim was 'to educate and inform', and that it was neither a relief organization nor a pressure group. It work was 'to generate the will to eliminate the persistence of hunger and starvation', not directly to provide food for the hungry. If enough people 'willed' hunger to end, then, Erhard stated, the problem would disappear of itself. Accordingly, the work of the Hunger Project was to disseminate literature: *A Shift in the Wind* was a newspaper about ending world hunger, and 'The Hunger Project Papers' was a series of occasional papers written by relevant experts. During the time of unrest in Cambodia, the Project spent $90,000 in advertising which exhorted people to contribute, and claimed to have elicited $1,000,000 in donations.

est's successors

est in its original form no longer exists: as Erhard put it, it 'retired'. Erhard expressed the intention of making his work more 'global': 'To have an original organization or set of organizations that can translate sourced intention into reality ... the central intention is to make the world work for everyone' (Hubner, 1990a, p. 19). This was done by the 'Centers Network', which was an unincorporated organization that took a number of other Erhard projects under its umbrella.

The *est* seminar was transformed in 1984 to The Forum, after Erhard sold his network to associates, who renamed it Landmark Education Corporation. The Chief Executive Officer of Landmark is his brother, Harry Rosenberg. At the time of writing, the seminar is known as the Landmark Forum. Although similar in style, the Landmark Forum has a number of important modifications. It tends to emphasize 'personal growth' ('transformation') rather than personal enlightenment, and it is slightly less demanding than the old-style *est* training. Hours are fractionally shorter, but still long; there are more comfort breaks, although still only one meal, in late afternoon. Trainers are less inclined to be aggressive and abusive.

After completion of The Forum, various follow-on courses are open to graduates. These include courses on communication – to which The Forum attaches very high importance – productivity at work, time management, parenting and human relationships. The

Forum boasts high customer satisfaction, with some 95 per cent of its clientele acknowledging that seminars had 'specific practical value' in many aspects of their lives.

Despite the various criticisms that have been made of The Forum, the vast majority of participants believe they have benefited from it. Landmark's own survey listed a number of aspects of life that the seminar addressed, and invited participants to rate it on a four-point scale: 'poor', 'fair', 'good' and 'excellent'. The results were as follows:

Has specific practical value for many aspects of my life	95%
Likely to have enduring value for me	94%
Well worth my time and effort	93%
Makes me better prepared for new situations and challenges that may arise in the future	93%
Is well designed to benefit most participants	93%
Well worth the cost	90%
Has helped me cope with a particular challenge or problem	86%
Has helped me clarify my goals, values, and strategies	85%

These are impressive results, although of course it might be argued that the source of the data is not unbiased. However, subsequent academic studies (Finkelstein *et al.*, 1982; Wruck and Eastley, 1997) appear to corroborate the claims that, by and large, participants are satisfied with the training they receive.

Is est a religion?

From what has been said thus far, one may wonder in what sense *est* can be regarded as a religion. *est* itself and the subsequent Landmark organization have denied being religious in character. Nonetheless, several books, both anti-cult and academic, now classify *est/* Landmark and other Human Potential groups as examples of new religions.

There are two main grounds for doing so. The first relates to the allegation that Erhard claimed divine or semi-divine status for himself. One former employee is quoted as saying, 'The Forum has a theory that Werner Erhard is Godlike' (Eugene Kim, quoted in *Cult Observer*, 4 April 1988). Allegedly, Erhard was once asked if he was like Moses, Jesus and the Buddha, and replied that he was more like the one who sent them! Erhard denies having said this, claiming that he makes no exclusive claims to be divine, but rather that 'being at Source' entails recognizing and utilizing the core Self, which is the godlike entity that each individual really is. Erhard claims, 'You are God.'

Second, Paul Heelas argues that the notion of being responsible for everything that happens in life takes one beyond the empirical realm of explanations. While I may be responsible for denting my car if I drive carelessly, it is not so obvious how a telephone salesperson can be responsible if he or she finds that, every time he or she dials a number, it is engaged. Heelas cites Tipton, who recounts one of Erhard's followers saying, 'There I sat, dialing the telephone, hour after hour – nobody home ... Finally, I realized that it was *me* who wasn't "home"' (Tipton, 1981, p. 214; quoted in Heelas, 1991, p. 32). One seminar leader is recorded as having said to trainees: 'I can exert my consciousness into the mineral, animal, human and cosmic realms, at any time, on any planet, in any galaxy, anywhere in the universe' (Kevin Garvey, 1980; quoted in Heelas, 1991, p. 32). Heelas therefore suggests that to attribute seemingly unlimited powers to the individual entails a belief in magic, which is held within *est*, The Forum and Landmark. In addition, Heelas points out that followers either work voluntarily or accept relatively low rates of pay, characteristic of the religious life.

It is not clear, however, whether apparent suggestions of unlimited human potential are to be taken literally or whether they are gross exaggerations aimed at boosting the confidence of the trainees. *est*/Landmark literature makes little reference to 'magic', and, on the few occasions when the word is used, it appears in a colloquial, metaphorical sense, sometimes within quotation marks ('the "magic" of Forum'). There is no evidence that Erhard was interested in magic or drew on the ideas of its modern practitioners, although it is possible that seminar leaders believe that the mind has paranormal powers, a phenomenon somewhat different from magic. Whatever the explanation of any such remarkable powers, the use of magic or the paranormal does not necessarily constitute specifically religious activity.

Just as the Maharishi has drawn on the Hindu tradition, Erhard has drawn on several forms of spirituality, including Zen, and some of his organizations have involved the promotion of religion. For example, they have funded lectures by several prominent religious figures, including the Dalai Lama, the sixteenth Gyalwa Karmapa, Swami Muktananda (a siddha yogi), and Douglas Harding, author of the Zen work *On Having No Head,* which greatly impressed Erhard. However, influence and support for forms of spirituality do not of themselves make an organization a religion: indeed a secular university might typically promote similar events.

Against the claim that *est* and Landmark are religions, it is also worth noting that Landmark is not a membership organization. Those who have undergone the *est* or The Forum seminars do not belong to any community of followers, but are simply people who have received a particular type of training. *est*/Landmark is therefore unlike the vast number of religions, where community is one of the principal characteristics, providing an environment in which people can share life's problems and celebrate life's significant events. Thus in *est*/Landmark there is no ritual, no festivals, no religious calendar to punctuate the year, and the chief life-cycle events of birth, marriage and death are not celebrated within the organization. As the promotional literature states, participants are free to follow their religion, or to have none.

In conclusion, we can say that *est* and Landmark made no claims to be religious, and have not attempted to change their participants' religious allegiance, which they can pursue simultaneously with undergoing the seminars. They have addressed human problems in a radical way, setting super-empirical goals, and addressing what some may regard as a spiritual aspect of human nature (the Core Self, the Source, which is at least godlike, if not divine). *est* and Landmark may have some of the attributes typically associated with religion, but it is doubtful whether they should be accorded full status as religious organizations.

Although I have argued that not all the groups covered within this chapter actually count as religions, the examples I have studied are nonetheless useful, since these case studies have aroused much comment on the part of anti-cult critics. Moreover, they certainly all possess an important spiritual dimension, and provide useful studies for determining where the edges of religion lie.

9. New Age, witchcraft and Paganism

The musical *Hair*, so daring and popular in the late 1960s, was well known for its proclamation that the Age of Aquarius was dawning. The cluster of ideas that is associated with the New Age movement, however, did not come together until over a decade later: most commentators associate 'New Age' with a movement that began in the 1980s.

It is difficult to offer a clear, coherent definition of 'New Age': anyone who has visited a New Age shop will recognize the multiplicity of topics, viewpoints and paraphernalia that are associated with it. Its variety and eclecticism are as much part of its inherent nature as they are part of its appeal. A cursory browse through a New Age bookshop's shelves will yield a plethora of material on meditation, visualization, interpretation of dreams, self-improvement, astrology, Tarot and crystals. The paranormal is well covered, with material on extrasensory perception, telepathy, clairvoyance, psychometry, divination (runes, Tarot, dowsing) precognition, out-of-the-body experiences, and more. The New Age interest in alternative spirituality includes channelling, spirit guides and angels, as well as eastern religions such as Hinduism, Buddhism, Sufism and Taoism. Traditional writings like the *I Ching* (the 'Book of Changes', the ancient Chinese oracle), the *Tao Te Ching* and the Bhagavad Gita tend to be featured, together with Buddhist writings, principally from the Zen and Tibetan traditions.

Amidst so much diversity it can be difficult to pin down the 'New Age' to a precise definition. The term itself refers to the Age of Aquarius which succeeds the Age of Pisces. According to astrologers, each zodiacal age lasts for a period of approximately 2000 years, when a new zodiacal constellation comes to dominate the planet

Earth. Because the 12 constellations that make up the zodiac do not occupy clear 30-degree sections of the sky, no exact date can be given for the changeover from Pisces to Aquarius. Dates range from as early as 1898 to 2915; hence some New Agers hold that the New Age has already come, others that it is expected, and others still that the earth is at the changeover point.

The 2000-year time-span is significant, for approximately 2000 years have elapsed since the advent of Christianity. To many New Agers, Christianity is represented by the Age of Pisces, and is hence to be regarded as a thing of the past. To many Christianity involves a highly structured authority: in the case of Roman Catholicism, for example, its hierarchy of bishops, archbishops and cardinals. Throughout its history Christianity has insisted on its creeds and confessions, persecuted its opponents and heretics, and provided strict instruction on ethical behaviour. It is of the very essence of the New Age to reject all this. The New Age has no formal institutional structure; indeed its amorphous nature even makes it difficult to define accurately what its elements are. No doubt it is partly because of its implicit claim to be post-Christian that the New Age is singularly disliked by evangelical Christians. Indeed one evangelical critic states that the New Age is the most serious present-day threat to the Christian faith (Berry, 1988, p. 3). However, the perceived threat is also due in part to the amorphous character of the New Age phenomenon: since it is not clear precisely what is New Age and what is not, there is a risk that New Age ideas and paraphernalia may inadvertently find their way into the Christian Church, compromising the pure gospel message.

The New Age does not merely offer an implicit critique of Christianity: New Agers tend to view all forms of institutionalized religion with suspicion. It is therefore important not to classify the New Age as yet another new religious movement. Paul Heelas writes: 'Some see the New Age Movement as a New Religious Movement (NRM). It is not. Neither is it a collection of NRMs' (Heelas, 1986, p. 9).

The New Age's characteristic rejection of institutional religion, its absence of any agreed creed, and the absence of any authoritative hierarchy encourage seeking rather than any certainty (like that of the traditional Roman Catholic or the evangelical Protestant) that one has found the absolute final truth. For the New Ager, the search is as interesting and rewarding as any experience of finding, and the enormous range of spiritual paths, practices and paraphernalia serves to encourage an eclecticism on the seeker's part. It is even possible to be part of the New Age and simultaneously part of some more established religious tradition. I recently met one New Ager at a New Kadampa Buddhist group; on visiting her home I found a kind of shrine over which Sai Baba appeared to preside and on which, amidst various New Age crystals, she dedicated religious books that she was about to read, one of which was the well-known Hindu scripture, the Bhagavad Gita. She was also an ardent follower of Stephen Turoff, a highly acclaimed New Age healer. There are no New Age authorities to determine whether this is a harmonious medley of world religious ecumenism, or whether it is a hotchpotch of inconsistencies: the onus rests with the individual seeker.

It is this symbiosis of ideas that has enabled New Ager Marilyn Ferguson to entitle her important sociological study of the New Age *The Aquarian Conspiracy* (1980/1987): the word 'conspiracy', as she points out, literally means 'breathing together', which encapsulates the way in which the plethora of New Age themes co-exist. In the absence of any central authority or headquarters, Ferguson points out that New Agers operate by means of 'networking' – another favourite New Age word. Information is shared by means of New Age journals: *Cadeuceus, Kindred Spirit* and *Resurgence* are examples of national publications in Britain, as well as a variety of local network publications. Events like the Festival of Mind, Body and Spirit provide opportunities for New Agers to disseminate information as well as celebrate their spirituality. The typical New Age shop carries copious advertising by local counter-cultural groups and individuals, spanning shamanists, channellers, healers and more established religious groups such as forms of Buddhism.

One typical feature of the New Age is a positive, indeed optimistic, view of the self. The self is certainly not to be disparaged, as in Calvinist doctrines of original sin. Far from being sinful and 'totally depraved', the self is even regarded by some New Agers as divine. As Shirley MacLaine said, 'I am god, I am god, I am god.' This does not mean that all human beings are perfect, but rather that they have potential, and should strive for their optimal state of well-being. It also implies that human beings are to be valued for what they are, whether they are male or female, black or white, straight or gay: accordingly, it is common to find a substantial amount of literature in New Age bookshops championing feminism and gay rights.

Striving for human betterment manifests itself in a variety of New Age interests. One such interest is healing, and there is much exploration of spiritual healing and forms of alternative therapy. These range from the advocacy of homeopathic and herbal remedies to the practices of spiritual healers. At the time of writing one of the most widely practised is Reiki – a healing technique emanating from Japan that practises the laying on of hands. New Agers have little interest in the kind of miracle working that is supposedly performed by Christian evangelists like Morris Cerullo. Spiritual healing is to be distinguished from curing, the latter being targeted at specific physical or mental disorders. Healing, by contrast, relates to the whole self: in the process of healing, the patient (or client) may not necessarily receive a cure for a specific ailment, but may be assisted to come to terms with the ailment, and have his or her whole state of being improved by the process.

Self-improvement goes beyond the alleviation of illness. The New Age seeks to provide a range of possibilities for general self-improvement. *You Can Heal Your Life* by Louise L. Hay became a cult book, offering methods for affirming one's self, empowering oneself for success and so on. While mainstream Christianity has extolled the virtues of humility and self-denial, 'empowerment' is a favourite word of New Agers: the self *is* of worth, and can be enabled to make positive and worthwhile achievements. It should not be surprising therefore that New Age ideas extend into 'human potential', which includes interpersonal skills, business skills, assertiveness and neuro-linguistic programming – all subjects that have significantly gained momentum in the conventional world of business in mainstream society. New Age ideas too extend into the fields of education and politics: the interest in Steiner is an example of the former, and the support for organizations like Friends of the Earth, Greenpeace and the Green Party is evidence of the latter.

Just as the New Age seeks to move beyond mainstream Christianity, it typically questions traditional authorities in science and medicine, substituting less conventional alternatives. Western science has proceeded by means of empirical observation, logic, hypothesis testing and methods of reasoning which are often attributed to the 'left-hand side of the brain'. New Age teachings suggest that over the centuries our scientifically dominated cultures have neglected the more intuitive aspects of the mind. Consequently, New Age ideas tend to utilize the brain's 'right-hand side' –

emphasizing intuition, creativity, imagination, compassion, healing and so forth. This change of emphasis in part derives from a perceived need to develop the whole of the mind, intuitive as well as logical; in part too it derives from a dissatisfaction with traditional scientific ways of looking at the world. For example, despite advances in modern medicine, new drugs have generated harmful side-effects, and new diseases such as AIDS have arisen, defying cure. The New Age does not profess to cure what allopathic medicine cannot, but its emphasis on holistic healing is intended to ensure optimal well-being in times of ill health, and its revival of herbalism and homeopathy are alleged at least to be natural and harmless.

A number of antecedent strands contributed to the rise of the New Age. The beatnik and hippie counter-culture had largely blown itself out, and seekers had to look for some alternative spirituality. Abraham Maslow's notion of a hierarchy of needs culminating in the spiritual is often identified as an important influence, as is Teilhard de Chardin's notion of an evolutionary spirituality. Kuhn's notion of the 'paradigm shift' signalling a transition from one way of understanding the world to another radically different set of assumptions and hypotheses suggested a quest for alternative modes of understanding. The rise of ecological awareness, heralded by the Club of Rome's gloomy report *Limits to Growth* in 1972, focused attention on the plight of the planet and the need to cherish the earth. Marshall McLuhan's notion of the 'global village' in which all the earth's inhabitants were brought closer and became interdependent was another contributory theme. Added to these, the 1970s saw an increased interest in the paranormal: Lyall Watson's *Supernature* and Uri Geller's spoon-bending on television aroused much public curiosity. Maybe conventional science had not explained everything satisfactorily, and some new quest for meaning was needed.

Although open to eastern ideas, the New Age was not born from the world-renouncing philosophies of Indian gurus. On the contrary, the New Age is singularly world-affirming: it seldom extols the virtues of poverty or austerity, or commends the lifestyle of the monk or the sadhu. Indeed, the very hub of the New Age movement lies within the world of business, its mecca being the New Age shop – a commercial profit-making enterprise, without which New Agers would be unable to possess the books and artefacts they need for their spiritual journey or personal development.

The Findhorn community

Two case studies of the New Age will serve to highlight some of its features. Situated in Forres in Inverness-shire in Scotland, the Findhorn community is one of the most widely known New Age communities in Britain. The initial prompting for the founding of such a centre took place in Glastonbury in 1953, when Eileen Caddy, one of Findhorn's founder-leaders, claims to have heard a voice saying, 'Be still and know that I am God.' This was to be the first of many communications with the divine reportedly experienced by the Findhorn leaders.

The Findhorn community was not founded immediately upon Eileen Caddy's experience, but some nine years later, when her husband Peter, who had managed a local hotel, found himself out of work. After numerous unsuccessful job interviews and four years of unemployment, an official from the National Assistance Board came to see Peter. At the end of the interview, he asked if the latter thought that it was God who was preventing him from gaining employment. Peter agreed, and was met with the response, 'Well, then, presumably if we cut off your money, God will provide for you' (Findhorn Community, 1976/1988, p. 3).

The Caddys took this as a challenge, and began to cultivate the land in the caravan park in which they were staying. They had no formal knowledge of gardening, and the quality of the land was extremely poor, being a mixture of sand and gravel, and overgrown with couch grass. Being on the banks of the Moray Firth, the land was exposed to high winds and cold weather. Together with a friend and colleague Dorothy Maclean, the Caddys began to cultivate the ground. Having no money to buy artificial fertilizers, they used entirely organic methods, making compost from organic waste and obtaining manure from local farmers. Eileen and Dorothy relied on the 'God within' for guidance, and both of them committed the guidance they received to writing.

Some two months after the Caddys had commenced their horticultural explorations, Dorothy received a revelation during a private meditation session. It was the spirit of one of the members of the plant kingdom, known as a 'deva' to the early Findhorn community – the deva of the pea, which offered help in the cultivation of the garden. This experience began the practice of co-operation with nature: the devas of a multiplicity of plants and

320

vegetables manifested themselves to Dorothy and Eileen, affording revelations about the methods that should be used to plant them and the conditions under which they should be grown. At times, their advice entailed conventional methods which the Caddys, being inexperienced, simply did not know; at other times, the devas' requests contradicted the information given in professional gardening books.

The communications with the plant devas were not confined to practical gardening tips. On the contrary, the principle of co-operation with nature is the key to understanding Findhorn's philosophy. Eileen Caddy was familiar with Peter Tompkins's *The Secret Life of Plants,* a somewhat controversial 'fringe science' book in which the author claimed that plants have consciousness, and hence enjoy relationships with each other, their environment, and human beings. Communications from plant sprits, then, are not exclusively for human benefit, but serve to indicate what is conducive to the plants' well-being. The well-being of a plant may conflict with conventional methods of gardening, in which case some accommodation is needed. Pruning may stimulate growth, but it is painful to the plant: the gardener must therefore make some adjustment to his or her gardening methods. The question of pruning sweet peas arose at an early stage for the Caddys, who – apparently guided by the devas – came to the view that humans should acquire a greater appreciation of plants in their natural form, rather than in the more formalized shapes and arrangements that one finds in parks.

The Caddys implemented the advice, with remarkable results. Within two seasons fruit and vegetables were growing prolifically, with a surplus to the Caddys' personal requirements that could be sold to local residents. The early days of Findhorn are remembered for their outsize cabbages, which weighed as much as 40 pounds, ten times the normal weight of a cabbage. Even expert horticulturists who visited Findhorn were amazed and baffled by such remarkable growth in an environment in which one would have expected little, if any, fruit and vegetables, to germinate. The outsize cabbages even caused some Christian evangelical critics to suggest that they were violations of nature and therefore the work of the devil!

At first the Caddys focused their activities on gardening, without publicizing their communications with the nature spirits. However, in 1968 Sir George Trevelyan visited the community with a view to making a radio programme about it. Sir George could not accept the explanation that the Findhorn garden's success was attributable only to the compost and hard work: there must, he said, be a 'Factor X' that accounted for the phenomena. At this juncture Peter Caddy divulged the experiences of the devas, and was surprised to find that their explanation received a sympathetic hearing.

The cosmology of the early Findhorn community is crucial to understanding its development. Eileen Caddy drew more heavily on Judaeo-Christian tradition than the other founder members; for example, she used the biblical creation story to illustrate God's sovereignty over nature, human responsibility for it, and one's duty of care and gratitude for it. She compared the cultivation of the Findhorn garden with Noah's following God's instructions to build the ark: the early Findhorn community was a modern-day example of people experiencing divine providence by hearing God's voice and obeying it. It was Dorothy Maclean who emphasized the devas that inhabited the plant life, communicating with the spirits that inhabited the flowers, the vegetables and the trees. 'Deva', Findhorn explains, means 'shining one', and experiences of devas were said to be accompanied by experiences of bright light.

Robert Ogilvie Crombie (1899–1975), known as 'Roc' for short, was a friend of the Caddys and joined the Findhorn community in its earliest years. Roc was particularly influential in developing Findhorn's cosmology to encompass a range of 'para-physicals' of which the devas were but one category. In addition to the devas, there was a 'Landscape Angel' who offered advice on the general layout of the garden, and was consulted on numerous occasions. The hierarchy of para-physicals was believed to range from gnomes and fairies at the 'earthiest' level to angels and archangels at the top. Presiding over all the para-physicals was the god Kurmos, or Pan, whom Roc first directly encountered in 1966 in the grounds of Inverleith House in Edinburgh. This was to prove to be the first of numerous similar experiences. On one such encounter Pan introduced him to the myriad of nature spirits that inhabit the earth:

> The moment he stepped into me the woods became alive with myriad beings – elementals, nymphs, dryads, fauns, elves, gnomes, fairies and so on, far too numerous to catalogue. They varied in size from tiny little beings a fraction of an inch in height – like the ones I saw swarming about on a clump of toadstools – to beautiful elfin creatures, three or four feet tall. Some of them danced round me in a ring; all were

welcoming and full of rejoicing. (Findhorn Community, 1976/1988, p. 119)

The dilemmas involved in the development of Findhorn were largely viewed in terms of the relationships between humans and para-physicals, and between the para-physicals themselves. Thus damage done to vegetation was perceived as displeasing the deva that presided over that particular aspect of plant life. The act of cropping and eating fruit and vegetables was in itself a spiritual problem, only resolvable by due consultation with the plant devas. On this particular question, it was judged that in nature compromise was needed: the devas indicated that it was acceptable to do harm to plant life in order to eat, but that it was important to show gratitude for one's food. The cultivation of vegetables entailed that the Findhorn diet was principally vegetarian, but not exclusively so: the founder-leaders had been meat-eaters, and concluded – again in consultation with the para-physicals – that changes in human behaviour, such as the espousal of vegetarianism, could not be expected to happen all at once, but rather involved a gradual process of self-improvement. On one occasion a member of the community, without authorization, used a bulldozer to clear a patch of ground that was needed to build a greenhouse. As Peter Caddy reported, 'what an uproar it brought from the nature spirits' (Findhorn Community, 1976/1988, p. 19).

To those who inhabit a more conventional reality which is not populated by gnomes, fairies, elves, devas and the like, and who do not hear voices of para-physicals proffering advice, the question arises as to whether the Caddys, Dorothy Maclean and Robert Ogilvie Crombie 'really believed' in a pantheistic universe that was vibrant with such life forms. Dorothy relates that her communications were not relayed in audible words that could be heard either by herself or by anyone else who was present at the time, but rather as 'thoughts of inspiration' which she translated into human language. Moreover, the physical world is an emanation of the para-physical world, its 'energy'; thus there is no dualistic separation between physical and para-physical. As the Findhorn community explains:

> The human mind formulates great hierarchies and ever greater beings, yet the whole truth is simpler still. The truth is within me and within you – the whole of it. Where anything exists, God is. Not part of God but God indivisible. (Findhorn Community, 1976/1988, p. 88)

Thus we have an account of the Self–God relationship which has striking affinities with advaita Hindu philosophy. God has many forms, but yet is one; God may appear to be worshipped as if God is distinct from the self and the world, but yet is one with it; God is me, and I am God; what is outside is also within – if indeed one should talk of 'inside' and 'outside' at all.

Mention should be made of David Spangler, who settled at Findhorn in 1970, having lectured in the USA on spiritual and esoteric subjects. Spangler was responsible for introducing Findhorn's programme of seminars and classes, which now constitute the main reason for visitors coming to Findhorn today. The community organizes seminars and workshops on arts and crafts, creative writing and yoga, amongst various other topics, the aim being to encourage participants to discover their hidden talents, to develop their potential, and also to improve their business skills. In common with much of the New Age, Findhorn encourages seekers to think positively about themselves and to develop their human potential.

Findhorn is not only important as a well-known New Age centre, which has now expanded as far as Russia in recent times. The early Findhorn community was remarkably innovative, unlike later New Age organizations which have jumped aboard the bandwagon of New Ageism. Findhorn began to practise ecology substantially before the rise of the well-known environmental organizations. At the time of its inception, the Club of Rome had not delivered its *Limits to Growth* report (1972), and Friends of the Earth and Greenpeace – the two best-known British environmental pressure groups – did not begin their rise until the 1970s. The World Wildlife Fund, the earliest of the environmental groups, only came on the scene in 1971.

Dorothy Maclean's conviction that the cosmos is populated with plant spirits and other forms of deity is on the one hand a return to a belief in animism, which some scholars have attributed to primal societies. On the other hand, Findhorn's world-view is forward-looking, anticipating, for example, James Lovelock's 'Gaia hypothesis', which hit the public in 1979. Gaia was the earth mother-goddess, and Lovelock contended that the universe as a whole was not an inanimate object, but 'alive'. Maclean's idea that the earth spirits could be contacted, and could offer advice on human affairs, helped to give momentum to those New Agers who have sought guidance for life through 'channels'. Findhorn's belief in human potential, and its drawing on eastern as well as western sources of spirituality, establishes its credentials as one of the early New Age communities in Britain.

Much has changed at Findhorn, however. Peter and Eileen Caddy split up and divorced. Spangler has since moved on. Giant cabbages no longer grow, and the fruit and vegetables are of quite normal size, although cultivation of the soil is still important, not only for food but for developing the spiritual life of those who offer labour at Findhorn, enabling them to 'get back to nature'. Originally a project to enable the Caddys to escape from poverty and become self-sufficient, Findhorn is now quite a large business enterprise. Courses are not cheap, costing in many cases hundreds of pounds for a few days' board and tuition.

Glastonbury

By way of contrast with Findhorn, the town of Glastonbury in Somerset, England, offers an alternative venue for capturing the spirit of the New Age. Situated 132 miles from London, the town is a fascinating blend of old and new spirituality, having probably been a centre of ancient Celtic religion, and boasting a long Christian history, while at the same time offering visitors an overwhelming choice of New Age ideas, artefacts and practices. The town is relatively small, with some 9000 residents and many visitors. The main tourist attractions consist of an Abbey, Glastonbury Tor (some 525 feet high), the White Spring, the Chalice Well and Wearyall Hill (both of which are associated with Joseph of Arimathaea), as well as the numerous New Age venues and activities. For those who are prepared for a somewhat muddy walk beyond the outskirts of the town, there are two ancient oak trees known as Gog and Magog.

The surrounding area was once mainly marshland, with lagoons connecting to the Bristol Channel, and is believed to have once been an island – hence its alternative name, the Isle of Avalon. The town lies at the foot of a number of small hills. A village has probably existed there since prehistoric times: evidence of some 60 to 70 huts has been discovered, together with a number of artefacts, including bowls which, it is conjectured, may have been used for drinking wine at religious festivals. In the course of its history, Glastonbury has been associated with a number of Christian saints: St Brigid, St

Patrick (who may or may not be the same Patrick as the one who brought Christianity to the Irish), and St Dunstan, and the long Christian tradition is evidenced by the impressive Abbey in the heart of the town.

Contrastingly, a brief journey through Glastonbury will reveal its preoccupation with what is new as well as what is ancient. Shop fronts frequently change, but at the time of writing the visitor will find several New Age shops, each having different specialisms. One specializes in books and New Age magazines, with a particular emphasis on Glastonbury itself and its remarkable properties. Another focuses on crystals, while a third is called 'The Green Man and the Goddess', and is principally a bookshop specializing in goddess religion and earth spirituality. There is an Orthodox shop, which sells Christian books and icons, and is run by leaders of the Celtic Orthodox Church. A hemp shop sells goods associated with cannabis-smoking (although by law it cannot supply customers with cannabis itself). The National Federation of Spiritual Healers has a prominent shop front, and provides information and advice about local healers and counsellors. There are several cafés, serving vegetarian and whole foods, and an alleyway leads to a complex of premises called The Avalon Foundation, formerly known as the University of Avalon, until the British government insisted that the term 'university' may be used only by degree-awarding higher education establishments with a royal charter. In many shop fronts there are advertisements and leaflets for Glastonbury's varied spiritual activities: various forms of Buddhist meditation, astrology, Tarot, 'sacred landscapes', healing, angels – indeed all the activities that one typically associates with the New Age. The staff of Archangel Michael's Soul Therapy Centre are dressed in Tibetan Buddhist robes and offer 'etheric healing': a technique that involves sitting inside a pyramid-like device and holding an electric *dorje*. The pyramid is said to have been designed by Sanat Kumara, the Buddha Maitreya and Jesus Christ. (I am told that the town's inhabitants consider this bizarre, even by Glastonbury standards!)

Glastonbury is particularly famous for the annual Glastonbury Festival, which originated in 1914 under the name of the National Festival Theatre of Music and Drama. As Glastonbury increasingly attracted New Age pilgrims, the Festival in its present form was revived in 1971: its current venue is a large field in the nearby village of Pilton, some five miles away, and boasts the claim to be the largest rock festival in Europe. As well as the rock bands, New Age and other spiritual groups use the opportunity to promote their brands of spirituality.

In recent times Glastonbury has been associated with UFOs, and various sightings have been claimed within the area. Not surprisingly, some of the Glastonbury pilgrims have an interest in crop circles, and the town hosts an annual conference on the subject (Howard-Gordon, 1982/1987, p. 106).

A great fire at Glastonbury Abbey in 1184 destroyed its entire library, thus depriving later generations of important primary sources relating to the town and the church there. Although regrettable, this loss has enabled posterity to engage in all kinds of speculations, giving momentum to the various Glastonbury myths. Not surprisingly, there are mutually contradictory versions of these myths and interpretations — sometimes even within the same guidebook! In the spirit of the New Age, there is no authoritative account of Glastonbury phenomena, and those who are inspired by Glastonbury can decide which myths and interpretations to believe and appropriate, or whether to doubt them all.

Glastonbury boasts a long Christian tradition, while also claiming to have been a centre of pre-Christian Celtic religion. These twin claims help to make it a place where an interest in spirituality can be combined with attempts to return to pre-Christian pagan ideas of earth spirituality, goddess worship and Celtic religion.

According to the Glastonbury legend, Christianity was brought there in 67 CE (some sources say 37 CE) by the coming of Joseph of Arimathaea, the wealthy noble who provided an opulent tomb in Jerusalem for Jesus' body (John 19:38-42). Jesus' disciple Philip is said to have sent Joseph to England to preach the gospel. He came with 12 disciples, bringing with him the Holy Grail – the cup used by Jesus and his 12 disciples at the Last Supper – and buried it at the foot of Glastonbury Tor. Slightly further on, the legend goes, Joseph stopped to rest on a hillock which is now known as Wearyall Hill; he rested his staff on the ground to lean on it, whereupon a hawthorn tree grew and started to blossom. The local king Arviragus donated land to Joseph and his followers, and they built a church of 'wattle and daub' (wood and mud) there. His 12 followers received 12 'hydes' of land (a hyde being 160 acres), where they build huts of mud and wattle, and lived simple lives of self-denial. They were known as the 'Anchorites', and, if the story were true, Glastonbury would have been the first place in Britain at which the Christian gospel was preached.

Although some Glastonburians accept the Joseph of Arimathaea legend as historically true, its earliest versions appear to emanate from medieval times, around 1250. Alfred, Lord Tennyson gave the Joseph stories further impetus in his *Morte d'Arthur:*

> The cup, the cup itself from which our Lord
> Drank at the last sad supper with His own;
> This from the blessed land of Aramat,
> After the day of darkness, when the dead
> Went wandering over Mariah – the good Saint,
> Arimathaean Joseph, journeying brought
> To Glastonbury.

This story of the grail is associated with the Chalice Well which is set at the foot of the Tor. There a well, whose shaft was probably constructed in the twelfth century, pours out some 25,000 gallons of water each day, and never dries, even in the worst times of drought. Over time, the waters have left a reddish-brown deposit in the well and on the ground over which it has flowed, and some Glastonburians see this as indicating that the well flows from the grail, the source of Christ's blood. The waters of the well, which pilgrims may gather freely, are believed to have miraculous powers, and there are many stories of remarkable cures that have been gained there.

Glastonbury's Arthurian legends

Tennyson's *Morte d'Arthur* serves as a reminder of the associations between the legends of King Arthur and Glastonbury. The inclusion of Arthurian ideas in the British New Age scene stems from the legends of this local king and folk hero who, together with his 'knights of the round table' journeys in quest of the Holy Grail, brought by Joseph of Arimathaea.

Whether King Arthur is myth or history has been much debated. Whatever the historicity of the Arthurian legends, he is not exclusively connected with Glastonbury, and, particularly in Cornwall (in the extreme South-West of England) there are rival sites, such as Tintagel and St Mary's Mount, a tidal island connecting to the village of Marazion. As one might expect, the sources that purport to give evidence of his existence are not scholarly writings that use the normal canons of historiography, and those who associate Arthur with Glastonbury are keener to press ahead with developing the town as a Arthurian centre, rather than rebutting rival claims.

The King Arthur legends consist of a quest for the grail. Such a quest is not simply a matter of finding the geographical location of buried treasure; according to tradition, one can only be successful in locating the grail if one has proved oneself worthy of so doing. Arthur's quest is therefore associated with loyalty, courage and chivalry, with fending off evil opponents who would thwart the knights' efforts, and with the quest for Camelot, the ideal perfect city. Thus, according to Geoffrey of Monmouth's *History of the Kings of Britain* (*c*. 1135), Arthur conquers Norway and Gaul, and fights Mordred in Cornwall, from whence he was brought to the Isle of Avalon, where his injuries were treated and his health restored. Arthur finally crosses the River of Death, at which a hand appears from the water to receive his famous sword Excalibur: this spot is located at Pomparles Bridge, some five miles from Glastonbury. ('Pomparles' is possibly a corruption of 'pons perilis' – 'dangerous bridge'.)

The grave of King Arthur and his consort Queen Guinevere was supposedly found in Glastonbury in 1191. A leaden cross bore an inscription which read, 'Here lies buried the renowned King Arthur with Guinevere his fortunate wife in the Isle of Avalon.' The grave was reopened in 1278, and Arthur's remains were reburied in front of the Abbey's high altar, where they remained until 1539, when King Henry VIII's dissolution of the monasteries left the vast majority of monastic properties, including Glastonbury Abbey, in ruins. King Arthur's coat of arms remains the emblem of the Abbey: one Arthurian legend records that the Virgin Mary appeared to Arthur and presented him with a crystal cross, which is supposedly preserved as a relic within the Abbey.

Glastonbury's pre-Christian tradition

I have focused mainly on the Christian tradition in Glastonbury, but Glastonbury's rise as a New Age Centre depends equally, if not more, on the claims that it has been a centre of pre-Christian Celtic religion. Several indicators of this exist. Within the precincts of the

Abbey lies an 'egg stone', a possible symbol of pre-Christian cosmology: it was not uncommon for Christian missionaries to 'Christianize' such stones, incorporating them within Christian shrines in this way. The Chalice Well may owe its origins, not to Joseph of Arimathaea, but to ancient goddess religion, where it possibly supplied the 'womb waters' of a goddess. The emphasis on the Virgin Mary, which is enshrined in Glastonbury's Christian myths, may be a further indicator of pre-Christian goddess worship. It is not uncommon for one female form of divinity to replace another when missionizing occurs, and it would be likely that Christian missionaries would wish to focus their attention on a centre where the competing pre-existing religion was strong.

Some of Glastonbury's apparently Christian features are as explicable in terms of Celtic religion as they are of Christianity. It has been speculated that Arthur was not a historical king, but originally a 'wind spirit', a leader of the Wild Hunt, who engaged in a search for the souls of the departed; an alternative suggestion is that he was a god of fertility, like the 'Green Man', a being who symbolizes fertility and who captures the popular spiritual imagination in Glastonbury and elsewhere. Alternatively, the name 'Arthur' itself has been argued to be a form of 'Arth Fawr', meaning 'Great Bear' – a possible reference to the stellar constellation, and thus relating to astrology. It may be no coincidence that the modern astronomical name for the northern hemisphere's brightest star is 'Arcturus'. One writer suggests that the notion of a Holy Grail may not originate from any chalice used at Christ's Last Supper, but may in some way relate to the Tarot's suit of cups. While it is more likely that this aspect of the Tarot derived from Christianity (the Tarot contains numerous Christian symbols and allusions), such connections and speculations enable the various aspects of Christian and non-Christian spirituality to intertwine and merge imperceptibly into each other.

Further evidence of Glastonbury's pagan roots may lie in the importance attached to trees. In previous centuries an avenue of oaks led up to the Tor, until they were cut down around 1906 to make way for farm land – an act which would certainly not be tolerated in today's climate of conservation! The famous Glastonbury thorn may originally have been associated with pagan festivals; indeed the original tree may have been a 'may tree', which would come into flower around the May Day pagan festival of Beltane. (The name

'Beltane' is associated with the goddess who is variously known as Beltis, Belit or Ba'alat.) The Christmas flowering would mark the winter solstice or Yule, which was only made to coincide with Christmas after the advent of Christianity. Some have speculated that the ancient trees Gog and Magog represent evil powers which the invocation of the goddess or other benign spirits might serve to fend off.

The Christian myth of St Collen is important in recognizing the connection between Glastonbury's Christian and pre-Christian spirituality. A ninth-century Welsh biographer recounts that Collen, a Christian hermit, was visited by two emissaries of Gwyn Ap Nudd, the king of the fairies, who invited him to the king's castle. Being a Christian saint, Collen equated fairies with demons, and took the precaution of taking holy water with him. When the fairies offered him food, he resolutely declined, believing in the power of fairy food to prevent his return. Instead, he sprinkled his holy water on the castle, as a consequence of which both the fairy castle and its fairies disappeared. The story is presumably a myth that demonstrates the victory of Christianity over the pagan religions, but its telling signals an interest in both religions.

There are other possible fairy connections. The name 'Avalon' itself may derive from 'Avallha', a Celtic demi-god who presided over the underworld. Some have connected the notion of the underworld with the fairies' glass mountain or spiral castle, the place at which the earth's energies meet the powers of death. The obvious point in Glastonbury for the meeting of such powers is, of course, its Tor. The sides of the Tor are terraced, and some have seen in its contours a spiral maze, allegedly constructed between 3000 and 2000 BCE as a means of invoking the goddess. Many Glastonburians have speculated that inside the Tor there exists a secret labyrinth of tunnels, a kind of gateway to the underworld.

It should be no surprise to find an interest in astrology within Glastonbury, and indeed the whole surrounding countryside is regarded by many as a mirror image of the stellar constellations, and known as the 'Glastonbury zodiac'. The Glastonbury zodiac was 'discovered' in 1935, and, ever since then, many Glastonbury pilgrims have claimed to see from the top of the Tor the shapes of the various zodiacal patterns in each of 12 directions. These 12 sections of the zodiac blend with the Joseph of Arimathaea legend of the 12 hydes which were given to the 12 disciples. Numerologically, the number 12 signifies the number of labours of Hercules (connecting with the Tor's hypothetical labyrinth) and the number of steps of initiation required for discovering the Holy Grail.

One final comment on Glastonbury concerns an alleged Druid connection. It is said that the Druids had an ancient college at Glastonbury, at which they taught their ceremonies and rituals. Some declare that the White Well, situated at the foot of the Tor, along from the Chalice Well, was the entrance to an ancient Druid cave. It has also been suggested that the ground plan of Glastonbury Abbey coincides remarkably with that of Stonehenge.

In sum, Glastonbury offers a fascinating array and amalgam of spiritualities. Unlike Findhorn, however, Glastonbury is an established historic town. So its community is pre-existent, although since the rise of the New Age it has drawn many healers, alternative therapists, vendors of New Age products, and spiritual groups. Unlike Findhorn, the community is not defined by founder-leaders like the Caddys. It is determined by its history, although this of course does not prevent new and innovative groups from alighting on the town.

Witchcraft and Paganism

Witchcraft, Paganism and Wicca, although sometimes taken to be aspects of the New Age, are to be sharply distinguished from it. As we have seen, the New Age is eclectic, without clear boundaries, and is characterized by spiritual seeking. By contrast, Wicca is a definite form of religion, with clearly defined practices (although these may vary from one group, or coven, to another), and which is the result of one's spiritual search rather than part of the search itself; it is for 'finders' rather than 'seekers'.

Although witchcraft or Wicca is a specific spiritual path, there is no single version of Wicca, and indeed the term is associated with a cluster of several related concepts, which are not easy to untangle: Paganism, goddess spirituality, Druidism, magic (or 'magick'), Celtic religion and shamanism. There are also those who would see witchcraft as being related to sorcery, occultism and even Satanism. At a popular level, many of these concepts are conflated, or at least not clearly distinguished, not least by Christian evangelical critics.

The word 'witchcraft' derives from the Anglo-Saxon word *wiccecraeft,* which is a compound of *wicca,* meaning 'witch' or 'wizard', and *craeft,* meaning 'power' or 'art'. Hence present-day Wiccans have revived the ancient word for 'witch'. The popular stereotype of the witch is of the old woman who brews potions in cauldrons, casts malevolent spells, and travels the sky at night on a broomstick – particularly at Hallowe'en – and owns a black cat as a companion or 'witches' familiar'. This stereotype can still be found in some of the older reference works on religion. For example, the contributor to Virgilius Ferm's *An Encyclopedia of Religion* writes:

> Witchcraft in general consists in the use of magic to injure the bodies or goods of others. Though witches may practice 'white' magic, their activities are generally believed to be malevolent and the witches themselves to derive their powers from devils or other evil spirits. By reason of their magic powers witches are reputed to be able to produce or cure disease, to induce love or aversion, to 'conjure' others, to give life to inanimate objects, to bring about storms and sell winds, and to fly through the air. They are often associated with toads or black cats, which are supposed to embody their 'familiar' demons. (Ferm, 1945/1976, p. 827).

The history of witchcraft

Wiccans will point out that, throughout the Church's history, there have been 'wise women' and magical practices, some of which have even been condoned by the Church. On balance, however, the Church regarded witchcraft as a rival set of practices, gave various pronouncements, and hunted down those who were said to practise magical arts. During Christianity's first millennium penalties were mild; however, in 1320 Pope John XXII issued a papal bull proscribing ritual magic, and in 1437 and 1445 Pope Eugene IV issued bulls prescribing severe penalties for witches who used their powers to cause bad weather. In 1484 Pope Innocent VIII issued the bull *Summis Desiderantes,* which expressed support for proceedings against witches by the Inquisition, and which heralded a wave of persecution and torture of witches. In 1486 two Dominican inquisitors, Kraemer and Sprengler, published the famous *Malleus Maleficarum* ('the hammer of the evildoers'). It should be noted that 'maleficarum' is the feminine form of the noun, and hence referred to witches and not evildoers more widely. The marks of the witch included having entered into a pact with the Devil; formally renouncing Christ; expressing such renunciation by desecrating the sacraments, or by trampling or spitting on crucifixes; holding secret meetings under cover of darkness; flying by night; and orgies, ritual killing of babies, and cannibalism. Other accusations against witches included blighting crops, causing animal deaths, illnesses and storms. (It is interesting to note that such accusations still prevail; even in the past two decades, practitioners of witchcraft have been blamed for animals found dead on Dartmoor in England.)

In reality, it is much more probable that the so-called 'witches' were 'wise woman' who could be consulted oracularly in matters relating to health and love. The potions they prepared were probably herbal remedies for illnesses or aphrodisiacs. (The term 'witch doctor', which has sometimes been applied to a tribal medicine man, indicates a relationship between witchcraft and healing.) What may well have offended the ecclesiastical authorities was the fact that the so-called witches were apparently usurping power by assuming authority and offering advice to those who more properly should have sought it in a male-dominated Church.

The Renaissance led to a greater questioning of the Church's authority, and such questioning gave some impetus to a greater interest in magic. A number of magical orders took their rise: the Martinists, the Illuminati, the Rosicrucians and the Freemasons. However, the Protestant Reformation did not signal a change of attitude to witches: Luther insisted that they should be burned at the stake, and the Calvinists continued to persecute them. After all, scripture did not legitimate their activities any more than the Catholic Church: 'Thou shalt not suffer a witch to live' was God's instruction to Moses (Exodus 22: 18).

The history of Judaeo-Christianity consists of rejection both of the fertility cults, whereby human beings used religion to control nature, and of the goddess. The only gesture towards goddess veneration is the cult of Mary, chiefly found in Roman Catholicism, although she is plainly subordinated to the deity, and desexualized as the perpetual virgin. Wiccans note that an important theme of Europe's pre-Christian religions was nature as well as goddess veneration, and Wicca is therefore an attempt to return to one's pre-Christian roots.

British pre-Christian religion is often associated with Druidism, which wiccans sometimes claim as a link between the ancient religions of the Indus valley and witchcraft. Such claims have to be treated with caution. Although the very ancient monuments of Stonehenge and Avebury in Wiltshire are popularly associated with the Druids, no first-hand records of Druidism survive, and any information we have about them is transmitted through opponents of their culture, most notably the Romans. What is certain is that they existed, and were known to the Romans in the first century BCE; as to their beliefs and practices we can only guess on the basis of extremely flimsy evidence.

The name 'Druid' itself has been given a variety of interpretations: 'servant of truth', 'all-knowing wise man', 'equal in honour' and 'oak' – the last of these alluding to the ancient Celtic tradition of venerating the oak tree, a cult which may have been associated with figures like the Green Man, which has experienced a revival with the advent of the New Age. The Father of the Druid pantheon was Taranis (the oak god), assisted by Belenos (the sun god), Cernunos (the god of the hunt, who becomes associated with the horned god Pan), Lugh (the god of many skills), and Esus (the pastoral god who enables the working of magic). Vivianne Crowley (1989) suggests that the Druids constituted the priesthood of the Celts, and Sadleir (1992) believes that they were Magi – philosopher-magicians who possessed a special gnosis, and who practised astrology and homeopathy. Their astrological expertise gave them the ability to define closely the cycle of the sun, moon and planets, and hence Druidism supposedly included the celebration of the seasons of the year.

Just as the seasons exhibit a cycle of fertility, birth, growth, fruition and death, it has been suggested that the Druids held that a similar process applied to the human soul. The soul, which is eternal, is capable of evolution – hence a belief in human potential – and goes through an eternal cycle. After death, it remains contactable, and renews itself in a Summerland, after which it is reborn, to grow, flourish and die again.

In the absence of direct evidence, all this has to remain speculative. Whatever the neo-Druids' claims to authenticity, Druidism experienced a revival in the eighteenth century in the form of a number of Druid cults in Europe. Henry Hurle's 'Ancient Order of Druids' was one early example in Britain; other later groups include the British Circle of the Universal Bond and the Order of Bards, Ovates and Druids. Some members of the Hermetic Order of the Golden Dawn – to which occultist and magician Aleister Crowley (1875–1947) belonged – were also attracted to Druidism.

The recent interest in witchcraft was revived by the now famous study, *The Witch-Cult in Western Europe* (1921), by Margaret

Murray (1863–1963). Although an academic work, it aroused public attention, principally because Murray argued against the traditional notion of the witch as the devil worshipper, arguing instead that witchcraft was the remnant of a pre-Christian tradition that once flourished in Europe. This tradition, she alleged, was a fertility cult belonging to Europe's pre-Christian era. Murray's theory is now largely discredited, largely because her work was based on dubious source material, including Charles Leland's *Aradia: The Gospel of the Witches,* published in 1899 and now known to be a spurious work. However, the popularity of Murray's study achieved two important results: it challenged the traditional image of the witch as the Devil's disciple, and it gave momentum to serious interest in witchcraft among some members of the public. When the British government 30 years later revoked the various witchcraft Acts, replacing these with the Fraudulent Mediums Act of 1951, a number of practising witches were then able to practise their craft openly, without fear of prosecution. As a consequence, witchcraft gained momentum in Britain during the 1950s, and became popular in the USA in the 1960s. Although most of these witches claimed to have been initiated into a lineage of covens going back to pre-Christian times, such claims are almost certainly spurious, and there is no evidence of links going back earlier than around the 1930s.

Many twentieth-century witches were unhappy with the term 'witchcraft' or 'witch', largely because of its negative connotations. Consequently, the Old English term 'wicca' was substituted. Claiming, as several did, to be reviving an ancient pre-Christian religion, the term 'paganism' has also come into use in certain circles. The root meaning of 'pagan' (Latin *paganus*) was a country dweller. Country dwellers, being removed from city life, did not practise the religions of the wealthier and more educated city dwellers, such as the Graeco-Roman civic religions, the mystery religions, and finally Christianity when it spread through the Roman Empire; instead they practised their own rites associated with rural life. Thus, until the somewhat later conversion of the country dwellers, 'pagan' came to be synonymous with those who did not embrace the Christian faith. Three features probably characterized the pagan religions: they contrasted with the state religions and the religions of the city-dwellers; they were probably related to fertility; and, since rustics are generally deemed to be less literate than city inhabitants, the pagan religions are largely undocumented. Wiccans such as Vivianne

Crowley have claimed that modern Wicca is a combination of Paganism (the religion) and witchcraft (the craft). However, as I have suggested, it is not possible to trace Wicca to ancient witchcraft, and, since ancient Paganism was non-literate, it is not possible to ascertain with certainty what rites were practised and what festivals were observed before Christianity swept across Europe.

The twentieth-century revival of witchcraft

A number of different strands of Wicca came into prominence in the 1950s and later. Gerald Brosseau Gardner (1884–1964) was a civil servant who spent most of his working life in Asia. He became fascinated by Asian magicians, and his interest in magic – eastern and western – caused him to study western occultism, principally through Theosophy and Freemasonry when he returned to England in the late 1930s, and also through some of the writings of Aleister Crowley. Gardner claimed that at one of the Theosophical group's meetings he encountered a number of witches, who introduced him to their priestess, Dorothy Clutterbuck, and that 'Old Dorothy' (as she was known) initiated him in 1939. Melton (1992), among others, has suggested that this account may be embellished: it is more likely, he believes, that the group of witches was Gardner's own creation. Gardner's account may well be a device for claiming to have a wiccan lineage.

Gardner published information about witchcraft in the guise of a novel entitled *High's Magic Aid*, in 1949, under the pseudonym 'Scire', his wiccan name. This was followed in 1954 by his *Witchcraft Today*, a more explicit treatment of the theme, and with a foreword written by Margaret Murray. (Since the British witchcraft laws had been repealed by that time, Gardner could be more open.) Gardner is the fountain-head of the Gardnerian tradition of witchcraft, and assumed the title 'king of the witches'. He organized his group of followers into a coven, which is the basic unit in which most present-day wiccans are organized: normally containing about 12 in number, a coven may be as small as four people, but is not normally larger than 26.

Gardner's rituals appear to have been based on some of the magical rites he encountered in Asia. In 1936 Gardner, while still in Asia, had written a book entitled *Kris and Other Malay Weapons*: the *kris* was a Malay magical knife, and this appears to have been the

337

precursor of the wiccan 'athame', the ceremonial knife that is thrust into the cup at a wiccan rite, symbolizing the union of male and female. Gardner's coven observed the moon's quarter days, and was focused on the goddess and the horned god. The coven practised their rites naked, or 'skyclad', to use the more usual wiccan terminology. (The term 'skyclad' originates from the Digambara school of Jainism, where the world-renouncing monk abandons all possessions, including clothing.) Gardner continued to revise his ceremonial manual throughout the remainder of his life.

Several of Gardner's initiates went on to give their own initiations. This led to some breakaway groups, the two most important of which are those of Alexander Sanders (1926–88), with his wife Maxine, and Sybil Leek. Sanders was more interested in ritual magic, and attracted a following of young intellectuals. After Gardner's death he claimed the title 'king of the witches' for himself. Both Sanders and Leek abandoned the practice of ritual nudity, substituting ceremonial robes for their covens' rites.

A number of other traditions of wicca are worth mentioning. Some covens have a 'cultural' focus, emphasizing a particular tradition of deity. These may be Saxon deities, most commonly those in the Celtic Norse or Druidic traditions, or they may be Egyptian. Some wiccan groups focus on the goddess Diana, who is often viewed as having a threefold form, representing the three stages of one's life – youth, adulthood and old age, symbolized by Kore (the maiden), Diana (the mother) and Hecate (the crone). Hecate is frequently portrayed as the consort of the horned god Pan.

The Dianic groups merge into the feminist wiccans. Some, although by no means all, of the Dianic covens are entirely female, and view wicca's emphasis on the goddess and its rejection of male-dominated Christianity with its male deity as a means of liberating women. One of the principal exponents of this form of wicca is Zsuszsanna Budapest, noteworthy for her substitution of the terms 'womon' and 'wimmin' for 'woman' and 'women'. The logic behind this is that the more conventional words 'woman' and 'women' are derivative from 'man' and 'men', and that such inadvertent references to the male gender should be eliminated. Following the lead of Naomi Goldenberg, Budapest also prefers to speak of 'thealogy' rather than 'theology' for similar reasons: *theos* is a masculine noun in Greek, and does not accurately encapsulate the activity of theorizing about the goddess.

In addition to these various forms of wicca, there is the tradition of the hereditary coven, in which initiation is transmitted within the family. Finally, there is the 'hedge witch' – someone who practises witchcraft alone, without the need of a supportive coven.

The teachings of Wicca/Paganism

Wicca is more about experiencing and enjoying nature, rather than explicitly formulating doctrines and formally studying or imparting them. Nonetheless, despite considerable variations among the many covens, there is a distinctive world-view that is characteristic of the wiccan. Paganism has been said to be a combination of eastern magic, western magic, Freemasonry, goddess spirituality.

Wicca combines the religious ideas of Paganism with the witches' 'craft', and the masculine images of God from the Celtic pre-Christian religions with the goddess. It can therefore be viewed as polytheistic, although such a characterization must be qualified in two ways. First, in common with the Hindu, pagans would typically claim that all gods are the one god, and that all the forms of the goddess are the one goddess. Second, it is an open question as to whether these forms of deity are 'out there', or whether they are to be understood mythologically as ways of understanding the self, the God within. As Vivianne Crowley writes:

> The Gods are considered to be expressions of the divine within humanity. The Gods are also considered to be divine forces operating in the universe. Whether they are seen as aspects of an impersonal life force or as cosmic beings with an individuality will depend on our own inner experiences and each individual will interpret this differently. (Crowley, 1989, p. 154)

Whatever one's understanding of God, truth is to be understood psychologically as well as metaphysically. Divinity is not to be understood as something that exists apart from the human self, a remote god who demands constant adulation and sacrifice from followers, and who has to be mediated through a special class of people known as the priesthood. In Wicca there is no distinction between priest and people – only degrees of initiation. In a wiccan ceremony there is no congregation who act as onlookers while priests and chosen office-bearers act out the divine drama of the worship; one cannot participate in a wiccan rite as a spectator, since such rites exclusively involve those who have received at least the first degree of initiation.

The rites of each coven are defined in a 'Book of Shadows' which is kept by the high priest or priestess. This book is passed on from one generation of witches to another: it is not published or duplicated, but is copied by hand. Unlike those religious traditions who attach supreme importance to the preservation of the sacred text as it gets transmitted, wiccans allow their Book of Shadows to undergo modifications through time, and regard it as perfectly acceptable that new rites are defined for new needs, and that additional material is added. Thus Vivianne Crowley does not perceive it as a problem that her own understanding of Wicca should incorporate eastern concepts such as the chakras, the forces of yin and yang, and the occasional reference to Ramakrishna.

Despite variations, there are important common elements in wiccan rites. Observation of the seasons is paramount, and in the vast majority of covens the solstices, equinoxes and 'quarter days' are celebrated. This gives eight principal festivals at equal intervals throughout the solar year: Beltane (1 May), Lammas (Lughnassadh) (1 August), Samhain – Hallowe'en, the Celtic Saturnalia (31 October), Imbolc (1 February), with the two solstices and equinoxes (Ostrata – 21 March; Litha – 22 June; Modron – 21 September; Yule – 21 December). This festival calendar reflects the solar year. Additionally, the lunar cycle is marked by observance of 'sabbaths' (esbats) at each full moon day (the so-called 'witches' sabbaths').

Rites typically commence with by casting or drawing of a circle in the space awaiting opening. This is usually out in the open, although sometimes an indoor temple is used. The priest or priestess greets the four cardinal directions, and the coven invokes the assistance of the gods or goddesses. This is followed by singing and dancing. The ceremony concludes with 'feasting' – traditionally 'cakes and ale', although bread and wine are often used. Finally the opened space is 'cleared', indicating that the rite is now complete and that the space is now returned to its secular purposes. Rites of passage are celebrated within the context of the coven, the best known of these being 'hand-fasting', the ceremony by which a couple bond themselves in marriage. Witches may also engage in their own personal rites, involving meditation, prayer, divination, the casting of spells or healings.

There are three degrees of initiation. In the first one is accepted as a member of the coven. After one has belonged to the coven for a year and a day, one is eligible for second-degree initiation, in which the initiate becomes an 'accomplished witch'. In the Gardnerian tradition only second- and third-degree witches attend, while in the Alexandrian tradition all members of the coven take part. The third-degree initiation is often called the 'Great Rite', enabling the initiate to gain entry into priesthood. The rite is noteworthy for the ritual sex that is employed. Different covens have different practices: the rite may be carried out either 'in token' or 'in true' – in other words, either symbolically or in reality. Vivianne Crowley reports that in some covens, including her own, the practice is for the initiating priest(ess) to perform the rite 'in token' with the acolyte, who then performs it 'in true' with his or her partner.

Witchcraft and Satanism

Some remarks are needed regarding the relationship between Wicca and Satanism. In so far as wiccans claim to revive a pre-Christian tradition, they do not embrace a theology which has any reference to Satan at all. Satanism, by contrast, is dependent on Christianity, accepting its traditional belief in a Devil who rebelled against God, and continues to engage in combat with him. Satanic rites could not exist without corresponding rites to draw on: there could be no Black Masses if there did not already exist the Christian sacrament of the Mass or eucharist. Witchcraft, Wicca and Paganism do not draw on Christianity for their rites, and any apparent similarities between pagan and satanic symbols (such as the pentagram or the horned god) should not be taken to imply that the two forms of religion are inter-related. Although the wiccan rejection of Christianity and its God may be perceived as 'satanic' by their critics, who may believe that they are unwittingly doing the work of the Devil, a religion which evokes such value judgements on the part of evangelical Christians is not to be conflated with deliberate and explicit worship of Satan, which is the hallmark of the Satanist. While there undoubtedly exist Satanist groups, who largely base themselves on *The Satanic Bible* by Anton La Vey (1930–97), they are few in number, and, according to Harvey, have a total membership of no more than about 100 in Britain (Harvey, 1995, p. 284).

10. The counter-cult movement

It is generally believed that new religions 'demand a response'. In most discussions of new religions it is not long before words like 'problem', 'challenge' and 'threat' appear. Notwithstanding the west's ideals of a free society where freedom of speech is permitted, new religious movements have tested liberal democracy's limits of tolerance. It is widely believed that the activities of NRMs need to be curtailed, if not by legislation, at least by warnings, forceful counter-argument, and in some cases litigation and even direct action.

In the earlier parts of the twentieth century, until the early 1970s, there was no real organized opposition to NRMs. In Britain the Society for the Propagation of Christian Knowledge and the Church Book Room Press both published series of booklets, addressing the older NRMs. The standard textbook was Horton Davies's *Christian Deviations* (1954/1965), a rather slender volume, not altogether accurate, but certainly more restrained than some of the later critiques of the post-1970s wave of NRMs.

The early 1970s saw quite a change in the NRM scene. The number of NRMs dramatically increased, and the impact of eastern thought began to make itself felt. With the exception of Theosophy, the old wave of new religions tended to be New Christian in character, offering their distinctive interpretations of the Bible. Improved global communication and the wider dissemination of eastern writings ensured that ideas from religions other than Christianity now became widely available to the general public. The Beatles' entanglements with the Maharishi and ISKCON tended to give such interests a seal of respectability. The demise of the hippie counter-culture caused ex-hippies to look for some alternative form of spirituality to fill the gap that hippiedom had left.

The new NRMs' evangelization tactics were more aggressive. The older NRMs had confined themselves to leafleting, by staffing Christian Science reading rooms, or – in its 'pushiest' forms – by door-to-door evangelism, which remains the practice of the Latter-day Saints and the Jehovah's Witnesses. One effect of door-to-door work was that it targeted the adult members of families; by contrast, the practices of certain newer religions in approaching people in streets, at bus stations, at airports and on university campuses ensured a wider target population which included young adults. The young were now perceived to be at risk.

Targeting the young was linked to community living, the typical lifestyle of the Unification Church, ISKCON and the (then) Children of God. Community living is hardly a live option for an older generation, who are on a career ladder, have bought homes and established families; but it is a possibility for a younger generation, with no such commitments. A community sometimes imposed special dietary regulations, such as ISKCON's strict vegetarianism. The decision to live in a community sometimes had the effect of disrupting education and career intentions, although not quite as much as NRMs' critics suppose: many Unificationists, for example, completed their degrees in the 1970s and some were actively encouraged to undertake postgraduate study while remaining full-time members. In some cases such as ISKCON and (then) Rajneesh, community living was combined with distinctive attire which caused followers to stand out in the society outside their commune. Compared with the new wave of NRMs, the older ones were quite conventional, only demanding minor adjustments to one's lifestyle, such as giving up alcohol.

Religious communities need finance. In some cases, joining a new NRM could mean handing over one's entire possessions; the Children of God did this, not only for practical reasons, but as a means of emulating the practice of the early Church which the Book of Acts describes (Acts 4:32–6). Some of the newer NRMs took to collecting monies from the general public, either by seeking donations or by selling goods such as flowers and candles (in the case of the UC) or religious books (ISKCON's practice). Such collections were not always legal, and in a number of instances the religious group did not adequately identify itself: the Unification Church, for example, claimed in the 1970s to be an ecumenical group supporting all forms of Christianity, rather than using any of their own names. The public could thus be lured into inadvertently financing religious groups that they would probably have been unwilling to support if they had known their true identity.

In short, the new wave of NRMs posed a much more serious threat to the dominant culture than the older 'Christian deviations'.

The post-1960s scene and NRMs

British society too changed during the post-war years: secularization, immigration and increased global communication altered the religious face of Britain. The progressive decline in church attendance, which started during the early 1960s, entailed a progressive lack of interest in theological critiques of new religions. In earlier years when it could be said that Britain was a 'Christian country', it was not uncommon for the Sunday preacher to denounce the errors of the Jehovah's Witnesses, or for Witnesses on door-to-door ministry to engage householders in discussion about the Trinity. Today relatively few citizens are in a position to sustain any such debate, and the Witnesses themselves have changed their publicity material accordingly: while they continue to publish material on the Trinitarian debate, their introductory literature focuses more generally on one's need for God, and addresses secularism and materialism rather than mainstream Christian doctrine.

The changing nature of new religions affected public attitudes too. Community living entailed living away from home, and hence new religions were accused of splitting up families. This phenomenon was no doubt little different from the way family members parted company as a result of embarking on university education or by taking up a post abroad within a multinational company, but the unconventional nature of the NRMs understandably instilled apprehensiveness on the part of a convert's parents and friends.

The 1960s witnessed the atrocities committed by Charles Manson. Although it is questionable whether his 'family' should be classified as a religious group, the Manson murders, in some people's minds at least, illustrated the sinister lengths to which 'cultic' activity might go. Their worst fears were confirmed when the Jonestown tragedy occurred in 1978, just as the anti-cult movement was beginning to gain momentum. The Jonestown massacre provided the vindication of the anti-cultists' gloomy prophecies: they were now able to claim that 'cults' were not merely bizarre or disruptive to family life and conventional living, but were positively dangerous, putting people's lives at grave risk. From Jonestown onwards almost any piece of counter-cult publicity made reference to Jim Jones and the Peoples Temple, and the pronouncements of other religious groups came under close scrutiny by anti-cultists who claimed to find evidence that other movements might require similar self-sacrifices on the part of their members. One notable example was the rumour, spread by anti-cultists, that Unification Church members had a suicide pact, since they were required to affirm regularly in their Pledge ceremony, 'I will fight with my life.'

Despite secularization taking its toll, evangelical publishing continued. Following Horton Davies's lead, the 1960s saw the appearance of Antony Hoekema's *The Four Major Cults* (1963) – the four being Christian Science, Jehovah's Witnesses, Mormonism and Seventh-day Adventism – and Walter Martin's *The Kingdom of the Cults* (1965/1985), all written from a mainstream Christian perspective. Other examples of counter-cult literature were NRM-specific works, such as Walter Martin's *The Maze of Mormonism* (1978). This particular genre of publishing is by no means dead, and continues in the work of Don McDowell and Josh Stuart (1986), Edmond C. Gruss (1974/1994) and Bob Larson (1989), amongst others. Alongside this genre of religious literature grew secular anti-cultist writing, such as that of Steven Hassan (1990) and of Joan Ross and Michael Langone (1988), who took up general themes relating to NRMs, such as 'brainwashing' and family problems. This literature was supplemented by a spate of ex-member material, often a 'great escape' story of how the author had successfully fled or been 'rescued' from an NRM – usually the Unification Church (Heftmann (1982), Williams (1987), Swatland and Swatland (1982)).

However, mere words were deemed to be insufficient. 'Something had to be done' to 'rescue' friends and family, and accordingly the 1970s saw the rise of a number of organized anti-cult groups. In a chapter in Bryan Wilson's *New Religious Movements: Challenge and Response* (1999), I have distinguished four categories of counter-cult group: (1) secular counter-cult organizations; (2) Christian evangelical counter-cult groups; (3) NRM-specific groups; and (4) organizations that offer the services of deprogrammers. Examples of secular groups include the American Family Foundation in the USA, and FAIR (Family Action Information and Resource) and the Cult

Information Centre in Britain. Of the best-known Christian evangelical groups there exist the Spiritual Counterfeits Project in California, the Dialog Center in Denmark, and the Deo Gloria Trust and the Reachout Trust in Britain. NRM-specific groups have tended to be fairly short-lived, giving way to the larger organizations of the first two varieties. Past examples have included Counter Scientology Europe, CONCERN (primarily for parents and ex-members of the Children of God), and EMERGE (for ex-Unificationists). The fourth group – the deprogrammers – are not content to offer counselling and produce counter-cult literature to stem the flow of NRM membership, but offer their services to abduct members by the use of force – usually for payment – offering to 'restore' them 'to normality'. This type of group was originally spearheaded in the USA by Ted Patrick, who describes his exploits in some detail in an autobiographical work entitled *Let Our Children Go!* (Patrick, 1976). In Britain, deprogrammer Martin Faiers, a former Unificationist leader, has for several years organized COMA (Council on Mind Abuse). (The British organization COMA should be distinguished from an American organization of the same time, which is unconnected to COMA UK.)

The various counter-cult organizations frequently co-operate with each other, and often intertwine in quite a complex way. Thus Johannes Aagaard, who runs the predominantly Christian Dialog Center in Denmark, also serves on the American Family Foundation's Board of Directors. Kenneth Frampton, who founded the Deo Gloria Trust – a Christian evangelical organization – apparently gave Ian Haworth financial support to establish the (non-religious) Cult Information Centre in Britain in 1987. Groups that have focused on specific NRMs have sometimes widened their frame of reference with the passage of time: for example, FAIR initially targeted the Unification Church, and Ted Patrick's original concern was with the (former) Children of God. From time to time organizations that have been officially opposed to deprogramming have found that they have had deprogrammers in their number, often to their embarrassment.

Deprogramming

The first substantial attempt to put together a 'rescue' organization was by Ted Patrick (b. 1930), who founded FreeCOG – later to become the Citizens' Freedom Foundation – in 1971. Patrick is often referred to as the 'father of deprogramming', being the first to offer the service of abducting members from NRMs and 'rehabilitating' them. Patrick is a black fundamentalist Christian, who left high school at age 15 and worked his way through a variety of jobs, eventually becoming a community relations officer in San Diego. In this role Patrick came across various complaints about the Children of God, which had been evangelizing in the town. Since CoG was not well known at that time, Patrick decided to infiltrate the group, masquerading as a convert.

Patrick's Citizen's Freedom Foundation gave way to the Cult Awareness Network in 1974. Officially CAN denied association with deprogramming, although its board of directors has included names who have been actively involved in deprogramming activities, as well as those who advocated the practice. Patrick himself was one of the co-founders, and his methods have been used, amongst others, by Steven Hassan (an ex-Unificationist turned deprogrammer) and Rick Ross, who has on several occasions been convicted.

Having undertaken the abduction, deprogrammers typically maintain a constant presence with the victim, who is often subjected to sleep and food deprivation, and who remains under the physical restraint of the captors. Some deprogrammers take a delight in mutilating the symbols of the victim's faith: Patrick tells of how he cut off an ISKCON devotee's sikha (top-knot), and in another passage his co-author Dulack boasts of his treatment of the Rev. Moon's image:

> He talks quietly, slowly, almost inaudibly. As he talks, he works with a felt-tip pen on a photograph of Sun Myung Moon that he has taken from his briefcase. He draws a pair of horns on Moon's head, then a moustache, pointed ears, making a caricature of the Devil out of the image the boy has been conditioned to love and revere. (Patrick, 1976, p. 24)

Deprogrammers' techniques are not subtle, but then they are not experts in Religious Studies, and in any case tend to regard the teachings of the new religions as gobbledegook. Their reasoning is that, since the teachings of most NRMs are obviously absurd, the only way seekers can be induced to join is by means of 'brainwashing'. Deprived by the 'cult' of their powers of reasoning, conventional reason cannot serve as an antidote. The only remaining way to bring 'recruits' back to normality is by physical coercion and attempting to undo the brainwashing process. The 'brainwashing' theory receives

347

little credence in academic circles, and hence the counter-cultists tend to rely on the evidence of a small minority of psychiatrists who support mind control theories, the most widely publicized of whom are Louis Jolyon West, Margaret Thaler Singer and Robert J. Lifton.

Deprogramming is of course illegal, and several deprogrammers, including Patrick, have been charged and convicted with these crimes. Where it is unsuccessful, it can be extremely damaging to family relationships: when an NRM member realizes that his or her parents have commissioned a forcible abduction, any remaining trust is lost, and the movement inevitably becomes more reluctant to allow contact with one's family, since contact may well pose a threat to one's remaining within the movement.

The deprogrammers' degree of success has been much debated. As Barker (1989) points out, the illegal nature of the activity makes it difficult to collect reliable statistics, although David Bromley and James Richardson (1983), in a study of 397 cases amongst Unification Church members, concluded that 64 per cent of deprogramming was 'successful'. However, as both Barker and Bromley agree, the apparent successes in deprogramming may be exaggerated, since there are reasons to suppose that a significant number of deprogramming victims may have been ready to leave the NRM in any case. As both writers point out, those who have been in the Unification Church for less than two months are much easier prey than those who have been in the movement for over four years, thus indicating that there are degrees of commitment to NRMs and that, inevitably, the higher the commitment the less effective are the efforts of the deprogrammers.

For many years the Church of Scientology had targeted the Cult Awareness Network, publishing a considerable volume of material denouncing its policies. In June 1996 CAN was bankrupted, largely as a result of lawsuits brought against the organization by Scientologists. Ironically, the name and assets were purchased by the Church of Scientology, who now continue to run CAN in a radically different way!

American Family Foundation

Founded in 1979, the American Family Foundation is somewhat more moderate that the former Cult Awareness Network. Although the

Church of Scientology has described it somewhat unkindly as CAN's 'sister organization', AFF is not comprised of deprogrammers, but defines its identity as a 'secular, not-for-profit, tax-exempt research center and educational organization'. AFF defines its purpose as focusing on 'cultic' groups and other groups that are deemed to practise 'psychological manipulation' or 'high-control' tactics.

AFF's main focus is on 'education', targeting particularly clergy (mainly Christian and Jewish) and educators. Its International Cult Education Program aims to disseminate information about 'cults' and also to enable its members to organize 'cult-education programs'. A further aim is to generate public discussion about 'cults', achieved through its 'Project Alert'. AFF is responsible for the publication of a number of journals in the field of NRMs, notably the *Cult Observer*, the *Cultic Studies Journal* (a research publication), its own newsletter (*AFF News*) – also available on-line – and *AFF News Briefs*, which are e-mailed to subscribers. AFF hosts a very detailed web site, with an impressive range of over 100 hypertext links, not all of which are by any means connected to other counter-cult organizations; in some cases NRMs' own home pages are linked to AFF.

AFF boasts an annual 5000 enquiries, most of which are about NRMs, but some of which are about psychological manipulation more widely. It has a network of some 100 counsellors, who, it claims, are professionals in various fields: education, psychology, religion, journalism and law. AFF organizes or sponsors 'recovery workshops' from those who wish to exit from NRMs, and offers the ex-member access to lawyers, psychotherapists and other support groups that are able to offer assistance.

Britain's counter-cult movement

Britain's best-known counter-cult organization is FAIR – originally an acronym for 'Family Action Information and Rescue'. FAIR was founded in 1976 by Paul Rose, Member of Parliament for Manchester. Rose had received a number of complaints from parents of Unification Church members, and came to believe that organized action was needed. FAIR's activities mainly involve disseminating information through leaflets, information sheets, a quarterly newsletter and public meetings. FAIR not only seeks to raise public consciousness, but offers advice to parents and relatives, urging them to write to politicians and to demand explanations from NRM leaders. Its campaigning tactics no doubt account for the fact that FAIR has twice applied for charitable status and been turned down.

FAIR is run entirely by volunteers, relying on donations and frequently complaining of financial hardship. It is therefore in no position to afford to employ professional counsellors, although its officers refer enquirers to a network of people whom it judges to be in a position to give advice, such as clergy and ex-members. FAIR maintains links with two other cult-monitoring organizations: the Cults Information Centre and Catalyst. The former is a small but vociferous organization run by its 'General Secretary' Ian Haworth, while the latter is more distinctively Christian in orientation, organized by Graham Baldwin, once a part-time lay chaplain at a London university.

None of these organizations actively recommends deprogramming, although Haworth is reported to have said, 'We aren't pushing that specific route, and we're not saying you shouldn't do it' (*Daily Mercury* (Guelph, Ontario), 1 February 1987). Baldwin prefers to offer 'exit counselling', which appears to involve offering advice to those who are on the brink of leaving NRMs, encouraging them to make the break. Although FAIR has stated that it opposes deprogramming, a breakaway group arose in 1985, calling itself 'Cultists Anonymous', and recommending a tougher line against 'cults', including deprogramming. CA stated that its officers remained anonymous for fear of reprisals by 'the cults', but it soon became well known that one of its principal leaders was Lord Rodney, who had previously arranged for his daughter – an NRM member – to be deprogrammed. During CA's period of existence, Lord Rodney had accepted the role of Chair within FAIR, and in 1987 FAIR's treasurer Cyril Vosper took part in a deprogramming, for which he received a prison sentence. CA rejoined FAIR in 1991, the breach having apparently been healed.

These organizations all portray a negative image of 'the cult'. Apart from the more recent distinction between 'religious' and 'therapy' cults, the counter-cultists tend to view NRMs as essentially similar in character, displaying the 'marks of the cult' that their literature typically lists (see Chapter 1). The counter-cult movement tends to espouse the 'brainwashing' theory to account for conversions, and to claim that anyone is potentially vulnerable when faced with the overtures of a 'cult'. As I have argued, such suppositions run

THE COUNTER-CULT MOVEMENT

counter to the findings of academic researchers, and hence they either ignore or dismiss such research claiming that it is ivory-towerish and that, unlike themselves, academics do not come into contact with the 'cult victims'. The movement therefore tends to rely on the testimonies of distressed parents, ignoring the fact that many parents are either happy about or indifferent to their sons' and daughters' NRM membership, and that some of those parents are even sufficiently impressed to convert to the movements themselves. In order to maintain this negative image of NRMs, the counter-cultists not only rely substantially on ex-member testimony, but on a particular type of ex-member, namely those who are vociferously hostile to the movement they have quit. No doubt it is inevitable to some extent that members who experience gradual loss of interest in an NRM and simply leave quietly will not reappear in an anti-cult context. In sum, the counter-cult movement is largely made up of those who have been influenced by the human face of the NRM phenomenon. Apart from those members of the clergy who are part of the movement, few have qualifications in religious studies, sociology or counselling, as far as I am aware. Despite the lack of formal credentials, however, a small number of counter-cultists describe themselves as 'cult experts', offering their opinions to the media, and securing publicity when an NRM-related news story hits the headlines.

INFORM

Faced with a hostile counter-cult movement that in many cases feeds enquirers' fears rather than allays them, a number of clergy and academics believed that there was a need for disseminating cooler, more impartial information about NRMs to the public. In 1986 Eileen Barker took the initiative in founding INFORM (Information Network Focus on Religious Movements) and elicited the support of the Archbishop of Canterbury. The Home Office had received a number of parental complaints relating to NRMs, but had been unwilling to offer funds to existing counter-cult groups. The prospect of a somewhat more balanced organization persuaded the Home Office to offer six years' start-up funding, followed by an annual consultancy fee. INFORM, which is based at the London School of Economics and Political Science, collects information on NRMs, which it makes available to researchers as well as to those with practical problems. It does not itself offer counselling, but puts enquirers in touch with a national network of qualified experts who are available to respond to enquiries or offer help.

Another important organization is CESNUR (Centre for the Study of New Religions), directed by Massimo Introvigne at the University of Turin. CESNUR operates at a more global level than INFORM, and, as the name implies, it is more concerned with academic study than with counselling. Its various international conferences, however, not only bring academics together, but a wide variety of interest groups, including politicians and counter-cultists. A large Internet site offers a wealth of information for the researcher.

Christian responses

Despite the concerns about brainwashing, lifestyle, splitting up families and finance – the key concerns of the secular counter-cultists – questions of truth still remain. It is understandable therefore that the evangelical Christian critique of new religions is still prominent, manifesting itself in a continuing volume of Christian counter-cult publications, and in a number of organizations that are dedicated to promoting the Christian faith – usually in its evangelical Protestant variety – as a superior alternative to the doctrines of the NRMs.

Spiritual Counterfeits Project

One of the most prominent Christian counter-cult organization is the Spiritual Counterfeits Project, situated in Berkeley, California. SCP arose as a result of some members of the 1960s' counter-culture, having experimented with forms of eastern spirituality, deciding to throw in their lot with evangelical Christianity. Having already experienced belonging to eastern traditions, they regarded themselves as being in an excellent position to comment on the American counter-culture's spirituality and to win its adherents back to Christ.

SCP began its rise in 1973, when it distributed tracts to the Guru Maharaji's followers at their 'Millennium '73' event at the Houston Astrodome. This heralded a ministry to combat the 'cults', the occult and – in due course – the New Age. In 1975 SCP travelled through numerous parts of the USA in its own special bus, speaking out against the snares of the new faiths that had alighted on the country. It was the SCP that was responsible for instigating legal proceedings against Transcendental Meditation, causing its subsequent ban in state schools.

SCP claims to be one of the earliest organizations to warn of the dangers of the New Age. The rise of channelling was the first indicator of a revived interest in occult phenomena, and SCP went on to deplore the way in which New Age activities percolated through into business organizations, schools, family life and even the Church.

Europe: Dialog Center

Particularly prominent amongst the counter-cult organizations in Europe is the Dialog Center in Denmark. Headed by Johannes Aagaard, it was founded in 1973 in response to the rise of NRMs, initially in Denmark, but also throughout the world. Aagaard has somewhat more regard for academics than many counter-cultists, and this is signalled by his preference for the term 'new religious movements' rather than 'cults'.

The term 'dialogue' is perhaps somewhat of a misnomer, suggesting that one of the prime functions of the Dialog Center is to organize meetings between mainstream Christians and NRM members, along the lines of the present-day inter-faith movement, in which there is non-judgemental discussion in an atmosphere of friendship and trust. On the contrary, the Dialog Center's policy firmly states, 'In relation to the neo-religiosity, our intention is to realize a dialog in confrontation.'

The 'dialogue' which the Dialog Center does recommend is between NRM members and their families. In spite of its insistence on the truth of mainstream Christianity, Aagaard and his sympathizers suggest more of a low-key approach between families and members, recommending them to discuss what aspects of the new religion appealed to them, and maintaining a friendly rapport throughout their period of membership, and an open door for them if and when they decide to return. The Dialog Center has stated firmly its opposition to deprogramming, believing that it is counter-productive, relatively ineffective, and damaging to good relationships between family and NRM member.

From an evangelical Christian perspective of course, it is not merely NRMs that are in error, but all the other major world religions. The Dialog Center's focus is therefore not exclusively confined to NRMs: one of its principal wings, the Dialog Center International, operates in 20 countries, and has particularly focused on Bombay, Delhi and Bangkok, where it engages in its apologetic to Hindus and Buddhists. A project called 'A Buddhist Christian Dialog' addresses Buddhism, albeit in an apologetic rather than dialogical way.

Britain: Deo Gloria Outreach and Reachout Trust

Meanwhile, back in Britain, the main Christian counter-cult groups are Deo Gloria Outreach and the Reachout Trust. Deo Gloria was founded (as previously mentioned) by Kenneth Frampton, whose two sons joined the (then) Children of God. Although Deo Gloria is still in existence at the time of writing, its activities are confined to a rather limited production of literature, and it no longer assumes a role either in active campaigning or in the organization of counter-cult training. Such activities are undertaken by the somewhat more active Reachout Trust, which organizes training seminars and produces educational materials.

Reachout took its rise in 1981, when its founder, Doug Harris lived opposite the rugby stadium in Twickenham, near London, where the Jehovah's Witnesses held their annual Convention. As an evangelical Christian, Harris felt that he could not allow such a large number of people to go unchallenged, when he believed them to be in such serious error. With a few fellow Christians of similar ilk, he stood outside the stadium attempting to distribute leaflets to the attendees. One imagines that these pickets were not highly successful, since Jehovah's Witnesses are strongly encouraged to avoid reading material that is hostile to the organization, and I know of no reports of any would-be attendee who turned back as a consequence of Reachout's activities. Whatever the results, the pickets could at least reassure themselves that they were 'witnessing for Christ' and offering the Jehovah's Witnesses the opportunity of sharing the gospel, in the way in which Harris and his supporters understood it. If this evangelical Christian witness did not initiate a decline in attendance at JW Conventions, this band of Christian evangelicals grew, and the literature distribution programme grew into demonstration marches through the town, and the setting up of Reachout as a formal organization.

Reachout contains a number of ex-members of NRMs, principally from the Jehovah's Witnesses and the Mormons. It is more probable that they have left as a result of personal disillusionment with these organizations, rather than through Reachout's activities. At any rate, these ex-members serve as a resource for Reachout, often leading seminars and pointing out to their (usually mainstream Christian) audiences the presumed errors of these movements, and how they believe mainstream Christians might respond to JW and Mormon missionaries who come to one's door.

Since Reachout's main objective is to win the 'cult member' for Christ, it accepts the same conclusion as the Dialog Center: it is not only those who belong to the 'counterfeit Christian' cults that need Christ's redeeming work. The logical conclusion, which Reachout accepts, is that all those who do not accept evangelical Christianity are in need of redemption, and, although Reachout's principal ministry is to JWs and Mormons, its publications offer critiques, not only of other 'counterfeit Christian groups' or of 'cults' but of mainstream religions such as Buddhism, Hinduism and Islam.

Official responses

All these organizations originate from individuals or groups of Christians who share a concern about the spread of NRMs, and who are not acting on behalf of any mainstream Christian denomination. Mention must therefore made of more official Christian bodies' response to the NRM phenomenon.

Since the rise of the new wave of NRMs roughly coincided with the arrival of Hindus, Muslims and Sikhs in Britain and the accompanying rise of the inter-faith movement, some of the mainstream churches raised the question of whether the newly devised principles of inter-religious dialogue could also be applied to NRMs as well as traditional world religions. While many Christians remained un-convinced, at least the World Council of Churches had championed the right of other religious groups to define themselves, and not to be subjected to prejudice, stereotyping or misinformation, adding explicitly that this applied 'whether those neighbours be of long established religious, cultural or ideological traditions or members of new religious groups' (British Council of Churches, 1981, p. 8).

Notwithstanding these guidelines, the Roman Catholic Church produced a rather negative official report in 1986, entitled 'Sects: The Pastoral Challenge'. Although short, it was abridged and is more publicly accessible under the title *New Religious Movements: A Challenge to the Church*, published by the Catholic Truth Society (1986). The Vatican Report was compiled by sending a questionnaire to episcopal conferences in 1984, and collating the bishops' replies. One bishop's response, quoted in the report, is plainly plagiarized from an article by Eileen Barker, and undetected! Although the report is often hailed as a landmark in defining the Roman Catholic Church's position, it really did no more than rehearse the usual stereotypes associated with NRM membership. Those who joined the 'sects' were described as 'footloose', 'vulnerable' and typically young; university campuses were identified as 'breeding grounds', and 'recruitment' was effected by indoctrination, 'love bombing' and 'flirty fishing'. The report firmly rejected dialogue, concluding that, 'It is necessary to inform the faithful, especially the young, to put them on their guard ...' (Saliba, 1995, p. 193).

Various other Christian bodies created forums for discussion on NRMs. The British Council of Churches held a consultation in London in 1986, attended by representatives from all the major denominations except Eastern Orthodoxy. Opinions were varied, and no firm policy emerged. In the same year the Lutheran World Federation and the World Council of Churches organized a consultation, this time at global level, and the report and papers ranged from the highly critical contributions of Reinhart Hummel and Johannes Aagaard to the much more conciliatory position of Kenneth Cracknell, who urged that, 'There are no limits to be set to dialogue' (Brockway and Rajashekar, 1986, p. 157).

The Church of Scotland had commissioned its Panel on Doctrine to look into the Unification Church's theology in 1978, and, predictably, received a negative evaluation, declaring the UC's teachings to be heretical. In 1982 the United Reformed Church in England published a small booklet entitled *Who Are They? New Religious Groups*, which was cautious, but endeavoured to avoid the usual stereotypes (Chryssides *et al.*, 1982). A small group from the URC's Mission and Other Faiths Committee agreed to a 'dialogue' meeting with the Unification Church in 1986. Although the meeting itself was cordial, the reaction of the URC's subsequent General Assembly, on receiving the report, was not: one delegate described the discussion as a 'blood bath'!

In 1989 the Church of England received a report from the Board for Mission and Unity on NRMs. This was somewhat more balanced than the Vatican Report, and drew extensively on advice given by INFORM. The report was cautionary, accusing some (unnamed) groups of secrecy and pointing out that eastern doctrines like reincarnation were incompatible with Christianity. The report concluded with a 'Draft Code of Practice' which the Board recommended to the NRMs. This enjoined them not to withhold their identity when canvassing, not to fund-raise under false pretences, and to abandon 'immoral means of persuasion such as "heavenly deception", "flirty fishing", sleep deprivation, food deprivation, hypnosis, or any form of emotional, psychological or spiritual "blackmail"' (Church of England, 1989, p. 10). One Unification Church leader remarked to me that, although he believed his church could comply with the code, to ask for compliance on such matters implied that they had been guilty.

In sum, while western Christian denominations have attempted to give a fair and balanced approach to NRMs, they have justifiably been critical, and at times hostile. It would also be true to add that lay members, who have not acquainted themselves with the NRM situation to the same degree as their leaders, are more prone to influence from media hostility and stereotyping.

Legal and political responses

For many critics, counter-cult organizations and Christian critiques are insufficient, and many who belong to the counter-cult movement wish to see legal and political action against the new religions. Recent years have seen numerous examples of litigation. Sun Myung Moon's conviction for tax evasion in 1983 is one of the most frequently cited examples, and the Unification Church's critics frequently use this example as evidence that the UC, as well as other NRMs, is guilty of financial irregularities and seeks to defraud. While there can be no doubt that the Rev. Moon was guilty of an offence under US taxation law, a number of mainstream Christian leaders were prepared to offer their support: some took part in a vigil outside the prison in Danbury, Connecticut and a number even volunteered to spend a night imprisoned with him. Whether or not Moon's conviction was discriminatory continues to be argued: Moon himself stated that if he had been white and American instead of yellow and Korean no action would have been taken. Apparently the UC's practice of placing church funds in an account in the leader's personal name was not uncommon amongst mainstream Christian clergy, who feared that they might also be prosecuted for similar financial irregularities.

A further legal battle involving the Unification Church occurred in 1981, when the British national tabloid newspaper, the *Daily Mail*, published an article bearing the headline, 'The church that splits up families'. The UC, having been the object of much public hatred and criticism by that time, decided that enough was enough, and that it would sue the newspaper for libel. The legal battle that ensued involved what was then the longest libel trial in British legal history, lasting six months in all. Not only did the Unification Church lose its case; apart from inevitable financial losses and the fact that the verdict confirmed the public's worst fears about the UC, the judge ordered that the charitable status of the UC should be investigated. In 1986 a summons from Britain's Attorney General arrived, itemizing a number of points on which the UC's charitable status might be rescinded. These included the charge that the UC was effectively a political organization, and that it was contrary to the public interest, being hostile to the Christian faith, deceitful, and requiring 'obedience to the uncontrolled authority of Sun Myung Moon'. Unificationists were jubilant in 1988, when the Attorney General announced that he had decided to drop the case, owing to 'insufficient evidence'. On this occasion, a number of mainstream Christian leaders, who had been following the case of the UC's charitable status with keen interest, made representation to the Attorney General to persuade him to drop the charges. There were two principal reasons: they believed that the charges against the UC were inherently unfair, and they also feared that a successful prosecution could establish a dangerous precedent. After all, mainstream Christianity often found itself actively involved in political activities, an example being the anti-apartheid movement in South Africa at that time.

Legal cases involving NRMs have involved both civil and criminal law. Following various child abuse scares in several countries, The

Family found itself the victim of a number of armed raids in Spain, Argentina, Australia and France, as a result of which a total of 326 children were taken into care. No evidence was found, and the children were returned to their community after several months. There is some evidence that individuals have been encouraged to sue NRMs after leaving, often for large sums of money. In 1986 one disgruntled ex-Scientologist decided to sue the Church of Scientology for no less than 39 million dollars, the reported ground being that it had failed to improve her eyesight. Although that particular attempt at litigation was unsuccessful, some counter-cult activities have either brought or encouraged similar law suits in the hope that an NRM might eventually become bankrupt.

The counter-cult movement did not remain content with the full force of existing law being brought to bear on NRMs. Pressure had to be exerted on politicians, they believed, so that NRMs' activities could be more strictly controlled. Equally, the NRMs themselves, perceiving the potential threats posed by political interference, attempted to influence politicians, presenting their case for religious freedom, gathering petitions and seeking to elicit the support of academics, members of the clergy and other sympathizers within the inter-faith movement.

From the politicians' point of view, 'cults' were hardly a major concern, compared with the main issues on which elections are fought, namely education, health and the state of the economy. On balance, however, more votes were to be gained by sympathizing with the counter-cult position, since the public at large were much more inclined to regard NRMs as bizarre and threatening. Overzealous government intervention could be problematic, however: state interference with religion is considered highly unacceptable in Britain and the USA. Non-discriminatory legislation on religion could easily rebound on mainstream religious traditions, and there was a risk that any political action aimed at NRMs could inadvertently affect mainstream immigrant religions and thus involve charges of racism. The 'cult problem' had certainly to be tackled with care.

One seemingly innocuous means of addressing the issue was for governments to commission reports. The first substantial attempt in this regard was the Cottrell Report to the European Parliament, presented in 1983 in draft form, and finally ratified in 1984. The report specifically mentioned the Unification Church, which continued to cause concern and had already been discussed within the Parliament. The report was originally entitled 'Motion for a resolution on the influence of the new religious movements within the European Community', but the expression 'new religious movements' was dropped in favour of 'new organizations operating under the protection afforded to religious bodies'. The counter-cult movement inherently disliked the former term, and in any case argued that certain groups were effectively business companies or political organizations masquerading as religions.

The Cottrell Report paid verbal homage to European Convention for the Protection of Human Rights and Fundamental Freedoms, and emphasized that 'full freedom of religion' was a fundamental principle within the European Community. What followed, however, was a 'code of practice' to which new religions were expected to agree. Cottrell emphasized that this code was a 'voluntary' one, but none of the most prominent NRMs was consulted about its content, and felt singularly unable to endorse it. Amongst the recommendations, it was proposed that those who intended joining an NRM should have 'an adequate period of reflection on the financial or personal commitment involved', that contacts with one's family must be maintained, that NRMs should make their principles 'immediately clear' and that they should be 'required by law' to provide the relevant authorities with addresses of members and details concerning their whereabouts.

The motion was passed by a substantial majority, with European counter-cultists applauding the decision. However, mainstream religious bodies such as the British Council of Churches were not nearly so enthusiastic, viewing the report as discriminatory. After all, mainstream churches would not normally agree to release information about members' whereabouts, and evangelists such as Billy Graham, whose preaching was lauded by mainstream evangelical Christians, emphasized the urgency of accepting the gospel: periods of reflection could result in one's decision being left too late, since Christ might return at any point in the meantime.

The Cottrell Report had little substantial effect on NRMs, except to give them additional evidence to support their claims to be victims of discrimination. The European Parliament's decision had advisory status only, and did not result in immediate legislation within any member state. The French government went as far as to commission its own report which appeared the following year: the Vivien Report on Sects. (Apart from Britain where the term 'cult' is popularly used, the word 'sect' is favoured in Europe.) The report recommended the appointment of a 'top official' who would monitor the NRM situation, informing the public and ensuring mediation for families who had become estranged through NRMs.

More serious restrictions on NRMs came in the 1990s, however, within the EU, Eastern Europe and the former Soviet Union. There were various reasons for this. The multiple suicide – or murder – in the Order of the Solar Temple in 1994 was the first instance of anything of the kind happening in Europe: hitherto mass deaths were related to religious communities on the other side of the Atlantic.

The 1990s also witnessed the demise of communism in Eastern Europe and the opening up of the former Soviet Union, with its new policies of glasnost and perestroika. Russia passed a law on the freedom of conscience and religion in 1990. To the new religions this signalled great cause for encouragement: not only could they now, they thought, freely evangelize in these countries, but several of them were convinced that the 40 years of communist rule had created a spiritual hunger which they could now help to satisfy. For the Unification Church in particular the fall of communism was vindication of its teaching that the victory of democracy over communism was part of the victory of God over Satan.

Unfortunately for the NRMs, several factors militated against this optimism. Eastern Europe and Russia had little experience of religious pluralism, the principal religious groups being the Orthodox Church in the former Soviet Union, and Roman Catholicism and forms of Protestantism dominating Eastern Europe. After 40 years of communist repression, when the religious communities in Eastern Europe and the former USSR talked of religious freedom they largely meant the freedom to practise religion which they had enjoyed before the communists came to power. Religious freedom meant rolling back the clock rather than acclaiming a new pluralism, which embraced the new religions.

The NRMs' progress in the former USSR was adversely affected in the 1990s by two other factors. One was Aum Shinrikyo, whose members were accused of the Tokyo underground poison gas murders in 1995: a substantial proportion of the group's members resided in Russia and the Ukraine. The White Brotherhood had also been the cause of controversy, culminating in Brotherhood members invading Kiev Cathedral in 1995.

The 1990s saw further reports and enquiries regarding NRMs in various countries. The French National Assembly commissioned an investigative report which appeared in 1995; a report from the Parliamentary Commission in Belgium was completed in 1997; in Germany the Enquete Commission was set up in 1996, and completed its report in 1998; Switzerland's Canton of Geneva set up a Sect Commission; and in Austria a Parliamentary Inquiry was held in 1998, although this was only a one-day event. At a federal level, the Council of Europe set up an investigation into 'sects', headed by Mr Nastase, former communist ministry of religious affairs director in Romania. In 1996 the European Parliament considered a new report compiled by rapporteur Mrs Berger of Romania; this report, which called for public education and for availability of information about NRMs and their members, was rejected, and is unlikely to be reconsidered in the life span of the present parliament.

These various reports tended principally to target the Unification Church, ISKCON, the Church of Scientology and The Family, although both the French and Belgium governments clearly believed that the sheer number of NRMs was a threat: France listed 172 'dangerous cults', and Belgium 187. There was, however, some confusion regarding what an NRM, a 'cult' or 'sect' actually is. Belgium included Opus Dei and The Work (both Roman Catholic groups), the Assemblies of God (one of the main branches of Pentecostalism), some mainstream Buddhist groups and the Hasidim.

The main concerns about groups were these. NRMs were said to exploit people financially, to 'launder' money and to avoid taxes. They were harmful to the health of members, sometimes offering alternative pseudo-medical therapies in place of proper medical treatment. Jehovah's Witnesses received particular mention by France's Parliamentary Commission on account of their refusal to accept blood transfusions. NRMs were accused of aggressive proselytizing methods: the 'brainwashing' theory has continued to influence politicians, although it must be said that the German Enquete Commission concluded that it did not exist. NRMs were viewed as disruptive of family life, and often caused social isolation, for instance when they insisted on providing their own education for children. Members were said to be exploited by poor working conditions and by underpayment, which arguably infringed their employment rights. Where members did not work full-time for the 'sect', they 'infiltrated' state institutions and business organizations. (It is not clear what such criticism amounts to: presumably an NRM member who has a government job or who is employed in a firm is considered to be 'infiltrating'.) NRMs were even accused of illegal activities spanning drug trafficking, child abuse, rape, illegal practice of medicine, tax evasion and incitement to suicide. Ironically, NRMs were also accused of harassing their critics.

It would be foolish to deny that any of these crimes had ever been committed within NRMs. However, members generally felt that such lists of crimes involved them in guilt by association, and implied that these practices were rife. As one informant from The Family pointed out, mainstream Christianity is not without its own child molesters, as has been witnessed by recent scandals that have come to light about Roman Catholic priests who have been entrusted with the education of young boys.

The various political debates resulted in a number of measures. A common conclusion, adopted by Britain, France, Belgium and Switzerland among other European countries, is that there should be greater public awareness about the nature of NRMs. The United Kingdom Passport Agency now issues advice to those receiving new passports, warning travellers of the risk of being caught up in a 'cult' and suggesting courses of action if one wishes to 'escape', and a number of German states have produced pamphlets that warn of the dangers posed by Scientology.

Another common response has been to require religions to register with the state. In most countries that adopt this policy, registration is subject to the religious organization having a certain minimum number of members or a tradition going back a specified number of years, or (more commonly) both. The required size can be as low as 100, as in Macedonia, or as high as 16,000 (Austria's requirement), and its required established length varies from 15 years (Russia's current proposal) to 100 years (the Polish requirement). Austria's requirements were particularly stringent: religious groups who were allowed to register would be subjected to a probationary period – 20 years in the case of totally new groups, and 10 years for groups who were reapplying – and, although its 300-member requirement for probationary status might seem generous, that number had to be composed of Austrian residents, and must exclude those who simultaneously belong to another registered group. This requirement therefore excluded foreign missionaries, and – for example – those who might become Scientologists but continue to remain members of another recognized religious community.

Such requirements militate against new religious movements, most of whom cannot claim a long tradition, and, at least in their early stages of existence, have not yet achieved the required membership target. Some countries have required more than membership thresholds and length of existence: in Greece and Austria there is a requirement of loyalty to the state. (Russia is currently considering a similar proposal.) This effectively excludes the Jehovah's Witnesses, who do not vote, and who have consistently refused to participate in military service or armed conflict, although under the membership and age criteria they would have qualified.

In the debate about registration, it is sometimes thought that failure to register is tantamount to a prohibition on practising one's faith, and indeed NRMs sometimes speak as if this were the case. This is not so; indeed it is particularly evident to the authorities in the former communist regimes that it is virtually impossible to stamp out the religious practices of the faithful. What they can do, however, is to encourage certain types of religious allegiance or render them more difficult. In the case of registration, some countries, such as Hungary, allocate a small proportion of their budget to religious organizations; successful registration therefore entitles a group to receive state benefit, which is denied to unregistered groups. The sum of money involved is not particularly large, and, since the state subsidy is allocated in proportion to a group's membership it is doubtful whether any NRMs, if successfully registered, would gain more than £1000 per year. (Some NRMs do not want state subsidy in any case, for example the Mormons and the Jehovah's Witnesses.) More serious is the situation that prevails in Greece, where it is necessary to be a 'known religion' in order to hold a public meeting, or to receive planning permission for building work.

Despite the fact that the Enquete Commission's conclusions appeared to suggest that there was not a great 'cult problem', the Church of Scientology claims to be experiencing a particularly difficult period in Germany. The civil service refuses to admit Scientologists, or indeed members of any other minority religious groups. The Bavarian government passed explicitly anti-Scientology legislation in 1996, requiring any state employee to swear under oath that he or she is not a Scientologist.

NRMs – where now?

At the time of writing there are many unresolved issues relating to NRMs. Faced with the threat of increased political intervention, many NRMs have been fighting back, championing their rights to religious freedom, and claiming that they are persecuted minorities. The fact that these threats to their future are communal has resulted in several alliances being formed amongst NRMs who, at their inception, simply pursued their own independent agendas. It is now abundantly clear that the spiritual life cannot be pursued in isolation from the outside world, and that coalitions for religious freedom can help serve these common interests. Academic conferences increasingly provide a forum for NRM leaders to meet each other, and to enlist whatever support they can find amongst the academic community. Even organizations such as the Jehovah's Witnesses, who formerly kept apart from others, are now increasingly coming out into the open and forging external links.

In the face of anti-cult criticism, a number of new religions have improved their practices, being less prone to concealing their identity or raising funds illegally. As members grow older, membership demands grow less stringent, and the last two decades have seen less emphasis on community living and more emphasis on combining spirituality with a conventional lifestyle. Doctrines have adapted, as a consequence of reflection, new spiritual experiences and at times the need to cope with unrealized expectations. Contrary to popular belief, I doubt if the advent of the new millennium will in itself make a significant difference to the vast majority of NRMs, only a very small handful of which have predicted a spectacular end to human affairs at such a precise date. Internal problems regarding leadership (in the case of the Unification Church) and dealing with schism (in the case of ISKCON) are more likely to form the more immediate agenda.

As time passes, new religions become old, with second- and third-generation memberships. With the passage of time, they become less threatening, and a more established part of society's religious scene. They may therefore incur less opposition, although from the evangelical Christians' perspective they will remain in error and still need to be presented with the gospel. And who can tell what further new wave of NRMs will come on the scene? One thing is for certain: given the volatility of the NRM phenomenon, no book can ever claim to have the final word.

Appendix 1

Statistical data

It is often said that NRMs are growing at an alarming rate. Some basic statistical information will give an impression of the numerical strength of the movements that have been covered in this book.

Statistics must be treated with caution. There is no uniform way in which religious groups declare their statistics: this can vary from counting membership, measuring attendance or people's self-definition of their allegiance. Some groups are membership organizations, whereas others simply have a loose following. Levels of commitment vary: at the lowest level, a 'member' may simply be someone born into a certain family or just be on a mailing list; at the highest level is the full-time worker. Some groups can change their definitions of belonging over time. Membership can also be affected by international migrations of members.

To complicate matters further, the statistics come from a variety of sources, and relate to different years. There is reason to believe too that not all extant statistical data have been collected reliably (as in the case of the Soka Gakkai below). I have selected the best available, providing a range where adjudication is impossible, but obviously it could be misleading to compare different groups on the basis of this information.

Baha'i
  Britain: 6000 (1997) (Weller, 1997)
  World: 6,000,000 (1999)[1]

Brahma Kumaris
  Britain: 1200 'regular students'[5]
  Outside India: 5715 (1992) (Whaling, 1995)
  World: over 450,000 (1999)[5]

Christian Science
   Britain: no figures available
   World: 400,000 (1998)[2]
      (active: 100,000 (1997))[1]

est
   Britain: 8000 (1987)[4]
   World: 1,000,000 (1996)[3]

The Family
   Britain: 290 (of whom 140 are full-time 'charter members') (1995)[5]
   World: 10,183 charter members and 2871 'fellow members' (1999)[5]

Findhorn
   World (mainly Britain): 250 (1985)[1]

ISKCON
   Britain: 200–300 families of initiates, including celibates;
      10,000 familes of life members; 60,000 attendees at Krishna's
      Birthday (1998)[5]
   World: 1,000,000 (1998)[2]
      8000 full-time (1998)[3]

Jehovah's Witnesses
   Britain: Memorial attendance: 214,351 (1998)[5]
   World: Memorial attendance: 13,896,312 (1998)[5]

Jesus Army
   Britain: 2600 (1999)[5]
   Outside Britain: virtually nil[6]

Latter-day Saints
   Britain: 180,000 (1998)[5]
   World: 10,000,000 (1998)[2]

New Kadampa Tradition
   Britain: 3000 (1999)[5]
   World: 5000 (1999)[5]

Osho
   Britain: 600–3000 (1999)[5]
   World: 200,000 (1998)[2]

Rastafarians
   Britain: 5000 (1987)[4]
   World: 700,000 (1998)[1]

Sai Baba
  Britain: 4000 active devotees linked to a Sai Centre (1999)[5]
  World 10,000,000[3]

Scientology
  Britain: 300,000 (1987)[4]
  World: estimates vary widely, from 1,000,000 to 8,000,000;
    Leaders in Los Angeles claim around 5,600,000 (1998)
  World full-time: 11,310 (1997)[5]
  World new participants: 642,596 (1997)[5]

Soka Gakkai
  Britain: 6800 'on paper', of whom 5000 are estimated to be active;
    5150 gohonzons have been issued (1999)[5]
  World: estimates vary widely:
  8,100,000 (1995)[3]
  12,000,000 (1996)[1]

Spiritualism
  Britain: 20,000 full members of the Spiritualist National Union
    (1999)[5]
  60,000 regular SNU members (1999)[5]
  World: 150,000 (1972)[1]

Subud
  Britain: 1794 (1989)[5]
  World: 12,000 (1999)[5]

Theosophy
  Britain: 1000 in Theosophical Society (1999) plus 200 in other
    Theosophical groups (Kevin Tingay's estimate)
  World: 34,000 (1998)[5]

Transcendental Meditation
  Britain: 150,000 (1999)[5]
  World: estimates vary from 50,000 (1993)[3] to 3,000,000 (1996)[1]

Unification Church (Family Federation)
  Britain: 1000 including Associate Members (1999)[5]
  600–700 committed members (1999)[5]
  World: estimates vary from 1,000,000 to[7] 3,000,000 (1999)[5]

Western Buddhist Order
  Britain: 1343 (459 ordained, plus 884 mitras) (1999)[5]

World: 459 ordained members and 884 mitras (1999)[5]

Witchcraft
    England: 30,000 (1987)[1]
    World: estimates vary from 50,000 to 800,000 (1996)[1]

Notes

1. From Preston D. Hunter's Adherents web site: http://www.adherents.com
2. From Ontario Consulants for Religious Tolerance web site: http://www.religioustolerance.org
3. From University of Virginia New Religious Movements new religious movements web site (1998): http://cti.itc.virginia.edu/~jkh8X/soc257/
4. From Clarke, 1987, p. 11.
5. Data from religious organization.
6. Author's estimate.

Appendix 2

Compendium

It has not been possible to give adequate coverage to all the most prominent NRMs that have a presence in the west. What follows are very brief summaries giving key information regarding organizations that are not discussed at length in the main text. Somewhat more detailed treatment of most can be found in Annett (1976) and Barrett (1996).

Aetherius Society

The Aetherius Society is a UFO-religion, founded in 1955 by Sir George King, an adept at kundalini yogi. King's psychic powers are believed to enable him to contact 'cosmic masters'. The movement teaches the possibility of spiritual evolution, whereby one can acquire a more subtle body, or else remain on earth to serve humankind as one of the Great White Brotherhood. It is also possible to experience rebirth in another planet. The eventual goal is merging with all life forms, including the celestial bodies.

Ananda Marga

Ananda Marga was founded in India in 1955 by Shri Prabhat Ranjan Sarkar (1921–90), also known as Sri Sri Ananda Murti or Baba Guru. It is a Saivite organization, with a celibate order and a lay membership who are encouraged to be moderate in sexual activity. Practices include meditation and yoga, and various social programmes.

Arcane School

Founded by Alice Bailey (1880-1949), the Arcane School taught an esoteric 'Ageless Wisdom', originally channelled to Bailey by Tibetan

Masters Koot Hoomi and Djwhal Khul. At one time a member of the Theosophical Society, Bailey taught a common essence of world faiths, and looked forward to the imminent coming of Maitreya, which she equated with the Second Coming of Christ, the next avatar of Krishna, the Jewish messiah and the Imam Mahdi. After leaving the Theosophical Society, she and her husband Foster Bailey founded the Lucis Trust (1922) and the Arcane School (1923), which continued until 1977. The Lucis Trust continues the work of the Arcane School, together with World Goodwill and Triangles.

Church Universal and Triumphant (Summit Lighthouse)
CUT was set up by Mark L. Prophet in 1958, who, together with his wife Elizabeth Clare Prophet, claims to have received divine messages from El Morya (a 'Messenger') and Ascended Master Saint-Germain. CUT regards itself as belonging to the Judaeo-Christian tradition, but holds that there are important teachings of Jesus that have become lost, particularly regarding some years in which he studied in India and Tibet. These are recounted in *The Lost Years of Jesus* and *The Lost Teachings of Jesus*. Apparently Jesus taught that there is a divine spark within everyone, the realization of which can free one from the cycle of reincarnation. CUT believes in a Great White Brotherhood, which offers guidance: the Prophets did not claim to be Ascended Masters, but merely Messengers. The central practice of CUT is invoking 'the violet flame' of the Holy Spirit.

Churches of Christ
The International Churches of Christ began their rise in Boston in 1979. They are evangelical and fundamentalist in theology, laying emphasis on commitment to 'discipleship', which is signified by adult baptism. The growth of the Church of Christ has been accomplished by a policy of church planting in other cities, initially in the USA and then worldwide. The first International Church of Christ in Britain was established in London in 1982, and drew on those members of the Churches of Christ (formerly a mainstream denomination) that declined to merge with the United Reformed Church. ICOC made itself controversial on account of its 'discipling' – subjecting members to spiritual oversight by a more senior member.

Eckankar

Hindu-Sikh in origin, the movement is led by a succession of 'Eck Masters', of which its founder Paul Twitchell (1909–71) is said to be the 971st. Twitchell claimed to have learned about Eckankar in 1949 from a spiritual encounter with Tibetan Master Rebazar Tarzs. After belonging to the Self-Revelation Church of Absolute Monism (a Hindu-related group) and the Church of Scientology, Twitchell established Eckankar in the USA in 1965. 'Eckankar' is defined as 'the ancient science of Soul Travel', which enables the soul to aspire to higher astral planes. After Twitchell's death, the lineage of Eck masters continued with Darwin Gross (until 1981) and currently Harold Klemp.

Elan Vital

Elan Vital is a continuation of the Divine Light Mission, founded by Shri Hans Ji Maharaj (d. 1966). On his death, his youngest son Prem Pal Singh Maharaj (b. 1957) assumed the leadership at age eight, becoming known as the 'boy guru'. In 1971 he visited London, and DLM gained in popularity; followers were known as 'premies' (lovers of God), and his teachings are known as 'The Knowledge'. Although born a Hindu, Maharaji no longer claims to be one, and has progressively adopted a western lifestyle, having married an American follower in 1974. The movement was reconstituted as Elan Vital in 1991. Many followers do not consider it to be a religion, and meetings generally consist of screening videos of Maharaji's talks.

Exegesis/Programmes Ltd

Exegesis began its rise in 1976 as Infinity Trainings. It bore similarities to *est,* offering 'enlightenment' and 'personal transformation' through a programme of seminars. It existed as a human potential organization until 1984, when it folded, largely because of opposition from the Home Office in Britain. It re-emerged as a telesales company under the name of Programmes Ltd.

Healthy, Happy, Holy (3HO)

Also known as Sikh Dharma, the organization was founded in the USA in 1971 by Siri Singh Sahib Harbhajan Khalsa (Yogi Bhajan). The organization emphasizes health, based on the practice of kundalini yoga. New members undergo the Sikh amrit ('baptism') ceremony and accept the five Ks, in common with Khalsa Sikhs.

There are currently 4000 active members, mainly in the USA and Canada. Community life in ashrams was once popular, but has declined since the early 1990s.

Mahikari

Founded in 1959 by Yoshikazu Okada, Mahikari now has worldwide branches. Yoshikazu is believed to be empowered to transmit God's light to others, especially for healing. Initially the use of this light was confined to a few holy people, but God has now granted its use to everyone, since humanity is at a time of crisis. A three-day seminar gives the follower authorization to use this light.

Meher Baba

Meher Baba (Merwan Sheriar Irani) (1894-1969) was born into a Parsee family in Poona. He claimed self-realization at age 18, and was given recognition by Shirdi Sai Baba. He taught universal love and devotion in Bombay in the early 1920s, but then became silent for the remainder of his life. His most famous book, *God Speaks*, was dictated in silence by means of an alphabet board and hand gestures. Claiming that God should be sought through action, he set up schools and hospitals. He is hailed as an avatar.

Messianic Jews

The Messianic Jews movement dates substantially from the 1960s, being influenced by 'Jews for Jesus'. Being a Messianic Jew enables one to combine one's presumed Jewish identity with a faith in Jesus. Messianic Jews use their own messianic synagogues, observing the traditional Jewish festivals. They do not celebrate Christmas and Easter. Politically, Messianic Jews tend to be Zionist. Attitudes to the Jewish Torah are somewhat ambivalent, but generally more liberal than Orthodox and Reform Jews. There are some 250,000 adherents worldwide.

Mother Meera

Mother Meera has been described as a 'female Sai Baba', and is regarded as an avatar and a Divine Mother. Born in 1960 in South India, she offers divine light and knowledge, but does not give teachings – only darshan, which is believed to bestow love and grace. Her aim 'is to help humans and to make them happy, peaceful, contented, harmonious and loving'. Her ashram is situated between Cologne and Frankfurt.

Oneness Pentecostalism

Oneness Pentecostalism began its rise from the Assemblies of God in 1914. It affirms the unity of God rather than the Trinity, finding no scriptural basis for the latter. In 1916 the Assemblies of God formulated a 'Statement of Fundamental Truths', which excluded a number of 'Oneness' movements. There have been numerous splits and mergers in Oneness Pentecostalism. At the time of writing the major groups include Pentecostal Assemblies of Jesus Christ, Pentecostalist Assemblies of the World, and United Pentecostal Church International. In all there are some 90 Oneness Pentecostalist denominations in 57 countries; its strongest allegiance is in the USA and Canada, as well as South Asia and Oceania.

Raël

Born as Claude Vorilhon in 1946, Raël's birth heralds the new Age of Aquarius. Raël supersedes Jesus and the Church, which belong to the Age of Pisces. Raëllianism is a UFO-religion, based on its founder-leader's claims to have encountered the Madech – extra-terrestrials who first appeared to him on 13 December 1973. In 1975 Raël is believed to have been taken to the Planet of Eternal Life and given further revelations regarding sustaining life on this planet. His writings include *My Encounters with Extra-Terrestrials,* which offers an interpretation of the Judaeo-Christian Bible in terms of visitations by beings from outer space. The organization plans to build an embassy to receive extra-terrestials, ideally in Israel, but elsewhere if permission is refused. Raëllians currently claim a mere 40 members and 200 'sympathizers' in Britain.

School of Economic Science

SES does not regard itself as a religion, but gained much negative publicity from the publication of *Secret Cult* by Peter Hounam and Andrew Hogg in 1984. Founded in 1937 by Andrew MacLaren, a Member of Parliament from 1922 to 1945, its leadership passed to Leon (Leonardo da Vinci) MacLaren (1910–94). Leon MacLaren was influenced by the Maharishi Mahesh Yogi and Sri Shantanand Saraswati, an exponent of *advaita vedanta.* SES runs classes in philosophy, by which is meant Vedic philosophy, with some

Christian and esoteric elements, together with the practice of meditation. SES was at its most popular during the 1960s and 1970s, and now has a following of some 4000 students. It is exclusively a British organization.

Sri Chinmoy
A Bengali, born in 1931, Sri Chinmoy was brought up in Aurobindo Ashram from age 12. His centre in New York, where he currently lives, was set up in the 1960s. While regarding himself as a Hindu and drawing substantially on Hindu scriptures, he teaches the love of God outside religion, strongly emphasizing meditation and world peace. In addition to his extensive writings, Sri Chinmoy has composed songs and holds peace concerts. He makes no claim to be an avatar, but has high-level links with world leaders, being official Spiritual Adviser to the United Nations. The movement is not large, claiming some 5000 followers worldwide in 1996.

Unity School of Christianity
An offshoot of the New Thought movement, founded by Charles and Myrtle Fillmore in 1889, the organization believes in the healing power of prayer. Claiming to 'transcend religious denominations', its teachings are non-dogmatic. Its founders claimed to have been healed from injuries received in childhood by practising 'affirmative prayer': 'I am a child of God, therefore I do not inherit sickness.' Their apparent success secured a following, and there are now groups worldwide, with a headquarters at Unity Village, Missouri, near Kansas City.

Word-Faith Movement
Drawing on the teachings of Charles Capps (1976), the Word-Faith Movement believes in positive affirmation, preaching 'prosperity theology'. Words can become vehicles for spiritual power, changing the physical and spiritual world, like God's creative word. Thus it is possible to create wealth through one's personal belief. The movement is influenced by New Thought, and more recently Kenneth Copeland's *The Laws of Prosperity*. John Avanzini's School of Biblical Economics is part of this movement.

Worldwide Church of God
Herbert W. Armstrong (1892–1986), WGC's founder, first gained

public attention as a radio preacher during the 1930s. He introduced *The World Tomorrow* until 1955. Today WCG is best known for its magazine, the *Plain Truth,* which comments on current affairs, viewing them as fulfilments of biblical prophecy. A fundamentalist movement, WCG gives equal emphasis to the Hebrew Scriptures, observing the sabbath, the traditional Jewish festivals, dietary laws and tithing. Having a small membership, it meets in homes rather than purpose-built premises. Its current leader is Joseph W. Tkach Jr.

Yogananda
Yogananda (1893–1952) was a Bengali who inaugurated the Self-Realization Fellowship. He lectured on kriya yoga in the USA and later in Europe, and his *Autobiography of a Yogi,* published in 1946, has been translated into 18 languages and is still widely read. Amongst his following, Mahatma Gandhi asked to be initiated into kriya yoga.

Bibliography

Where two dates are given in an entry, the first refers to the original date of publication, and the second to the edition used in this book.

Agehananda Bharati, Swami (1981) *Hindu Views and Ways and the Hindu-Muslim Interface: An Anthropological Assessment*. New Delhi: Munshiram Manoharlal.

Allan, John (1980) *TM: A Cosmic Confidence Trick*. Leicester: Inter-Varsity Press

Annett, Stephen (1976) *The Many Ways of Being*. London: Abacus.

Anon (1993) 'Cult Awareness Network and the Waco religious shoot-out'. *Unification News*, April, p. 23.

Appleton, Sue (n.d., *c.* 1991) *Was Bhagwan Shree Rajneesh Poisoned by Ronald Reagan's America?* Cologne: Rebel Publishing House.

Arrington, L.J. (1979) *The Mormon Experience: A History of the Latter-day Saints*. London: Allen and Unwin.

Atkins, Gaius Glenn (1923) *Modern Cults and Religious Movements*. Old Tappan, NJ: Fleming H. Revell.

Baha'i International Community (1992). *The Baha'is: A Profile of the Baha'i Faith and Its Worldwide Community*. New York: Baha'i International Community.

Bainbridge, W.S. (1997) *The Sociology of Religious Movements*. London: Routledge.

Bancroft, Anne (1976/1989) *Twentieth-Century Mystics and Sages*. London: Arkana.

Bancroft, Anne (1985) *New Religious World*. London: Macdonald.

Barker, Eileen (ed.) (1982) *New Religious Movements: A Perspective for Understanding Society*. New York: Edwin Mellen Press.

Barker, Eileen (1983) 'New religious movements in Britain: content and membership'. *Social Compass,* vol. 30, no. 1, pp. 33–48.

Barker, Eileen (1984) *The Making of a Moonie: Brainwashing or Choice?* Oxford: Blackwell.

Barker, Eileen (1986) 'Religious movements: cult and anti-cult since Jonestown'. *Annual Review of Sociology,* vol. 12, pp. 329–46.

Barker, Eileen (1986). 'Religious Movements: Cult and Anticult since Jonestown.' *Annual Review of Sociology*, No. 12, pp. 329–46.

Barker, Eileen (1989) *New Religious Movements: A Practical Introduction.* London: HMSO.

Barrett, David V. (1996) *Sects, 'Cults' and Alternative Religions: A World Survey and Sourcebook.* London: Cassell.

Barrett, Leonard E. (1974) *Soul-Force: African Heritage in Afro-American Religion.* New York: Anchor Press.

Barrow, P. (1991) *Mormons and the Bible: The Place of the Latter-day Saints in American Religion.* Oxford: Oxford University Press.

Bartley, W.W., III (1978) *Werner Erhard: The Transformation of a Man.* New York: Potter.

Batchelor, Stephen (1998) 'Letting daylight into magic: the life and times of Dorje Shugden'. *Tricycle: The Buddhist Review*, Spring, pp. 60–6.

Becker, Howard (1932) *Systematic Sociology on the Basis of the Beziehungslehre and Gebildelehre of Leopold von Wiese.* New York: Wiley.

Beckford, James (1985) *Cult Controversies: The Societal Response to New Religious Movements.* London and New York: Tavistock.

Beckford, James (ed.) (1986) *New Religious Movements and Rapid Social Change.* London: Sage.

Beier, L. (1981) *Mormons, Christian Scientists and Jehovah's Witnesses.* London: Ward Lock.

Beit-Hallahmi, Benjamin (1993) *The Illustrated Encyclopedia of Active New Religions, Sects and Cults.* New York: Rosen Publishing Group.

Bennett, J.G. (1958) *Concerning Subud.* London: Hodder and Stoughton.

Berry, Harold J. (1988) *New Age Movement.* Lincoln, NE: Back to the Bible.

'Bert' (n.d.) 'Flirty fishing – the inside story: one man's personal experience'. London: The Family.

Blewett, W.E. (n.d., *c.* 1985) 'The Human Potential Movement, *Est* and the life training'. Lewisville, TX: Church of the Annunciation. Unpublished MS for diocesan circulation.

Bloomfield, Harold H., Cain, Michael and Jaffe, Dennis (1985) *TM: Discovering Inner Energy and Overcoming Stress.* New York: Delacorte.

Boulton, Wallace (ed.) (1995) *The Impact of Toronto.* Crowborough: Monarch.

Bowen, D. (1988) *The Sathya Sai Baba Community in Bradford.* Leeds: University of Leeds Monographs.

Bowker, John (ed.) (1997) *The Oxford Dictionary of World Religions.* Oxford and New York: Oxford University Press.

Braden, Charles S. (1949) *These Also Believe: A Study of Modern American Cults and Minority Religious Movements.* New York: Macmillan.

Brahma Kumaris (1989/1994) *Inner Beauty: A Book of Virtues.* Pandav Bhawan, Mount Abu: Brahma Kumaris World Spiritual University.

Brahma Kumaris (1997) 'Brahma Kumaris World Spiritual Organization'. http://www.brahmakumariswso.com/ [as on 8 January].

Brahma Kumaris (n.d., a) *Brahma Baba – Who Started a Unique Spiritual Revolution*. Pandav Bhavan, Mount Abu, India: Prajapita Brahma Kumaris.

Brahma Kumaris (n.d., b) *Vision of a Better World*. Pandav Bhawan, Mount Abu: Brahma Kumaris World Spiritual University.

Breen, Michael (1997) *Sun Myung Moon: The Early Years 1920–53*. Hurstpierpoint, West Sussex: Refuge Books.

British Council of Churches (1981) *Relations with People of Other Faiths: Guidelines on Dialogue in Britain*. London: British Council of Churches.

Brockway, Allan R. and Rajashekar, J. Paul (eds) (1986). *New Religious Movements and the Churches*. Geneva: WCC Publications.

Bromley, David G. and Richardson, James T. (eds) (1983) *The Brainwashing/Deprogramming Controversy: Sociological, Psychological, Legal and Historical Perspectives*. New York and Toronto: Edwin Mellen Press.

Brooks, Charles R. (1992) *The Hare Krishnas in India*. Delhi: Motilal Banarsidass.

Bruce, S. (1995) *Religion in Modern Britain*. Oxford: Oxford University Press.

Buddhist Society (1991) *The Buddhist Directory: A Directory of Buddhist Groups and Centres and Other Related Organisations in the United Kingdom and Ireland*. 5th edition. London: The Buddhist Society.

Burrell, M. (1972) *Wide of the Truth: Mormons, What They Believe*. London: Morgan and Scott.

Burrell, M. (1983) *Learning about the Mormons*. London: Mowbray.

Burrell, M. and Stafford Wright, J. (1973) *Some Modern Faiths*. London: Varsity Press.

Bushman, Richard L. (1984) *Joseph Smith and the Beginnings of Mormonism*. Urbana and Chicago: University of Illinois Press.

Butterworth, J. (1981) *Cults and New Faiths*. Tring, Hertfordshire: Lion Publishing.

Button, John and Bloom, William (eds) (1992) *The Seeker's Guide: A New Age Resource Book*. London: Aquarian.

Campbell, Colin (1972) 'The cult, the cultic milieu and secularization'. In Hill (1972), pp. 119–36.

Campbell, Eileen and Brennan, J.H. (1990/1994) *Dictionary of Mind, Body and Spirit: Ideas, People and Places*. London: Aquarian.

Cashmore, E. (1979) *Rastaman: The Rastafarian Movement in England*. London: Allen and Unwin.

Catholic Truth Society (1986) 'Sects: the pastoral challenge'. *Briefing 86*, vol. 16, no. 2, 6 June, pp. 142–52. Republished as *New Religious Movements: A Challenge to the Church*. London: Incorporated Catholic Truth Society.

Causton, Richard (1988) *Nichiren Shoshu Buddhism*. London: Rider.

Central Somerset Gazette (1936) *The Central Somerset Gazette Concise Guide to Glastonbury and Neighbourhood*. Glastonbury: Avalon Press.

Chevreau, Guy (1994) *Catch the Fire: The Toronto Blessing – An Experience of Renewal and Revival*. London: HarperCollins.

Chidester, David (1988) *Salvation and Suicide: An Interpretation of the Peoples Temple and Jonestown*. Bloomington: Indiana University Press.

Chryssides, G.D. (1985) 'TM – a science for Christians, too?' *Reform*, July, p. 9.

Chryssides, George D. (1987) 'Reviewing the New Religions' (review article). *World Faiths Insight*, New Series 15, February, pp. 49–52.

Chryssides, George D. (1988a) *The Path of Buddhism*. Edinburgh: St Andrew Press.

Chryssides, George D. (1988b) 'Buddhism goes west'. *World Faiths Insight*, New Series 20, October, pp. 37–45.

Chryssides, George D. (1990) 'Can new faiths be reasonable?' In *Research Project on New Religious Movements*, Rome, International Federation of Catholic Universities, pp. 9–29.

Chryssides, George D. (1991) *The Advent of Sun Myung Moon: The Origins, Beliefs and Practices of the Unification Church*. London: Macmillan.

Chryssides, George D. (1994a) 'Britain's changing faiths: adaptation in a new environment'. In Parsons (1994), pp. 56–84.

Chryssides, George D. (1994b) ' "Don't get too involved!" – methodological issues in the study of new religious movements'. *The Journal of Beliefs and Values,* vol. 15, no. 2, pp. 15–18.

Chryssides, George D. (1994c) 'New religious movements: some problems of definition'. *Diskus*, vol. 2, no. 2.
http://www.uni-marburg.de/fb11/religionwissenschaft/journal/diskus

Chryssides, George D. (1998) *The Elements of Unitarianism*. Shaftesbury: Element.

Chryssides, George D. (ed.) (1999) *Unitarian Perspectives on Contemporary Religious Thought*. London: Lindsey Press.

Chryssides, G.D., Lamb, C. and Marsden, M. (1982) 'Who are they? New religious groups'. London: United Reformed Church.

Church of England (1989) *New Religious Movements: A Report by the Board for Mission and Unity*. London: General Synod of the Church of England, GS Misc 317.

Church of Jesus Christ of Latter-day Saints (n.d., *c.* 1990) 'What is the Book of Mormon?' Salt Lake City: Church of Jesus Christ of Latter-day Saints.

Church of Scientology (1994) *The Scientology Handbook: Based on the Works of L. Ron Hubbard*. Hollywood, CA: Author Services.

Church of Scientology (1995) 'Jonestown: the big lie'. *Freedom*, vol. 27, issue 2, pp. 24–7.

Church of Scientology (1998a) *What is Scientology?* Los Angeles: Bridge Publications.

Church of Scientology (1998b) *Scientology: Theology and Practice of a Contemporary Religion*. Los Angeles: Bridge Publications.

Clark, John (1978) 'Problems in referral of cult members'. *Journal of the National Association of Private Psychiatric Hospitals*, vol. 9, no. 4, pp. 27–9.

Clarke, Peter B. (1986) *Black Paradise: The Rastafarian Movement*. Wellingborough: Aquarian.

Clarke, Peter B. (ed.) (1987) *The New Evangelists: Recruitment, Methods and Aims of New Religious Movements*. London: Ethnographica.

Conway, F. and Siegelman, J. (1978) *Snapping: America's Epidemic of Sudden Personality Change*. Philadelphia and New York: Lippincott.

Cooper, Roger (1982) *The Baha'is of Iran*. London: Minority Rights Group.

Cooper, Simon and Farrant, Mike (1997) *Fire in Our Hearts: The Story of the Jesus Fellowship*. Northampton: Multiply Publications.

Cowan, Jim (ed.) (1982) *The Buddhism of the Sun*. Richmond, Surrey: NSUK.

Crabtree, Herbert (1932) *Some Religious Cults and Movements of To-day and Their Contribution to the Religion of To-morrow*. London: Lindsey Press.

Crompton, R. (1996) *Counting the Days to Armageddon: The Jehovah's Witnesses and the Second Presence of Christ*. London: Lutterworth.

Crowley, Vivianne (1989) *Wicca: The Old Religion in the New Age*. London: Aquarian.

Davies, Horton (1954/1965) *Christian Deviations: The Challenge of the New Spiritual Movements*. London: SCM.

Denniston, Denise (1986/1997) *The TM Book: How to Enjoy the Rest of Your Life*. Fairfield, IA: Fairfield Press.

Department of Philosophy and Religion, University of North Dakota (1999) 'Alternate considerations of Jonestown and the People's Temple'. http://www.und.nodak.edu/dept/philrel/jonestown/ as at 25 April 1999.

Deus, J.C. (1997) 'Is the Dalai Lama a wolf in sheep's clothing?'. *Más Allá de la Ciencia*, no. 103, September. Translated from Spanish on Internet: http://www.tibet-internal.com/MasAlla.html [as at 5 March 1998].

Drury, Nevill (1989) *The Elements of Human Potential*. Shaftesbury: Element.

Durkheim, Emile (1915/1971) *The Elementary Forms of the Religious Life*. London: George Allen and Unwin.

Eliade, M. (1993) *Encyclopedia of Religion*, vol. 13. New York: Collier-Macmillan.

Esslemont, J.E. (1923/1974) *Baha'u'llah and the New Era*. London: Baha'i Publishing Trust.

Evans, Christopher (1973) *Cults of Unreason*. London: Harrap.

FAIR (1990) 'Cults: Are You Vulnerable?' London: Family Action Information and Rescue.

Family, The (1992a) *Our Statements: The Fundamental Beliefs and Essential Doctrines of The Fellowship of Indepndent Missionary Communities Commonly known as The Family*. Zurich: World Services.

Family, The (1992b) *Position and Policy Statement'*. Zurich: World Services.

Ferguson, Marilyn (1980/1987) *The Aquarian Conspiracy: Personal and Social Transformation in Our Time*. New York: Putnam.

Ferm, Virgilius (ed.) (1945/1976) *An Encyclopedia of Religion*. Westport, CT: Greenwood Press.

Findhorn Community (1976/1988) *The Findhorn Garden: Pioneering a New Vision of Humanity and Nature in Cooperation*. Forres, Scotland: Findhorn Press.

Finkelstein, P., Wenegrat, B. and Yalom, I. (1982) 'Large group awareness training'. *Annual Review of Psychology*, vol. 33, pp. 515–39.

Forem, Jack (1974) *Transcendental Meditation: Maharishi Mahesh Yogi and the Science of Creative Intelligence*. London: George Allen and Unwin.

Gadhia, D.J. (1989) *The Divine Grace of Lord Sri Sathya Sai Baba*. Wolverhampton: Sri Sathya Sai Baba Centre.

Galanter, M. (1979) 'The "Moonies": a psychological study of conversion and membership in a contemporary religious sect'. *American Journal of Psychiatry*, vol. 136, no. 2, pp. 165–70.

Gardner, John Fentress (1992) *American Heralds of the Spirit: Emerson, Whitman and Melville*. Hudson, NY: Lindisfarne Press.

Gee, P. and Fulton, J. (eds) (1991) *Religions and Power: Decline and Growth*. British Sociological Association, Sociology of Religion Study Group.

Geldard, Richard (1993) *The Esoteric Emerson: The Spiritual Teachings of Ralph Waldo Emerson*. Hudson, NY: Lindisfarne Press.

Geldard, Richard (1995) *The Vision of Emerson*. Shaftesbury: Element.

Gill-Kozul, Carol (ed.) (1995) *Living Values: A Guidebook*. London: Brahma Kumaris World Spiritual University.

Gomes, Alan W. (1995) *Unmasking the Cults*. Carlisle: OM Publishing.

Griggs, Barbara (1993) 'Peace of mind'. *Country Living*, November. Reprinted as a Transcendental Meditation leaflet.

Gruss, Edmond C. (1974/1994) *Cults and the Occult*. 3rd edition. Phillipsburg, NJ: Presbyterian and Reformed Publishing Company.

Gyatso, Geshe Kelsang (1991) *Heart Jewel: A Commentary to the Essential Practice of the New Kadampa Tradition of Mahayana Buddhism*. London: Tharpa.

Hall, John R. (1987) *Gone from the Promised Land: Jonestown in American Cultural History*. New Brunswick, NJ: Transaction.

Hanegraaff, Wouter J. (1996) *New Age Religion and Western Culture: Esotericism in the Mirror of Secular Thought*. Leiden, New York and Cologne: E.J. Brill.

Hardy, Alister (1979) *The Spiritual Nature of Man: A Study of Contemporary Religious Experience*. Oxford: Clarendon Press.

Harris, Doug (1995) *Cult Critiques*. Richmond, Surrey: Reachout Trust.

Harrison, Shirley (1990) *'Cults': The Battle for God*. London: Christopher Helm.

Harvey, Graham (1995) 'Satanism in Britain today'. *Journal of Contemporary Religion*, vol. 10, no. 3, pp. 283–96.

Harvey, Graham and Hardman, Charlotte (1996) *Paganism Today*. London: Thorsons.

Harvey, Graham (1997) *Listening People, Speaking Earth*. London: C. Hurst & Co.

Hassan, S. (1990) *Combatting Cult Mind Control*. Wellingborough: Aquarian.

Hassija, B.K. Jagdish Chander (n.d., a) *Devleopment of Self, or Human Resource Development for Success in Management through Spiritual Wisdom and Meditation*. Delhi: Brahma Kumaris Centre.

Hassija, B.K. Jagdish Chander (n.d., b) *Self-transformation, Universal-transformation and Harmony in Human Relations*. Delhi: Brahma Kumaris Centre.

Hatcher, William S. and Martin, J. Douglas (1986) *The Baha'i Faith: The Emerging Global Religion*. San Francisco: Harper and Row.

Hawkins, Craig S. (1998) *Goddess Worship, Witchcraft and Neo-Paganism*. Carlisle: OM Publishing.

Haworth, Ian (1993) 'Cults on campus'. London: Cults Information Centre.

Haworth, Ian (1994) 'Cult concerns: an overview of cults and their methods in the UK'. *Assignation*, vol. 11, no. 4, pp. 31–4.

Hay, Louise L. (1984) *You Can Heal Your Life*. Enfield: Eden Grove.

Hayagriva Dasa (1985) *The Hare Krishna Explosion: The Birth of Krishna Consciousness in America (1966–1969)*. New Vrindaban: Palace Press.

Heaven's Gate (1997) URL:
www.heavensgatetoo.com [as on 6 April 1997].

Heelas, Paul (1982) 'Californian self religions and socializing the subjective', in Barker (1982), pp. 69–85.

Heelas, Paul (1986) *The New Age Movement: The Celebration of the Self and the Sacralization of Modernity*. Oxford: Blackwell.

Heelas, Paul (1991) 'Cults for capitalism, self religions, magic, and the empowerment of business', in Gee and Fulton (1991), pp. 27–41.

Heelas, P. and Thompson, J. (1986) *The Way of the Heart*. Wellingborough: Aquarian.

Heftmann, Erica (1982) *Dark Side of the Moonies*. Harmondsworth: Penguin.

Hill, Michael (ed.) (1972) *A Sociological Yearbook of Religion in Britain: 5*. London: SCM.

Hill, Michael (1995) 'Sect', in Eliade (1993).

Hinnells, John (1998) *A New Handbook of Living Religions*. Harmondsworth: Penguin.

Hoekema, Anthony A. (1963) *The Four Major Cults: Christian Science, Jehovah's Witnesses, Mormonism, Seventh-day Adventism*. Exeter: Paternoster.

Hole, Christina (1977) *Witchcraft in England*. London: Book Club Associates.

Holy Bible, The (1978) New International Version. London: Hodder and Stoughton.

Hong, Nansook (1998) *In the Shadow of the Moons*. New York: Little, Brown.

Howard, Roland (1997) *Charismania: When Christian Fundamentalism Goes Wrong*. London: Mowbray.

Howard-Gordon, Frances (1982/1987) *Glastonbury: Maker of Myths*. Glastonbury: Gothic Image Publications.

Hubbard, L. Ron (1950) *Dianetics: The Modern Science of Mental Health*. Redhill, Surrey: New Era.

Hubbard, L. Ron (1955) 'The Hope of Man'. From the welcoming address by L. Ron Hubbard to the Congress of Eastern Scientologists at the Shoreham Hotel, Washington, DC on 3 June 1955. *Ability: The Magazine of Dianetics and Scientology*, mid-June, pp. 109–17.

Hubbard, L. Ron (1956/1968) *Scientology: The Fundamentals of Thought*. Letchworth: Publications Organization World Wide.

Hubner, John (1990a) 'Words of Werner'. *WEST* (*San Jose Mercury News*), 11 November, pp. 17–26.

Hubner, John (1990b) 'All in the family'. *WEST* (*San Jose Mercury News*), 18 November, pp. 8–18.

Humphreys, Christmas (1951) *Buddhism*. Harmondsworth: Penguin.

Humphreys, Christmas (1968) *Sixty Years of Buddhism in England*. London: Buddhist Society.

Institute of Natural Law and Order Inaugural Assembly (1977) 'The fulfilment of law, justice and rehabilitation through the development of Consciousness'. Weggis, Switzerland: Maharishi European Research University Press.

Introvigne, Massimo (1995) 'Ordeal by fire: the tragedy of the Solar Temple'. *Religion,* vol. 25, pp. 267–83.

Irvine, William C. (1970) *Heresies Exposed*. New York: Loizeaux.

Jackson, R. and Killingsley, D. (1988) *Approaches to Hinduism*. London: Murray.

Jesus Fellowship Church (1992) *Jesus: The Name. Jesus: The Foundation: An Introduction to the Faith and Aims of the Jesus Fellowship/Jesus Army and the New Creation Christian Community*. Nether Heyford, Northamptonshire: Jesus Fellowship Church.

Judah, J. Stillson (1974) *Hare Krishna and the Counter Culture*. New York: Wiley.

Kerns, Phil with Wead, Doug (1979) *People's Temple, People's Tomb*. Plainfield, NJ: Logos International.

Kersten, H. (1986/1994) *Jesus Lived in India: His Unknown Life before and after the Crucifixion*. Shaftesbury: Element.

King, Martin and Breault, Marc (1993) *Preacher of Death: The Shocking Inside Story of David Koresh and the Waco Siege*. London: Penguin.

Knott, Kim (1986) *My Sweet Lord: The Hare Krishna Movement*. Wellingborough: Aquarian.

Kroll, Una (1974/1976) *TM: A Signpost for the World*. London: Darton, Longman and Todd.

Kuhn, T.S. (1962/1970) *The Structure of Scientific Revolutions*. 2nd edition. Chicago and London: University of Chicago Press.

Kwak, Chung Hwan (1980) *Outline of the Principle Level 4*. New York: HSA-UWC.

Kwak, Chung Hwan (1985) *The Tradition*. New York: Rose of Sharon Press.

La Fontaine, J.S. (1994) *The Extent and Nature of Organised and Ritual Abuse*. London: HMSO.

Lamont, Stewart (1986) *Religion Inc.: The Church of Scientology*. London: Harrap.

Larson, Bob (1989) *Larson's New Book of Cults*. Wheaton, IL: Tyndale House.

Lash, John (1990) *The Seeker's Handbook: The Complete Guide to Spiritual Pathfinding*. New York: Harmony Books.

Lewis, James R. and Melton, J. Gordon (1994) *Sex, Slander, and Salvation: Investigating The Family/Children of God*. Stanford, CA: Center for Academic Publication.

Lofland, John (1966) *Doomsday Cult: A Study of Conversion, Proselytization, and Maintenance of Faith*. Englewood Cliffs, NJ: Prentice-Hall.

Lofland, John and Stark, R. (1965) 'Becoming a world-saver: a theory of conversion to a deviant perspective'. *American Sociological Review*, vol. 30, pp. 862–75.

Lopez, Donald S., Jr (1998a) 'Two sides of the same god'. *Tricycle: The Buddhist Review*, Spring, pp. 67–9.

Lopez, Donald S., Jr (1998b) 'An interview with Geshe Kelsang Gyatso'. *Tricycle: The Buddhist Review*, Spring, pp. 70–6.

Lopez, Donald S., Jr (1998c). 'An interview with Thubten Jigme Norbu'. *Tricycle: The Buddhist Review*, Spring, pp. 77–82.

Ludlow, D.H. (ed.) (1992) *Encyclopedia of Mormonism*. 5 vols. New York: Collier Macmillan.

Lyle, Robert (1983) *Subud*. Tunbridge Wells: Humanus.

Maaga, M.M. (1996) 'Triple erasure: women and power in Peoples Temple'. PhD dissertation, Drew University.

MacEoin, Denis (1998) 'Baha'ism', in Hinnells (1998), pp. 618–43.

Maharishi European Research University (1976) 'Enlightenment for ideal rehabilitation: expansion of consciousness as the basis of the restoration of creative intelligence – the effectiveness of the transcendental meditation programme for rehabilitation'. Presented at the Third International Conference on Drug Dependency, Liverpool, England, 6 April. Weggis, Switzerland: Maharishi European Research University Press.

Maharishi Mahesh Yogi (1963/1965) *Science of Being and Art of Living: Transcendental Meditation*. Harmondsworth: Penguin.

Maharishi Mahesh Yogi (1967/1976) *On the Bhagavad-Gita: A New Translation and Commentary, Chapters 1–6*. Harmondsworth: Penguin.

Mann, A.T. (1992) *Millennium Prophecies: Predictions for the Year 2000*. Shaftesbury: Element.

Martin, Walter (1965/1985) *The Kingdom of the Cults*. Minneapolis, MN: Bethany House.

Martin, Walter (1978) *The Maze of Mormonism*. Ventura, CA: Gospel Light Publications.

Matczak, S.A. (1982) *Unificationism*. New York: Edwin Mellen Press.

Mayer, Jean-François (1996) *Les Mythes du Temple Solaire*. Geneva: Georg.

Mayer, Jean-François (1999) 'Les chevaliers de l'Apocalypse: l'Ordre du Temple Solaire et ses adeptes', in Champion, Françoise and Cohen, Martine (eds) *Sectes et Démocratie*, Paris: Editions du Seuil, pp. 205–23.

Mayhew, H. (1971) *The Mormons; or Latter-day Saints: A Contemporary History*. New York: AMS Press.

McDowell, Josh and Stuart, Don (1986) *Understanding the Cults*. San Bernardino, CA: Here's Life Publications.

McDowell, Josh and Stuart, Don (1992) *The Deceivers: What Cults Believe; How They Lure Followers*. Amersham: Scripture Press.

Melton, J. Gordon (1992) *Encyclopedic Handbook of Cults in America*. New York and London: Garland.

Melton, J. Gordon (1996) *Encyclopedia of American Religions*. 5th edition. Detroit: Gale.

Melton, J. Gordon (1998) 'Modern alternative religions in the West', in Hinnells (1998), pp. 594–617.

Melton, J. Gordon and Moore, Robert L. (1982) *The Cult Experience: Responding to the New Religious Pluralism*. New York: Pilgrim Press.

Milgram, S. (1974) *Obedience to Authority: An Experimental View*. London: Tavistock.

Miller, Russell (1987) *Bare-faced Messiah: The True Story of L. Ron Hubbard*. London: Michael Joseph.

Momen, Moojan (1997) *A Short Introduction to the Baha'i Faith*. Oxford: Oneworld.

Moon, Sun Myung (1992) 'Becoming the leaders in building a world of peace'. 24 August. Little Angels Performing Arts Center, Seoul.

Moore, James (1991) *Gurdjieff: The Anatomy of a Myth*. Shaftesbury: Element.

Moore, Rebecca (1985) *A Sympathetic History of Jonestown: The Moore Family Involvement in Peoples Temple*. Lewiston, NY: Edwin Mellen Press.

Moore, Rebecca (1988) *In Defense of Peoples Temple*. Lewiston, NY: Edwin Mellen Press.

Moore, Rebecca and McGehee, Fielding (1989) *New Religious Movements, Mass Suicide, and Peoples Temple*. Lewiston, Lampeter, Queenston: Edwin Mellen Press.

Morrish, Ivor (1982) *Obeah, Christ and Rastaman: Jamaica and Its Religion*. Cambridge: James Clarke.

Mullan, Bob (1967) *The Mormons*. London: W.H. Allen.

Mullan, Bob (1983) *Life as Laughter: Following Bhagawan Shree Rajneesh*. London: Routledge.

Murphet, Howard (1971/1997) *Sai Baba, Man of Miracles*. Chennai: Macmillan India.

Murray, Margaret (1921) *The Witch-Cult in Western Europe: A Study in Anthropology*. Oxford: Clarendon Press.

Needleman, Jacob (1970) *The New Religions*. New York: Doubleday.

Nelson, Geoffrey K. (1987) *Cults, New Religions and Religious Creativity*. London: Routledge and Kegan Paul.

New Kadampa Tradition (1998a) 'New Kadampa Tradition. http://www.nkt.co.uk as on 24 April 1999.

New Kadampa Tradition (1998b) 'Manjushri Mahayana Buddhist Centre'. http://www.manjushri.force9.co.uk/ as on 24 April 1999.

New World Bible Translation Committee (1961/1984) *New World Translation of the Holy Scriptures*. Brooklyn, New York: Watchtower Bible and Tract Society of Pennsylvania.

Osho (1989) *I Celebrate Myself*. Cologne: Rebel Publishing House.

Otto, R. (1917) *The Idea of the Holy*. London: Oxford University Press.

Palmer, Susan J. (1996) 'Purity and danger in the Solar Temple'. *Journal of Contemporary Religion*, vol. 11, no. 3, pp. 303–18.

Parsons, Gerald (ed.) (1994) *The Growth of Religious Diversity: Britain from 1945. Volume II: Issues*. London: Routledge.

Patrick, T. with Dulack, T. (1976) *Let Our Children Go!* New York: Dutton.

Prebish, Charles S. (1993) *Historical Dictionary of Buddhism*. Metuchen, NJ and London: Scarecrow Press.

Puttick, Elizabeth (1997) *Women in New Religions: In Search of Community, Sexuality and Spiritual Power*. London: Routledge.

Rawlinson, Andrew (1997) *The Book of Enlightened Masters: Western Teachers in Eastern Traditions*. Chicago and La Salle, IL: Open Court.

Rieu, Dominic C.H. (1983) *A Life with a Life: An Introduction to Subud*. Tunbridge Wells: Humanus.

387

Robbins, Thomas (1989) 'The second wave of Jonestown literature: a review essay'. In Rebecca Moore and Fielding McGehee III (eds), *New Religious Movements, Mass Suicide and Peoples Temple: Scholarly Perspectives on a Tragedy*, Lewiston, NY: Edwin Mellen Press, pp. 113–34.

Robbins, Thomas and Palmer, Susan J. (1997) *Millennium, Messiahs and Mayhem*. New York and London: Routledge.

Ross, Joan Carol and Langone, Michael D. (1988) *Cults: What Parents Should Know*. Weston, MA: Carol Publishing Group/American Family Foundation.

Roth, Robert (1987/1994) *Maharishi Mahesh Yogi's TM Transcendental Meditation*. New York: Donald I. Fine.

Roundhill, J. (1973) *Meeting Jehovah's Witnesses*. London: Lutterworth.

Ruhela, S.P. (1994) *Sri Sathya Sai Baba and the Future of Mankind*. New Delhi: Vikas.

Russell, C.T. (1917) *The Finished Mystery*. Brooklyn, New York: International Bible Students' Association.

Russell, Peter (1976/1978) *The TM Technique*. London: Penguin.

Rutherford, J.F. (1920) *Millions Now Living Will Never Die*. Brooklyn, New York: International Bible Students' Association.

Sadleir, Steven S. (1992) *The Spiritual Seeker's Guide: The Complete Source for Religions and Spiritual Groups of the World*. Costa Mesa, CA: Allwon.

Saliba, John (1995) *Perspectives on New Religious Movements*. London: Geoffrey Chapman.

Sangharakshita, Venerable Maha Sthavira (1978) *Buddhism and Blasphemy: Buddhist Reflections on the 1977 Blasphemy Trial*. London: Windhorse.

Sangharakshita, Venerable Sthavira (1989) *The Ten Pillars of Buddhism*. Glasgow: Windhorse.

Satsvarupa dasa Goswami (1983) *Prabhupada*. Los Angeles: Bhaktivedanta Book Trust.

Shapiro, Eli (1977) 'Destructive cultism'. *American Family Physician*, vol. 15, no. 2, p. 83.

Shaw, David (1994) *Spying in Guruland: Inside Britain's Cults*. London: Fourth Estate.

Sheppherd, Joseph (1992) *The Elements of the Baha'i Faith*. Shaftesbury: Element.

Shubow, Robert (1981/1988) *The Voyagers: The True Story of a Race of Beings Far More Intelligent than Us*. London: Brahma Kumaris World Spiritual University.

Singer, M.T. and Schein, E.H. (1958) 'Projective test responses of prisoners of war following repatriation'. *Psychiatry*, vol. 21, no. 4, pp. 375–85.

Smart, Ninian (1995) *Worldviews: Crosscultural Explorations of Human Beliefs*. 2nd edition. Englewood Cliffs, NJ: Prentice-Hall.

Sontag, Frederick (1977) *Sun Myung Moon and the Unification Church*. Nashville, TN: Abingdon.

Starhawk (1979/1989) *The Spiral Dance: A Rebirth of the Ancient Religion of the Great Goddess*. San Francisco: HarperCollins.

Stark, R. and Bainbridge, W.S. (1996) *Religion, Deviance and Social Control*. New York: Routledge.

Stone, Donald (1975) 'The Human Potential Movement'. In Charles Y. Grock and Robert N. Bellah (eds), *The New Religious Consciousness*, Berkeley, CA: University of California Press, pp. 93–115.

Storr, Anthony (1996) *Feet of Clay: A Study of Gurus*. London: HarperCollins.

Stuart, Ossie (1998) 'African diaspora religion'. In Hinnells (1998), pp. 690–727.

Subhuti, Dharmachari (1983) *Buddhism for Today: A Portrait of a New Buddhist Movement*. Salisbury: Element.

Subhuti, Dharmachari (1994) *Sangharakshita: A New Voice in the Buddhist Tradition*. Birmingham: Windhorse.

Swatland, A. and Swatland, S. (1982) *Escape from the Moonies*. London: New English Library.

Thapa, Deepak (1998) 'It's Dalai Lama vs Shugden'. http://www.wouth-asia.com/himal/September/dorje.htm as on 5 March 1998.

Thayee, Shivamma (1992) *My Life with Sri Shirdi Sai Baba*. Faridabad: Sai Age Publications.

Times, The (1981) T. Lobsang Rampa (Obituary) 31 January, p. 14.

Tipton, S. (1981) 'The moral logic of the Human Potential Movement'. British Sociological Association, Sociology of Religion Study Group, April.

Transcendental Meditation (1995) 'Scientific Research on Transcendental Meditation and Maharishi Ayur-Veda: An Introduction and Overview, May 1995'. London: Transcendental Meditation.

Transcendental Meditation (n.d., *c.* 1995) 'Transcendental Meditation: Enjoy a Happy, Healthy, More Fulfilling Life'. London: Transcendental Meditation.

Troeltsch, E. (1931) *The Social Teachings of the Christian Church*. London: Macmillan.

Turner, Harold W. (1998) 'New religious movements in primal societies'. In Hinnells (1998), pp. 581–93.

Tylor, E.B. (1871/1929) *Primitive Culture,* vols 1 and 2. London: Murray.

von Bissing, Ronimund (1962). *Songs of Submission: On the Practice of Subud*. Greenwood, SC: Attic Press.

Wallis, Roy (1985) 'The sociology of the new religions'. *Social Studies Review*, vol. 1, no. 1, pp. 3–7.

Warner, J. (1967) *The Mormon Way*. Englewood Cliffs, NJ: Prentice-Hall.

Washington, Peter (1993) *Madame Blavatsky's Baboon: Theosophy and the Emergence of the Western Guru*. London: Secker and Warburg.

389

Watchtower Bible and Tract Society (1968) 'Are you looking forward to 1975?' *Watchtower*, 15 August. (Watchtower Library 1997 CD ROM.)

Watchtower Bible and Tract Society (1988) *Revelation*. Brooklyn, New York: Watchtower Bible and Tract Society of New York.

Watchtower Bible and Tract Society (1993) *Jehovah's Witnesses – Proclaimers of God's Kingdom*. Brooklyn, New York: Watchtower Bible and Tract Society of New York.

Watchtower Bible and Tract Society (1995) 'Saved from a "wicked generation" '. *Watchtower*, 1 November, pp. 10–15.

Watchtower Bible and Tract Society (1998) *1998 Yearbook of Jehovah's Witnesses*. Brooklyn, New York: Watchtower Bible and Tract Society of New York & International Bible Students' Association.

Weber, Max (1922/1965) *The Sociology of Religion*. London: Methuen.

Weber, Max (1930/1976) *The Protestant Ethic and the Spirit of Capitalism*. London: Allen and Unwin.

Weightman, Simon (1977) *Seekers and Scholars*. Milton Keynes: Open University Press.

Weller, Paul (ed.) (1997) *Religions in the UK: A Multi-Faith Directory*. Derby: University of Derby Press.

Wessinger, Catherine (1998) '1978 — Jonestown'. Draft essay to be published in Catherine Wessinger (forthcoming), *How the Millennium Comes Violently*. Located at URL: http://www.und.nodak.edu/dept/philrel/jonestown/jt1978.html last revised 15 January 1998.

Western Buddhist Order (1975) *Puja*. London: Friends of the Western Buddhist Order.

Whaling, Frank (1995) 'The Brahma Kumaris'. *Journal of Contemporary Religion,* vol. 10, no. 1, pp. 3–28.

Williams, J. with Porter D. (1987) *The Locust Years*. London: Hodder and Stoughton.

Williams, Paul (1996) 'Dorje Shugden'. *The Middle Way*, vol. 71, no. 2, pp. 130–2.

Wilson, Bryan (1959) 'An analysis of sect development'. *American Sociological Review*, vol. 24, pp. 3–15.

Wilson, Bryan (1961) *Sects and Society: A Sociological Study of the Elim Tabernacle, Christian Science and Christadelphians*. Berkeley, CA: University of California Press.

Wilson, Bryan (1983) *The Social Impact of New Religious Movements*. New York: Rose of Sharon Press.

Wilson, Bryan (ed.) (1999) *New Religious Movements: Challenge and Response*. London: Routledge.

Wilson, Bryan and Dobbelaere, Karel (1998) *A Time to Chant: The Soka Gakkai Buddhists in Britain*. Oxford: Clarendon Press.

Wilson, Colin and Wilson, Damon (1992) *World Famous Cults and Fanatics*. London: Magpie.

Wruck, K.H. and Eastley, M.F. (1997) 'Landmark Education Corporation: selling a paradigm shift'. Boston: *Harvard Business School*, 3 November.

Yinger, J.M. (1946/1961) *Religion in the Struggle for Power: A Study in the Sociology of Religion*. Sociological Series, no. 3. Durham, NC: Duke University Press.

Yinger, J.M. (1970) *The Scientific Study of Religion*. London: Collier-Macmillan.

Young, Wendy Warren (1987) 'The aims and methods of "est" and "The Centres Network"', in Clarke (1987), pp. 131–47.

Index

Bab, the 245–6, 249, 255, 258–9
Babism 247, 259
Baha'is 17, 244–59, 366
Baha'u'llah 245–7, 249, 250, 251,
253, 254, 255, 256, 258, 259
Bailey, Alice 370–1
Bainbridge, William 31
Baldwin, Graham 350
baptism
adult 47, 155–6, 160, 371
for the dead 117–18
in Holy Spirit 22, 122, 140, 150–1
infant 4
Jehovah's Witness 102
of Jesus 73, 114, 128
in Jesus Army 155–6, 160
in LDS 114, 115
Baptists 149, 155, 160–1
Barker, Eileen 12, 13, 20, 21, 348,
351, 356
Barrett, D.V. 259, 274 302, 370
Bartley, W.W.III 282
Beatles 173, 293–4, 342
Becker, Howard 7, 8, 9
Beit-Hallami, Binyamin 67
Bellaton, Dominique 64
Bennett, John G. 93, 261, 264, 266
Berg, David Brandt 124, 135–9, 163
Berg, Maria 136, 141, 142
Bernard of Clairvaux 59, 64
Besant, Annie Wood 91–2
Bhagavad Gita 20, 82, 84, 91, 165,
166, 167, 169, 170, 172, 174, 176,
189–90, 203, 302, 315, 317
bhakti 168, 169, 174, 183, 198, 203
bhakti yoga 164, 187
Bhaktisiddhanta Saraswati 170–1,
175
Bible
authority of whole 51
baptism in 155–6
concept of covenant in 156
Emerson and 82, 84
end-time prophecies in 146–8
Garvey and 270
Heaven's Gate interpretation
of 67–8, 69–70, 75
Hebrew 28, 32, 52, 376
higher criticism and 120
interpretation of in New Christian
groups 162–3

Jehovah's Witnesses and 3, 28,
94, 96, 98–9, 101, 104, 105, 107
King James (Authorized) Version
viii
in mission 29
New International Version viii
New World Translatiion viii, 100
'Old Testament' vii–viii
Rael and 374
Rastafarianism and 271–5, 276
Sai Baba and 188
Swedenborg and 80
typological interpretation of 49,
52–4
in Unification Church 127, 129
Bible Students *see* Jehovah's
Witnesses
birthdays 96, 103, 191, 214
Black Power 244, 270, 272, 277
Blavatsky, Helena Petrovna 77,
87–91, 93, 225
Blessing, the 17, 125, 131, 132–3,
134, 163
blood transfusion 5, 105–6, 362
bodhisattvas 230–1, 236, 240, 242
Brahma Kumaris 166, 192–202, 366
brainwashing 3, 20, 23, 33, 34–5,
43, 45, 124, 211, 345, 347–8, 350,
352, 362
Branch Davidians 33, 46, 48–56
Breault, Marc 55
British Council of Churches 356,
360
Bromley, David 348
Budapest, Zsuzsanna 338
Buddha 38, 88, 89, 174, 184, 204,
207, 214, 215, 217, 225, 227, 230,
249, 258, 295, 312
buddha-nature 205, 211, 212–13, 219
Buddhism 11, 13, 15, 19, 31, 32, 70,
87, 90, 91, 124, 181, 202, 204–43,
244, 257, 260, 281, 286, 290, 315,
317, 326, 354, 355, 362; *see also*
New Kadampa; Nichiren
Shoshu; Pure Land; Tibetan; Zen

Caddy, Eileen and Peter 320–3, 325,
332
California 34, 38, 40, 42, 135, 136,
304, 346, 352
Calvin, John 118, 126, 278, 317, 334